# Formative Years of Communist International
# and
# the *Metamorphosis* of Bolshevism

# Formative Years of Communist International and the *Metamorphosis* of Bolshevism

Arun Kumar Sinha

AAKAR

FORMATIVE YEARS OF COMMUNIST INTERNATIONAL AND THE *METAMORPHOSIS* OF BOLSHEVISM
Arun Kumar Sinha



First Published 2017

ISBN 978-93-5002-524-6



*Published by*
**AAKAR BOOKS**
28 E Pocket IV, Mayur Vihar Phase I
Delhi 110 091, India
Email: aakarbooks@gmail.com

*Laser Typeset at*
Arpit Printographers, Delhi 110 032

*Printed at*
Sapra Brothers, Delhi

*In memory of the thousands of Martyrs around the world, who laid down the most precious moments of their life to* ***realize the dream of Communist Society.***

*"It is often said that 'the germ of all Stalinism was in Bolshevism at its beginning'. Well, I have no objection. Only, Bolshevism also contained many other germs, a mass of other germs, and those who lived through the enthusiasm of the first years of the first victorious socialist revolution ought not to forget it. To judge the living man by the death germs which the autopsy reveals in the corpse - and which he may have carried in him since his birth - is that very sensible?"*

– **Victor Serge, *From Lenin to Stalin*, 1937**

# Contents

# Acknowledgement

This writing, originally planned as a long essay, has turned into the shape of a book. The initial drafts were prepared around December 2015 and were meant to be more of a self-clarification. I can record gratefully that the drafts went through many revisions because a few of my friends took care to read through the drafts minutely and offer precise suggestions. Above all, the writing got the benefit of access to the sources of references available in the public domain *freely*. It is a pleasure to realize that these documents and pamphlets are now *widely* available for public viewing and reading, mere possession of which would have landed the revolutionaries in Europe in serious persecution by their governments some eighty years ago.

This advancement of human society, albeit under bourgeoisie civilization, in dissemination of knowledge, information, thought process not only in all the other spheres of life but also in matters of great conflicts related to transcending the *barbarism* inherent in the capitalist society is the pointer that *socialism* is doable, *socialism* is not just a utopia existing only in the myriad contemplation of visionaries.

Therefore, I thankfully acknowledge the numerous websites which are the sources of inspiration and information in preparing this writing; in that sense this writing is an expression of collective, voluntary *labour*. I have mentioned only some of the websites with respect to the specific references in the manuscript. The responsibility for any error in citing the historical facts in the writing, of course, lies with the author.

I am thankful to Goutam Sen, a veteran in espousing the trend of viewpoints expressed in this work and a relentless champion of the emancipation of the workers by *themselves*, for kindly consenting to write the foreword to this work. Last but not the least, I am thankful to K.K. Saxena of Aakar Books, Delhi in taking interest to publish this work with painful, meticulous editing and formatting of the text.

January 2017 AKS
Kolkata, India

# Foreword

No single event in the world, other than the October Revolution in Russia, has aroused so much interest and drawn so much attention of both the camps of the revolutionaries and those representing the status quo during almost last one hundred years. Naturally, a plethora of literature has been produced regarding assessment and evaluation of the great historic event.

It is now a well established historical fact that the great revolution in Russia inspired immediately the workers and toiling masses all over the world to revolt. In particular, revolutions broke out in a number of countries like Germany, Hungary, Latvia, etc. At the same time, one cannot fail to notice how the capitalists of the world got united to smash the incipient Russian revolution by economic, political and military means. The fierce opposition of the reactionaries within Russia against the revolution with the support and aid of the capitalist nation states are also well-documented in history.

We all know that the historic October Revolution took place in a backward capitalist country that too was dominated by the petty bourgeois production relations. It is true that the Russian working class took power through the October revolution in 1917, but the working class faced a Herculean task to accomplish the socialist revolution. It is to be further noted that, as pre-revolutionary Russia was a peasantry dominated country, the working class there was minority amongst the population. (This obviously put serious constraints upon the practice of democracy and socialist transformation). The three major demands of October Revolution were bread, land and peace. Amongst these demands the issue of land was in essence capitalist in nature, whereas the issues of bread and peace, although in the ultimate analysis have socialist content, in the immediate sense they were not socialist in character. Thus overall socialist content of the revolution from the beginning was weak, despite the strong existence of factory-council movement and other positive initiatives towards social control. For obvious reasons, all the leading personalities of the Russian revolution, whatsoever differences among them, were unanimous on a single point: either international proletarian revolution, especially revolutions in advanced capitalist countries of Europe would come to its support or the revolution was doomed to be failure.

Despite some initial sprouts, the revolution in the West did not materialize. In Hungary and Bavaria Soviet governments actually seized state-power – although only for a brief period. The German Revolution was crushed; hundreds of the revolutionaries including great revolutionary personalities like Rosa Luxemburg and Karl Liebknecht were killed by the Weimar Republic. The Hungarian revolution could not be accomplished. The possibility of international revolution was extinguished. Thus in this state of isolation the Russian revolution faced the most difficult situation. The Soviet state took a complex and zigzag path for its survival. In retrospect, it may be said that some of the steps were too retrogressive; but at that time, one may conclude that, in the midst of the complex events the victorious side within the revolutionary camp undertook those steps which were seemed to be unavoidable under the prevailing "extreme exigency" to save the revolutionary fort. Though the irony of history is that, in the long run, 'socialism' was achieved, but the fort was 'dispossessed' from within.

The rule of a single Communist Party with a highly bureaucratized form finally triumphed and became a 'socialist' model. This model of establishing socialism 'from above' was highly publicized and followed from one country to the other. The necessity of power taken by the working class and introducing socialism 'from below' was abandoned. This model at the same time undermined the international content of socialist revolution and helped to formulate the theory of socialism in one country. Thus when the Parties with nomenclature 'Communist' took power either in China or in the countries of East Europe, the major section of communists became jubilant—socialism is not far away!

The victorious side saw the history of the victory and success of 'socialism' through its own glass and wrote it in its own way; and both the Communist Party leadership and rank and file communists by and large accepted that version. Yet there were notes of dissents from the very beginning. The hard fact is—everything could not be suppressed and put under carpet, A section of the far-sighted and un—swayed communists not only found other side of the story, but also raised many serious questions about what were going wrong. In hindsight, one may comment that all the dissenting voices might not or did not lead to 'correct' assertion and formulation, yet it has to be candidly admitted that with respect to the prevailing *closed door* regime those were commendable job.

People outside the closed coterie of the 'communist' power first got a 'free access' to peep into some of the age-old suppressed facts only during Khrushchev-era of the so-called period of de-Stalinization. After this, the reforms initiated by Gorbachev revealed a bit more. It is only recently when the old archives have been made open for public access, the inquisitive persons are in liberty to go through all the facts, debates and controversies during the *closed door* regime.

After the ignominious collapse of the "Communist" regime in Soviet Russia and the countries of Eastern Europe and market-oriented turn of "socialist" China, two developments have occurred. On the one hand, there is a great "hurray" of the bourgeois milieu to declare capitalism as 'the end of history' and socialism is 'dead', 'defeated' and 'rejected' as a system, goal or idea. On the other, even the most ardent supporters of communism have to admit that "there was something wrong somewhere". Naturally, many 'solved' issues are being unsolved; fresh and enthusiastic attempts are made to unearth many buried facts. A new scope for re-search and re-evaluation has been opened.

The author of the current work, Arun Sinha has accessed all types of literature available to explore and pen down the narrative of the tumultuous days immediately after the October Revolution. Although the author in this work deals with the issue of objective and subjective causes for the ultimate defeat of the Russian socialist revolution, his principal objective is very specific—i.e., to delineate the *metamorphosis* of the Bolshevik Party through the initial years of the revolution and the implication of this *metamorphosis* on the formative years of the Communist International, popularly known as the Third International.

## I

In order to revisit the trajectory of the Russian revolution, it is most important to differentiate the dynamics of the bourgeois *democratic* revolution from the proletarian *socialist* revolution and locate the unique problematic part of the *socialist* revolution. In case of the bourgeois democratic revolution, the political revolution --that is the class-shift in state-power (from absolute monarchy/feudal or any other form of autocratic regime to a democratic regime) is the last act of the revolution. In this case, it is taken for granted that the capitalist production relations have already taken their roots in the society; and although there may remain some reforms to be accomplished, the democratic revolution is an *end in itself*. In case of the *socialist* revolution, the political revolution (that is class-shift in state-power, smashing of the old state-power and attainment of the proletarian class power) is only the beginning of the revolution. There may develop urge for *socialism* within the capitalist society because of its inherent contradiction, but there is no question of *socialist* production relations to be born within the womb of capitalism in a piecemeal way.

At this juncture, the difference between bourgeois democracy-cum-dictatorship and proletarian democracy-cum-dictatorship may be enunciated. It is a common understanding among the Marxists that the bourgeois democracy bears the stamp of the bourgeois class because, in the overall and ultimate analysis, *capital* and moneybag always dictate the terms of every aspect of society. At the same time, this democracy is well-equipped with various oppressive institutions to throttle the rights and aspirations of the working class and other toiling masses. Therefore, bourgeois democracy always becomes *equivalent* to bourgeois dictatorship. The dictatorship of the proletariat on the other hand has to attain the characteristics of proletarian democracy so that all the members of the class and the *class as a whole* will enjoy democracy so that while resisting the onslaught of the counter revolution, they would get a chance in continuing the *socialist* transformation. This is the real and vibrant soul of the *socialist* revolution and a path to implement the revolutionary outcry: *Workers' emancipation is the act of the workers themselves.*

It is now well documented that there were contending opinions on the post-revolutionary path to be followed both within the Bolshevik Party and outside; and also internationally both within the Soviet Russia and outside. One may also conjecture that if the other side would have won and could decide the course, how far the fate of the process of socio-economic transformation would have been different. But it may be safely concluded that so far the ultimate result is concerned, there would have been no difference: if the international *socialist* revolution did not happen, the Russian revolution would have to face a defeat.

## II

At the outset, the Russian revolution not only opened up a new horizon of possibilities, it aroused high expectations towards its declared goals. Decrees were passed one after another to strengthen the "workers' control" in industrial production centers. Decrees were passed on the Judiciary to remove the old judges from office, and they were replaced either by popular vote or by the Soviets. Decrees were passed to simplify marriage and divorce laws; children born out of the wedlock were given the same right as the offspring born without the marriage ceremony. Separation of the church from the state was decreed. Right of the nations to self-determination extending up to the right to secession was promulgated. One may argue that most of the above decrees were not particularly *socialist* in character, but one has to admit that those measures were sufficiently radical to be hailed, particularly under the extreme difficult situation the revolution faced in the socio-economic and political context of post-revolutionary Russia.

The Russian Bolsheviks did not however intend to wait for the revolution abroad. For the time being anyway, the tasks at hand in Russia were determined, not by the Bolshevik leaders, but by the international imperialist powers. Those had begun a "crusade" against the Soviet Republic. White and foreign armies had to be driven back before any other questions could be considered. By a mixture of popular support, revolutionary ardor, and pure will, the counter-revolutionary forces were driven out. But the price paid was enormous. What suffered above all was the industrial and agricultural production. The dislocation of industrial production also brought dislocation of the working class. In purely quantitative terms, the class that had led the revolution, the class whose democratic processes had constituted the living core of Soviet power, was halved in importance. In real terms, the situation was even worse.

But what was to be the fate of the revolution, if the class that had rose to achieve it ceased to exist in any meaningful sense? This was not a problem that the Bolshevik leaders could have foreseen. They had always said that isolation of the revolution would result in its destruction by foreign armies and domestic counter-revolution. In the changed situation at the aftermath of the Civil War, the new state-power had survived; but radical changes were being produced in the internal composition of the state-power. The democratic reforms in the Red army were also receded due to the Civil War. The old experts who were not hostile were inducted in the army to serve the military; and democratic election within army was deferred. This process finally transformed the red army into the standing army. Everything 'red' in the red army faded away gradually to pave the way for its transformation into a formal standing army with defined hierarchy. Under extreme exigency, one-man-management took start from the year 1920 onwards despite opposition from a considerable section of the advanced workers. As explained by a close and sympathetic observer:

> In all this the Bolsheviks had no choice. They could not give up power just because the class they represented had dissolved itself while fighting to defend that power. Nor could they tolerate the propagation of ideas that undermined the basis of its power – precisely because the working class itself no longer existed as an agency collectively organized so as to be able to determine its own interests.
>
> [Chris Harman, Russia: How the Revolution was Lost, *International Socialism*, No. 30, Autumn 1967]

Instead of being "the self-conscious, independent movement of the immense majority in the interest of the immense majority", the revolution in Russia had reached the stage where it involved the exploitation of the rural countryside by the dire needs of the urban population and for maintaining the Red Army, by exercising naked physical force of the state. It was clear to almost all the groups in the Bolshevik Party that such policy of exercising force on the rural population meant the revolution remained always in danger of being overthrown by the peasant insurrections.

There seemed to be only one course open. That was to accept many of the demands of the peasantry, while maintaining a strong, centralised state apparatus. The New Economic Policy (NEP) was attempted to accomplice this purpose. Its aim was to reconcile peasants to the regime and to encourage economic development by giving a limited range of freedom to private commodity production. The state and the state-owned industries were to operate just as one of the elements in an economy governed by the needs of peasant production and the play of the market forces. It is explained in the current work: "It was named 'New' as this was not the economic policy of the Bolsheviks on the eve of revolution, rather the result of an afterthought ... facing the concrete reality of rural Russia". Lenin tried his utmost to explain before the delegates of the Communist International in the Third Congress about what were the compulsions for the Bolshevik leadership at the end of the Civil War "to help the peasants at any price".

In order to maintain control over the Russian society, the Bolshevik party had been forced to use thousands of the members of the old Tsarist bureaucracy. Out of necessity the Soviet State of 1917 had been replaced by the single-party State from 1920 onwards. The Soviets that remained were increasingly being transformed just into a front for Bolshevik power.

These stark changes in the composition of the Soviet State may be understood if we make a comparative study. At the outset no single party did reign supreme in the Soviets. There was free election with a right to recall of the elected representative; the compositions of the political trends within the Soviets were in a flux. The democratic scenario among the elected members of the Soviets in those initial days was well depicted by John Reed in his writing on *The Structure of Soviet State*. He wrote,

> No political body more sensitive and responsive to the popular will was ever invented. And this was necessary, for in time of revolution the popular will changes with great rapidity. For example, during the first weeks of December, 1917 there were parades and demonstrations in favour of Constituent Assembly, that is to say, against the Soviet Power. One of these parades was fired on by irresponsible Red Guards, several people were killed. The reaction to this stupid violence was immediate. Within twelve hours the complexion of Petrograd Soviet changed. More than a dozen of Bolshevik deputies were withdrawn and replaced by Mensheviks. And it was there for three weeks before public sentiment subsided before Mensheviks were retired one by one and Bolsheviks sent back.

Thus it is evident that the Soviet state was not based on the rule of a single-party system in the beginning; there were competing political parties.

It may not be out of context to note that the admission of the international content of socialist revolution was not only limited within the leaders of the Bolshevik or Communists at large, it had its roots amongst advanced section of the workers. When news of breaking out of revolution in Germany in 1918 came to Russia, the Russian workers came out in the street with a festive mood, rejoicing and shouting slogans in favor of German revolutionary workers. The reference to German revolution and an interesting discussion on it in Sinha's deliberation is not only relevant but also is thought provoking. It may also ignite the interest of the readers for further studies of the German revolution.

.......

It will be very much unwise, unethical and un-Marxist if one accuses the Bolshevik leadership, especially its celebrated leaders like Lenin, Trotsky, Zinoviev, Bukharin, *et al* that they did not follow the theory which they believed and propagated before the revolution, *or*, the path they followed was non-Marxist. No great struggle, no revolutionary movement, no epical revolution has ever followed and will follow any theory, whatsoever 'scientific" or "correct" or "sanctified" it might be. Rather every real and great movement would provide rich materials for evolving new and enlightened theories as guides to act for the future course of action. It is unfortunate for the activists in the era of post-Russian revolution that the theorization made out of necessity and exigencies for defending and continuing the Russian socialist revolution actually produced a number of theories which are retrogressive in nature or are propositions simply not to be hailed and followed.

## III

The author referred to a number of inputs (including comments, memoirs and quotations) while analyzing the development of the October Revolution and its continuation. These references may help the readers to evaluate and re-evaluate the relevant course of history, particularly the development of the Third International.

It is well known that Rosa Luxemburg was an ardent supporter of the Russian socialist revolution. During September and October 1918, while in prison, she penned down her critique on the agrarian policy, the nationality question and the question of democracy and dictatorship to communicate her concern for the fate of the Russian revolution. In retrospect, some may defend the Bolsheviks' land policy in the logic that they had no other option but to make those concessions to the millions of peasants. Others may trace the origin of the agrarian crisis of the late 20s and 30s of the last century and degeneration of the Russian revolution in this very erroneous Bolshevik policy. All of us are well acquainted with the old controversy over the right of self-determination of nations where Luxemburg differed radically with the Bolshevik leadership. Though many critics have tried to highlight where she was wrong, many others seem to agree about the rightful stress of her arguments on proletarian internationalism and international proletarian class unity. The most important point of Luxemburg's criticism was on the Bolshevik's later attempt to equate the dictatorship of the proletariat with that of the Communist Party, not only in practice, but also in paving this concept into theory. Her criticism on this account, if regarded as trenchant and farsighted in her time, seems to be prophetic, in retrospect.

The important socialist activists and theoreticians of the Workers' Council movement, Anton Pannekoek and Herman Gorter had been castigated and obliterated for being "Left-wing Communist" for a couple of decades by the victorious communist side. Thanks to the author of this book, he not only re-searched, but also re-surfaced the old criticism of Pannekoek and Gorter, which may help the readers to grasp the relevant issues discussed. The emphatic focus of Pannekoek on the independent class initiative of the workers in the developed countries is self-evident, when he wrote,

> Such an aim cannot be attained by an ignorant mass, confident followers of a party presenting itself as an expert leadership. It can be attained only if the workers themselves, the entire class, understand the conditions, ways and means of their fight; when every man knows from his own judgment, what to do.

Gorter, on the other hand, constantly stressed the contrasts between Russia and Western Europe, to defend his views that whilst the Bolshevik revolution was appropriate for Russia, it would not necessarily work in the West.

It is interesting to find that the author did not restrict his review within the circle of the contemporaries of the October Revolution, but extended his critique to the later commentaries on the Russian revolution. In this direction, the author reviewed the polemics between Charles Bettelheim and Paul Sweezy on dictatorship of the proletariat and dynamics of the transitional phase among the Marxists during the worldwide turbulent periods of the 1970's. Whatsoever interesting and thought provoking their contribution may be, the controversy whether the transition itself is equivalent to socialism or not, could not be resolved.

## IV

At this juncture it would not be out of context to mention a few relevant points of the current work in a nutshell.

- One may or may not admit that all the steps taken in those initial stages of the Soviet regime were *socialist* in content. And similarly, one may or may not agree with all the explanations provided by the ruling Bolsheviks in those initial years. But the readers must acknowledge the effort of the author to unearth the debates and the controversies surrounding the steps taken in those years. All these revelations have given us a chance to judge the merits and demerits of the practice and the theoretical implications of revolutionary democracy in the initial stage of transition.

- The chapter on analysis of the international situation by Lenin in the Second Congress of the Communist International contains interesting observations on John Maynard Keynes. Keynes made a detailed estimate of the balance sheet of the liabilities that the cost of war imposed upon the belligerent countries. Keynes also warned about the historical significance of the possible alliance of "Bolshevism" and "Spartacism" in Russia and Germany respectively. The interested readers will find valuable inputs from these references and will have an idea how the bourgeois think-tank personified in Keynes comprehended the impact of the war and the revolutions in Europe after the First World War.
- The Bolshevik expectation of revolutions in the West was not fulfilled. Naturally, such miscarriage of expectations provoked analysis within the Communist International to the pertinent question that why the working class of the developed countries were hesitant and diffident in marching forward with the banner of revolution. To Lenin and the leadership of the Third International in general, the answer was the "Opportunism in the upper ranks of the working class movement." The author, in this context, has included an important and lively discussion on this issue. By taking recourse to the classical Marxist understanding he has shown how the working class through its struggle become united and constitutes as a class for itself. This understanding does not accommodate the concept of "opportunism" among the working class. The author showed that the experience of German revolution, especially the leading role of the Berlin Shop Stewards also does not match with the above theorization of opportunism among the working class.
- At the same time the author pointed out with various references that while defending the steps in favor of state capitalism "the biggest fallacy ... was Lenin's defense of ...primitive accumulation of Russian state capital dictated by the need of the weak state and underdeveloped

> capitalism as an original practice of 'socialism'". He has also quoted from Lenin: "Freedom to trade means freedom for capitalism, but it also means a new form of capitalism. We are doing this quite openly. It is state capitalism." The quotation continues, "But state capitalism in a society where power belongs to capital, and state capitalism in a proletarian state are two different concepts." In this context the author referred the analysis of both, Eugen Verga, the acknowledged economist of CI and Paul Mattick, a close observer and critique of the steps taken by the Bolsheviks in post-revolutionary Russia.

We may conclude by saying that the author deserves credit for studying anew the course of the history of the Russian revolution to locate the *metamorphosis* of the Bolshevik Party through the initial years of the revolution and its imprint on the formative years of the Third Communist International. One may or may not agree with all the comments and conclusions drawn by the author, his meticulous reading of the subject may illuminate us in many aspects, if not all, especially in the Centenary year of the Russian October Revolution. Let us welcome his serious and honest endeavor.

Kolkata, March 2017 **Goutam Sen**

# 1
# Introduction

Communist International (CI), popularly known as the Third International was formed primarily at the initiative of the Bolsheviks in Russia. The First Congress of CI was convened in the Kremlin Palace, Moscow from March 2-6, 1919. Vladimir Lenin stressed the need of a new International in *April Theses*[1] as soon as he landed in Petrograd (St. Petersburg) in April 1917 after the February Revolution, along with his comrades from exile in Europe. The urge for a new International of the working class was felt as the leaders of the Second International, such as Karl Kautsky, Philipp Scheidemann, Rudolf Hilferding of Germany, Otto Bauer of Austria, Ramsay Macdonald of Great Britain, Georgi Plekhanov, Irakli Tsereteli, Fedor Dan of Russia, Jules Guesde of France, etc. all pledged support to their respective national governments in the First World War (WWI). Their support to the WWI effectively dragged the working class belonging to different nations in Europe at bayonet points of each other on the opposite sides of the trenches of war. In his work [Lenin, 1974a], Lenin identified the Internationalist groups among the working class of Europe who could be part of the new International, such as the "Spartacus" group in Germany, the group "gathered around the Bremen paper, *Arbeiterpolitik*", and

> the Scottish public school teacher and Socialist, MacLean, who has been sentenced to hard labour by the bourgeois government of England for his revolutionary activity against the war; hundreds of English Socialists who are in jail for the same offence....
>
> in Holland, the party of the "Tribunists," those who publish the daily paper *Tribune* (Anton Pannekoek, Herman Gorter, Wynkoop, and

> Henriette Roland-Holst, who, though a centrist at Zimmerwald, has now joined our ranks); in Sweden, the party of the youth or the Left with leaders such as Lindhagen, Ture Nerman, Carlson, Strom and S. Hoglund, who at Zimmerwald was personally active in the organization of the Zimmerwald Left, and who is now serving a prison term for his activity against the war. .... [Lenin, 1974a, p. 79]

Of course, many others he mentioned.

The activities of CI in the formative years were intimately related to the developments in Russia after the October 1917 revolution. The very close bondage of the Third International with the Russian revolution was both its strength and weakness. The strength was embedded in the deep enthusiasm among the delegates of CI who assembled in Moscow with the hope to witness *socialism* in their own eyes, and abolition of *state* in practice in Soviet Russia. Many of the delegates in the First Congress did not subscribe to communistic principles as the Bolsheviks in Russia, and represented anarchist, syndicalist trends of the working class movements in Europe. Several of them were treated as fugitives in their own countries. They could find themselves as free international citizens in Soviet Moscow for the first time as a large part of their political life passed under disguise. In that sense, the Congress in the Moscow assembly represented a truly international communion of revolutionaries. Victor Serge, an anarchist militant coming from Spain wrote,

> The entire first phase of the Russian Revolution seems to me today to have been dominated by the utter honesty of Lenin and his group. It was this that attracted all of us to him, regardless of our nationality and our viewpoint. In Spain early in 1917, I discussed the Russian Revolution with a group of militants who were even then talking of seizing Barcelona and setting up a new Commune (one day in July we posted its program on the walls). ....We were not Marxists, yet in the distorted echoes of Lenin's words that reached us, we could discern a remarkable integrity. [Serge, 1937, p. 9]

The weakness of the tie-up was Soviet Russia being the *only state* where dictatorship of the proletariat was exercised during the days of its genesis as a state when the urban working class in Russia held political power. It is crucial to keep this assertion in mind while reflecting on the initial developments of CI. It was the first time and a profound time in the history of human civilization that attempts were made to organize society depending principally on certain predictions and projections of two authors. The analysis of Karl Marx and Friedrich Engels regarding the historical progress of society was debated not only among the tutored pedants of European "socialism", but also among the exploited and oppressed "*masses*" in relatively underdeveloped Russia who aspired to contribute in building society from their own, direct experiences. The victorious workers in Russia were desperately looking for the impending victory of the proletariat in more economically developed Germany. As a recent research account shows, everybody in the workers' camp were pinning their hopes on the workers' and soldiers' revolution in Germany that lasted from November 1918 till January 1919, and most of them were in Russia.

> For both leaders and the rank and file, revolutionary Germany was the centre of their world-revolutionary mental map[7]. In Soviet Russia, the German revolution of 1918-19 was accompanied by extensive press coverage, demonstrations and calls for solidarity[8]. When the Spartacist leaders Karl Liebknecht and Rosa Luxemburg were murdered in Berlin in January 1919, they were celebrated as martyrs of socialism throughout Soviet Russia, with acts of public grievance even in the most remote areas.[9] [Albert, 2011, pp. 111-112]

Our subsequent discussion focuses on the significant impact of the failure of the workers' and soldiers' revolution in Germany and other places of Europe on the "socialist" practices in Soviet Russia. However, the important point here is the portrayal of Soviet Russia as the *lone* sentinel of "socialist" practices had a huge adverse impact on the transformation of CI as an extension of Bolshevism. Dictatorship of the proletariat was a natural, colloquial phrase among the revolutionaries who assembled in Moscow in March 1919. Deliberations on this subject was the major issue among the traditional "socialist" parties of Europe[2] who till the other day were the prevailing deities before the working class of Europe, and of course, the eventuality of dictatorship of the proletariat was like a horror movie before the bourgeoisie and existing governments in Europe. Contrary to the expectation of the revolutionaries assembled in the First Congress of CI, practice of this idea was left to the Bolshevik interpretation of the newly raised Soviet state-policies formulated under heavy odds of international isolation. Bolshevik practices were a subject of intense criticism by the traditional "socialist" parties who repudiated even the basic idea that the working class can constitute itself as the ruling class of society. Significantly, practice of dictatorship of the proletariat by the Bolsheviks and their theoretical justifications and interpretation were subjects of intense scrutiny by the contemporary communist revolutionaries from Western Europe who assembled in Moscow under the umbrella of CI. *Metamorphosis* of Bolshevism about the understanding and practices of state-craft, about "socialist" organization of society, and subsequent interpretation of Soviet Russia as the *role model* of "socialism" left an indelible imprint over the working class movements in Europe. More significantly, this *metamorphosis* of the programmes of "socialism" made a huge adverse impact on the emerging working class movements in the colonies that were under various forms of imperialists' control.

Embarrassing questions may be raised here regarding the relevance of raking up this nearly century-old history now that many of the facets of *metamorphosis* of Bolshevism are well established and well understood. How are the queries on this past history going to help answering the questions of *socialism* today and the associated struggle of the working class against capitalism? The blunt answer to these questions is the brutal truth that none of the major issues that arose in the formative years of CI could be resolved by providing resounding answers during the living and actual practices of "socialist" organization of society in that period. Expectations ran high that such "socialist" reorganization would lead to a viable, alternative society based on the dominant role of the working class without capital and capitalism in future.

The reasons behind the failure of Soviet Russia as a regime heading towards *socialism* even in its formative years are generally understood in terms of the very limited exercise of workers' democracy, in terms of the hegemony of the absolutist *Party* in all affairs of society, of lack of democracy in social practices. Rarely discussed is the meaning of *socialist* production relations, the significance of the revolution in ushering them under dictatorship of the proletariat, and the interrelation of *socialist* production relations with the exercise of workers' democracy. Seldom is raised the issues of *transitional society* under dictatorship of the proletariat where the proletariat exercises freedom in bringing in *socialist* production relations which compete with the capitalist production relations hitherto existing in society. How did Soviet Russia face these questions, and what was the theoretical explanation of the *transitional society* by the Bolsheviks before the delegates of CI in subsequent sessions of the Congresses? How did they address the dichotomy and divergence of their actual practices of "socialism" in the *transitional society* which were miles apart in theory and practice from the vision of Marx on *socialism*? Moreover, the question of *socialist* revolution like every other revolution in history is not the question of production relations alone. We also need to explore the preparation of the working class of Europe in their ideological conviction in ushering the supremacy of *socialism* over the prevailing bourgeoisie ideology in society. Were they ideologically prepared in their revolutionary efforts to seize power so as to provide an alternative *state* which was to wither away along with the *transitional society*? Most unfortunately, as our present critique will show subsequently these questions were neither addressed in the deliberations of CI, nor have yet been answered in a convincing manner before the international working class. In a different fashion and with more specific contemporary reference to the events of the "Arab Spring" of 2011, Gabriel Kuhn asked [Kuhn, 2012],

> It was so apparent that many of the Arab revolutionaries faced questions that were essentially the same that the German revolutionaries had faced almost a hundred years earlier—or, for that matter, pretty much all revolutionaries throughout history: What do we do once the tyrant is gone? How do we facilitate a true transition of power? How do we establish political and economic institutions that really alter the forms of government and production? What is the role of the military and the police? [Kuhn, 2012, p. xiii]

Naturally, such a void in the realm of the theory of social and economic organization of *socialism*, and the defeat of the practices beforehand under the illusory guise of "victory" has left the international working class bewildered and diffident. In fact, the international working class has been compelled to compromise and adjust its own class interests with the dominant interests of the bourgeoisie in every part of the world, in every sphere of activity.

It is not that the world has not witnessed revolutions in the long period after WWI – there were many revolutions and revolutionary prospects particularly after the Second World War (WWII), the most significant being the overthrow of the Kuomintang regime in China by the guerrilla army that went through a glorious, arduous path of *Long March* under the leadership of the "communist" party of China. Today, it requires no long argumentation to say that the actual practices of "socialism" under the rule of such victorious "communist" parties had not much in common with the prospects and issues of *socialism* that were on the practical agenda of the working class of Europe after the WWI, and also in the living and animated debates generated in the formative years of CI.

There has been in recent years, a renewed interest in the Russian revolution and the associated international working class movement of that time. Substantial documentation of the CI is now available, particularly after opening of the state archives in erstwhile "socialist" states to the researchers [Degras, 1971], [Riddell, 2016], [Riddell, 1986]. There is a work in 1997 [Fernandez, 1997] that reviewed extensively the germinating political economy of Soviet Russia and a broad spectrum of international schools of criticism. In 2005, documents from the archives of erstwhile Soviet Russia were collated to throw light on the crucial formative period of the Soviet state, i.e., from 1917-1921 [Kowalski, 2005]. In 2006, a book was published of 656 pages that contain only the annotated bibliography of the books, documents, and theses on the Russian revolution focusing on the period of 1917-21, [Smele, 2006] the period that is under our consideration. However, *limited reviews and critiques* have been devoted to the number of theses accepted in the Congresses of CI in its formative period. They later became the hallmarks and signposts of "communist" practices all over the world. It requires no eloquent argument over the fact that history weighs in the moments of fierce wars, the opposing contingents in the warring camps bring forth their past glories in their campaigns. At the height of the age of enlightenment, Victor Hugo said (1852), "An invasion of armies can be resisted, but not an idea whose time has come." *Socialism* was a practical idea before the revolting proletariat of Europe as a sequel to the WWI, and they were incessantly reminded of the Paris Commune, a new form of *state* that arose during the uprising of the Paris workers in March 1871. The glorious existence of the Commune ended in 72 days with the massacre of revolting workers by the joint army of the French and German capitalists. Therefore, introspection over the key theses in the formative period of CI is necessary to draw the critical lessons of the theory and practice of "socialism", particularly in the light of the defeat of their actual exercises.

## 1.1 Working Class Revolutions in Europe after the WWI and the Genesis of CI

Here, we must highlight the civil war-like situation in Europe as a consequence of the WWI which resulted in several attempts of revolution by the working class in Europe, the most significant among them being in Russia, Germany, and Hungary. In his opening remarks to the First Congress of CI Lenin stated, "Not only in Russia, but in the most developed capitalist countries of Europe, Germany for example, civil war is a fact." [Lenin, 1972a, p. 9] He was not exaggerating. In 1919, Soviet Russia faced a violent Civil War as a consequence of a countrywide internal onslaught by the forces of counterrevolution that was supported by fourteen "civilized" nation-states of Europe. While presenting his report on the international situation at the Second Congress in July 1920, Lenin remarked, "Among the official British documents there is a paper which scrupulously enumerates all the states (fourteen in all) which some six months ago in December 1919, pledged themselves to take Moscow and Petrograd." [Lenin, 1972a, p. 41] To these "civilized"! state-powers of Europe the new Soviet Russia was a rogue regime of Bolsheviks, and Holy Russia! was to be resurrected by them from this rogue rule.

The attempts by these European nation-states to dislodge the Soviet government in Russia backfired as civil unrest was raging in their own backyards. Industrial workers in war-torn Europe were spontaneous in their support of the Soviet rule in Russia. The after effects of war left a devastating impact over the psyche of the common "*masses*" of Europe. They witnessed the real, true face of capitalism in dragging the life of the millions compulsively to death and destruction. The workers and battle-fatigued soldiers of Europe severely questioned the rule of capital by spontaneously raising the flag of revolt. Soviet rule in their own places caught instant imagination after observing the flow of events in Soviet Russia beginning with the October Revolution of 1917. That was an epochal period of history when the events of every month took the strides of decades in an otherwise usually placid time. The most significant events in Europe in the period after the WWI were proclamation of Soviet rule in Hungary and Germany.

### *1.1.1 Brief overview of the workers' and soldiers' revolution in Hungary and Germany in 1919*

The Soviet Republic of Hungary was proclaimed on March 21, 1919. It was preceded by a democratic revolution when the monarchy was abolished in the wake of numerous strikes in the factories in and around Budapest and revolt of the soldiers in October 1918. Hungary was declared a republic with a coalition government headed by Count Michael Karloyi. The social democratic party (SDP) was most influential in Budapest during this coalition regime [Deak, 1968]. Matters came to a head in February and March 1919, when this SDP-led government faced opposition from the newly constituted Hungarian communist party, formed only four months before and was headed by the former journalist, Béla Kun. The SDP-led government capitulated before the pressure of demands from the workers and soldiers for a Soviet form of state. It was a piquant situation. Without a single shot being fired, and no fighting, not even a street demonstration, power passed from the Karloyi government to a Revolutionary Governing Soviet (with Béla Kun at its head). The Soviet Republic of Hungary lasted for 133 days [Cunningham, 2004].

In Germany, the naval retinues of the North Sea fleet refused to obey the orders for a suicidal attack against an overwhelmingly superior British fleet. On November 2, 1918 the fleet was ordered to be docked in Kiel, the port city of North Germany. The following day, violent unrest spread over the docks and factories of Kiel. The Governor of Kiel was forced to resign, and control of the town passed to an elected Workers' and Sailors' Council. On November 9, revolution swept throughout Berlin, the capital of imperial

Germany. Columns of workers, comprising armed detachments, converged at the city centre in a series of huge demonstrations. Karl Liebknecht, the lone deputy in the Reichstag who on December 2, 1914 voted against "war credits" and was sent for military conscription, and now the leader of the splinter group *Spartakusbund* (Spartacus League) proclaimed from the balcony of the Imperial Palace,

> The day of the revolution has come. We have enforced peace. Peace has been concluded in this moment. The old has gone. The rule of the Hohenzollern, who have resided in this palace for centuries, is over. In this very hour we proclaim the Free Socialist Republic of German.... [Liebknecht, 2000]

On the same day Philipp Scheidemann, leader of the largest social democratic party (SPD) of Europe and a cabinet member of the Kaiser's Government, announced from the balcony of the Reichstag that Germany was a republic. Incidentally, Philip Scheidermann was the person who strongly advocated the participation of his party in the Kaiser's war efforts. Kaiser Wilhelm II was away in Belgium, and was notified of the proclamation of the republic. The Kaiser officially abdicated his throne on November 28, 1918 [Kuhn, 2012, p. 29]. Dual power came into existence in Germany; on one side there was the Weimar Republic whose first president was Friedrich Ebert, the vastly influential and manipulative politician from SPD. On the other hand, there was the Workers' and Soldiers' Council clamouring for Soviet power. The First General Congress of the Workers' and Soldiers' Councils of Germany was held in Berlin on December 16, 1918 with Richard Müller, the leader of the revolutionary stewards as Chairman of the Executive Council of the Workers' and Soldiers' Councils of Great Berlin. The first and second demands in the report of the Chairman of the Congress were,

1. The political power lies in the hands of the workers' and soldiers' councils in the German Socialist Republic. It is their duty to maintain and to expand the achievements of the revolution and to suppress the counterrevolution.
2. Until an assembly of delegates of all workers' and soldiers' councils has elected an Executive Council of the German

> Socialist Republic, the Executive Council of Great Berlin fulfils this role. [Kuhn, 2012, p. 36]

The revolution ended in a bloodbath that lasted between January 9-15, 1919; the premature armed insurrection called by the newly formed communist party of Germany (KPD) was suppressed by the armed counter-offensive of *Freikorps* brigades, handpicked by Gustav Noske, SPD leader and the interior minister of the Weimar Republic. The cold blooded murder of the unarmed leaders of the insurrection, Rosa Luxemburg, Karl Liebknecht, Leo Jogiches, and others by the "socialist" (!) government of the Weimar Republic terminated the revolution.

In the countries where Soviets did not come into existence, workers either formed organizations dumping the leadership of the so-called "socialists", or compelled their leaders to support the new initiative of bringing together the working class organizations of Europe in the form of the Third International. The First Congress of the CI was convened against the backdrop of huge disillusionment of workers and soldiers of Europe with the war efforts of their governments on both sides of the warring camps. Indignation of the workers towards the traditional leaders of "socialism" who had comprised the Second International, and had actively supported the war efforts of their national governments was not mere political propaganda by the revolutionaries who assembled under the banner of the CI in Moscow. It was a fact of life in European urban centres which was reflected in the "*mass*" desertion of the workers from this "socialist" camp. For example, the Congress of the 700,000-member strong Independent Social-Democratic Party of Germany (USPD) held at Halle, Germany in October 1920 saw the majority of the delegates switching their affiliation to the Third International after a four-hour long oration by Gregori Zinoviev, the Bolshevik Chairman of the Presidium of CI.[3]

### 1.2 A Brief Tour of CI in the Formative Years

The revolutionaries who assembled in Moscow in March 1919 during the First Congress of CI came with ambitious hopes of world revolution. By the formation of CI they saw the proclamation of the anti-war conference held in Zimmerwald, Switzerland in

September 1915 against participation of the working class in the war being realized in practice. The resolution of the Zimmerwald *Left* was only an expression of intent by the "*Left*" tendencies, an insignificant minority of the SDPs of Europe. Only forty-two delegates attended the Zimmerwald conference representing ten countries from Europe and European Russia [Riddell, 2008, p. 8]. The proclamation urged the international proletariat to wage an irreconcilable *class struggle* against their national governments.

> It is the task and the duty of the Socialists of the belligerent countries to take up this struggle with full force; it is the task and the duty of the Socialists of the neutral states to support their brothers in this struggle against bloody barbarism with every effective means. [Manifesto, 1915]

The enthusiasm for the world proletarian revolution reached its peak at the Second Congress of CI held in Petrograd and Moscow, July-August 1920. The First Congress in which the resolution announcing formation of the CI was passed and the first *Manifesto* of CI was released was essentially a preparatory meeting with minimal participation from the parties and organizations outside the periphery of erstwhile imperial Russia. "It was attended by 35 delegates with voting powers, representing 19 parties and organizations, and by 19 delegates, representing 16 organizations, with a consultative voice" [Degras, 1971, p. 6] from 22 countries [Riddell, 2008, p. 9]. Only one delegate from the recently formed Communist Party of Germany (KPD) was present whose mandate was actually to oppose the convocation of the First Congress [Rosmer, 1973, p. 66]. The French and the English contingents were present with consultative votes. On the other hand, the Second Congress had attracted sizeable participation and interest of the working class organizations of varied nature from all over Europe, United States of America, and also a delegation from the countries under colonial rule representing the Eastern part of the world. The official number of delegates accounted was 218. "Delegates came from 37 countries, representing not only small groupings but also several parties with tens of thousands of members and strong ties with the broad working class movement." [Riddell, 2008, p. 11] Another account states, "The congress was attended by 217 delegates from 41 countries, of whom 169 had voting powers. Of these, 136 represented communist parties, which also had 15 delegates with consultative voice." [Degras, 1971, p. 109]

It is interesting to note the British working class was represented by several tendencies in the Congress, namely the Shop Stewards Committee, British socialist party and "Left-wing" communist party members such as Sylvia Pankhurst. Similarly, USPD the breakaway factions of SPD in Germany with a significant support base among the working class sent a delegation apart from KPD in Germany. France was represented by both the Committee for the Third International and a delegation from the Socialist party. The invitation from the Executive Committee of CI (ECCI) clearly mentioned the revolutionary syndicalists to participate in the Congress. "An invitation is also extended to all groups of revolutionary syndicalists, the IWW unions, and other organizations with which the ECCI has entered into relations..." [Degras, 1971, p. 103] In fact, a letter of invitation from ECCI was sent to the International Workers of the World (IWW) in January 1920, the largest proletarian organization of USA with a distinct syndicalist outlook to join the Second Congress. The wide spectrum of participation of the revolutionary sections of the working class in the Congress made even Lenin ecstatic before the Congress was opened. In a speech before the Moscow Soviet on March 6, 1920 to celebrate the first anniversary of the formation of CI, Lenin said,

> During this year the Communist International has been successful beyond all expectation; we may say boldly that at the tithe of its foundation no one expected such immense successes. [Lenin, 1974b, p. 417]

Responding to the sense and variety of participation a new version of the *Manifesto* of CI was released. The other significant resolution in the Congress was the adoption of the infamous "21 conditions for admission to CI". The intention behind framing these statutes for communist parties from all over the world was to stop admission of the leaders of the Second International to the newly formed CI who were veering towards it sensing the inclination and mood of the "*masses*" of workers in Europe. In effect, it was imposition of the Bolshevik view of political organization of the working class that was hotly contested by several representatives from the European working class during the debates of the Second and Third Congress of CI.

The Third Congress of CI held in Moscow in June-July 1921 received the largest delegation from European parties but at the same time the enthusiasm for world revolution started plummeting at the end of the sessions. "The third Comintern congress, held from June 22 to July 12, 1921, was attended by 509 delegates from 48 countries, of whom 291 had full voting rights." [Degras, 1971, p. 224] The Congress saw acrimonious debates between the French and the German delegations on the issue of the failure of "March Action" organized by the offshoots of KPD in Germany. The Third Congress was held following the infamous Tenth Congress of the Bolshevik party in Russia held in March 1921 that formally banned the existence of platforms and factions within the party. The Congress was held following the suppression of the sailors' uprising in Kronstadt Fort in Petrograd nearly at the same time. The Congress saw expulsion of the Italian socialist party from the Third International. It was in the Third Congress that Lenin formulated the New Economic Policy (NEP) in Soviet Russia before the assembly of the communists of the world. By the time the Fourth Congress was held in Moscow, in November-December 1922, Soviet Russia had already completed five years of existence. Prospects of the working class revolution in Europe receded in the distant horizon[4], and the sessions in the Congress were showing all signs of Bolshevik dominance in the ideas and practices of CI. It was the last Congress that Lenin could participate, and he was found cautioning against the implications of *russification* of CI.

> At the Third Congress, in 1921, we adopted a resolution on the organisational structure of the Communist Parties and on the methods and content of their activities. The resolution is an excellent one, but it is almost entirely Russian, that is to say everything in it is based on Russian conditions. This is its good point, but also its failing. It is failing because I am sure that no foreigner can read it. I have read it again before saying this. In the first place, it is too long, containing fifty or more points. Foreigners are not usually able to read such things. Secondly, even if they read it, they will not understand it because it is too Russian. Not because it is written in Russian – it has been excellently translated into all languages – but because it is thoroughly imbued with the Russian spirit. And thirdly, if by way of exception so foreigner does understand it, he cannot carry it out. This is its third defect. [Lenin, 1972b, pp. 142-143]

By the time the Fifth Congress of CI was held in Moscow, June–July 1924, the process of *russification* was complete. Joseph Stalin who was nowhere mentioned in the first four Congresses presented four reports. Leon Trotsky although he delivered three reports was already on the path of disgrace in his own Bolshevik party. It was the Congress of Gregori Zinoviev who was the President of ECCI in all throughout the five Congresses. His speeches constituted 65 of the 120 pages of minutes of proceedings in the Fifth Congress. [Communist Party of Great Britain, 1924]. Bolshevization of CI was complete but Bolshevism itself got *metamorphosed* at the same time. In place of the world revolution, "socialism in one country" occupied the centre stage of the agenda of the Bolshevik party in Russia.[5] Subsequently the agenda was followed up in the deliberations of CI.[6] We therefore, in this essay, consider the first four Congresses as the formative period of CI. We review the developments of political programmes of CI in the light of the *metamorphosis* of Bolshevism that left an indelible imprint not only over the development of CI but also over a large part of human civilization in the last century.

### 1.3 International Critiques of Bolshevism During the Formative Years of CI

One of the very early critiques of Bolshevik policies in post-revolution Russia was Rosa Luxemburg. Clara Zetkin, her long standing compatriot and a very active participant in the formation of CI had to say the following about Rosa in her obituary,

> She gave herself completely to the cause of Socialism, not only in her tragic death, but throughout her whole life, daily and hourly, through the struggles of many years ... She was the sharp sword, the living flame of revolution. [Cliff, 1959, Quote]

As early in September 1918, while in prison she drafted *The Russian Revolution*, an unfinished work that she did not have the opportunity to see in print in her lifetime. It was tragic and unfortunate that Luxemburg's work was never published by the Third International, whereas this was the first fairly balanced assessment of revolution in Russia and its implications on the impending German revolution from somebody outside Russia. In the first chapter of the essay, Luxemburg wrote,

> It is not Russia's unripeness which has been proved by the events of the war and the Russian Revolution, but the unripeness of the German proletariat for the fulfilment of its historic tasks. And to make this fully clear is the first task of a critical examination of the Russian Revolution....There is no doubt either that the wise heads at the helm of the Russian Revolution, that Lenin and Trotsky on their thorny path beset by traps of all kinds, have taken many, decisive step only with the greatest inner hesitation and with most violent inner opposition. And surely nothing can be farther from their thoughts than to believe that all the things they have done or left undone under the conditions of bitter compulsion and necessity in the midst of the roaring whirlpool of events, should be regarded by the International as a shining example of socialist policy toward which only uncritical admiration and zealous imitation are in order. It would be no less wrong to fear that a critical examination of the road so far taken by the Russian Revolution would serve to weaken the respect for and the attractive power of the example of the Russian Revolution, which alone can overcome the fatal inertia of the German masses. Nothing is farther from the truth. [Luxemburg, 2004, p. 284]

About the contemporary relevance of Luxemburg's criticism of the Russian revolution, Peter Hudis and Kevin B. Anderson wrote while introducing a selection of Rosa Luxemburg's works in *The Rosa Luxemburg Reader* as,

> It is a testament to Luxemburg's prescience that her critique of the Russian revolution, posed in such a radically different historical context, nevertheless speaks to a question that is on the minds of millions today—is there an alternative to both existing capitalism and its bureaucratic/totalitarian opponents? [Luxemburg, 2004, p. 25]

While the above statement testifies the relevance of the mighty question of human civilization today that was raised almost a century ago, it would have been fair and complete to say that the question was not raised by Luxemburg alone even at that time. Among the *groups* that Lenin considered including in the new International was the "Dutch Left Group" led by Anton Pannekoek, Herman Gorter among others. They were closely associated with the formation of KPD in Germany and later its breakaway "Left-wing" communist workers' party of Germany (KAPD). They made significant contributions to the critique of Bolshevism in the contemporary period as Luxemburg's criticisms. In response to

Lenin's attack on "Left Wing Communism" [Lenin, 1974c] in 1920, Pannekoek wrote in the same year a long rebuttal *World Revolution and Communist Tactics* where he highlighted the significance of ideological preparation of the working class while analysing the reasons for the defeat of the German revolution.

One of the early treatises on the debates and theses during the formative years of CI appeared in the form of the memoirs of Alfred Rosmer. Rosmer was a French anarchist who on his own moved over to Bolshevism, was a member of the ECCI of the Second Congress of CI, played a leading role in Red International of Labour Unions, and for a period was a member of the political bureau of the French communist party (PCF). His long association with Trotsky and later disassociation with him during the formation of the Fourth International are quite well known and extensively documented. While introducing the book *Moscow Under Lenin* in June 1972 to English readers, Tamara Deutscher, lifelong companion of Isaac Deutscher wrote,

> How did it happen, how could it have been that the party of revolution which was to lead toward the liberation of man, toward a classless society, gradually sank into the mire of a totalitarian regime? Was Leninism responsible for Stalinism? Did Stalin continue what Lenin let off? It was to answer such questions that Alfred Rosmer set out to write *Moscou Sous Lenine*. [Rosmer, 1973, p. vii]

We refer to Rosmer's work to show the level of dithering, ambivalence and confusions that prevailed in the critique of the revolutionaries who were directly associated with the formation of CI, and who soon distanced themselves as they could not digest the convulsions in CI in the light of the *metamorphosis* of Bolshevism. Echoing confidence of the international revolutionaries in the personal leadership of Lenin and Trotsky during the Second Congress of CI, Rosmer wrote,

> Though these books were written for a particular situation, they have lost none of their value. They can still profitably be read today and not only for their historical interest; many of the problems they deal with are still with us. In Moscow in 1920 they were, for the delegates, texts of incomparable richness. They were studied and discussed enthusiastically. Their authors had enormous prestige with the delegates. Lenin and Trotsky stood head and shoulders above the other men in October revolution."[7] [p. 59]

Unfortunately, the same Rosmer in the same work was tentative, befuddled, and torn between allegiance to the Russian revolution and despair at the prospect of its growing insensitivity to the world proletarian revolution. He wrote in the conclusion of the book,

> The period of transition, the passing from the feeble regime, which the revolutionaries needed only to finish off, to the new society which had to be built, was the most difficult test. [Rosmer, 1973, p. 224]

This 'period of transition' was supposed to be dictatorship of the proletariat. Did the revolutionaries pass 'the most difficult test'? In the same paragraph he wrote,

> If it no longer expressed the aspirations, if it was ignorant of the needs, of the men who had accepted it as a guide, then it is no longer possible to speak of the dictatorship of proletariat. From now on it was the dictatorship of a party, of a small group of men, of a dictatorship which became intolerable to those very men who were supposed to be the builders of the socialist society.

Rosmer did not answer the question whether dictatorship of the proletariat, the transition period to *socialism,* was meant to be led by *a single guiding party,* and if so what guaranteed it to remain steadfast to the aspirations of the working class? Rather he answered,

> One can write the history of a revolution only if one sympathises with it; otherwise one can collect a lot of facts and fail to see their meaning. If one treated the history of the Commune in this way, there would be not much left for socialists.

In another place he wrote, "It is not easy to distinguish the moment at which a revolution becomes a counter-revolution." [Rosmer, 1973, p. 227]

Today, we cannot rest by sympathizing with Rosmer's romantic overtures with the virtues of a revolution that occurred nearly a century ago. For nearly a century, the vices of the deafening level of propaganda of "socialism in one country" gripped the international working class, struggle against capitalism. This had led to the doctrine of volunteerism of a *vanguard Party,* made its existence an absolutely necessary precondition to achieve such fallacious versions of "socialism". We do not know whether Rosmer was aware of Lenin's astounding shift before and after the October

Revolution regarding the fundamental basis of social revolutions as understood by the laws of historical materialism. While commemorating the Paris Commune, Lenin wrote in 1911 the following in a eulogy:

> Two conditions, at least, are necessary for a victorious social revolution —highly developed productive forces and a proletariat adequately prepared for it. But in 1871 both these conditions were lacking. French capitalism was still poorly developed, and France was at that time mainly a petty-bourgeois country (artisans, peasants, shopkeepers, etc.). On the other hand, there was no workers' party; the working class had not gone through a long school of struggle and was unprepared, and for the most part did not even clearly visualise its tasks and the methods of fulfilling them. [Lenin, 1974d, p. 141]

Nearly twelve years after, an exasperated Lenin focused on the peculiar crisis situation in which the revolution in Russia found itself. He sought to overwrite the law of historical materialism in the above paragraph to emphasize that the victory over the crisis in Russia was in line with the creative extension of "Marxism". He wrote in *Pravda*, May 30, 1923,

> What if the complete hopelessness of the situation, by stimulating the efforts of the workers and peasants tenfold, offered us the opportunity to create the fundamental requisites of civilization in a different way from that of the West European countries? Has that altered the general line of development of world history? Has that altered the basic relations between the basic classes of all the countries that are being, or have been, drawn into the general course of world history? [Lenin, 1974e, p. 478]

To stress the compulsion of raising volunteerism of the workers and peasants of Russia 'tenfold', and to buttress the historical significance of "socialism" of the Russian variety he even had to invoke Napoleon in the same article.

> You say that civilization is necessary for the building of socialism. Very good. But why could we not first create such prerequisites of civilization in our country by the expulsion of the landowners and the Russian capitalists, and then start moving toward socialism? Where, in what books, have you read that such variations of the customary historical sequence of events are impermissible or impossible?

> Napoleon, I think, wrote: *"On s'engage et puis ... on voit."* rendered freely this means: "First engage in a serious battle and then see what happens." Well, we did first engage in a serious battle in October 1917, and then saw such details of development (from the standpoint of world history they were certainly details) as the Brest peace, the New Economic Policy, and so forth. And now there can be no doubt that in the main we have been victorious. [Lenin, 1974e, p. 480]

Today, after a century-old bitter experience of defeat under the delusion of being 'victorious', we can certainly say that the international proletariat did not share Lenin's ahistorical conviction of swimming against the hostile, high tide after jumping into it anyway. Neither can we draw solace by the justification of defeat of "socialism" in Russia referred to endlessly in the literature from the grim reality of the social factors. Rosmer wrote, "In Moscow, in 1920, we were facing reality," [Rosmer, 1973, p. 60], and went on to point out Civil War, famine, lack of support of the international revolution, the all out attack of the international bourgeoisie upon the Soviet state, etc. as the causes of failure of the revolution.

> All the moral and material resources of a country already drained and exhausted by war had had to be thrown into war for three years. It was an unforgivable illusion to expect things to happen differently and more easily elsewhere. The struggle would be even more bitter, since everywhere else the bourgeoisie was stronger. [Rosmer, 1973, p. 60]

Interestingly, we found our understanding of Lenin's assertion in 1923 being echoed by Charles Bettelheim, the French economist-philosopher. Bettelheim made a formidable name among the Western "Marxists" in the1970s by openly denouncing the post-WWII Soviet regime in Russia. His compatriot, Paul M. Sweezy wrote about him,

> Fortunately, there are few if any Marxists better qualified than Charles Bettleheim to help fill this need. The appearance of his book and the further extension of his ideas along the lines of the above critique should set the stage of a lively and fruitful discussion. [Sweezy, 1972, p. 26]

Bettelheim in his celebrated work *Class Struggle in the USSR 1917-23* wrote in the Introduction,

> Under these conditions, the fundamental problem for the Soviet proletariat to solve seemed to be that of increasing production as quickly as possible: in building "the material foundations of socialism" it was "guaranteed" that the corresponding production relations and the appropriate superstructure would also develop. Hence the slogans of the period: "Technique decides everything" and "Catch up with and surpass the most advanced capitalist countries."....
>
> The fact is that this "understanding" dominated the ideological and political conceptions of the European sections of the Third International, and thereby helped to conceal the existence of classes and of class struggle in the Soviet Union, thus encouraging people to seek "elsewhere" than in class contradictions the causes of the grave difficulties being experienced by the Soviet Union....
>
> For a whole generation, my own generation, the two theses mentioned above enjoyed a sort of "obviousness" which caused us to avoid analyzing the real contradictions and problems: even when these were not ignored, their "solution" was put off till later—it would in due course be provided by the development of the productive forces. [Bettelheim, 1977, pp. 26-27]

We note with satisfaction that Bettelheim seemed to point to the limited 'ideological and political conceptions of the European sections of the Third International', 'for a whole generation' above. He seemed to ponder here over the vital issues before the working class in a *transitional society* marching towards *socialism;* that is how to carry forward and develop the basis of *socialist* production relations in a *transitional society.* We have a great deal to say later in this essay about Bettelheim's and Sweezy's debate *On the Transition to Socialism.* Here, in passing we can comment that Bettelheim in his enviable volume of work never mentioned Lenin's vigorous attempts in 1923 to overwrite the laws of historical materialism as was understood by him in 1911. Neither did Bettelheim ever question Lenin's repeated harping on accumulation of capital and on state capitalism under Soviet rule in the sessions of the Third and the Fourth Congress of CI. We point out this fallacy in Bettelheim's work at the onset of our essay as our methodology and objective remain the same as Bettelheim's. He wrote,

> One of the aims of this book is, indeed, to endeavor, as is possible today with the advantage of hindsight, to provide a fuller characterization of the system of the dictatorship of the proletariat as

> it existed in Russia between 1917 and 1923 and subsequently. This should also make it possible to appreciate better the nature of the social relations and class struggles which determined the characteristics of the system and contributed to its later evolution. In this connection, we must turn back to Lenin's previously quoted formulation: "Ours is not actually a workers' state, but workers' and peasants' state. [Bettelheim, 1977, p. 99]

We have to question today, whether the Third International was prepared to take up this 'even more bitter' struggle elsewhere in the world as suggested by Rosmer. We cite here Fernando Claudin, the leading standard bearer of the "popular front" in the Spanish Civil War and political bureau member of the Spanish communist party. He was expelled from the party in February 1965 as a sequel to a prolonged debate within the higher echelons of the party. While reviewing the experience of the European "communist" movement under the guidance of the Third International, Claudin concluded in December 1969 the following:

> But what it is interesting to note here in this transposition of the Russian model is Lenin's grave underestimation of the influence of reformist politics and the reformist mentality among the proletariat of the advanced countries. I do not mean to say that Lenin underestimated the wide *extent* of the reformist phenomenon, but rather its *depth*, the firm roots that it possessed in the working-class masses of the West.
>
> This underestimation of the penetration of reformism into the Western proletariat was a symptom of theoretical shortcomings that were to have an effect on the political plane in the way the new revolutionary party was created, the way its structures and mode of working were conceived and its tasks were carried out. [Claudin, 1975, p. 58]

Claudin viewed here the '*depth*... of the penetration of reformism into the Western proletariat' through the looking glasses of Lenin's analysis of 'opportunism', of 'labour aristocracy' that Lenin elaborated in the sessions of the Second Congress of the Third International. Even in 1969, Claudin's criticism was limited only to 'reformism' among the working class movement, and not on the mechanism of modern capitalist production relations, the dominance of the monopoly capital, of finance capital and international financial institutions over the existence of the working class. Nonetheless, it was the admission in the other way of the fact that *class struggle* does not go through insurrections at every moment in history. It exists in the capitalist society with all its complexity even when its acuteness is not manifested in the fabric of society with an open call to arms by the opposing camps. The competition between, so to say, the revolutionary preparation and 'reformism' is basically the problems of winning over the resistance of the bourgeoisie in the continuum of a bitter, arduous and historical process. These social phenomena of capitalist political economy can *never be substituted or counterpoised* by the problems of organizational preparedness of the working class. The questions of organizational efforts of the proletariat for a *communist* (*socialist*) revolution are not the substitution or counter position of the problems of transition to a *socialist* society from a capitalist society, particularly in the developed countries.[8]

Today, we have to question whether the theoretical preparedness of CI was adequate to match the strength of the bourgeoisie in this bitter struggle over the issues of production relations in *socialism*, existence of *state*, ideology, organization of society as a cooperative of direct producers, etc. Were the approaches of CI to these issues clearly different and an alternative to the theoreticians and ideologues of the capitalist society? We have to look into the theoretical justifications of such approaches in the formative years of CI so that from the advantageous position of hindsight after the crass downfall of the movement we can be in a clearer position to formulate the agenda of *socialism* in the twenty-first century.

## 1.4 The Approach in Our Critique

As we have mentioned, a critique of the theoretical standpoints of CI cannot be done without taking into account an analysis of the transition of the Russian revolution which in turn led to the *metamorphosis* of Bolshevism. We will see in a subsequent discussion that the theoretical standpoints of CI towards the international working class revolutions were formulated largely by drawing upon the Russian experience. This was also Lenin's parting observation. As of now, the international critiques of Bolshevism during those initial years of revolutionary upheaval in Russia are found to fall in *four major* categories: *i*) wholehearted support to the Bolshevik interpretation of *state* after revolution and the criticisms restricted towards the subsequent monolithic nature of the *Party* and state administration, *ii*) rejection of not only the Bolshevik interpretation of *state* in totality but also the historical relevance of revolution in Russia considering that to be a *putsch* by an extremist minority in the political spectrum, *iii*) conceding the necessity of dictatorship of the proletariat but rejecting political hegemony of a vanguard *Party*, and *iv*) rejecting dictatorship of the proletariat altogether as an obsolete and irrelevant concept. A dispassionate analysis of the documents adopted in the sessions of CI is therefore required to assess the arguments behind the above currents of criticisms.

While we evaluate the programmes of CI in the context of the Bolshevik interpretation of "socialism", we constantly remind ourselves of the privileges of hindsight as we look back and try to analyse the tumultuous events some hundred years ago and the arguments that were placed with conviction. Our aim here is to gather the relevance of the arguments to justify and reason for the revolutionary *class identity* of the proletariat against world capitalism even though we recognize the failure of the heroic attempts of the working class immediately after the WWI.

Although it is difficult to do justice in a single essay, our effort here is to analyse with respect to *socialism* the basic theses that were adopted in the formative years of CI. These were namely the theses on *i*) bourgeoisie democracy and proletarian dictatorship (1919), *ii*) international situation and the role of communist parties (1920), *iii*) national and colonial question (1920), and *iv*) state capitalism in Russia (1921, 1922). In our review we first take up the theses *i*) from Lenin which was adopted in 1919. Apart from the theoretical arguments, we examine the steps of socio-economic reorganization that the Bolsheviks exercised in the name of dictatorship of the proletariat. We also review the issues of practice of workers' democracy, ideology, juridical and political rights that should follow in theses on dictatorship of the proletariat. As a continuation of our review we critically examine Marx's idea of *communism*, transition to a *communist* society from capitalism, and Lenin's interpretation of *state* in a *transitional society*. All these reviews are based on the documents adopted in the Congresses of CI, and related more recent commentaries on the subject. Later, we critically review the theses adopted in the subsequent Congresses as concrete examples of practices of "socialism", and the general guidelines for preparation of the working class in its struggle for overthrowing the hegemony of capital in the society. To broaden the scope of our critique, we simultaneously review the contemporary criticisms of Bolshevism, so as to provide the reader with a comprehensive understanding of the conditions of political revolutions that the working class was poised for in Europe after the WWI. We discuss extensively the German revolution in our review as in many ways the prospects of a European revolution after the WWI hinged on the fate of the German revolution. As a concluding part of the essay, we review the "Colonial Theses" adopted in the Second Congress of CI that had a pivotal role in guiding "communist" participation in the national liberation struggles in the colonies and semi-colonies.

Before we proceed further, we seek apologies in advance from the reader on two counts. The first is due to the extensive use of quotations. We understand that the subject under discussion is highly polemical among the activists of social revolution. Therefore, we have referred to the authors in as much detail as possible in the space of a single essay so as to avoid the misunderstanding of quoting out of context. The second reason is the possible overlap and repetition of the arguments in the following Chapters. Although these theses are reviewed as independent entities, they were actually the interrelated programmes of social revolutions for the international working class.

## NOTES

1. As known in the annals of Bolshevism the *April Theses* were the principles and tactics enunciated by Lenin to guide the Bolsheviks during the transition from the bourgeoisie revolution in February-March 1917 to the *socialist revolution* in October 1917. The theses were presented as the guiding principles for a "proposed platform of a proletarian party".
2. We refer here to the Berne International that was held in Berne, Switzerland in February 1919. The purpose of the Conference was to resurrect the Second International after the WWI. Karl Kautsky, Rudolf Hilferding and Edward Bernstein played a major role in the Berne

Conference who were referred by Lenin in his theses in the First Congress of CI in Moscow, March 1919. The members of the Berne Conference advocated their support for democracy and liberty, and condemned dictatorship of any variety.

3. Apart from the Halle (Germany) Congress, John Riddell referred to three other workers' convention/congress in three different countries: Toulon (France), Livorno (Italy), and Prague (Czechoslovakia) in the records of the Third Congress of CI [Riddell, 2016], where the workers' representatives switched loyalty to the Third International. Riddell noted in the Halle Congress of the French socialist party held during December 25-30, 1920 "The Comintern rallied 70 percent of the Congress delegates and, after the Congress, 60 percent of the membership." [Riddell, 2016, p. 10] In the Livorno Congress of the Italian socialist party in January 1921, there was a split.

    The Congress vote gave the Unitarians a comfortable majority, with 98,028 mandates, the Communists received 58,783 and Turati's Socialist Concentration, 14,695. The Left thereupon walked out and organised itself as the Communist Party of Italy (PCI); the ECCI immediately recognised it as Comintern's Italian Section. [Riddell, 2016, p. 12]

4. We refer here to Fernando Claudin's assessment in his seminal work *Communist Movement: from Comintern to Cominform*. He wrote,

    When the Third Congress of the Comintern met, in the summer of 1921, it had begun very clearly to appear that the 'final struggle' would have to be postponed. The real world was separating itself from the world-as-thought. Something has cracked in Lenin's theoretical schema, and this 'something' could not but have serious consequences for the tool that have been created precisely to serve this schema, the Communist International.[Claudin, 1975, p. 56]

5. In making this statement, we take the cue from Charles Bettelheim, a staunch votary of *Leninism*. He wrote,

    Stalin, taking up a thesis of Lenin's [50], reaffirmed that it was possible to undertake the building of socialism in the USSR without making this dependent on the victory of the proletarian revolution in Europe or in the rest of the world.... [Bettelheim, 1977, p. 40]

6. We again take recourse to Claudin's work to corroborate this statement. He wrote,

    With the defeat of Trotskyism in the Soviet Union and in the Communist parties of all countries, the theory of socialism in a single country became the official doctrine of the Comintern. It underlies the conception of the world revolution that is given in the programme of the Comintern approved by its Sixth Congress (1928). [Claudin, 1975, p. 74]

7. Rosmer here referred to the books authored by Lenin and Trotsky that were distributed among the delegates of the Second Congress of CI. He wrote,

   A few days after we arrived in Moscow, we received two books that had just been published by the Communist International. They were *Left-Wing Communism, An Infantile Disorder* by Lenin, and *Terrorism and Communism*, a reply by Trotsky to a work of Kautsky's which had appeared with the same title. The two books formed a sort of introduction and commentary on the Theses prepared for the Congress. [Rosmer, 1973, p. 49]

8. In making this statement that is pivotal in our arguments in the present essay, we find similar views in Claudin's work. Claudin wrote,

   To sum up: the divorce, revealed by practice, between Lenin's ideas about the proletariat of the industrialized capitalist countries and the actual behaviour of this proletariat shows up (as well as the psychological aspect that has been mentioned) the absence, in Marxist theory, of an answer to certain political and theoretical problems concerning the road to revolutions in these types of society. [Claudin, 1975, p. 61]

   However, Claudin hardly did justice to his declared objective that his review of the practices of the Third International was 'to make a critical analysis of the political theory and practice of Marxism since the October revolution'. Except some thirteen pages under the subtitle "Moribund Capitalism" in the Second Chapter titled "The Crisis of Theory", the entire work was devoted to criticism of the political doctrines of "Thermidor", the degenerated Russian absolutist state, in relation to the international communist movement. Claudin produced an analysis devoted to the political economy, the production relations in Soviet Russia that forced the *metamorphosis* of Bolshevism into such degenerated practices.

## REFERENCES

V.I. Lenin. *Tasks of Proletariat in Our Revolution*. *Collected Works*, Vol. 24, 2nd ed. Progress Publishers, Moscow, 1974a.

Victor Serge. *From Lenin to Stalin*. Pioneer Publishers, New York, 1937.

Gleb J. Albert. 'German October Is Approaching': Internationalism, Activists, and the Soviet State in 1923. *Revolutionary Russia*, 24(2):111–142, 2011. doi: 10.1080/09546545.2011.620360.

Gabriel Kuhn, Editor. *All Power to the Councils! A Documentary History of the German Revolution of 1918-1919*. The Merlin Press Ltd, Wales, 2012.

Jane Degras, Editor. *The Communist International 1919-1943 Documents.* Volume I. Routledge, 1971.

John Riddell. *To the Masses: Proceedings of the Third Congress of the Communist International, 1921*. Haymarket Books, Chicago, 2016.

John Riddell, Editor. *The German Revolution and the Debate on Soviet Power: Documents, 1918-1919; Preparing the Founding Congress*. 1-6. Pathfinder Press, Atlanta, 1986.

Neil C. Fernandez. *Capitalism and Class Struggle in the USSR: A Marxist Theory*. Ashgate, Farnham, 1997.

Ronald Kowalski. *The Russian Revolution and Civil War 1917-1921: Sources in History*. Routledge, New York, 2005.

Jonathan Smele. *The Russian Revolution and Civil War 1917-1921: An Annotated Bibliography*. Bloomsbury Academic, London, 2006.

V.I. Lenin. Speech at the Opening Session of the Congress, March 2, 1919. In *Speeches at Congress of the Communist International*. Progress Publishers, Moscow, 1972a.

Istavan Deak. Budapest and the Hungarian Revolutions of 1918-1919. *The Slavonic and East European Review*, 46,(106):129–140, 1968.

John Cunningham. Hungary 1919-133 Days of Workers' Rule, 2004. URL: *http://www.workersliberty.org/node/2322*.

Karl Liebknecht. Proclamation of the Free Socialist Republic, November 9, 1918, 2000. URL : *http://www.zum.de/psm/weimar/iebknecht.php*.

John Riddell. Comintern: Revolutionary Internationalism in Lenin's Time. *Socialist Voice Pamphlet*, South Branch Publications, Canada, 2008.

Zimmerwald Manifesto. International Socialist Conference at Zimmerwald, September 21, 1915. URL: *https://www.marxists.org/history/international/social-democracy/zimmerwald/manifesto-1915.htm*.

Alfred Rosmer. *Moscow Under Lenin*. Monthly Review Press, New York, 1973.

V.I. Lenin. Speech at a Meeting of the Moscow Soviet in Celebration of the First Anniversary of the Third International. *Collected Works*, Vol. 30, 2nd ed. Progress Publishers, Moscow, 1974b.

V.I. Lenin. Five Years of the Russian Revolution and the Prospects of the World Revolution. In *Speeches at Congress of the Communist International*. Progress Publishers, Moscow, 1972b.

Communist Party of Great Britain. Fifth Congress of the Communist International, abridged report of meetings held at Moscow June 17 to July 8, 1924. URL: *http://isreview.org/issue/93/zinovievism-and-degeneration-world-communism*.

Tony Cliff. Rosa Luxemburg's Place in History, 1959. URL: *https://www.marxists.org/archive/cliff/works/1969/rosalux/9-history.htm*.

Rosa Luxemburg. The Russian Revolution. In Peter Hudis and Kevin B. Anderson, Editors, *The Rosa Luxemburg Reader*, Chapter 14. Monthly Review Press, New York, 2004.

V.I. Lenin. *"Left Wing" Communism - An Infantile Disorder*. Collected Works, Vol. 31, 2nd Ed. Progress Publishers, Moscow, 1974c.

V.I. Lenin. *In Memory of the Commune*. Collected Works, Vol. 17, 2nd ed. Progress Publishers, Moscow, 1974d.

V.I. Lenin. *Our Revolution (Appropos of N. Sukhanov's Notes). Collected Works*, Vol. 33, 2nd ed. Progress Publishers, Moscow, 1974e.

Paul M. Sweezy. A Reply. In Paul M. Sweezy, editor, *On the Transition to Socialism*. Monthly Review Press, New York, 1972.

Charles Bettelheim. *Class Struggle in the USSR, First Period: 1917-1923*. Part I. Monthly Review Press, New York, 1977.

Fernando Claudin. *The Communist Movement: From Comintern to Cominform*. Monthly Review Press, New York, 1975.

# 2

# Theses on Bourgeois Democracy and Dictatorship of the Proletariat

Lenin's theses on bourgeois democracy and dictatorship of the proletariat[1] and the subsequent *Manifesto of Communist International* in the First Congress of CI are significant for a number of reasons. The issues regarding an alternative society to capitalism and the general features of administration of such a society were addressed in Lenin's theses in a practical sense (*a matter of actual practice*). Subsequently, in the *Manifesto* [Communist International, 1919] that was drafted by Trotsky and was signed by the presidium members of the First Congress including Lenin the issues were addressed in a more specific manner.

The theses were presented against the background of catastrophe of the WWI that devastated the economies of European civil society. The theses brought out in clear terms the nature of political hegemony of the capitalist class in bourgeois democracy. The lives of the millions who were put to death and untold sufferings were forced upon for the sole purpose of existence of the war industry, of finance capital, of aggression of capital in the new arrangement of colonies of Africa and Asia and subjugation of the people thereof. Enormous causality that was enforced upon the people of Europe by the war made them realize that "in no civilized capitalist country does 'democracy in general' exist; all that exists is bourgeois democracy, and it is not a question of 'dictatorship in general', but of the dictatorship of the oppressed class, i.e. the proletariat, over its oppressors and exploiters, i.e. the bourgeoisie" [Lenin, 1972a, p. 11]. This central theme of *class dictatorship* by the proletariat was stressed with full force in Lenin's theses as the alternative to this man-made horror of war.

Lenin wrote, "It was in the name of "freedom and equality" that the bourgeoisie waged the war, and in the name of "freedom and equality" that the munitions manufacturers piled up fabulous fortunes." [Lenin, 1972a, p. 16] In view of the social crisis that emanated from the war, Lenin established, "In capitalist society, whenever there is any serious aggravation of the class struggle intrinsic to that society, there can be no alternative but the dictatorship of the bourgeoisie or the dictatorship of the proletariat." [Lenin, 1972a, p. 17]

Taken out of context, these statements may be interpreted as part of standard political vocabulary, but the fact of the matter of the political situation in post-war Europe was only reiterated in these statements. Without analysing the details of history, we can vouch that similar words and understanding of Lenin came from the Spartacus group who initiated the insurrection in Berlin in January 1919. The programme of the Spartacus group was drafted by Luxemburg and reads as follows:

> All this resistance must be broken step by step, with an iron fist and ruthless energy. The violence of the bourgeois counterrevolution must be confronted with the revolutionary violence of the proletariat. .... The fight for socialism is the mightiest civil war in world history, and the proletarian revolution must procure the necessary tools for this civil war; it must learn to use them—to struggle and to win. [Luxemburg, 2004a, pp. 352-353]

As immediate demands of revolution in Germany the programme reads,

> The Spartacus League demands:
>
> **I** As immediate measures to protect the Revolution:
>
> 1. Disarmament of the entire police force and of all officers and non-proletarian soldiers; disarmament of all members of the ruling classes.
> 2. Confiscation of all weapons and munitions stocks as well as armaments factories by workers' and soldiers' councils.
> 3. Arming of the entire adult male proletarian population as a workers' militia. Creation of a Red Guard of proletarians as an active part of the militia for the constant protection of the Revolution against counterrevolutionary attacks and subversions. [Luxemburg, 2004a, p. 353]

These were words not only of a political programme, they were actually put into practice by the Executive Council of the Workers' and Soldiers' Councils of Great Berlin during the brief existence of dual power in Germany. In the speech given before the First General Congress of the Workers' and Soldiers' Councils of Germany, December 16, 1918, Müller observed,

> The revolution overthrew the old governmental system, and the power of the state is now contained in the workers' and soldiers' councils that took its place. The domination of the imperialists and the bourgeoisie has been undermined. The new order rests on the shoulders of the workers' and soldiers' councils and it is their task to ensure social and political developments living up to socialist ideas and principles. The Executive Council of the Workers' and Soldiers' Councils of Great Berlin was implemented as the provisionary central organ of the German workers' and soldiers' councils and it was recognized as such. It became the revolution's visible expression... [Kuhn, 2012, p. 32]
>
> We were convinced that it was necessary to form a central council for Germany. The German socialist republic needed a central political organ, a defender of the sovereignty of the working masses. On this basis, we published the declaration that I cited above, putting all regional, national, military, etc. boards under our control and asserting our central role in administering the country. [Kuhn, 2012, p. 34]

This sketch of the revolutionary programmes in Germany in somewhat detail shows that dictatorship of the proletariat in the *council form of governance* with elected delegation of the workers and soldiers was an *automatic* institutional form of choice for governance by the revolutionary sections of workers and soldiers wherever they could raise the battle against bourgeoisie democracy to the level of seizing the state-power. This was attempted in the same period after the Russian revolution in Finland, in Austria, in Bavaria, and in Hungary although the Soviet power there existed for only brief durations.

The second point we want to highlight is the remarkable sense of fraternization and internationalism prevalent among the representatives of the working class that seldom came to notice in the subsequent years of workers' struggle in the twentieth century (except for a brief period in the Spanish Civil War). Speaking about the situation in Germany, Lenin wrote in his theses,

> The murder of Karl Liebknecht and Rosa Luxemburg is an event of epoch-making significance not only because of the tragic death of these finest people and leaders of the truly proletarian, Communist International, but also because the class nature of an advanced European state—it can be said without exaggeration, an advanced state on a world-wide scale has been conclusively exposed. [Lenin, 1972a, p. 16]

While elaborating on the attitude of ruling governments of Europe towards Bolshevik tendencies among the workers in their places, Lenin wrote,

> Throughout the civilized world we see Bolsheviks being exiled, persecuted and thrown into prison. This is the case, for example in Switzerland, one of the freest bourgeoisie republics, and in America, where there have been anti-Bolshevik pogroms, etc. [Lenin, 1972a, p. 17]

Luxemburg in her assessment of the Russian revolution reciprocated this argument of the political hegemony of the capitalist class in bourgeois democracy *vis-a-vis* the dictatorship of the proletariat.

> Moreover, the Bolsheviks immediately set as the aim of this seizure of power a complete, far-reaching revolutionary program: not the safeguarding of bourgeois democracy, but a dictatorship of the proletariat for the purpose of realizing socialism. Thereby they won for themselves the imperishable historic distinction of having for the first time proclaimed the final aim of socialism as the direct program of practical politics. .... Their October uprising was not only the actual salvation of the Russian Revolution; it was also the salvation of the honor of international socialism. [Luxemburg, 2004a, p. 290]

Anton Pannekoek in 1920, expressed similar views while analysing the specific nature of the problems before the working class revolutions in Europe on the international significance of the Russian revolution, albeit in a different fashion in his critique of Bolshevism in Russia.

> The Russian revolution brought the proletariat political control in so astonishingly rapid an upturn that it took Western European observers completely by surprise at the time, and although the reasons for it are clearly identifiable, it has come to seem more and more astonishing in view of the difficulties that we are now experiencing in Western

> Europe. Its initial effect was inevitably that in the first flush of enthusiasm, the difficulties facing the revolution in Western Europe were underestimated. Before the eyes of the world proletariat, the Russian revolution unveiled the principles of the new order in all the radiance and purity of their power—the dictatorship of the proletariat, the soviet system as a new mode of democracy, the reorganization of industry, agriculture and education. In many respects, it gave a picture of the nature and content of the proletarian revolution so simple, clear and comprehensive, so idyllic one might almost say, that nothing could seem easier than to follow this example. However, the German revolution has shown that this was not so simple, and the forces which came to the fore in Germany are by and large at work throughout the rest of Europe. [Pannekoek, 1978]

The third point of significance in Lenin's theses is the interpretation of the Soviet form of administration as the dissolution or withering away of *state.* Lenin stressed the need and actual working of the *state* as the instrument required for subjugating the capitalists, minority population of yesterday's exploiters. At the same time, the objective of this form of *state* was to dissolve among the "*mass*" organizations of the proletariat. Lenin drew a parallel between the Paris Commune and Soviet state in his theses.

> And it is now, when the Soviet movement is embracing the entire world and continuing the work of the Commune for all to see, that the traitors to socialism are forgetting the concrete experience and concrete lessons of the Paris Commune and repeating the old bourgeoisie rubbish about "democracy in general". The Commune was not a parliamentary institution. [Lenin, 1972a, p. 13]

According to Lenin in the theses, the Soviet form of governance was "a self-governing mass workers' organization in which there was no division between legislative and executive powers." He elaborated upon this concept later in the theses by saying,

> The substance of Soviet government is that the permanent and only foundation of state power, i.e. the entire machinery of state, is the mass-scale organization of the classes oppressed by capitalism, i.e. the workers and the semi-proletarians (peasants who do not exploit the labor of others and regularly resort to the sale of at least a part of their own labor-power). [Lenin, 1972a, p. 19]

Then, as a concrete form of governance he exemplified,

> Soviet power, i.e., the dictatorship of the proletariat, on the other hand, is so organized as to bring the working people close to the machinery of government. That too, is the purpose of combining the legislative and executive authority under the Soviet organization of the state and of replacing territorial constituencies by production units—the factory. [Lenin, 1972a, p. 19]

Again he reiterated,

> Destruction of state power is the aim set by all socialists, including Marx above all. Genuine democracy, i.e. liberty and equality, is unrealizable unless this aim is achieved. But its practical achievement is possible only through Soviet, or proletarian democracy, for by enlisting the mass organizations of the working people in constant and unfailing participation in the administration of the state, it immediately begins to prepare the complete withering away of any state. [Lenin, 1972a, p. 20]

That the mechanism of *state* becomes irrelevant for all practical, social purposes and loses its separate entity and authority in the Soviet system was best explained in the *Manifesto* of CI that rightfully took the baton from its predecessor drafted by Marx and Engels. "We communists, the representatives of the revolutionary proletariat of various countries of Europe, America, and Asia, who have gathered in Soviet Moscow, feel and consider ourselves to be the heirs and executors of the cause whose programme was announced 72 years ago." [Communist International, 1919] It proceeded to write,

> the proletariat, on the contrary, as the overwhelming majority of the people, openly exercises its class power by means of its mass organizations and through its councils, in order to wipe out the privileges of the bourgeoisie and to secure the transition, rather the transformation, into a classless communistic commonwealth....In the Council system the mass organizations rule and through them the mass itself, in as much as the Councils drew constantly increasing number of workers into the State administration; and only by this process will the entire working population gradually become part of the government. The council system also builds itself directly on the mass organizations of the proletariat, on the council themselves, the revolutionary trade unions, the cooperatives, etc. .... Above all this union is fostered by the fact that in the Council system elections are based not on arbitrary territorial districts, but on units of production. [p. 24]

The dialectical process of negation of *state* as a *political entity* in the *socialist* society was the fulcrum in the writings of Luxemburg before her very untimely and unnatural death. Just before the insurrection in Germany, while defending the political programme of the Spartacus group during the First Congress of KPD[2], Luxemburg wrote,

> The establishment of the socialist order of society is the mightiest task which has ever fallen to a class and to a revolution in the history of the world. This task requires a complete transformation of the state and a complete overthrow of the economic and social foundations of society. .... [Luxemburg, 2004a, p. 350]
>
> Only through constant, vital, reciprocal contact between the masses of the people and their organs, the workers' and soldiers' councils, can the activity of the people fill the state with a socialist spirit.... [p. 351]
>
> The socialization of society can be achieved only through tenacious, tireless struggle by the working mass along its entire front, on all points where labor and capital, people and bourgeois class rule, can see the whites of one another's eyes. The emancipation of the working class must be the work of the working class itself. [p. 351]

We have given several references to the role of *state* primarily to show that the understanding and perceptions were uniform among the revolutionaries at the beginning of the Third International. Once the proletarian revolutions are capable of overpowering the might of the bourgeoisie to exercise its own dictatorship in the society they immediately work for dissolution of *state* among the 'mass organizations' of the proletariat. The communist revolutionaries who assembled under the umbrella of CI sincerely looked up to Marx's theoretical contributions that highlighted the importance of "*smashing*" the old, bourgeoisie state by dictatorship of the proletariat in the light of the experience of the Paris Commune, once the proletariat can attain the position of the *ruling class* in society. At the same time their vision was the *new* state would cease to exist in the proper sense of the term. It would become the organ of administration of the fruits of revolution by engaging the bountiful creativity of the exploited population as a collective entity of direct producers, which is hitherto untapped and is disallowed in deciding the course of the society. It is worth mentioning that there was minimal reference to the role of the organized political of CI formation, the *communist party*, in both these primary documents of the First Congress. Only at the end of Lenin's theses, he advised for attaining the majority of the *communists* in the Soviets that might come up in the course of revolution. That was logical for any political entity to strive for attaining a majority among the elected delegates so as to pursue their programme of action.

In our present time, these contributions towards dictatorship of the proletariat from the First Congress of CI are important to remember on two counts. On the one hand, from the mid-1970s of the 20th century several "communist" parties of Europe formally abrogated the concept of dictatorship of the proletariat considering this to be obsolete.[3] Subsequently, many of the parties formally disowned their own existence after the demise of the "socialist" regimes in East Europe.[4] While introducing Etienne Balibar's defence of dictatorship of the proletariat to the English readership, Grahame Lock wrote sarcastically in 1977,

> And if—as the French, Italian, Spanish, Portuguese and Japanese Communist Parties, among others, believe—there are in any case good reasons from a Marxist point of view for abandoning the dictatorship of the proletariat, then what possible reason could any British Communist have for disagreeing?
>
> But not only is the term *dictatorship of the proletariat* apparently old-fashioned and out-of-date; it is also distasteful. For how can the Left condemn the 'dictatorships' in Chile or Argentina, Iran or South Korea, etc., while proposing to install its own dictatorship? And if the term *dictatorship* is unpleasant, its partner *proletariat*—is seemingly plainly absurd (just try suggesting to a British factory worker that he is a 'proletarian' . . ). [Balibar, 2011, pp. 8-9]

This argument leads to theses that at least in the developed capitalist economies the working class have lost relevance as a separate *political entity*. They have no independent role apart from toeing and tailing the policies of the traditional labour and social-democratic parties that the workers deserted or were about to desert during the revolutions in Germany and Russia after the WWI. In fact, fundamentally this was not a new argument—it was present from the time of Edward Bernstien at the beginning of the 20th century. Later, Karl Kautsky, Georgi Plekhanov, and a host of

European social-democrats of the Second International severely criticized Bolshevism in Russia as a practice of dictatorship of the proletariat. While criticizing Bolshevism as "terrorism", they actually stood guard in masterminding the murder of the host of German revolutionaries and massacre of the revolutionary workers and soldiers in their own countries. *Or*, they remained silent to these ghastly incidents when the state-power was crushing the workers' uprising in Germany on the plea that the working class was unprepared to lead a revolution. In that sense, repudiation of the revolutionary role of the working class in Europe runs counter to modern history also in the post-WWI Europe during the crisis of its civil societies.

On the other hand, there have been several occasions in modern Europe where the workers rose to register their class initiatives. The most illustrative example was of course, the seizure of factories in Italy in September 1920, when metal workers, automobile workers, railway workers occupied the factories of industrial towns of Italy in Milan, Turin, Naples, Genoa, Florence, Palermo. "Within three days 400,000 workers were in occupation. As the movement spread to other sectors, the total rose to over half a million. Everyone was stunned by the response." [Williams, 1975, p. 241] During the Third Congress of CI in June-July 1921, this massive occupation of factories by the workers in Italy led Lenin to question the Italian delegation. He asked,

> The Italian Communists are not always Communists to a sufficient degree. Did a single Communist show his mettle when the workers seized the factories in Italy?[44] No. At that time, there was yet no communism in Italy; there was a certain amount of anarchism, but no Marxian communism. [Lenin, 1972b, p. 93]

Of course, by 'Marxian communism' Lenin was highlighting the significance of overthrowing the bourgeoisie state in Italy which was a necessary, political call of action awaiting the response of the occupation movement of the factories that never got materialized. The question of confronting the state-power was brought repeatedly into focus on numerous occasions whenever the working class in European countries came to the forefront of *class struggle*. It was raised in Budapest, Hungary where the workers' uprising began on October 23, 1956. The working class defeated the police and installed a new government, which lasted 18 days before being crushed by the Soviet tanks. In France, in May 1968, when the workers in the Renault factory at Cléon (near Rouen) and at Flins (north-west of Paris) occupied the factory premises, and fraternization was quick to follow from the students of Sorbonne University.[5] In Gdansk, in 1980 the workers occupied the Lenin Shipyard raising the banner of revolt by demanding the recognition of Solidarity, their independent trade union. These events from the recent past are mentioned to register whenever the workers' initiatives bring themselves face-to-face with the state-power of the bourgeoisie, the class initiative of the workers cannot stop *only* in the occupation of the production units. That remains the instinctive and the most direct, immediate response from the working class. The initiative must raise itself to an *alternative state* of its own by replacing the old state-power qualitatively. Political assertion of the working class as the *new ruling class* necessarily remains *a precondition* to realize the *new* organs of authority in the society. The evidence of class initiatives witnessed in the workers' revolts reject the thesis of obsolescence of their separate social, political identity as promoted by the traditional political parties of labour. Dictatorship of the proletariat remains a fundamental historical responsibility before the working class.

Evidently, the questions that come to the forefront are why the failure of revolt of the working class in Europe after the WWI became repeated phenomena? Why could the formation of the Third International not arrest defeat of the impending workers' revolutions in so many places of Europe? Why was the working class in Russia left isolated after the seizure of state-power, and was able to hold on only for a brief period? Why even with the declarations and theoretical arguments posited in Lenin's theses could the *metamorphosis* of Soviet societies into totalitarian entities not be arrested? Well, the answers to these direct questions partly (any theorization of the failure or success of revolution is bound to be only an incomplete, part answer) lie in the *metamorphosis* of Bolshevism that had a huge influence on the subsequent proceedings of CI. Closer scrutiny of Lenin's theses and other concurrent writings of several other critics of CI highlight several glaring inconsistencies and often contradictory positions in them.

It is important to assert that revolutions *do not follow or happen according to textbooks.* The most profound historical evidence of this assertion is the failure of the German revolution where the working class was more mature in the trade union struggle than their Russian counterpart. The Russian working class, at least, could hold on to new state-power for a brief period. The theoretical arguments of the Bolsheviks underwent drastic slippery shifts when they faced the harsh reality of actual practice beyond the revolution. They were not in a position to relate to their own experiences about the challenges of transition to *socialism* in an underdeveloped economy with the limitations of understanding of Marx and Engels. During the formation of the Third International the leaders of CI heavily banked on the analysis of capitalist society that was particularly due to Marx, and on the subsequent political projections mostly developed by Engels as executor of their joint theoretical venture. What turned out to be more important for the leaders of CI was to face the reality of holding on to state-power in Russia after the defeat of revolutions in Europe in general, and in Germany in particular, than rethinking or questioning the projections of Marx and Engels.

We now present a point-by-point analysis of the inconsistencies and limitations of understanding of the historical process of evolution of dictatorship of the proletariat as reflected in the documents of CI and other concurrent materials.

## 2.1 On the Revolutionary Nature of *Socialist* Production Relations under Dictatorship of the Proletariat

Upon closer perusal of Lenin's theses on dictatorship of the proletariat in the First Congress of CI, it is difficult to ignore the extremely political nature of his arguments. It is true what Lenin was arguing here about the "*smashing*" of state-power of the existing bourgeoisie democracy that is undoubtedly a political question. The question is related to the struggle for power between two antagonistic classes of modern capitalist society. But dictatorship of the proletariat is also at the same time the beginning of *socialist* society, the process of dissolution of *state*. We have shown above how Lenin focused on the Soviet form of organization of *state* that was supposed to offer "precisely such a change as provides an unparalleled extension of the actual employment of democracy by those oppressed by capitalism—the toiling classes." [Lenin, 1972a, p. 18]

This 'unparalleled extension of the actual employment of democracy by those oppressed by capitalism' is only realizable when the mode of production and exchanges unequivocally guarantee *free* association of the direct producers. Society relinquishes the *law of value* that alienates the direct producer from his or her own labour, and ceases to have an ombudsman authority above itself by the name of the state. Thereby, society at large liberates itself from the domain of politics. This was Marx's vision about *communist* society in his arguments against Proudhon when he wrote,

> The working class, in the course of its development, will substitute for the old civil society an association which will exclude classes and their antagonism, and there will be no more political power properly so-called, since political power is precisely the official expression of antagonism in civil society. [Marx, 1955, p. 80]

Marx was consistent in his vision of the mode of production in *communist* (*socialist*) society. Even before his detailed analysis and critique of capitalism in *Capital* he stressed the alternative social nature of production and the union of producers in *The German Ideology*. He wrote,

> This appropriation is further determined by the manner in which it must be effected. It can only be effected through a union, which by the character of the proletariat itself can again only be a universal one, and through a revolution, in which, on the one hand, the power of the earlier mode of production and intercourse and social organization is overthrown, and, on the other hand, there develops the universal character and the energy of the proletariat, without which the revolution cannot be accomplished; and in which, further, the proletariat rids itself of everything that still clings to it from its previous position in society.
>
> Only at this stage does self-activity coincide with material life, which corresponds to the development of individuals into complete individuals and the casting-off of all natural limitations.The transformation of labour into self-activity corresponds to the transformation of the earlier limited intercourse into the intercourse of individuals as such. With the appropriation of the total productive

> forces through united individuals, private property comes to an end. Whilst previously in history a particular condition always appeared as accidental, now the isolation of individuals and the particular private gain of each man have themselves become accidental. [Marx, 2000, pp. 194-195]

We want to emphasize here this holistic and yet at the same time precise interpretation of revolution that transforms social production completely at a hitherto unfound plane was not at all present in Lenin's arguments for dictatorship of the proletariat. Whereas in the case of Marx it was only a projection based on the analysis of the mode of production under capitalism and criticism of the ideology that sustains alienation of the producer, "socialism" was a matter of actual practice in the case of Lenin. Therefore, his arguments undoubtedly were much more relevant and significant from the point of view of actual reorganization of production relations towards *socialism*. By being silent on the *socialist* mode of production in a theses on dictatorship of the proletariat, Lenin missed the essential revolutionary kernel of *socialism*; that is the problems of engaging society in such a way that 'private gain of each man have themselves becomes accidental'.[6] The engagement of society towards the fundamental transformation of the mode of production is the essence of *revolutionary practice* that Marx enunciated in his Third Theses on Feuerbach as, "The coincidence of the changing of circumstances and of human activity or self-changing can be conceived and rationally understood only as *revolutionary practice*." Therefore, dictatorship of the proletariat is completely *anew* not only because without a revolution the old state-power cannot be abolished, but also and more significantly because the *revolutionary practice* of the proletariat as a *ruling class* can only exist by transforming themselves into a community of producers directly consuming the yield of their social production. It is a transition where labour of the individual subsumes in the collective labour of society without possessing the tag of exchange of *value*, where private gain in terms of expropriation of surplus *value* becomes only an accident, and not the general rule of production in society. *Socialism* is a society that represents freedom to perform labour, a society that focuses on emancipation of labour from the yoke of performing labour for somebody (including the statist overlord) else's "profit" having no stake or concern to the process or the outcome of labour. Dictatorship of the proletariat provides the foundations and moves forward towards such a society of *free* cooperative producers. Only in this sense the organ of administration ceases to be a *state* in the historical evolution of the institution along the course of human civilization. The emphasis that Marx put on dictatorship of the proletariat as a 'necessary transit point' to a *new* society can be seen here to bring out the consistency in him as the modern pathfinder towards a classless humane society. Marx wrote in *The Class Struggle in France 1848-50,*

> This socialism is the *declaration of the permanence of the revolution, the class dictatorship* of the proletariat as the necessary transit point to the *abolition of class distinctions generally,* [Marx, 1969a, p. 223]

Lenin was not alone in failing to provide a precise programme for socialization of labour under dictatorship of the proletariat in the First Congress of CI; it was missed by his collaborators and contemporary critics alike. Except for Rosa Luxemburg in her brief article *The Socialization of Society* which she wrote while in jail in December 1918, this essential aspect of labour being 'life's prime want' in *socialism* was not touched by either the leaders of CI or their critics. Luxemburg wrote,

> In a socialist society, where everyone works together for their own well-being, the *health* of the workforce and its *enthusiasm for work* must be given the greatest consideration at work. Short working hours that do not exceed the normal capability, healthy workrooms, all methods of recuperation and a variety of work must be introduced in order that everyone enjoys doing their part. [Luxemburg, 2004b, p. 347]

This dynamic and intrinsic connection between the voluntary nature of labour of an individual that is the source of enjoyment, and an unparalleled freedom of the producers of social labour in *socialism* was never brought out even in Luxemburg's criticism of the Bolsheviks in the Russian revolution when she pointed out the grave want of democracy in post-revolution Russian society. Dictatorship of the proletariat remained the *obverse* phenomenon of bourgeoisie democracy; a mechanism of class rule by retaining the wings and arms of subjugation. Therefore, it degenerated into the sum and substance of state-craft in a new form. Lenin wrote in the same theses,

> Proletarian dictatorship is similar to the dictatorship of other classes in that it arises out of the need, as every other dictatorship does, to forcibly suppress the resistance of the class that is losing its political sway....In contrast, proletarian dictatorship is the forcible suppression of the resistance of the exploiters, i.e. an insignificant minority of population, the landowners and capitalists. [Lenin, 1972a, p. 18]

In spite of referring to the *state* being withered away by engaging the "*masses*" from the basic production units in matters of administration, Lenin's theses remained silent on how the role of exchange *value* would get minimized in production and distribution. He did not comment on how wage-labour would get transformed into free labour and would cease to be *commodity*, how centralization of the means of productions and the means of consumption at the hands of Soviet administration would be effective in making them social, and at the same time *free* at the disposal of the individual producer. The revolutionaries who assembled in Moscow were on the lookout for such answers from the living practice of "socialism" in Russia which unfortunately were missing in the documents placed before them in the sessions of the Congress.

It would be interesting to note here that such yardsticks or parameters of progress of *socialist* production relations in a *transitional society* were brought into discussion (one should say "revived") by Sweezy and Bettelheim during their debates. Bettelheim stressed in the discussion,

> It is fundamentally true that the existence of *commodity relations* is an obstacle to the domination by the producers over their products and that the full development of these relations leads to the control over the immediate producers by the bourgeoisie, and therefore to the non-domination by the producers over the conditions of their existence. It is therefore fundamentally true that the elimination of commodity relations figures among the *historical tasks* that the proletariat must accomplish in the course of building socialism. [Bettelheim, 1972a, p. 40]

We will have the opportunity later to look into the paradigm '*historical tasks*' that was called for 'building socialism' while we discuss Lenin's interpretation of *state* in Section 2.4. Here, we record that it would be wrong and historically inaccurate to assert that the Bolshevik and the CI leadership ignored the issues of introducing "socialist" relations of production under dictatorship of the proletariat. Lenin's several writings on the eve of the revolution and after regarding reorganization of production and raising productivity of labour under dictatorship of the proletariat such as [Lenin, 1972c], [Lenin, 1974a], his subsequent theses in the sessions of the later Congresses of CI, and above all his treatise on *The State and Revolution* reveal the dichotomy and contradictions in the stated positions on these subjects. They ironically gravitated towards policies of an *absolutist* state denouncing what was the article of faith with Bolshevism on the eve of the revolution.

Large-scale centralization of the means of production and distribution, of financial institutions, and the workers' and synonymously Soviets' control on accounting and production were pivotal to Lenin's views regarding "socialist" relations of production. On the eve of the October Revolution, Lenin categorically expressed his views on the workers' role in production relations under dictatorship of the proletariat. He wrote,

> The chief difficulty facing the proletarian revolution is the establishment on a country-wide scale of the most precise and most conscientious accounting and control, of *workers' control* of the production and distribution of goods. .... When we say: "workers' control", always *juxtaposing* this slogan to dictatorship of the proletariat, always putting it *immediately after* the latter, we thereby explain what kind of state we mean....If it is of the proletariat, if we are speaking of a proletarian state, *that is*, of the proletarian dictatorship, then workers' control *can* become the country-wide, all-embracing, omnipresent, most precise and most conscientious *accounting* of the production and distribution of goods.
>
> This is the chief difficulty, the chief task that faces the proletarian, i.e. socialist revolution. Without the Soviets, this task would be impracticable, at least in Russia. [Lenin, 1972c, pp. 104-105]

This understanding about the workers' control, i.e. taking control of '*accounting* of the production and distribution of goods' was more precise and specific in [Lenin, 1974b], which was a sort of manual of instructions before the Soviet government.[7] Here, Lenin's instruction to the Soviets was

> We have decreed and introduced throughout Russia the highest type of state—Soviet power. Under no circumstances, however, can we rest content with what we have achieved, because we have only just started the transition to socialism, we have not yet done the decisive thing in this respect. The decisive thing is the organisation of the strictest and country-wide accounting and control of production and distribution of goods....Until workers' control has become a fact, until the advanced workers have organised and carried out a victorious and ruthless crusade against the violators of this control, or against those who are careless in matters of control, it will be impossible to pass from the first step (from workers' control) to the second step towards socialism, i.e. to pass on to workers' regulation of production. The socialist state can arise only as a network of producers' and consumers' communes, which conscientiously keep account of their production and consumption, economise on labour, and steadily raise the productivity of labour, thus making it possible to reduce the working day to seven, six and even fewer hours. [Lenin, 1974b, pp. 254-255]

It is abundantly clear that by the workers' control under dictatorship of the proletariat, Lenin specifically meant workers' participation in the nationwide accounting of production and utilization of the means of production and consumption. Although having accurate data and estimate of production is important to understand the state of affairs of economy this is only a primitive dimension of *socialist* economy. To conceive the transition to "socialist" society as a nationwide association of auditors of production is at best rudimentary. It is true in the above quoted paragraph the Lenin also visualized 'to pass from the first step (from workers' control) to the second step towards socialism, i.e. to pass on to workers' regulation of production.' It requires the workers' control over the policy for fixation of the rules and systems of exchanges between social products, the workers' control over the transformation of existing divisions of social labour, the workers' control over the prioritization of modernization of the means of production so as to facilitate the practice and environment of nationwide 'workers' regulation of production'.

Unfortunately, neither Lenin's theses in the sessions of CI or his writings elsewhere shed any light on these vital issues of ushering *socialist* relations of production. On the other hand, these questions were left to be responded by the centralization of the means of production and consumption as the panacea of "socialist" economy. The suggestions were evident in the proclamations of the *Manifesto* released in the First Congress of CI.

> The task of the Proletarian Dictatorship in the economic field can only be fulfilled to the extent that the proletariat is enabled to create centralized organs of management and to institute workers control. To this end it must make use of its mass organizations which are in closest relation to the process of production. In the field of distribution the Proletarian Dictatorship must re-establish commerce by an accurate distribution of products; to which end the following methods are to be considered: the socialization of wholesale establishments, the taking over of all bourgeoisie-State and municipal apparatus of distribution, control of the great cooperative societies, which organizations will still have an important role in the production epoch; the gradual centralization of all these organs and their conversion into a systematic rational distribution of products. [Communist International, 1919, pp. 28-29]

One is left to wonder how centralization of the means of production and distribution *in itself* solves the problem of alienation of labour from its social content unless the "*masses*" of workers are involved in planning the policy for exchange of products, their prioritization, and a host of other such issues that are immediately involved in social productions and exchanges. We want to make it clear that the basic principle of *each according to his labour* and 'accurate distribution of products' are not addressed *only* by keeping account of gross production and consumption *or* by centralization of the sources of production and distribution. To address these fundamental issues of *socialism*, the divisions of labour that can augment the forward movement of society as a whole are to be prioritized such that labour becomes voluntary in a progressive manner. As a consequence, the separation between mental and physical labour gets progressively reduced. At the same time, *socialism requires* abolition of the divisions of labour that keep the international working class divided and at loggerheads. *Socialism* requires cessation of the divisions of labour that the working class inherits as a legacy of a past, decadent society where labour is only an alienated component of a social production process over which the "*masses*" of the workers have no control. This requires abandoning those divisions of labour that relieve the working class "in ridding itself of all the muck of ages and become fitted to found society anew." [Marx, 2000]

To emphasize our argument that centralization of the means of production and distribution *per se* may not facilitate socialization of labour under dictatorship of the proletariat we again refer to the discussion between Bettelheim and Sweezy, as they raised this significant issue of transition to *socialism*. While refuting the argument that the existence of the paradigm of "plan" *vis-a-vis* "market" is a strong indicator for "socialism" being implemented in society, Bettelheim wrote,

> The foregoing means that what is decisive—from the point of view of socialism—is not the mode of *"regulation"* of the economy, but rather the nature of the *class in power*. In still other terms, the fundamental question is not whether the "market" or the "plan" (therefore also the "state") controls the economy but the *nature of the class which holds power*. If the role of the state in directing the economy is given first priority, the role of the nature of class power is relegated in the second place, which is to say that the *essential* is left aside.*
>
> On the economic level, the existence of the market (in effect, of *commodity relationships*) is a *condition of possibility* of bourgeoisie domination, while on the political level, the state, as a form of existence of political power, is also a *condition of possibility* of bourgeoisie domination. In this regard, "market" and "state" are not in fundamental conflict but rather complement each other; the principal role falls now to the one, now to the other, according to the nature of the economic, social, and political contradictions of each moment. [Bettelheim, 1972a, p. 44]

Bettelheim very rightly stressed a fundamental problem of *transitional society* in the above quoted paragraphs. The problem emanates from the competition and opposition the *new* organization of *socialist* modes of exchange faces from the economy based on commodity relationship and "profit" existing in the society. However, Bettelheim visualized the evolution of *state* under dictatorship of the proletariat as a bourgeoisie, capitalist state *only* —'*condition of possibility* of bourgeoisie domination'. This was also our apprehension about Lenin's presentation on dictatorship of the proletariat as an *obverse* phenomenon of bourgeoisie democracy. To be sure, the answer to this apprehension is that dictatorship of the proletariat is a *quasi-state*, a *state* in transition towards dissolution, and not existing for strengthening the apparatus and instruments of oppression. This is only possible when the vital question *'nature of the class which holds power'* is resolved by bringing in all the platforms of "*mass*" activities of the workers towards matters of governance of society. The contours and objectives of *socialist* production we presented above must couple with the decision-making process which follows from the workers' control over the implementation of the programmes of socialization of labour.

It may be argued while stressing 'country-wide accounting and control of production and distribution of goods', Lenin did not mean a *socialist* society but a transitional form of social organization under dictatorship of the proletariat. We want to stress that this was not the case. Lenin argued that at least in the case of transition to "socialism" for Russian society, it was required to trace the path backwards, that is, the acceptance of existing capitalist production relations. In fact, Lenin himself made it clear while prioritizing the role of managers and specialists in deciding the above issues of production relations we cited. In the same pamphlet on *Immediate Tasks of the Soviet Government*, he concluded,

> Now we have to resort to the old bourgeois method and to agree to pay a very high price for the "services" of the top bourgeois experts. All those who are familiar with the subject appreciate this, but not all ponder over the significance of this measure being adopted by the proletarian state. Clearly, this measure is a compromise, a departure from the principles of the Paris Commune and of every proletarian power, which call for the reduction of all salaries to the level of the wages of the average worker, which urge that careerism be fought not merely in words, but in deeds. Moreover, it is clear that this measure not only implies the cessation—in a certain field and to a certain degree—of the offensive against capital (for capital is not a sum of money, but a definite social relation); it is also *a step backward* on the part of our socialist Soviet state power, which from the very outset proclaimed and pursued the policy of reducing high salaries to the level of the wages of the average worker. [Lenin, 1974b, pp. 248-249]

On the other hand, what he advocated for the workers was returning to the piece-rate system of production, a reverting to the

'Taylor system' of production, a hierarchy based decision-making process in the production system, propositions that went against what was the *essence* of *socialist* revolution. He wrote,

> We must raise the question of piece-work[106] and apply and test it in practice; we must raise the question of applying much of what is scientific and progressive in the Taylor system; we must make wages correspond to the total amount of goods turned out, or to the amount of work done by the railways, the water transport system, etc., etc.... The possibility of building socialism depends exactly upon our success in combining the Soviet power and the Soviet organization of administration with the up-to-date achievements of capitalism. We must organize in Russia the study and teaching of the Taylor system and systematically try it out and adapt it to our own ends....We must learn to combine the "public meeting" democracy of the working people—turbulent, surging, overflowing its banks like a spring flood—with *iron* discipline while at work, with *unquestioning obedience* to the will of a single person, the Soviet leader, while at work. [Lenin, 1974b, pp. 258-259]

While Lenin articulated on combining the Soviet system of administration with 'up-to-date achievements of capitalism', 'with *iron* discipline while at work', Trotsky was more aggressive in urging military conscription of labour. As a rebuttal to Karl Kautsky's condemnation of the Bolshevik practices in Russia after the revolution, Trotsky wrote the pamphlet *Terrorism and Communism: A Reply to Karl Kautsky*. In chapter 8 of the pamphlet under the heading "Report on the Organization of Labor" he wrote,

> The foundations of the militarization of labor are those forms of State compulsion without which the replacement of capitalist economy by the Socialist will forever remain an empty sound. Why do we speak of militarization? Of course, this is only an analogy—but an analogy very rich in content. No social organization except the army has ever considered itself justified in subordinating citizens to itself in such a measure, and to control them by its will on all sides to such a degree, as the State of the proletarian dictatorship considers itself justified in doing, and does. Only the army—just because in its way it used to decide questions of the life or death of nations, States, and ruling classes—was endowed with powers of demanding from each and all complete submission to its problems, aims, regulations, and orders. And it achieved this to the greater degree, the more the problems of

> military organization coincided with the requirements of social development.
>
> The question of the life or death of Soviet Russia is at present being settled on the labor front; our economic, and together with them our professional and productive organizations, have the right to demand from their members all that devotion, discipline, and executive thoroughness, which hitherto only the army required. [Trotsky, 2006]

Trotsky's proposition of the militarization of labour was not accepted within the Bolshevik party itself because of strident resistance from the rank-and-file and the leaders. Still, the fact that this proposal was included in the pamphlet for distribution among the delegates of the international working class in CI speaks volumes about the intention of the author and the leadership of CI. One may even argue here that Trotsky urged this proposition because of his rich experience in handling the raging Civil War in Russia in 1918-20 to safeguard the revolution and its success. That does not justify the recommendation for enforcing military discipline among the workers for increasing gross output of production to liberate them from the yoke of militarism that the World War enforced upon them and against what the workers fought bitterly to attain the revolution. Trotsky and Lenin forgot that paying 'a very high price for the "services" of the top bourgeois experts' (the expertise they accumulated as *capital* in the historical process of knowledge formation!) while at the same time enforcing '*iron* discipline while at work', asking for 'the right to demand from their members all that devotion, discipline, and executive thoroughness, which hitherto only the army required' from the working class does in no way elevate them to a new production relation. The workers did not lay down their lives for a regime of labour conscription under instruction from the yesterday's experts; their labour cannot be called voluntary in this respect. Rather they went for revolution to enforce their right in decision-making, what to produce and what not to produce, to rebuild their society as their own.

### *2.1.1 The Bolshevik policy in overhauling the financial institutions*

Let us now pay attention to the Bolshevik policy for the financial institutions such as banks. Like his policies of the nationwide control and accounting of industrial production, Lenin focused on the centralization of banking operations under Soviet rule in the form of nationalization of banks as a step forward to "socialism". To be fair to Lenin, initially he did not mean nationalization of banks to be "socialism", but definitely a step towards "socialism". Lenin wrote, "Control over a bank, the merging of all banks in one, is *not yet* socialism, but it is *a step towards* socialism." [Lenin, 1974c, p. 53] Initially, he meant the banks' crucial role in accounting and control which can be directly inherited from capitalism to organize the "socialist" society. On the eve of the revolution, he wrote,

> Capitalism has created an accounting *apparatus* in the shape of the banks, syndicates, postal service, consumers' societies, and office employees' unions. *Without big banks socialism would be impossible.* .... A single State Bank, the biggest of the big, with branches in every rural district, in every factory, will constitute as much as nine-tenths of the *socialist* apparatus. This will be country-wide *book-keeping*, country-wide *accounting* of the production and distribution of goods, this will be, so to speak, something in the nature of the *skeleton* of socialist society. [Lenin, 1972c, p. 106]

In a significant turnaround after the revolution, he was much more pragmatic in the sense that he specifically focused on the *actual functions of banks* as a source of huge capital under monopoly control of the new state. Just after the revolution (October 1917), he wrote,

> Only by nationalizing the banks *can* the state *put itself in a position* to know where and how, whence and when, millions and billions of rubles flow. And only control over the banks, over the centre, over the pivot and chief mechanism of capitalist circulation, would make it possible to organize real and not fictitious control over all economic life, over the production and distribution of staple goods, and organize that "regulation of economic life" which otherwise is inevitably doomed to remain a ministerial phrase designed to fool the common people. Only control over banking operations, provided they were concentrated in a single state bank, would make it possible, if certain other easily-practicable measures were adopted, to organize the effective collection of income tax in such a way as to prevent the concealment of property and incomes; for at present the income tax is very largely a fiction. [Lenin, 1974a, p. 335]

Now, banks are the storehouses of 'millions and billions of rubles' definitely not just for keeping accounts of them, but for providing credits and earning "profits" in terms of interest on credits. Banks are meant for financial transactions either by means of fictitious or virtual transfer of money for speculative trading or by providing credits in real terms by transfer of assets in the form of gold or any other precious metal. If the banks are not meant to earn "profits" in the form of interest on credits they simply do not remain banks—they turn into social organizations for transferring national assets to the numerous avenues of social labour prioritized in the Soviet system of administration. It is worthwhile to note that one of the tasks Lenin had in mind for centralized banking operations was 'to organize the effective collection of income tax in such a way as to prevent the concealment of property and incomes.' This is the regular practice of any sensible capitalist economy to identify defaulters and fraudsters who hoodwink the governments from paying income-tax for their unscrupulous financial dealings. If Lenin meant the second option, that is transforming the banks as social organizations for transferring their assets to "socialist" reorganization then how did he assert that the money in the banks would not become irrelevant as the medium of circulation and exchanges? In the same article he wrote,

> The ownership of the capital wielded by and concentrated in the banks is certified by printed and written certificates called shares, bonds, bills, receipts, etc. Not a single one of these certificates would be invalidated or altered if the banks were nationalized, i.e. if all the banks were amalgamated into a single state bank. Whoever owned fifteen rubles on a savings account would continue to be the owner of fifteen rubles after the nationalization of the banks; and whoever had fifteen million rubles would continue after the nationalization of the banks to have fifteen million rubles in the form of shares, bonds, bills, and commercial certificates and so on. [Lenin, 1974a, p. 334]

Not only for nationalization of banks, in the same article Lenin had exhorted for the nationalization of insurance business as a stepping stone to "socialism".

> Nationalization of the banks would greatly facilitate the simultaneous nationalization of the insurance business, i.e. the amalgamation of all the insurance companies into one, the centralization of their

> operations, and state control over them. Here, too, congresses of insurance company employees could carry out this amalgamation immediately and without any great effort, provided a revolutionary-democratic government decreed this and ordered directors and big shareholders to effect the amalgamation without the slightest delay and held every one of them strictly accountable for it. The capitalists have invested hundreds of millions of rubles in the insurance business; the work is all done by the employees. The amalgamation of this business would lead to lower insurance premiums, would provide a host of facilities and conveniences for the insured and would make it possible to increase their number without increasing expenditure of effort and funds. [Lenin, 1974a, pp. 338-339]

There is no ambiguity as to what Lenin meant by nationalization of the banks and the insurance business. Lenin understood state or nationalized ownership of the capital in the banks, insurance, syndicates, etc. to be synonymous with national assets being under the control of dictatorship of the proletariat by dint of decrees under Soviet rule. That this understanding is devoid of logic in all respects is evident when Lenin remained silent on certain basic issues such as trading the currencies in international financial markets. How was the exchange rate of the Russian ruble fixed in the international *currency* market even with state monopoly over supply of rubles? How could Lenin ensure the stability of the price of either kopeks or millions of rubles in the banks, if the ruble itself got devalued in the international *currency* market? Secondly, even if one agrees that insurance premium would be less with the state monopoly, how would it be any different from the premium paid to a capitalist insurance enterprise, except that the former was subsidized by the state and that the new directors (!) of this business were elected by the shareholders who were employees of the nationalized amalgam of the insurance sector? There are innumerable number of co-operative societies of the workers and employees in the enterprises of any capitalist economy that work on the same principle.

In fact, according to Lenin's own admission before the Fourth Congress of CI, the major achievement of the Soviet state in five years was the stabilization of the Russian ruble in the international *currency* market and the arrest of hyper inflation in the Soviet economy. In his address on the experience of five years of the Russian revolution he observed,

> First of all, I shall deal with our financial system and our famous Russian ruble. I think we can say that Russian rubles are famous, if only for the reason that their number now in circulation exceeds a quadrillion. That is something! It is an astronomical figure....But what is really important is the problem of stabilizing the ruble. We are now grappling with this problem, our best forces are working on it and we attach decisive importance to it....On this question, I think I can cite some fairly important and decisive data. In 1921 the rate of exchange of the paper ruble remained stable for a period of less than three months. This year, 1922, which has not yet drawn to a close, the rate remained stable for a period of five months. [Lenin, 1972d, pp. 135-136]

It may be said without further explanation that after five years of the existence of Soviet Russia, Lenin took credit as the Premier of the new state for stabilizing the ruble, the Soviet *currency* in the world monetary trading system. In no sense did Lenin mention the withering of the capitalist system of banks, or its leading role in nationwide accounting that he was so eagerly looking forward before the revolution. Progressive abolition of *currency* as a medium of exchange was not his priority. Rather, his outlook was to strengthen the centralized state monopoly of the banking and insurance business system by keeping strict regulation over the circulation and control of flow of capital for which he urged the employees, the unions in the banking system to play the role of watchdog! By no means had this policy endangered capitalism as a production relation in Soviet Russia. On the contrary, this only strengthened state monopoly over circulation of capital and fixation of its unit value (ruble) in international financial exchanges.

Even if one agrees to consider the argument that the employees' supervision and control over the banking system would have placed the assets in the hands of the Soviets in the long run, one must look into what actually occurred in the history of the early years of Soviet Russia. Here again, Lenin's vision was to reaffirm the employees as members of the Soviet state apparatus by means of decree.

> By a single decree of the proletarian government these employees can and must be transferred to the status of state employees, in the same way as the watchdogs of capitalism like Briand and other bourgeois ministers, by a single decree, transfer railwaymen on strike

> to the status of state employees....The conversion of the bank, syndicate, commercial, etc., etc., rank-and-file employees into state employees is quite feasible both technically (thanks to the preliminary work performed for us by capitalism, including finance capitalism) and politically, provided the *Soviets* exercise control and supervision. [Lenin, 1972c, pp. 106-107]

As a contrast, we quote here from the early history of Soviet banking to testify for the actual events following such decrees:

> On the day following the Bolshevik seizure of power all commercial banks closed down.'[7] Their staffs received salaries for three months in advance, with the understanding that they would abstain from performing their duties as long as a Soviet government was in power, joining the concerted action of the employees of the State Bank and all other government financial institutions and ministries in refusing to serve the new regime. This boycott was fully effective. The few operations that commercial banks did undertake in the weeks following the October Revolution were directed solely toward protecting their assets while contributing to the general paralysis of economic life that, Lenin's opponents hoped, would bring down the new regime.... Manifestly, the effective boycott by the bulk of bank employees made the use of the banking system as "the skeleton of socialist society" a practical impossibility.,[8] However, during the months that followed, the total disorganization of all banking operations was gradually overcome and by the end of 1917 the cash department of the State Bank was functioning again and some discount and lending operations were taking place. [Gravy, 1977, p. 23]

As is evident from the actual experience of the initial days of Soviet rule in Russia, a *socialist* society cannot be built by simply inheriting the old divisions of labour, by continuing the old practices of monetary exchange and circulation. Here, in the banking sector, the Soviet state-power was not challenged by the bourgeoisie whose political resistance was already on the decline, but by the very employees whom Lenin intended to be the stakeholders of the Soviet state by issuing decrees. Progressive irrelevance and obsolescence of the practice and tradition of circulation of money in the *transitional society* is exactly what is meant by 'ridding itself of all the muck of ages and become fitted to found society anew'. In the historical perspective of the post-revolutionary days in Russia both the Bolsheviks and the bank employees in Russia were not prepared for that eventuality.

### *2.1.2 The Bolshevik policy on the housing and food questions*

Not only in the case of production relations which decided directly the fate of revolution, Lenin's and the Bolshevik policies in matters of direct social concerns such as housing, food rationing, etc. were at best irrational and primitive with respect to the vision of *socialist* society. Lenin enforced the principle of dictatorship of the proletariat in determining social class heritages and belongings to the point of directly targeting the individuals in erstwhile privileged positions. He advocated direct invasion and occupation of the houses and mansions of the erstwhile privileged as a means of addressing the housing problem for the workers and the urban downtrodden. On the eve of the revolution, Lenin wrote (we reproduce the full paragraph),

> The proletarian state has to forcibly move a very poor family into a rich man's flat. Let us suppose that our squad of workers' militia is fifteen strong; two sailors, two soldiers, two class-conscious workers (of whom, let us suppose, only one is a member of our Party, or a sympathizer), one intellectual, and eight from the poor working people, of whom at least five must be women, domestic servants, unskilled labourers, and so forth. The squad arrives at the rich man's flat, inspects it and finds that it consists of five rooms occupied by two men and two women—"You must squeeze up a bit into two rooms this winter, citizens, and prepare two rooms for two families now living in cellars. Until the time, with the aid of engineers (you are an engineer, aren't you?), we have built good dwellings for everybody, you will have to squeeze up a little. Your telephone will serve ten families. This will save a hundred hours of work wasted on shopping, and so forth. Now in your family there are two unemployed persons who can perform light work: a citizeness fifty-five years of age and a citizen fourteen years of age. They will be on duty for three hours a day supervising the proper distribution of provisions for ten families and keeping the necessary account of this. The student citizen in our squad will now write out this state order in two copies and you will be kind enough to give us a signed declaration that you will faithfully carry it out."
>
> This, in my opinion, can illustrate how the distinction between the old bourgeois and the new socialist state apparatus and state administration could be illustrated. [Lenin, 1972c, p. 112]

It is not known how far the Soviet state succeeded in solving the acute housing problem of the urban downtrodden by such forcible occupation of the mansions of the erstwhile privileged community. One observation, however, can be made assuredly. Such policy definitely turned the erstwhile privileged occupants of the mansions to curse their misfortune of being in Russia, leading to their exodus from Russia during the revolution. On the other hand, their deserted mansions became the targets of competition among the selected urban poor as the new privileged occupants. Such a policy did not reflect upliftment in terms of the recognition of belonging to the *class* of the downtrodden; instead the revolution degenerated into the awarding of privileges to certain individuals at the cost of certain erstwhile privileged members of society.

Supply and distribution of food articles and fuel is another area that brought disparity within the working class in sharp focus after the revolution. The new Soviet regime faced immense crisis over food supply in the years just after the revolution because of Civil War. Recent researches that bring out the level of workers' resentment and protests as well as the ways in which the new administration tackled such crises are strikingly similar to eyewitness accounts recorded years ago under conditions of enormous hardship. What is more important, they point to the unfair and unjust policies towards the working class population that the new regime was forced to adopt even when they called for sacrifice among the working class on behalf of dictatorship of the proletariat. To tackle the catastrophe of Civil War, Lenin advocated 'universal labour conscription' to support the Red Army. He justified conscription as this was asked under the rule of Soviets.

> In Germany it is the Junkers (landowners) and capitalists who are introducing universal labour conscription, and therefore it inevitably becomes war-time penal servitude for the workers.
>
> But take the same institution and think over its significance in a revolutionary-democratic state. Universal labour conscription, introduced, regulated and directed by the Soviets of Workers', Soldiers' and Peasants' Deputies, will *still not* be socialism, but it will *no longer* be capitalism. It will be a tremendous *step towards* socialism, a step from which, if complete democracy is preserved, there can no longer be any retreat back to capitalism, without unparalleled violence being committed against the masses. [Lenin, 1974a, pp. 363-364]

But did the workers and the urban downtrodden enjoy the right and access to even such basic and essential requirement of food supply? How was the policy of food distribution decided even in the case of acute food rationing, and what was the reaction of the working class? We quote here from recent researches on such basic questions of working class society in Soviet Moscow that reflect very rudely to the actual conditions of subsistence of the working class under the very regime for which they fought all the existing powers on the earth.

> During the civil war and through 1920, relations between workers and 'their' state were determined, more than anything, by the food shortage in the cities, which made inequality in distribution inevitable. The food shortage resulted from the constant decline in the proportion of land sown for food production, itself caused by civil war, peasant hostility to state requisitioning of grain, and the contraction of trade. The main method of food supply in Moscow, from 1918 until 1922, was rationing system, under which grain and other agricultural products requisitioned from the peasantry were centralized by the food supply commissariat and distributed to the Red army and the urban population. There were fierce disputes over how rationing should be organized, which amounted, essentially, to competitions between different types of inequality....In 1919, an additional 'labour ration' was introduced for factory workers; then factories of 'special importance' were upgraded to military ration status; then the principle of 'reserved' (*bronnirovannye*) ration was introduced, under which the food supply authorities were supposed to ensure that those designated received their rations no matter what; then came academic ration, a special ration for Red army men's families, and so on. Corruption, and trade in fake ration cards was rife. An early manifestation of Soviet state officials' privilege was corrupt access to extra rations, which fuelled working-class resentment and demands for 'equalization of rations'.[21] ....There was widespread concern among workers that inequalities in the rationing system worked in favour of party officials and the embryonic ruling elite and this inspired the demand for equalization of rations, i.e. that all urban wage-earners should receive the same. [Pirani, 2008, pp. 26-27]

Next, we bring the accounts of Victor Serge who like Rosmer was a French anarchist émigré of Russian origin. He was not only an active participant in the formation of CI but also was one who literally took part in the front line for protecting Red Petrograd in the face of white army's invasion. In his memoirs he recounted,

> In fact, in order to eat it was necessary to resort, daily and without interruption, to the black market; the Communists did it like everyone else. Banknotes were no longer worth anything, and ingenious theoreticians spoke of the coming abolition of money. .... The rations issued by the State cooperatives were minute: black bread (or sometimes a few cupfuls of oats instead), a few herrings each month, a very small quantity of sugar for people in the "first category" (workers and soldiers), and none at all for the third category (non-workers).
>
> The words of St. Paul that were posted up everywhere—HE THAT DOTH NOT WORK, NEITHER SHALL HE EAT!—became ironical, because if you wanted any food you really had to resort to the black market instead of working. .... Winter was a torture (there is no other word for it) for the townspeople: no heating, no lighting, and the ravages of famine. Children and feeble old folk died in their thousands. Typhus was carried everywhere by lice, and took its frightful toll. All this I saw and lived through, for a great while indeed. Inside Petrograd's grand apartments, now abandoned, people were crowded in one room, living on top of one another around a little stove of brick or cast iron which would be standing on the floor, its flue belching smoke through an opening in the window. Fuel for it would come from the floorboards of rooms nearby, from the last stick o f furniture available, or else from books. Entire libraries disappeared in this way. I myself burned the collected *Laws of the Empire* as fuel for a neighboring family, a task that gave me considerable satisfaction. People dined on a pittance of oatmeal or half-rotten horsemeat, a lump of sugar would be divided in tiny fragments among a family, and a single mouthful taken out of turn would start angry scenes. The local Commune did everything it could to keep the children fed, but what it managed was pitiful. [Serge, 2012, pp. 135-136]

For the readers' sake we note here that Serge wrote the first draft of these memoirs in the later period during his banishment to the Ural mountains under the very regime that produced 'a mass of other germs', that he found life worth living among the tremendous hardships he scripted above. Not only he, numerous others as Rosmer wrote, 'were facing reality' in Soviet Moscow in 1919-20. The workers were getting restive and resentful as the recent, modern research shows a striking similarity with Serge's accounts. We resort to lengthy quotes from these references to provide some flesh and blood in our bid to abstract arguments on production relations that were actually prevailing even when the Soviet state was embryonic, in its formative years. These features of the new state apparatus in germination definitely caught the eyes of the émigré revolutionaries from Europe. Their conscience bled and dithered at the sight of transformation of the Bolshevik revolutionaries into ruthless, pragmatic and statist administrators.

## 2.2 On *Revolutionary Democracy* under Dictatorship of the Proletariat

The actual practice of democracy in post-revolution Russia is a well-traversed topic that may be found in the critiques of the contemporaries' produced right after the revolution. Luxemburg commented on the want of democracy in the body politic of post-October Russia as, "... the rule of the Jacobins (the postponement of the Soviet Congress from three-month periods to six-month period). Yes, we can go even further: such conditions must inevitably cause a brutalization of public life: attempted assassinations, shooting of hostages, etc." [Luxemburg, 2004a, p. 307]

We do not deny that freedom of access to political practice is undoubtedly one aspect of democracy in general, and is reflected in Luxemburg's comment. As we elaborated above the first step of the proletariat as the *ruling class* therefore lies in the historical initiative of forming and strengthening the Soviet form of political institutions evolving from the production units. We recollect here as Marx and Engels proclaimed in the *Communist Manifesto* that "the first step in the revolution by the working class, is to raise the proletariat to the position of ruling class, to win the battle of democracy."

However, the practice of democracy in the case of the *transitional society* or for that matter in any society cannot and should not be discussed in isolation of the mode of production in the prevailing conditions. The precondition for the proletariat to win 'the battle of democracy' lies in exercising unfettered freedom to overhaul and transform the existing productions relations. Therefore, it cannot but be the practice of *revolutionary democracy* for the working class under its own rule. Unfortunately, this fundamental aspect of the practice of democracy as the revolution in the domain of production relations is not generally discussed in the critiques of the Russian revolution. It is generally referred and understood as a political question *per se*, a question of holding on to state-power.[8]

Historian Eric Hobsbawm wrote, "In short, the mode of production is the base of our understanding of the variety of human societies, and their interactions, as well as their historical dynamics." [Hobsbawm, 1997, p. 165] Following Hobsbawm's argument, we wish to focus on two specific features of *revolutionary democracy*. One, *revolutionary democracy* as was understood by the Bolsheviks in their policy of class alliances between the proletariat and the peasantry; second, the impact of the Bolshevik statist policies towards the degeneration of revolutionary practices within CI even in the formative years.

### *2.2.1 Bolshevik understanding of class alliance and revolutionary democracy*

We are not the first to coin the paradigm *revolutionary democracy*, it was done by Engels. As Hal Draper observes in detail[9], "In a polemic against Henizen, Engels developed a conception of the revolutionary Democracy *as a bloc of lower classes led by the proletariat, mobilizing against the bourgeoisie as well against absolutism, on the basis of a transitional type of program.*" [Draper, 2011a, p. 186] He quoted Engels as (a part of a long quote),

> In all civilized countries, Democracy has the political rule of the proletariat as its necessary result, and the political rule of the proletariat is the first presupposition of all Communist measures. As long as Democracy has not yet been won, so long therefore do Communists and Democrats fight together, and so long are the interests of the Democrats likewise those of Communists. Till then the difference between the two parties are purely theoretical in nature and can very well be discussed theoretically without thereby disturbing their common action in any way.

Lenin corroborated this understanding of *revolutionary democracy* as a political alliance among the parties with revolutionary programmes that do not consider *socialism* as the immediate goal. He wrote,

> Either in the interest of the landowners and capitalists, in which case we have not a revolutionary democratic, but a reactionary-bureaucratic state, an imperialist republic.
>
> Or in the interest of revolutionary democracy—and then *it is a step towards socialism*. [Lenin, 1974a, p. 362]

In the same article, he went on specifically to distinguish between the revolutionary democrats and the revolutionary proletariat.

> And the attitude of the proletariat to the peasants in such a situation confirms the old Bolshevik concept, correspondingly modifying it, that the peasants must be wrested from the influence of the bourgeoisie. That is the sole guarantee of salvation for the revolution.
>
> And the peasants are the most numerous section of the entire petty-bourgeois mass. Our Socialist-Revolutionaries and Mensheviks have assumed the reactionary function of keeping the peasants under the influence of the bourgeoisie and leading them to a coalition with the bourgeoisie, and not with the proletariat.
>
> The masses are learning rapidly from the experience of the revolution. And the reactionary policy of the Socialist-Revolutionaries and Mensheviks is meeting with failure: they have been beaten in the Soviets of both Petrograd and Moscow.[120] [Lenin, 1974a, p. 368]

This is essentially the famous concept of the stages of revolution moving from *democracy* to *socialist* revolution with the proletariat taking the leading role to wrest power from the bourgeoisie. Lenin's arguments regarding *revolutionary democracy* are in conformity with Engels' view above; that is a transitional, temporary alliance or bloc among political parties formed towards attaining democracy for the exploited classes. Here, it would be interesting to note what Hal Draper observed on Engels' formulation that at least was not contributed by Marx.

> We have seen that, repeatedly and vigorously, articles by Engels had included the petty-bourgeoisie as a constituent of the anti-bourgeoise bloc of the Democracy. This was to be a bloc of the proletariat, small peasantry, and petty bourgeoisie: so Engels had explained in his article against Henizen and in his draft of the Manifesto. But this conception nowhere appears in the Manifesto itself. [Draper, 2011a, p. 197]

So, how does according to Lenin and Engels, *revolutionary democracy* differ from *socialism* or *communism*? How according to them does the proletariat win 'the battle for democracy'? Well, as we have seen above Engels wrote, 'Democracy has the political rule of the proletariat as its necessary result, and the political rule of the proletariat is the first presupposition of all Communist measures'. This was also Lenin's assertion as we have seen earlier that by 'political rule of the proletariat' he meant dictatorship of the proletariat, "*smashing*" the political, administrative, punitive bourgeoisie state apparatus. The tough question however remains what happens to the alliance between the democrats and *communists* as the *communists* put forward their political programme towards *socialism*?

It will be not out of context here to see how Marx interpreted the transition towards winning 'the battle of democracy'. Marx wrote in 1850,

> The proletariat rallies more and more round *revolutionary socialism*, round *Communism*, for which the bourgeoisie has itself invented the name of *Blanqui*. This socialism is the *declaration of the permanence of the revolution, the class dictatorship* of the proletariat as the necessary transit point to the *abolition of class distinctions generally*, to the abolition of all the relations of production on which they rest, to the abolition of all the social relations that correspond to these production relations, to the revolutionizing of all the ideas that results from these social relations. [Marx, 1969a, pp. 223-224]

Here, Marx's thrust and concern is towards the class interests of the proletariat in continuing the revolution (the way he saw revolution is of *permanent nature*), interpretation of '*class dictatorship*' as the freedom proletariat exercises in overhauling production relations, social relations, and even revolutionizing the sphere of ideas that they inherit as the relics of the past society cannot be overlooked. Compared with Lenin's and Engels' interpretation one cannot gloss over the consistency of Marx in *not making* democracy *solely* a political question for the proletariat, a projection dealing not only in making and breaking political alliances. Rather, overhauling of all old, inherited social relations under the reign of dictatorship of the proletariat to the point of abolition of all classes as the vestiges of the past is the continuum Marx concluded as the historical tasks for the revolutionary proletariat. Therein unfolds the significance of democracy as the freedom to usher the struggle for *socialism* under the hegemony of the proletariat as the *form* and *right* of revolutionary practice.

If we now revert our attention from theoretical projection to actual practice, we have to say that Lenin had nothing to propose in his theses in the First Congress of CI on the important issue of alliance between different classes with divergent interests. He responded to the question of alliance with an approach of armed hostility towards the political adversaries and opponents of revolution. Lenin's concrete proposals on the actual transition of class alliances in Russia came later, in the Third and Fourth Congress of CI, when he proposed state capitalism and the New Economic Policy (NEP). These later proposals were there against the background of hostility of a large section of peasants towards the agrarian programme of the Bolsheviks during the Civil War. In his theses in the First Congress Lenin wrote,

> It follows that the Mensheviks were compelled to admit that there was no unity in their party, and that its members were either on the side of the bourgeoisie or on the side of the proletariat. The majority of the Mensheviks went over to the bourgeoisie and fought against us during the Civil war. We, of course, persecute Mensheviks, we even shoot them, when they waged war against us, fight against our Red Army and shoot our Red commanders. We responded the bourgeoisie war with the proletarian war—there can be no other way. [Lenin, 1972a, p. 24]

Lenin's open admission of bloody, internecine relations between the erstwhile fellow-travellers of revolution provides the pointer to the historic parting of ways between the "democrats" and the communists as the Bolsheviks moved ahead with their programme of "socialism". It cannot be denied that the Mensheviks and the Socialist-Revolutionaries (SRs) played an active and important role in the ousting of the Tsarist regime in the February Revolution of 1917.[10] The Mensheviks had considerable political influence over the workers in Petrograd till July 1917, the seat of the October Revolution. Many of them turned acutely hostile to the Bolshevik agrarian programme in the Civil War period. The uncomfortable question here is by marching alone and ahead of the political parties who participated in the February Revolution had the Bolsheviks really solved the teething question of transformation of the alliance between the peasantry and the proletariat towards "socialism"? The answer, from Lenin's own admission was unfortunately *no*.

Lenin openly and candidly admitted the failure of the Bolshevik agrarian policy during the Civil War before the delegates of the Fourth Congress of CI in November 1922. Lenin wrote in his review of Soviet Russia's five years,

> ....but in 1921, after we had passed through the most important stage of the Civil War—and passed through it victoriously—we felt the impact of a grave—I think it was the gravest—internal political crisis in Soviet Russia. This internal crisis brought to light discontent not only among a considerable section of the peasantry but also among the workers. This was the first and, I hope, the last time in the history of Soviet Russia that feeling ran high against us among large masses of peasants, not consciously but instinctively. What gave rise to this peculiar, and for us, of course, very unpleasant, situation? The reason for it was that in our economic offensive we had run too far ahead, that we have not provided ourselves with adequate resources, that the masses sensed what we ourselves were not then able to formulate consciously but what we admitted soon after, a few weeks later, namely that the direct transition to purely socialist forms, to purely socialist distribution, was beyond our available strength, and that if we were unable to effect a retreat so as to confine ourselves to easier tasks, we would face disaster. The crisis began, I think, in February 1921. In the spring of that year we decide unanimously—I did not observe any considerable disagreement among us on the question—to adopt the New Economic Policy. [Lenin, 1972d, pp. 134-135]

Not only in one place before a Congress of international revolutionaries, Lenin was candid enough to realize and admit 'namely that the direct transition to purely socialist forms, to purely socialist distribution, was beyond our available strength,' to the domestic audiences as well. Summarizing the achievements of the October Revolution in his often quoted article in *Pravda* in October 1921, Lenin wrote,

> Our last, but most important and most difficult task, the one we have done least about, is economic development, the laying of economic foundations for the new, socialist edifice on the site of the demolished feudal edifice and the semi-demolished capitalist edifice. It is in this most important and most difficult task that we have sustained the greatest number of reverses and have made most mistakes.... We expected—or perhaps it would be truer to say that we presumed without having given it adequate consideration—to be able to organise

> the state production and the state distribution of products on communist lines in a small-peasant country directly as ordered by the proletarian state. Experience has proved that we were wrong. It appears that a number of transitional stages were necessary—state capitalism and socialism—in order to *prepare*—to prepare by many years of effort—for the transition to communism. [Lenin, 1973a, pp. 57-58]

We hope, these two extensive references from Lenin's transparent admission would be sufficient here to show the failure of the practice of *revolutionary democracy* as understood by the Bolsheviks in post-October Russia. In a *transitional society*, a new struggle, a teething and strenuous struggle opens up to win over the petty bourgeoisie, the "*mass*" of the small-proprietors towards the vital interests of political power of the proletariat. One cannot deny the significance of the intensely engaged political expressions of *class struggle* that was fought among the rival political parties as the state-power is wrested from the bourgeoisie. We have witnessed this struggle among the political parties in post-war Russia, in Germany, in Hungary, in Italy through the intense vacillation, confusion among the allies of political formations those desired to hold on to existing political power, in their reluctance to strengthen the Soviet form of political power. In Russia, this struggle degenerated into bloody fratricide when different political parties (namely the SRs and the Bolsheviks), that were committed only yesterday to revolution clashed with each other with arms in hand for their respective agrarian programmes.

However, we again bring to focus that *revolutionary democracy* is not *solely* a political question, not *only* a question of swaying the non-proprietor "*masses*" in agricultural production (and who says only the peasant "*masses*", what about the employees, the urban petty bourgeoisie, the section of the workers who are still to take the call of *socialism*?) towards a unique political formation that culminated in strengthening the new state-power. Rather, as Marx visualized in all profoundness, *revolutionary democracy* is the unmitigated freedom the proletariat exercises to unfetter the peasant "*masses*" from various forms of capitalist production relations, towards collectivization, towards progressive decline of the economic categories such as *surplus value*, tax, and rent in agricultural production. *Revolutionary democracy* is the freedom proletariat exercises over the pre-capitalist and capitalist modes of agricultural production by socializing agricultural labour and products, by progressively downsizing the role of market, by surpassing the freedom of exchange (*and not by withholding the freedom*) of labour and products in the market, by making the social exchange of *value* through the market irrelevant in the society. Only in that way can democracy be revolutionary in ushering *socialist* production relations based upon a communion of direct producers. Otherwise, in every sense perpetuation of the monopoly of the state in agricultural production is either primitive accumulation by dint of sheer punitive measures of the state, *or*, it is supervision of the distribution of wage by the state towards the non-proprietors in agrarian economy.

Interestingly, similar observations on outlining the general course of development of "socialism" in a *transitional society* were made some fifty years ago by Sweezy during his debates with Bettelheim. Unfortunately, his observations regarding the dangers that an undeveloped agrarian economy faced during transition to "socialism" led to very different conclusions drawn by both of them at the end of their debate. Let us see Sweezy's observation on the subject. In an editorial in the journal *Monthly Review*, Sweezy wrote,

> We are not suggesting that production for profit can be immediately abolished, still less that a socialist society can hope to dispense with market relation in near future. But we are saying that production for profit must be systematically discouraged and rapidly reduced to the smallest possible compass, and that market relations must be strictly supervised and controlled lest, like a metastasizing cancer, they get out of hand and fatally undermine the health of the socialist body politic. [Sweezy, 1972, p. 27]

The discerning reader will notice that the *transitional society* was meant to be a 'socialist society' by Sweezy. In fact, perusing their debates one finds their understanding of "socialism" to be synonymous with dictatorship of the proletariat as interpreted by Lenin, 'a number of transitional stages were necessary—state capitalism and socialism—in order to *prepare*—to prepare by many years of effort—for the transition to communism.' We will deal with these serious confusions on the nomenclature of *transitional society* later in this Chapter when we review Marx's understanding of the transitional *state*. Apart from such confusions over terminology, could Sweezy conclude that such dangers of market economy, of revival of capitalism were averted in Soviet Russia during the pursuance of the "socialist" agrarian programmes of the Bolsheviks after the revolution? We do not know whether he was aware of the candid admissions of Lenin above. Even fifty years after the October Revolution, Sweezy was making naive, general statements when the course of events in Russian agrarian society compelled the Bolsheviks actually to revive 'state capitalism' by introducing the NEP.

There were two distinct positions of the Bolsheviks on this vital issue of alliance between the political and economic interests of the proletariat and the peasantry. Before the revolution, their standpoint was for a struggle to win over the peasantry from the political influence of the bourgeoisie towards the proletarian standpoint, towards *socialism* as opposed to bourgeoisie democracy. We have seen that Lenin wrote, 'the peasants must be wrested from the influence of the bourgeoisie'. This was Lenin's assertion after the February Revolution of 1917, while pressing fellow Bolsheviks to further advance the revolution after the overthrow of the Tsar's absolutist rule. He anticipated breaking of the alliance as the revolution further advanced towards "socialism". In April 1917, Lenin wrote while arguing with Lev Kamenev,

> What, then, is the first stage?
>
> It is the passing of state power to the bourgeoisie.
>
> Before the February-March revolution of 1917, state power in Russia was in the hands of one old class, namely, the feudal landed nobility, headed by Nicholas Romanov.
>
> After the revolution, the power is in the hands of a *different* class, a new class, namely, the *bourgeoisie.*
>
> The passing of state power from one *class* to another is the first, the principal, the basic sign of a *revolution,* both in the strictly scientific and in the practical political meaning of that term.
>
> To this extent, the bourgeois, or the bourgeois-democratic, revolution in Russia is *completed.*
>
> ....
>
> The revolutionary-democratic dictatorship of the proletariat and the peasantry" has *already* become a reality[3] in the Russian revolution,

> for this "formula" envisages only a *relation of classes*, and not a *concrete political institution implementing* this relation, this cooperation. "The Soviet of Workers' and Soldiers' Deputies"—there you have the "revolutionary-democratic dictatorship of the proletariat and the peasantry" already accomplished in reality.
>
> This formula is already antiquated. Events have moved it from tile realm of formulas into the realm of reality, clothed it with flesh and bone, concretized it and *thereby* modified it.
>
> A new and different task now faces us: to effect a split *within* this dictatorship between the proletarian elements (the anti-defencist, internationalist, "Communist" elements, who stand for a transition to the commune) and the *small-proprietor* or *petty-bourgeois* elements (Chkheidze, Tsereteli, Steklov, the Socialist-Revolutionaries and the other revolutionary defencists, who are opposed to moving towards the commune and are in favour of "supporting" the bourgeoisie and the bourgeois government).[4]
>
> The person who *now* speaks only of a "revolutionary democratic dictatorship of the proletariat and the peasantry" is behind the times, consequently, he has in effect *gone over* to the petty bourgeoisie against the proletarian class struggle; that person should be consigned to the archive of "Bolshevik" pre-revolutionary antiques (it may be called the archive of "old Bolsheviks"). [Lenin, 1974c, pp. 44-45]

We are constrained to quote a long passage from Lenin so that there is little scope of misinterpreting him on *revolutionary democracy*. As we stressed at the beginning of this subsection the concept was *only* a transitional political alliance so far as the aim was confined to fight the absolutist Tsarist regime. It ceased to exist so far as ascendancy of the class rule of the bourgeoisie in political terms of 'passing of state power from one *class* to another is the first, the principal, the basic sign of a *revolution'* was complete. In fact, he was so confident on his assertion of catalysing 'a split *within*' that he admonished Kamenev saying, 'The person who *now* speaks only of a "revolutionary democratic dictatorship of the proletariat and the peasantry" is behind the times, consequently, he has in effect *gone* over to the petty bourgeoisie against the proletarian class struggle;'

Ironically, the same Lenin asserted in the Third Congress before the delegates of CI as,

> The supreme principle of the dictatorship is the maintenance of the

> alliance between the proletariat and the peasantry in order that the proletariat may retain the leading role and its political power. [Lenin, 1972e, p. 117]

Not only in one place, while elaborating on the need for the NEP in Soviet Russia before the delegates of Third Congress of CI a year ago, Lenin wrote,

> In my thesis I tried to analyse *the problem of the relations between the proletariat and the peasantry*. For the first time in history there is a state with only two classes, the proletariat and the peasantry. The latter constitutes the overwhelming majority of the population. It is, of course, very backward. How do the relations between the peasantry and the proletariat, which holds the political power, find practical expression in the development of the revolution? The first form is alliance, closer alliance. This is a very difficult task, but at any rate it is economically and politically feasible. [Lenin, 1972e, p. 112]

In the paragraphs referred just above there was no mention of *class struggle* within the peasantry, no call to associate the landless labourers among the "*masses*" of peasantry towards the interests of the urban proletariat. Lenin was clearly exhorting the proletariat to keep the interest of the entire peasantry intact by forming a 'closer alliance' with them. Did he mean reverting back to the theory of *revolutionary democracy*? Was it a new realization about "socialism" where the political interests of the proletariat are best preserved by alliance with the interest of the entire peasantry? All these later realizations had nothing to do with a concise, mature theory of *socialism*. We have seen before it was the dire need of holding on to the new state-power in the face of the hostile reaction of the peasantry that forced Lenin to advocate such closer alliances with the entire peasant community. Lenin confessed before the Third Congress of CI,

> We confess that the initial form of this alliance was very primitive and that we made many mistakes. But we were obliged to act as quickly as possible, we had to organize the supplies for the army at all costs. During the Civil War we were cut off from all grain districts of Russia. [Lenin, 1972e, p. 115]

Lenin did not elaborate what were the 'many mistakes' committed during forcible grain acquisition from the peasants for the Red Army. The fallout of the agrarian programme named

*War Communism* was direct refusal of the peasants to part with grain to the state machinery that necessitated introduction of the NEP.

Lenin's statements do not reflect consensual alliance between two sections of the exploited "*masses*" in the society who were partners in the revolution the day before. They only reflect subjugation of the vast "*masses*" of the economically deprived population to the forces of the state. In Lenin's view, this peculiar representation of the alliance of classes with divergent interests was not going to happen through political parties having divergent political programmes. The alliance was supposed to be maintained by dint of the clout of a state-power that was self assured of the support of the proletariat for maintaining grain supply even when actually it was a case of forcible acquisition. Naturally, the questions arise where the dissenting and divergent voices of the aggrieved "*masses*" within the peasantry would have expressed their views? Were these dissents and divergence of same counterrevolutionary nature as the working class faced during the establishment of dictatorship of the proletariat?

Winning over the "*masses*" of non-proprietor or marginal proprietor population in the rural economy towards *socialism* is a question of *class struggle* that is a tortuous journey in the transformation of society. There was no mention in Lenin's theses all around of how these affected "*masses*" articulated their political demands under the Soviet rule. Even if we consider the "communist" party to be the vanguard section of the proletariat, it could not represent the economic and political interests of those sections of peasant "*masses*" who were looking for free play of capitalist production relations as the outcome of revolution. They could be won over only by allowing full freedom of articulation of their political demands while at the same time expanding the domain of socialized production and exchange that gradually diminished the role of the market. A reasonable hypothesis may be while the production relations advance effectively towards *socialism* and the society *de facto* renounces the capitalist attributes of the economy, the political rights of the opposition to such measures need to be protected as the democratic rights of opposing political parties. On both the counts, Soviet Russia followed the path contrary to *socialism*. While in terms of the ground realities of economy the Bolshevik party was forced to introduce the NEP in agriculture and espoused 'state capitalism' in industry, they minimized the role of Soviets as platforms of political struggle representing different class interests and programmes towards "socialism".

During his exchanges with Bettelheim, Sweezy realized this vital weakness in the nature of the "socialist" revolution in Russia, and in other countries where agriculture remained underdeveloped capitalist economy and the nation-states claimed to be "socialist" after the WWII. He wrote,

> For historical reasons which need not be detailed here, no revolution since the Russian Revolution of 1917 has come anywhere near fitting the classical Marxian schema. In most cases, the proletariat, small and weak to begin with, was shattered by repression and war; and all the new ruling parties were strongly influenced, if not all for the same reasons, by Soviet form and methods. Under these circumstances it seems to me to make little sense to say that the proletariat either was or could have been in power. What emerged in practice, probably inevitably, was a dictatorship proclaiming itself proletarian and socialist but actually drawn from several classes and struggling with the life-and-death tasks of running the economy and maintaining itself in power. [Sweezy, 1972, p. 52]

Our effort would have been superfluous fifty years after Sweezy's observation had not Sweezy and Bettelheim togther reached a bizzarre conclusion proceeding from the above observation. After prolonged correspondence they reached the conclusion that the ideological supremacy of the *Party*, custodian of the pure form of *Marxism-Leninsim* as a supreme ideology had maintained and advanced the proletarian chracter of the statist rule depicted above. In the next section of this Chapter, and in later Chapters we will closely look into this argument of ideological supremacy of the *Party* in a society that was branded to be "socialist" despite the absence of the socio-economic basis. However, the fact remains the policy of governance and administration pursued by the Bolsheviks during and after the Civil War period had not much to do with the *revolutionary* form of *democracy*. The Bolsheviks attempted to address the concerns of the peasantry ahead and above the heads of the existing political parties that had considerable influence, particularly among the middle and rich sections of the peasantry. In their effort to introduce "socialism" by the policy of grain monopoly of the state they could not achieve success as the peasantry refused to accept the policy.

Was there any other option open for the Russian revolution to pursue? This is a loaded, enigmatic question of history. First, we have seen in the introduction of this Chapter and in Chapter I that the efforts towards dictatorship of the proletariat were international phenomena whose achievements were most vibrant in post-war Germany and in Russia. This principal, international character of dictatorship of the proletariat was never in the picture in the debates of Bettelheim and Sweezy even though they had access to all the literature after fifty years of the Russian revolution. It was a shortcoming not only of these two scholars, most unfortunately even the "authoritative accounts" of Soviet history narrated the formation of CI as Sheer attempts of Lenin to settle personal accounts.[11] That the fate of Russian revolution was deeply intertwined to the international revolution was repeatedly asserted by the revolutionaries in Germany and in Russia. In a fervent appeal to the working class of countries in the Allied camp of war, Liebknecht wrote,

> The proletariat of the world must not allow the flame of the Socialist Revolution to be extinguished, or all its hopes and all its powers will perish. The failure of the Russian Socialist Republic will be the defeat of the proletariat of the whole world. [Liebknecht, 1919]

Luxemburg analyzed in her critique of Bolshevism in a different context as,

> This is the essential and enduring in Bolshevik policy. In this sense theirs is the immortal historical service of having marched at the head of the international proletariat with the conquest of political power and the practical placing of the problem of the realization of socialism, and of having advanced mightily the settlement of the score between capital and labor in the entire world. In Russia the problem could only be posed. It could not be solved in Russia. And in this sense, the future everywhere belongs to "Bolshevism". [Luxemburg, 2004c, p. 310]

That the practical problems of transition to *socialism* could only be posed in Russia, and the solution of these practical problems needed victory of *socialism* in Europe was also understood by Lenin in several places of his writings. While addressing the delegates in the Third Congress of CI in July 1921, he outlined the international perspective for survival of the Russian revolution in very clear terms.

> We thought: either the international revolution comes to our assistance, and in that case our victory will be fully assured, or we shall do our modest revolutionary work in the conviction that even in the event of defeat we shall have served the cause of the revolution and that our experience will benefit other revolutions. It was clear to us that without the support of the international world revolution the victory of the proletarian revolution was impossible. Before the revolution, and even after it, we thought: either revolution breaks out in the other countries, in the capitalistically more developed countries, immediately, or at least very quickly, or we must perish. In spite of this conviction, we did all we possibly could do to preserve the Soviet system under all circumstances, come what may, because we knew that we were not working for ourselves, but also for the international revolution. [Lenin, 1972e, p. 108]

This was a brilliant, sincere exposition of the future of the working class revolution in a country where capitalism in agriculture was passing through a primitive stage of evolution as compared to the developed economies of Europe. As we stressed earlier there are neither textbooks for revolutions to happen nor are they the results of a fervent wish of the revolutionaries. Defeated European revolutions particularly in Germany could not help the workers of Russia in their valiant efforts to usher transition to international *socialism*. We will dwell on the reasons for the failure of the German revolution in our subsequent discussion in Chapter 4. It was evident by the time of the Third Congress of CI in 1921 that dictatorship of the proletariat in Russia remained an isolated island among the series of defeats of the European working class.

Second, the Russian revolution not only suffered international isolation, the working class was isolated and devastated within Russia itself. In his theses in 1921 quoted above it is noteworthy that Lenin was repeatedly referring to 'we'. Earlier at all places, Lenin wrote as the spokesperson of the revolutionary proletariat, but while addressing the delegates of CI, Lenin only referred to the Bolsheviks as 'we'. By July 1921, the Bolsheviks stood isolated in the political spectrum of Russia as we have seen in the history of fratricide among the political parties. We may remember here Engels' writing on the peasant war in Germany.

> The worst thing that can befall a leader of an extreme party is to be compelled to take over a government in an epoch when the movement is not yet ripe for the domination of the class which he represents and for the realisation of the measures which that domination would imply. [Engels, 1926, English translation]

It is mentioned in [Serge, 2012] that Lenin repeated such statement considering the situation in which the Russian revolution found itself. We do not place such comments here as we do not have the primary source. However, it is a fact in every sense of the word that Russian workers made genuine, sincere efforts towards *socialism* during the post-war turbulent days. Their stellar role will always remain a beacon before the international working class. Although the October Revolution in 1917 is generally recorded in historical documents as the workers' revolution in Russia, in all practical terms that was only the beginning of workers' revolutionary initiative in Russia. Before the October Revolution, Lenin reasoned while arguing with Kamenev the need of revolutionary measures as,

> What *compels* such steps?
>
> Famine. Economic disorganisation. Imminent collapse. The horrors of war. The horrors of the wounds inflicted on mankind by the war. [Lenin, 1974c, p. 54]

The most tragic irony the Russian proletariat faced was exactly Lenin's fears turned into reality after the October Revolution for continuous three years till 1921 when the new state found relative stability among the comity of capitalist states of the world. The first detachments of the Red Army came from the contingents of the working class in Petrograd who withstood the onslaught of the trained military of white guards, and later the army of the fourteen states of Europe. A vivid description of the heroic effort of the Petrograd working class to save Red Petrograd from the onslaught of the white army under General Yudenich may be found in [Serge, 2012], and there are numerous such accounts of history. The four years of Civil War and *War Communism* decimated the best sons and daughters of Russia's working class when dictatorship of the proletariat became more of a notional character in the social context. Introducing the reasons for the NEP in a theses in the Third Congress of CI, Lenin had to admit,

> The dictatorship of the proletariat does not signify a cessation of class struggle, but its continuation in a new form and with new weapons. ....The difficulties of transition, and the influence of the bourgeoisie, inevitably cause the mood of this mass to change from time to time. Upon the proletariat, enfeebled and to a certain extent declassed by the destruction of the large-scale machine industry, which is its vital foundation, devolves the very difficult but paramount historic task of holding out in spite of these vacillations, and carrying out to victory its cause of emancipating labour from the yoke of capital. [Lenin, 1972f, p. 88]

Here, it is to be noted that by 'mass' Lenin meant 'the small farmer class', and by 'vacillations' of them he was pointing to the raging peasant revolts in the rural countryside of Russia at that time against forcible grain acquisition by the state. We have cited earlier the frustration with the economic situation and resentment among the urban working class regarding the food crisis whose relatively 'declassed' nature Lenin was referring to here. Initiative and vigour for *class struggle* in such a tragic, difficult situation did not remain with the *class* whose dictatorship faced the acid test. It became the onus and hinged on the commitment and sacrifice of the revolutionaries, the 'we' Lenin referred to earlier.

In a rapid turnaround, the crisis situation that hastened the statist character of the regime at the disposal of a *vanguard* contingent was regarded to be the virtue in late discourses, as Soviet Russia found relative stability, that Lenin used to refer as 'unstable equilibrium'. Even after fifty years of the revolution, erudite economists such as Sweezy and Bettelheim proclaimed the continuance of Soviet rule under the hegemony of a bureaucratic and alien clique to be dictatorship of the proletariat, the *'class in power'*. It is for this reason we stated the answer regarding the choices before the Russian revolution were loaded as we cannot recreate history according to our wish, and recommend certain prescriptions based on non-factual reading of history, the imaginary course of the suggested history that never happened. At the same time, while taking into account the historical narrative, we cannot also set aside a concrete analysis of the mode of production of post-revolution Russian society. We cannot console ourselves by stating that what happened in the defeat of revolution was the *only* course left before the Russian society.

### 2.2.2 Impact of the statist policies of the Bolsheviks on the revolutionary practices of CI

In a different context while analysing the reign of "terror" in post-revolution Russian society, Kautsky wrote, "For decades the Russian Socialists had made a virtue out of necessity, and espied in the backward character of their agrarian problems a certain advantage." [Kautsky, 1919, p. 82] While the Bolshevik leadership were exhorting the significance of Soviet Russia as the outpost of international "socialist" revolution of the working class before the delegates of CI, they were doing exactly the opposite of that in Russia as the immediate measures to bring economic stability. What was more disturbing, very soon they started theorizing their practice in Russia as general principles for international "socialism". The Bolsheviks were making tectonic shifts in their standpoints regarding dictatorship of the proletariat. To answer and justify their isolation in the political spectrum of Russia they cited the cardinal presence of the *communist party* as the mandatory requirement for transition to "socialism" in a country, for victory of the international struggle for "socialism", for the survival of the Soviet system in Russia and elsewhere while Lenin and Trotsky were acting as their leading proponents. It is difficult to draw any other conclusion from the bizarre shift of understanding if one compares the two manifestos issued after the First and Second Congress of CI. Under a heading 'Democracy and Dictatorship', Trotsky wrote in the first manifesto as,

> The dictatorship of the proletariat, which gives it the favoured position in the community, is only a provisional institution. As the opposition of the bourgeoisie is broken, as it is expropriated and gradually absorbed into the working groups, the proletarian dictatorship disappears, until finally the State dies and there is no more class distinction, [Communist International, 1919, pp. 23-24]

Not only did Trotsky stress the transitional nature of *state*, he, in fact, indicated dissolution of socialist parties within the Soviet form of organization of administration under dictatorship of the proletariat. He wrote,

> On the other hand, there are essential elements of the proletariat, heretofore not within the Socialist party, who stand now completely and absolutely on the platform of the Dictatorship of the Proletariat in the form of Council rule, for example the corresponding elements among the Syndicalists. [Communist International, 1919, p. 31]

This manifesto ended with a very interesting call for unity among the proletariat at the end, *"LONG LIVE THE INTERNATIONAL REPUBLIC OF THE PROLETARIAN COUNCILS!"*

It was a clarion call for the Soviet form of international organization of the working class irrespective of their national identities, independent of their varied political affiliations and their different occupations of all hues as wage labour, to unite on a platform for Soviet power against the bourgeoisie. This spirit of commonness of objectivity with the syndicalists was echoed in the letter of invitation to IWW that went under Zinoviev's signature in January 1920. He wrote,

> In order to destroy the capitalist State, to break the resistance of the capitalists, and to disarm the capitalist class, in order to seize the property of the capitalists and to hand it over to the entire working class—for all these tasks a government is necessary, a State, the dictatorship of the proletariat, through which the workers in their Soviets can eradicate the capitalist order with an iron hand.
>
> That is just what is happening in Soviet Russia. But the dictatorship of the proletariat is only a temporary measure. We communists also want to abolish the State. The State can exist only as long as the class struggle lasts....
>
> As the most important revolutionary-syndicalist organization among the revolutionary industrial unions in America, the IWW should take the initiative in seeking a basis for the unification of all unions with a class-conscious, revolutionary character, of all workers who recognize the class struggle, such as the Union of Industrial Workers, the One Big Union, and the few revolutionary unions in the AFL....
>
> As revolutionaries they should not repulse the attempts of the American communists to get agreement on joint revolutionary action. The political party and the industrial organization must work shoulder

> to shoulder for the common purpose—the abolition of capitalism by the dictatorship of the proletariat and the establishment of Soviets; the dissolution of classes and of the State. [Degras, 1971, pp. 73-74]

Sincerity and genuineness behind all these appeals for proletarian unity are bound to be questioned from the developments of the Second Congress of CI. Trotsky drafted this *Manifesto* and delivered the valedictory address of the Second Congress. Unlike the *Manifesto* for the First Congress, this was a report on the international situation of crisis of the capitalist economy, assessments over the emerging civil war in Europe (presenting at once a very rosy picture of the international proletarian revolution and colonial uprisings). It was more of a rabble rousing propaganda pamphlet. Most surprising was the analysis of Soviet rule in Russia and its international implications. While the first *Manifesto* stressed the nature of communistic society and the production relations to follow after the revolution, in the second *Manifesto* there was no mention of the working of the Soviet administration towards extension of democracy among the exploited population especially among the working class. Their inclusion and participation in the state administration, policy making, nature of electoral participation in Soviets, judicial systems, interplay of varied political tendencies in the Soviets—in short, there was no mention of how the proletariat was exercising democracy towards dissolution of *state* and was progressing towards a classless society that was meant to be the tasks of dictatorship of the proletariat in the first manifesto. Rather, in an inexplicable way, strengthening of the Red Army was found to be the virtue of the new state. The second *Manifesto* wrote,

> The development and consolidation of the Soviet power in Russia is the most momentous historical event of the period succeeding the foundation of the Communist International.
>
> In the eyes of class society the creation of an army has usually been regarded as the supreme test of industrial and State reconstruction. The weakness or the strength of the army has been regarded as evidence of the weakness or strength of industry and the State.
>
> In the midst of the strife the Soviet power has created a mighty armed force. The Red Army has demonstrated its superiority not alone in the struggle with old bourgeoisie monarchist Russia.... but also in the struggle with the national armies of the "democracies" which

> world imperialism is planting for its own interests (Finland, Estonia, Latvia, Poland). [Communist International, 1920, p. 20]

There was now no more admission of tracing backwards, of strengthening the wings of *state* in the adverse conditions of holding the fort of international "socialism", rather it was an appraisal of success of the heroic effort to form a new state, albeit under the *new* rule of the exploited class. But where was the manifestation of working of the new *class* in political power, the power of decision-making in the second *Manifesto*? Earlier we have found both Lenin and Trotsky were asking for labour conscription for revival and growth of industrial productivity. Now, the second *Manifesto* dealt with the virtues of centralization of authority and planning for increasing productivity of industry.

> The concentration of industry and the means of transportation in the hands of the government leads to standardizing of the industrial arts and make them common property of society. Only under a socialist regime is it possible to fix the minimum number of types of locomotive cars and steamers to be manufactured and repaired, and to carry on standards manufacture en masse of parts of machinery designed by periodic regulations, thus securing enormous advantage in the matter of productivity. Beside the imperialist assaults from abroad nothing stands in the way of Soviet Russia's further economic achievements, and nothing is going to prevent her scientific organization of industry and the introduction of the Taylor system, divested of course, of its capitalistic features of exploitation and sweating. [Communist International, 1920, p. 21]

While reading these statements in 1920, one cannot forget Lenin's instructions as the immediate tasks of the Soviet government [Lenin, 1974b] in 1918. The Russian model of practice of "socialism" was put forward as generalization of "communist" practices in the manifesto of CI. A statement full of jargon follows the above paragraph that is very difficult to interpret and understand. Except that the intention was to harp on the mission of resurrection of industry by a national government that was devastated in the war.

> While in the rest of the world national interests clashing with imperialist encroachments serve as the source of incessant conflicts, uprisings and wars, socialist Russia has shown how easily a Workers' Government can reconcile national requirements with industry

> interests by purging the former of chauvinism and the latter of imperialism. [Communist International, 1920, p. 21]

We have mentioned earlier that Russian society was yearning desperately for economic revival. The new state was bound to take this call to stop continuing instability and Civil War, to bring a semblance of order in the society and governance. While the new state administration was highlighting their success in turning the difficult tide before the Congress of CI, questions were bound to be raised on how the success of a national government in reviving capitalist production relations in a war ravaged underdeveloped economy was going to motivate the international working class for *socialism*. There was no mention at all in this second *Manifesto* of CI about the progress of democracy in Soviet society in the rush to catch up with industrially developed Europe. While the First Congress saw the Third International as a platform of Soviet republics, the Second Congress saw itself as a world *communist party* that was singular in the forefront of the world proletarian revolution.

> The Communist International is the revolutionary party of the International proletariat. It sweeps aside all those organisations and groups which beguile the proletariat, openly or in disguise, inducing it to kneel before the fetishes screening the dictatorship of the bourgeoisie, such as legality, democracy, national defence, etc. ....
>
> The Communist International is the international party of proletarian insurrection and proletarian dictatorship. It has no aims and problems other than those of the working class. .... [Communist International, 1920, pp. 29-30]

Thus, the Russian experience of isolation of the Bolsheviks after the revolution was thrust upon CI as the *only* political party, organized *vanguard* formation before the international proletariat to take the call of dictatorship of the proletariat. We have seen even in January of the same year, Zinoviev was addressing IWW of USA in a completely different manner and with different objectives. It is worth noting this huge shift within a year of its formation about the role and objective of CI was endorsed not only by Lenin as a member of the Russian delegation, it got approval of the representatives of socialist and "communist" parties from 32 countries many of whom were in the nascent stage of formation.

As in every other sphere of activity centralization of authority of ECCI was suggested in the Second Congress itself. The directives of ECCI were made binding on the "communist" parties by the twenty-one conditions of admission in CI drafted by Lenin considering CI as the leader of international "socialism". The 16th condition for inclusion in the Third International went as,

> All decisions of the Congresses of the Communist International, as well as the decisions of its Executive Committee, are binding on all parties affiliated to the Communist International. The Communist International, operating in the midst of most acute civil war, must have a far more centralized form of organization than that of the Second International. At the same time, the Communist International and its Executive Committee must, of course, in all their activities, take into consideration the diversity of conditions under which the various parties have to work and fight, and should issue universally binding only on questions on which passing of such decision is possible. [Piatnitsky, 1934, p. 31]

While the first part of the condition speaks clearly of the intent, the second part shows the reality that the affairs of "communist" parties of different countries were still not under control of the Bolsheviks. There were still many, particularly from Western Europe, who were reluctant to accept the Bolshevik directives for revolution and therefore consensus was still required. Within a brief time interval till the Fourth Congress was held the Third international became a vehicle of the proletarian movement "modelled" by the experience of the Russian revolution as the experiences of other revolutions became slowly irrelevant and faded out in their outward and visible defeat. These developments cannot be condoned and overlooked under the pretext of adverse, crisis situation of the Russian revolution. Nor can a conclusion be drawn that following the Russian charter was the *only choice* left before CI and the revolutionary sections of the international proletariat.

### 2.3 Ideological Tenets of Bolshevism and Dictatorship of the Proletariat

Our discussion till now is focused on socialist production relations and *revolutionary democracy* under dictatorship of the proletariat. The major weakness or limitation of understanding among the

Bolsheviks and consequently among the partners of CI about the transition to *socialism* revolved around these principal issues. Transition to *socialism* is evidently transformation of society to a *new* basis and form, and in any case production relations *alone* do not constitute a functional, living society. Crisis in capitalist society brings the contradictions within the production relations in sharp focus but these crises are neither restricted to production relations alone nor do they follow one-to-one correspondence to the social issues that are thrown up along with the crisis. For example, dropping of the atomic bombs in Hiroshima and Nagasaki by the American government at the end of the Second World War (WWII) was intended to register before the world the supremacy of capital of American origin. At the same time this action created a host of other critical issues of the survival of humanity that are still now equally important. The "*mass*" killing fields in Kampuchea brought before the world the horror of genocide in the name of introducing an egalitarian society. But these catastrophes also brought the crisis of human relations in much more sharper focus than only the production relations under the new regimes in the post-Vietnam war Southeast Asia could register. The recent rise of terrorist movements across the globe in the name of radical Islam may be interpreted as retaliatory attempts to counter the European model of civilization; but the barbarism inherent in these radical movements does not in any way substitute or surpass the need for a revolutionary critique of capitalism of European origin. At the onset of the WWI, Luxemburg wrote in *Junius Pamphlet* quoting Engels,

> Friedrich Engels once said, "Capitalist society faces a dilemma, either an advance to socialism or a reversion to barbarism."[21] What does a "reversion to barbarism" mean at the present stage of European civilization? ....Thus we stand today, as Friedrich Engels prophesied more than a generation ago, before the awful proposition: Either the triumph of imperialism and the destruction of all culture, and, as in ancient Rome, depopulation, desolation, degeneration, a vast cemetery; or, the victory of socialism, that is, the conscious struggle of the international proletariat against imperialism, against its methods, against war. [Luxemburg, 2004d, p. 321]

Unfortunately, after a century of the WWI the world has witnessed not only more barbarism, genocides by traditionally known variety of imperialism that were not even imagined in Luxemburg's time, but also the fact that millions of dead bodies were strewn in the trenches of Siberia after merciless shooting, and these "*mass*" murder camps were claimed to be the victory of "socialism". The contours of barbarism against humanity have turned out to be much wider and deeper than probably Engels and Luxemburg could have contemplated. These critical issues of the crisis of human civilization cannot be addressed by discussing the features of revolutionizing production relations *alone*.

Capitalism shaped and catalyzed the production relations that were inherent inside the society, but much more than that capitalist society brought forth modern civilization. Bourgeoisie civilization constituted a society that was not identified by hereditary privileges alone; rather it is a society where the capacity of an individual is revealed in the open in all shades of activity. While critically commenting on the particularly halting approach of reforms by the German bourgeoisie Marx wrote the following immortal description of bourgeois civilization.

> The revolutions of 1648 and 1789 were not English and French revolutions, they were revolutions in the European fashion. They did not represent the victory of a particular social class over the old political system; they proclaimed the political system of the new European society. The bourgeoisie was victorious in these revolutions, but the victory of the bourgeoisie was at that time the victory of a new social order, the victory of bourgeois ownership over feudal ownership, of nationality over provincialism, of competition over the guild, of partitioning [of the land] over primogeniture, of the rule of the landowner over the domination of the owner by the land, of enlightenment over superstition, of the family over the family name, of industry over heroic idleness, of bourgeois law over medieval privileges. The revolution of 1648 was the victory of the seventeenth century over the sixteenth century; the revolution of 1789 was the victory of the eighteenth century over the seventeenth. These revolutions reflected the needs of the world at that time rather than the needs of those parts of the world where they occurred, that is, England and France.
>
> There has been nothing of this in the Prussian March revolution. [Marx, 1969b, p. 139]

Reading the above passage of Marx one may be amused to find more bourgeoisies in him than the bourgeoisie themselves. He was bringing out here the historical significance of revolutions in England and France in ushering a new European civilization. The Prussian bourgeoisie in the nineteenth century had neither the capacity nor the intent to pursue revolution against Prussian absolutism. The European proletariat gaining from the experience of the street battles of Paris in 1848 were rising behind the bourgeoisie to demand its share in the revolution. Unfortunately, an alternate vision of civilization based on the collectives of direct producers in the new *socialist* society was sparsely present in the documents of the Bolsheviks and CI. The role of CI was restricted and narrowed down to a political platform for winning immediate political power albeit on behalf of the proletariat and that too following the experience of revolution in an undeveloped capitalist economy. Organization of society on a hitherto unfound platform that transcends interpretation of legality, morality, religion, family, ideology of "fetishism of commodities" of the bourgeoisie society require immense courage of conviction among the "*masses*" of the proletariat in the multiple dimensions of governance, culture, science, justice system, social nature of distribution of all amenities, i.e. to actively consider a society based on "the standpoint of the new is human society, or social humanity." (Thesis X) [Marx, 1969c] These are crucial questions of ideology, philosophy that are addressed not only by deciding production relations *alone* although that remains pivotal, fundamental and immediate in ushering a *socialist* society. The place of revolutionary ideology is cardinal in the exercise of freedom among the "*masses*" to consider and decide *their own rule* as the material basis of life process in the new form of society.

Revolutionary ideology in actual practice is the deliberation of all the issues we cited through the *new* social institutions that cannot be realized in bourgeoisie civilization. Luxemburg asserted and highlighted this aspect of revolutionary ideology in her critique of revolutionary practices in Russia.

> Socialist democracy begins simultaneously with the beginnings of the destruction of class rule and of the construction of socialism. It begins at the very moment of the seizure of power by the socialist

> party. It is the same thing as the dictatorship of the proletariat.
>
> Yes, dictatorship! But this dictatorship consists *in the manner of applying democracy*, not in its *elimination*, in energetic, resolute attacks upon the well-entrenched rights and economic relationships of bourgeois society, without which a socialist transformation cannot be accomplished. But this dictatorship must be the work of the class and not of a little leading minority in the name of the class—that is, it must proceed step by step out of the active participation of the masses; it must be under their direct influence, subjected to the control of complete public activity; it must arise out of the growing political training of the mass of the people. [Luxemburg, 2004c, p. 308]

There have been many discussions on the substitution and replacement of initiatives of the "*masses*" and practices of democracy in Russia by the Bolshevik party, notable among them are [Brinton, 1970], [Sen, 2000]. We here concentrate on the ideological tenets that influenced the theory and practice of Bolshevism in a society in transition from deeply underdeveloped capitalism to "socialism". The ideological moorings of Bolshevism soon were followed religiously in the practice of CI.

### *2.3.1 On the workers' assertion of rights under the Bolshevik regime*

Let us first consider the question of assertion of the workers' rights. There was a raging debate within the organized working class in Russia from 1919 -1921 regarding who should have decisive control over the production system. The debate was raised mainly by the trade union leaders such as Alexander Shliapnikov, Sergei Medvedev among others within the highly influential ranks of the All Russia Metalworkers' Union and the Bolshevik party. They had formally put up the *Theses of the Workers' Opposition* before the Tenth Congress of the Bolshevik Party.[12] Their submission included many Chair holding members of the central trade unions of Russia as signatories. Later, their standpoint was articulated in a more theoretical manner in the pamphlet *Workers' Opposition* by Alexandra Kollontai, a prominent old Bolshevik whose membership continued from 1898. This group representing the highly skilled, unionized workers went on to argue in the theses for more authority in matters of production, their management and for a decisive say in matters of industrial policy. We reproduce below some relevant passages from the theses.

> The practices of party congresses and state organs for the past two years have systematically narrowed the scope of the work of trade unions and brought almost to zero the influence of workers' unions in the Soviet government. The role of trade unions in the organization and administration of production in fact has been reduced to the role of an office of inquiry and recommendation, placing staff in administrative posts, between state organs and unions there is no agreement and conflicts overload party organizations. The unions still have neither a printing press nor paper. Journals of even the largest unions come out with a delay of several months. The state printing press gives lowest priority to work on behalf of unions. ....The belittling of the significance and actual role of the trade unions in Soviet Russia signifies the manifestation of bourgeois, class hostility toward the proletariat and must be quickly overcome....The system of building economic policy by a bureaucratic path, over the heads of organized producers, by means of functionaries, appointees, dubious specialists, has given birth to duality in management of the economy, involving constant conflicts between factory committees and the management of enterprises, between unions and economic organs. ....
>
> [This thesis] emphasizes that the unions must concentrate in their hands all management of the economy as a unified economic whole....The organization of management of the entire economy will belong to an All-Russian congress of producers, unified in professional production unions, which elects a central organ, governing the entire economy of the republic....All workers and employees, without distinction to position and profession, occupied in separate economic units, such as: factories, mines, transport services and in connection with all types of agriculture, are direct managers of property located within them, are answerable for its preservation and the expedient use of it before all laborers of the republic.... One of the indispensable conditions of the elevation of our national economy is the systematic implementation of the naturalization of wages, as a measure, ensuring the heightening of the productivity of labor and the betterment of the producers' lives...." [Shliapnikov, 1921]

We have quoted from separate parts of the theses to show some of its prominent statements. It clearly pointed to the insignificant role of the workers and their unions that prevailed in decision-making and managing the systems of industrial production. To stress the lack of opportunity for airing of views the theses submitted, 'The state printing press gives lowest priority to work on behalf of unions.' That such an important theses on reorganization of national economy and the role of the industrial working class was put up before the Congress of the Bolshevik party, and not in the Congress of Soviets undoubtedly testifies to the minor role of the Soviets as platforms and organs of active democratic practices. Second, in the name of 'heightening of the productivity' the unions brought the demand of 'naturalization of wages', which was a demand for the law of wages to be given a fair play in the "socialist" economy. In that sense, the thesis underscored the unions' greater role in deciding fair wages, as like the practices of trade union bargaining that happens in a capitalist system of wage-driven labour relations in production.

This issue of a greater say of the workers as demanded by the *Workers' Opposition group* was more cogently argued in Kollontai's pamphlet. At the very beginning of the pamphlet she could forcefully bring the question of *class* nature of ownership of the means of production and organization of production.

> Even if Soviet Russia succeeds in carrying out completely its project of general electrification, without introducing any essential change in the system of control and organization of the people's economy and production, it would only catch up with the advanced capitalist countries in the matter of development. [Kollontai, 1921, p. 19]

Then she brought out clearly the difference of approach between the *Party* leadership and the *group* she stood for.

> The whole controversy boils down to one basic question: Who shall build the Communist economy, and how shall it be built? This is, moreover: the essence of our programme: this is its heart. This question is just as important as the question of seizure of political power by the proletariat. ....
>
> The cardinal point of the controversy that is taking place between the Party leaders and the Workers' Opposition is this: to whom will our Party entrust the building of the Communist economy—to the Supreme Council of National Economy with all its bureaucratic branches? Or to the industrial unions? Comrade Trotsky wants 'to join' the trade unions to the Supreme Council of People's Economy, so that, with the assistance of the latter, it might be possible to swallow up the former. Comrades Lenin and Zinovieff, on the other hand,

> wanted to 'bring up' the masses to such a level of Communist understanding that they could be painlessly absorbed into the same Soviet institutions. Bukharin and the rest of the factions express essentially the same view. Variations exist only in the way they put it; the essence is the same. Only the Workers' Opposition expresses something entirely different, defends the proletarian class viewpoint in the very process of creation and realization of its tasks. The administrative economic body in the workers' republic during the present transitory period must be 'a body directly elected by the producers themselves. All the other administrative economic Soviet institutions should serve only as executive centres of the economic policy of the all-important economic body of the workers' republic..' [Kollontai, 1921, pp. 1, 15-16]

We will very soon see the views of Lenin and Trotsky on this crucial issue of the workers' control *vis-a-vis* the *Party*'s role. Before that a few comments on Kollontai's standpoint are in order. First, she was no different from the Bolshevik leadership in urging the *Party* to allow a larger role of the unions in managing the economy, 'to whom will our Party entrust the building of the Communist economy?'—she asked. Her demand was to put the 'Soviet institutions' subordinate to the policies framed in the 'All-Russian congress of producers' that we referred earlier in the theses of the *group*. But the Soviets came into existence as the natural choice of institutional forms of the elected representatives of the direct producers to frame such policies of *socialist* economy. Then, how did the suggestion to replace the Soviets by the unions as the authority for framing policies of industrial production arise? She repeated this argument in her pamphlet while referring to the 'Supreme Council of National Economy', a Soviet body promulgated under Soviet law.[13]

The question is why and how was this body transformed to be a bureaucratic apparatus in which the workers and their unions had very little say? It is evident from Kollontai's pamphlet and the theses of the *Workers' Opposition group* that the Soviets were losing relevance as the organs of workers' decisive say in matters of policies of national economy, as the dynamic platforms of "*mass*" participation that was anticipated and claimed in the first *Manifesto* of CI. 'In the Council system the mass organizations rule and through them the mass itself, in as much as the Councils drew constantly increasing number of workers into the State administration;' [Communist International, 1919] Soviet institutions those evolved during the revolutions from February to October 1917 (even till February 1918) as the organs of workers' political power were now perceived as the wings of bureaucratic state apparatus where the elected representatives of the workers had limited influence and say. The Bolshevik party substituted the Soviets as the seat of the political organ of the state to claim the final authority, and therefore appealing before its leadership through their unions for their rights was the last resort of these representatives of the organized working class. The working class got divested from its own *state* apparatus, and conversely, the state apparatus lost its *identity* as the political organ of dictatorship of the proletariat. Lenin's statement 'Soviet power, i.e. the dictatorship of the proletariat, on the other hand, is so organized as to bring the working people close to the machinery of government..' was losing relevance in the unelected, bureaucratic transformation of Soviet administration so that the workers found in the elected strength of their trade unions a last resort to survive just as it happens in other capitalist societies.

The above assessment about the reduced importance of the institution of Soviets in the eyes of the workers was not wrong. It became clear when Lenin and Trotsky advocated in full steam for the supremacy of the *Party* and not of the Soviets. While negating these demands of the unions for exercising rights in deciding policies of industrial production, Lenin spoke in December 1920,

> Within the system of the dictatorship of the proletariat, the trade unions stand, if I may say so, between the Party and the government. In the transition to socialism the dictatorship of the proletariat is inevitable, but it is not exercised by an organization which takes in all industrial workers. Why not? The answer is given in the theses of the Second Congress of the Communist International on the role of political parties in general. I will not go into this here. What happens is that the Party, shall we say, absorbs the vanguard of the proletariat, and this vanguard exercises the dictatorship of the proletariat. The dictatorship cannot be exercised or the functions of government performed without a foundation such as the trade unions. These functions, however, have to be performed through the medium of special institutions which are also of a new type, namely, the Soviets.....

> But the dictatorship of the proletariat cannot be exercised through an organisation embracing the whole of that class, because in all capitalist countries (and not only over here, in one of the most backward) the proletariat is still so divided, so degraded, and so corrupted in parts (by imperialism in some countries) that an organization taking in the whole proletariat cannot directly exercise proletarian dictatorship. It can be exercised only by a vanguard that has absorbed the revolutionary energy of the class. The whole is like an arrangement of cogwheels. Such is the basic mechanism of the dictatorship of the proletariat, and of the essentials of transition from capitalism to communism. [Lenin, 1973b, pp. 20-21]

Here, Lenin was crystal clear about the nature of working of the 'cogwheel', 'the basic mechanism of the dictatorship of the proletariat' that had three distinct components: *a*) political leadership of the *vanguard* of the proletariat in the form of *Party*, *b*) administrative policy making the role of Soviet state apparatus, *c*) the executioner role of the trade unions who remain a '*link* between the vanguard and the masses'. There was no ambiguity in Lenin that workers' right in deciding their own fate was actually hypothecated to the wisdom of the vanguard *Party* as the "*masses*" were uneducated and untrained in "socialist" policy making. Trade unions were there to assist the "*masses*" in the implementation of the programmes as was decided by the Soviets or *Party*, as 'schools of communism'—the role Lenin assigned to the trade unions. We wish to remind the reader here that this was the same Lenin who distinguished the Soviet form of administration from the bourgeoisie parliament in his theses in the First Congress as, 'That too, is the purpose of combining the legislative and executive authority under the Soviet organization of the state and of replacing territorial constituencies by production units—the factory.' The principal complaint of the elected representatives of the workers in the theses of the *Workers' Opposition group* was this contention of Lenin—being divested of their right to legislate, and the executive authority being assigned to the nominated bureaucracy growing within the Soviet administration.

Ironically, for both the *Workers' Opposition group* and the Bolshevik leadership the layers of Soviet organizations as "*mass*" platforms of political training for deciding *state* issues became irrelevant. Lenin viewed the trade unions as the linking organization to the "*masses*" of workers to train them to "socialist" practices. Only three years ago, these 'untrained' "*masses*" created the political institutions, have gone through the political education of two revolutions (in fact counting the aborted attempt in 1905, three revolutions) unseating the mighty Tsar and later the weak, provisional bourgeoisie government. It was the dream of these 'most backward' "*masses*" of the proletariat for a *new* society in Russia that hoisted the Bolsheviks and Lenin to state-power. Before the revolution and in the theses before the First Congress of CI, Lenin tirelessly advocated the Soviets as the *new* institutional form *akin* to the Paris Commune, the rich, superior platform of workers' democracy as opposed to bourgeoisie democracy. Three years after the revolution, he was evaluating the "*masses*" in the scale of their backwardness, their inability to understand and grasp the gravity of state policies, and therefore stressing the necessity of their *vanguards*. Again, these *vanguards* were not coalesced in the Soviets as elected representatives of the 'backward' "*masses*", they were to be absorbed in the *Party*, the know-all and never-to-falter leadership. The *metamorphosis* happened not only in Lenin, the entire Bolshevik party grovelled before the wisdom of Lenin in the Tenth Congress.[14] In hindsight, one reason behind the apprehension of the *Party* leadership might be the dissenting voice of the *Workers' Opposition group* that was bound to be another parallel power centre as they also demanded the Soviets to be subordinated to their authority. In that sense, the significance of the institutional form of dictatorship of the proletariat was lost to both the opposing camps in the Tenth Party Congress.

That we are not distorting Bolshevik understanding of the role of the Soviets under *Party*'s guidance and control should be clear from Trotsky's writings reproduced below. They were more blunt in exposition than Lenin as we have seen earlier. In the same pamphlet [Trotsky, 2006].

Trotsky wrote before the delegation of the Second Congress of CI as follows:

> If the party and the trade unions were organizations of preparation for the revolution, the Soviets are the weapon of the revolution itself. After its victory, the Soviets become the organs of power. The role of the party and the unions, without decreasing is nevertheless

essentially altered.

In the hands of the party is concentrated the general control. It does not immediately administer, since its apparatus is not adapted for this purpose. But it has the final word in all fundamental questions. Further, our practice has led to the result that, in all moot questions, generally—conflicts between departments and personal conflicts within departments—the last word belongs to the Central Committee of the party. This affords extreme economy of time and energy. ....

The exclusive role of the Communist Party under the conditions of a victorious proletarian revolution is quite comprehensible. The question is of the dictatorship of a class. In the composition of that class there enter various elements, heterogeneous moods, different levels of development. Yet the dictatorship pre-supposes unity of will, unity of direction, unity of action. By what other path then can it be attained? The revolutionary supremacy of the proletariat pre-supposes within the proletariat itself the political supremacy of a party, with a clear programme of action and a faultless internal discipline.

The policy of coalitions contradicts internally the regime of the revolutionary dictatorship. We have in view, not coalitions with bourgeois parties, of which of course there can be no talk, but a coalition of Communists with other "Socialist" organizations, representing different stages of backwardness and prejudice-of the laboring masses. (Chapter 8)

It is extremely surprising to find the same Trotsky here who only a year back indicated dissolution of the *Party*, and was prepared to stand on the same steps with the syndicalists on the platform of Soviets. A year after, he was unabashedly looking for a decisive, centralized leadership masked in the absolutism of 'unity of will, unity of direction, unity of action' of the *Party* so much so that he was reluctant to share its leading role even with any 'other "Socialist" organizations'. He did not even have confidence in the rank and file of the *Party* system when he proclaimed, 'the last word belongs to the Central Committee of the party'. Earlier we have seen he exhorted for military conscription of labour to enforce iron discipline and unity of will. Then, what remained of the Soviets as the forum of active *"mass"* participation, of decisive power of the working class? Exactly this was the query echoed in Luxemburg's criticism that we reproduce below.

When all this is eliminated, what really remains? In place of the

> representative bodies created by general, popular elections, Lenin and Trotsky have laid down the soviets as the only true representation of the laboring masses. But with the repression of political life in the land as a whole, life in the soviets must also become more and more crippled. Without general elections, without unrestricted freedom of press and assembly, without a free struggle of opinion, life dies out in every public institution, becomes a mere semblance of life, in which only the bureaucracy remains as the active element. Public life gradually falls asleep, a few dozen party leaders of inexhaustible energy and boundless experience direct and rule. [Luxemburg, 2004c, p. 307]

At this point, we have to settle some scores with Bettelheim and Sweezy. They jointly agreed with the infallibility of the *Party* as the sole guarantee towards transition to "socialism". We are bewildered to find Bettelheim arguing as

> The *dominant apparatus* of proletarian state power, therefore, is the *Marxist-Leninist party* and not the state apparatus. The Marxist-Leninist party is the true instrument of the dictatorship of the proletariat, and the crucial organizational form of a proletariat which has become the ruling class. [Bettelheim, 1972b, p. 64]

By this assertion, are we to believe that the Bolshevik clarion call "*All Power to Soviets*" between July and October 1917 was actually suggested to hoodwink the war-fatigued "*masses*" of the workers and soldiers? Was it a smokescreen put before the workers of Red Petrograd who rallied behind the Bolsheviks with this call in their heart and mind to protect its existence from the mighty white army of General Yudenich? Not only in Russia, the mandate for formation of the Revolutionary Council of workers and soldiers in Berlin in January 1919 was not for any party or group but for all the revolutionary "*masses*" in Germany who sided against the Weimar Republic of the bourgeoisie. Was the formation of the Council to be treated as an accident and not a proletarian state power and authority? Is the Paris Commune to be understood as an accident of history and not a revolutionary authority as no political party or group could claim the sole leadership to the Commune? Of course, Bettelheim was not so naive to suggest such wild conjectures. Before such confounding assertions as above he wrote,

> The essential aspect of the bourgeoisie state is the *separation* of the

> state apparatus from the masses; the state apparatus is "above" the masses, it controls them and represses them, whereas the working class state is no longer completely a state because it is the instrument of the exercise of power by the working masses themselves (herein resides the essence of the Paris Commune, the power of the Soviets, the Revolutionary Committees, etc.). [Bettelheim, 1972c, p. 45]

Bettelheim's statements are to be treated as pious intentions as such proclamations can be found fifty years before their writing also in *The State and Revolution* by Lenin, and in numerous Bolshevik literature on the eve of the October Revolution. The question before Bettelheim is how he could assert the infallibility of volunteerism of a dedicated group of people as the talisman for 'the true instrument of the dictatorship of the proletariat'? The assertion of Trotsky and Lenin we referred to were fifty years before Bettelheim's assertion. Those were far removed from interpreting the Soviets as the political organs of exercising dictatorship of the proletariat. Just after these general statements, Bettelheim reverted to his pet theme of the *vanguard* role of the "communist" party in protecting the 'working-class'.

> The power of the workers can obviously take different forms according to concrete historical conditions, principally according to the relation of class forces. This power can exert itself, notably, by the intermediary of a "vanguard detachment" of the proletariat, i.e., a Marxist-Lennist communist party; such a party exerts proletarian power to the degree that it is effectively a vanguard, a part of the working class which represents the totality of the class and acts in concert with it without aspiring to take the place of the working class.... [Bettelheim, 1972c, p. 45]

Of course, Bettelheim never explained under what circumstances 'The power of the workers' is exerted by 'a "vanguard detachment" of the proletariat' in place of the revolutionary institutions such as 'Paris Commune, the power of the Soviets, the Revolutionary Committees' those he mentioned just a paragraph above. The issue under the scanner is not only the political power of the state for suppression of the erstwhile bourgeoisie; the issue at hand is declaration of the hegemony of the 'vanguard detachment' in every matter of the society. Bettelheim proved by these assertions that he had not advanced an inch ahead of Rosemer who even two decades before him was looking for the salvation and relief for the 'working class' in the infallibility of the *Party*.

We took labour in examining Bettelheim's argument on the feasibility of dictatorship of the proletariat in an underdeveloped capitalist economy such as post-revolutionary Russia in some detail to show the basic philosophical construct of the leaders, the ideologues, the economists, the propagandists remained the same even five decades after the fate of the Russian revolution was sealed. The construct was the ingrained belief that the proletariat were unable as a *class* to manage their own affairs in a *new* society even if they had crossed the fire of actual revolutions in relatively quick succession of time interval. The bourgeoisie, notwithstanding their internal strife, may be able to manage "their" civilization based on the circulation of money and "profit". But the belief that was ingrained among all such elite representatives was the proletariat needed a tutor *or* a master *or* a salvation army for the transition to a *new* civilization. Is this ideological construct in the middle of the twentieth century fundamentally different from the fabled tales of Moses pronouncing the *Ten Commandments* or Muhammad pronouncing the *Hadith* to the faithful?

The subject of unpreparedness of the workers in making decisions (and not only execution of decisions) under the "socialist" economy was also examined by the leaders of the Second International. It will be interesting here to see Kautsky's observation on the preparedness for the proletarian revolution in general.

> It is not so easy to organize as it is to expropriate. The capitalist concern is a complex organization, which finds its intelligence in the capitalist himself, or in his representative. If it is desired to abolish capitalism, same form of organization must be created, which should be possible of functioning as well, if not better, without the capitalist head. This is not so simple as was the procedure of Philip IV or of Stenka Razin; for it demands a certain set of conditions of a material as well as o£ a psychical order, a high development of capitalistic organisation, not only of production but also of the export and import of raw materials. Moreover, it also demands a proletariat, which is conscious of its duties, not only towards its own neighbours and comrades, but also towards society as a whole—a proletariat, moreover, which has become accustomed to voluntary discipline and self-administration through long years of mass organization; and which, finally, is

> intelligent enough to distinguish the possible from the impossible, and the scientifically educated leader with character from an ignorant demi-god without a conscience. Wherever these conditions are not present, capitalism cannot with any success be permanently dissolved by Socialism. [Kautsky, 1919, p. 82]

It is ironical to find the two legends Lenin and Kautsky, bitter critics of each other and vying to claim the authority of proletarian leadership were unanimous on the basic pivotal point: *the proletariat was unprepared to build socialism.* According to both of them, the proletariat crucially needed the learned, "politically correct" leadership to attain "socialism". Whereas Luxemburg's understanding was far mature with respect to the needs and priorities of the *socialist* societies in terms of 'social humanity,' she could not relate ideological understanding with the actual, concrete programme to overhaul the existing production relations. Although Lenin spoke of the withering away of *state,* he either did not have the idea or the opportunity to see through the implications of his standpoint that turned out to be worshipping volunteerism of an elite minority with the progress of time, and was of course far what Marx envisaged for the *communist* society.

We would like to end this part of the discussion with a reference to Blanquism and its nature by Engels with respect to dictatorship of the proletariat although it is a misnomer to honour August Blanqui as the originator of the concept.[15]

> Brought up in the school of conspiracy, and held together by the strict discipline which went with it, they started out from the viewpoint that a relatively small number of resolute, well-organized men would be able, at a given favorable moment, not only to seize the helm of state, but also by a display of great, ruthless energy, to maintain power until they succeeded in sweeping the mass of the people into the revolution and ranging them round the small band of leaders. This involved, above all, the strictest, dictatorial centralization of all power in the hands of the revolutionary government. [Engels, 1891, *Postscript*]

We do not want to lead the reader to conclude that Lenin and Bolsheviks were modern Blanquists of the twentieth century. The above elaborate discussion then turns futile. No two momentous courses of events in history are the same, nor is the leadership in the course of those events equivalent in their vision and programmes. What remains connecting among the events distanced in historical settings are the ideological principles, moorings that dominate the approach of the leadership to those events. We have quoted Engels here to show that even with all sincerity and courage of the revolutionaries the Bolsheviks remained captive of their situation in which historically they were placed when they had the responsibility and opportunity to decide for the ideological foundation of the *new* society. Ideologically speaking, despite their earnestness they could not surpass Blanquism of the nineteenth century.

### 2.3.2 Political and juridical rights under the statist regime of Bolshevism

Revolutions are extreme approaches to solutions of social conflicts, but so are counterrevolutions *per se*. It is well documented in the history of the failures of the working class rebellion in Europe, particularly in Italy and in Germany, how counterrevolution soon took the centre stage of society. In March 1933, the Nazi party was the sole legal party in Germany claiming the authority with the excuse to prevent a communist uprising. In an apparent similarity, the Eleventh Congress of the Russian communist party in April 1922 sanctified the Bolshevik party in its new incarnation as the sole legal political party in Russia. The Tenth Congress that we earlier referred to banned the existence of all platforms inside the *Party* with Lenin and Bukharin leading the resolutions. In a belated admission in 1939 Trotsky wrote,

> It is true that the Bolshevik Party forbade factions at the Tenth Party Congress in March 1921, a time of mortal danger. One can argue whether or not this was correct. The subsequent course of development has in any case proved that this prohibition served as one of the starting points of the Party's degeneration. The bureaucracy presently made a bogey of the concept of 'faction', so as not to permit the Party either to think or breathe. Thus was formed the totalitarian regime which killed Bolshevism. [Trotsky, October 1939]

What was in Trotsky's mind regarding the 'time of mortal danger' in the spring of 1921? Those were theoretical articulations from the platform of unions regarding assertions of the workers' rights against the Bolshevik leadership, the armed mutiny of Kronstadt sailors (the same Kronstadt naval base that was the bastion of the October Revolution), the workers' strike movement in the factories of Petrograd and Moscow that went unabated in 1920-21, and the raging peasant rebellion against forcible grain acquisition by the state in the countryside, etc. To quote from the recent research work we referred to earlier,

> There was widespread concern among workers that inequalities in the rationing system worked in favour of party officials and the embryonic ruling elite—and this inspired the demand for equalization of rations, i.e., that all urban wage-earners should receive the same. [Pirani, 2008, p. 31]

Lenin admitted the grim scenario while introducing the reasons of the NEP before the delegates of CI in the Third Congress.

> I have already said that in the spring of 1921 the most appalling want caused by the fodder shortage prevailed among peasantry, which constitutes the majority of our population. .... The condition of the working class is extremely hard. It is suffering horribly. Those who have more political understanding, however, realise that in the interest of the dictatorship of the working class we must make tremendous effort to help the peasants at any price. The vanguard of the working class has realized this, but in that vanguard there are still people who cannot understand it, and who are too weary to understand it. [Lenin, 1972e, p. 117]

These several passages from the leaders of revolution, as well as from modern research portray the extremely grim reality before the Bolsheviks that we pointed out earlier. Their isolation was not only confined to the domestic political spectrum of Russia, their isolation from their core base of "*mass*" support was also evident. By their own admissions a sizeable population of the workers in urban centres and the sections of the peasantry were deeply disillusioned and resentful to the *new* regime.

Unfortunately, the approach of Bolshevism to this economic and civil crisis was unadulterated animosity to the political opposition. The political standpoints of the Bolsheviks were a testimony to the exasperation and groping in the darkness of hostility. Earlier we have seen Lenin's defence of mutual bloodsheds between the SRs and Bolsheviks. Now, let us look at Lenin's hostility towards even the non-party "*masses*" who dared to question the Bolshevik policy particularly in the rural areas. Lenin left no stone unturned in his famous pamphlet *Tax in Kind* in 1921 under the heading "POLITICAL SUMMARY AND DEDUCTIONS" to express his hostility to the Mensheviks and SRs.

> The events of the spring of 1921[78] once again revealed the role of the Socialist-Revolutionaries and Mensheviks: they help the vacillating petty-bourgeoisie element to recoil from the Bolsheviks, to cause a "shift of power" in favour of the capitalists and the landowners. *The Mensheviks and Socialist-Revolutionaries have now learned to don the "non-party"* disguise. This has been fully proved. Only fools now fail to see this and understand that we must not allow ourselves to be fooled. Non-party conferences are not a fetish. They are valuable if they help us to come closer to the impassive masses—the millions of working people still outside politics. They are harmful if they provide a platform for the Mensheviks and Socialist-Revolutionaries masquerading as "non-party" men. They are helping the mutinies, and the whiteguards. The place for Mensheviks and Socialist-Revolutionaries, avowed or in non-party guise, is not a non-Party conference but in Prison (or on foreign journals, side by side with the whiteguards; we are glad to let Martov go abroad). We can and must find other method of testing the mood of the masses and coming closer to them. We suggest those who want to play the parliamentary, constituent assembly and non-Party conference game, should go abroad; over there by Martov's side, they can try the "charms" of democracy and ask Wrangel's soldiers about them. We have no time for the "opposition" at "conference" game....[Lenin, 1973c, pp. 361-362]

Lest the reader may suspect us as votaries of Menshevism for placing this long reference from Lenin's pamphlet we may make it clear that we have no such intention. We understand the Russian revolution remains highly polemical even after a century, and to look for coherence with some existing trend is a well-entrenched tradition! It is a record of history that the Mensheviks and SRs in many places tried to settle the scores with the Bolsheviks during the Civil War by openly taking sides with the white guards in the trenches opposing the Red Army.

Here, the question is how Lenin can be defended in the above paragraph except probably suggesting that he was trying to lift the sagging morale of the Bolsheviks in the crisis situation by openly inciting them to brook no political opposition. The paragraph depicts vividly the fact that like Trotsky he had actually confidence in *nobody* except in their Central Committee. According to the above arguments anybody could be labelled a Menshevik or SR or at least a 'fool' who opposed the Bolshevik agrarian policy. Trotsky made this assertion in succint clear terms before the delegates of CI in the Second Congress.

> Today we have received a proposal from the Polish government to conclude peace. Who decides such questions? We have the Council of People's Commissars but it too must be subject to certain control. Whose control? The control of the working class as a formless, chaotic mass? No. The central committee of the party is convened in order to discuss the proposal and to decide whether it ought to be answered. And when we have to conduct war, organize new divisions and find the best elements for them—where do we turn? We turn to the party. To the central committee. The same thing applies to the agrarian question, the question of supplies, and all other questions. [Trotsky, 1924]

Like Trotsky in the above paragraph, the reader will notice Lenin had great contempt for any formal gathering like the 'non-Party Conferences' in which anybody dared to openly express reservation, dissent, or opposition to the programme of grain monopoly of the state. Second, by Lenin's own statement such conferences were not meant for active participation of the peasants (many of whom might have been avid supporters of Bolshevism) in state administration, they were meant by the Bolsheviks for 'testing the mood of the masses'. On the converse side, the hostility of the rural "*masses*" was so apparent that the Mensheviks or SRs could easily sway the so-called 'mood' so that Lenin had to forcefully recommend dissolution of such conferences. The latent irony here is Lenin at the same time was vigorously campaigning within the *Party* to abandon such 'suicidal' grain monopoly policy.

In any case, the Bolsheviks never encouraged continuation of the multiple political parties or groups in the Soviets that could reflect the struggle of divergent interests of the sections of peasantry and the different strata of the proletariat. In the previous subsection we have observed the great reluctance of the Bolshevik leadership to concede to the workers' rights through the trade union platforms.

Any subsidiary forum, leave aside political expressions of other parties, was vehemently opposed by the Bolshevik leadership after the instinctive rebellions in February 1921 of the affected "masses" across Russia became an embarrassing reality. In that desperate situation the political form of *class struggle* reflecting even sectional interests of the erstwhile exploited *"masses"* within the Soviet platforms became out of the agenda for the Bolsheviks.

However, the Bolsheviks were not *metamorphosed* to this despotic position in one day, instantly after the *revolution*. Lenin's own references point to the existence of multiple political parties in the Soviets till 1919. He had multiple references to Soviets as forums of 'explanatory' work among the peasant deputies. For example, in October 1918 there was a reprint of Lenin's pre-revolution pamphlet on *Political Parties in Russia and the Tasks of the Proletariat* where he grouped existing political parties in Russia into four headings and analysed their class basis and nature of their political programmes. As seen below, by his own analysis of group C and D, the vast petty-bourgeoisie peasant *"masses"* were divided in their loyalty among the SRs and the Bolsheviks.

> 2) WHAT CLASSES DO THESE PARTIES REPRESENT? WHAT CLASS STANDPOINT DO THEY EXPRESS?
>
> ....
>
> C. (S.D. and S.R.). Small proprietors, small and middle peasants, the petty bourgeoisie, and that section of the workers which has come under the influence of the bourgeoisie.
>
> D. ("Bolsheviks"). Class-conscious proletarians, wage-workers and the poor peasantry (semi-proletarians) standing close to them.
>
> 3) WHAT IS THEIR ATTITU DE TOWARDS SOCIALISM?
>
> ....
>
> C. (S.D. and S.R.). For socialism, but it is too early to think of it or to take any immediate practical steps for its realization.
>
> D. ("Bolsheviks"). For socialism. The Soviets must immediately take all possible practicable steps for its realization.[1] [Lenin, 1964, p. 93]

By his own admission in 1921, the Bolsheviks were not pursuing 'socialism' in agriculture, and were advocating alliance of the proletariat with the entire peasantry. Then, what made the SRs vanish from the political spectrum of Russia? It is well documented the "Left"- SRs temporarily shared the Soviet government, but like all other parties and groups participating in the revolution their participation in the Soviets later turned minimal. Clearly, a vast section of the peasantry lost their political, ideological representatives in the arena of *class struggle* by these developments of hounding, and liquidating political opposition. Their aspirations and right of democracy to intervene in the administration of the state became non-existent. We may examine here another statement made by Lenin that clearly shows the churning, wavering, switching over of the Soviet deputies towards the Bolshevik opinion during the onset of revolution.

> [120]On August 31 (September 13), 1917, the Petrograd Soviet for the first time passed, by a majority of 279 to 115, with 50 abstentions, a motion tabled by the Bolshevik group, emphatically rejecting the policy of compromise with the bourgeoisie. The resolution called for the transfer of all power to the Soviets and outlined a programme for revolutionary changes in the country. A few days later the Bolshevik Party won yet another major victory. On September 5 (18) the Moscow Soviet of Workers' and Soldiers' Deputies carried a similar Bolshevik motion by a majority of 355 votes. ([120]Editor's Note) [Lenin, 1974a, p. 368]

The question is why there was no mention in Lenin's theses of the living and bitter clash of opinion of the Soviet deputies during the spiralling economic crisis in February 1921 as was there on the eve of revolution? After all, our analysis in Section 2.2 has shown there was minimal difference in the agrarian programmes after the Civil War among the political parties whom Lenin assessed as the enemies of revolution. We have shown in Section 2.2 the dichotomy in the analysis of classes among the rural population, before and after the Civil War. Even if we go by Lenin's assessment, the class interests of the peasantry and the proletariat were vastly divergent after the revolution. The rich and middle peasants were looking for survival and regeneration of capitalism. The proletariat was looking for state ownership of all major means of production. Unfortunately, no political institution was there among the vast "masses" of beneficiaries of revolution to reflect upon these divergent objectives of the transformation of society. The institutional representation of *class struggle* would have educated and trained the peasant delegates about the objective of self-rule, and self-activity in the administration of society. On the other hand, we have just seen above that let alone institutions, the Bolsheviks strongly disapproved any formal gathering that would let a storm raised even in a cup of opposition. They faced all around isolation out of desperation to stick to the state-power; their efforts to introduce "socialism" in Russian society by forcing the exploited "*masses*" to acknowledge their initiative actually rebounded on them.

In the fundamental sense of social practice of democracy, Bolshevik leadership reflected a very dim view of the perspectives of *liberty* that historically were brought before society by the bourgeoisie revolutions of Europe. Definitely the growth of Bolshevism in Russia cannot be viewed without putting into context to the prevalent attributes of Russian society—that was the veritable want of *liberty* in the Russian society, the most prominent social, political feature under the centuries old monarchist-estate regime of the Tsar. Lenin wrote in the manual for Soviet Government, "If we measure our revolution by the scale of West-European revolutions we shall find that at the present moment we are approximately at the level reached in 1793 and 1871." [Lenin, 1974b] Here, he was referring to the underdevelopment of Russian political economy by comparing with the eighteenth century French bourgeoisie revolution, and the nineteenth century French workers' revolution in the Paris Commune. The revolutions of 1793 and 1871 did not only advance sea changes in the relations of production, they modernized the modes of exploitation in European society to unprecedented heights. In fact, it may be said the revolutions established a "scientific" basis to *class*-based exploitation which are yet to be confronted in a coherent, cogent manner with concrete alternatives. Associated with these modern mode of productions came institutional representation of *liberty*, freedom of individual, freedom of expression and association of opinion, freedom of the workers to agitate and organize strikes in the industries.

The Bolsheviks forgot and undermined the fact that the very idea of the proletarian revolution could not be there unless the working class experienced the idea of liberation in the European revolution that Marx commented upon. The revolutionary actions of the Paris Commune and the October Revolution were only the beginning of implementation of these ideas of *liberty* to which the proletariat of Russia committed themselves as the leader of the deprived in the society. It was a cruel irony of prevarication that while as a matter of theory Lenin espoused the cause of the Soviet form of administration he was vastly different in what he was actually demanding as a matter of practice. In the same piece of writing in October 1921 on the fourth anniversary of the October Revolution, Lenin wrote,

> The Soviet system provides the maximum democracy for the workers and peasants; at the same time, it marks a break with *bourgeois* democracy and the rise of a *new*, epoch-making *type* of democracy, namely, proletarian democracy, or the dictatorship of the proletariat. [Lenin, 1973a, p. 62]

As it happens in every stage of development of capitalist society, evolution of the political institutions closely follow the production relations concurrently available in the society. Development of political and social institutions of post-revolution Russia was no exception; they were deeply influenced by Bolshevik motivation of centralization of all production apparatus and amalgamation of all the arms of state under a centralized authority. While the Bolsheviks and a large section of class-conscious workers were ready to sacrifice themselves for the world revolution, the Russian society at large particularly the erstwhile oppressed "*masses*" of peasantry were desperately looking for economic stability and end of Civil War. The new found *liberty* of exercising their will in many instances brought the exploited "*masses*" and particularly the enlightened workers who directly participated in the revolution in confrontation with the approach of centralization of authority in the state apparatus and in the Bolshevik leadership. At the same time, these confrontations could not take the shape of political battles as by that time existence of political parties except the Bolshevik party had become illegal. The ideological construct of Bolshevism in post-Civil War Russia degenerated into a benevolent, despotic regime of dictatorship that had very little in common with *class dictatorship* that was the call of the October Revolution and even in Lenin's writing above. Not only were the political parties with divergent views forbidden, as we have seen even differing opinions among the organized working class pledging loyalty to the *Party* were banned and rebuffed at the Tenth Party Congress. So much was the fear of embarrassment among the Bolsheviks that the appeal of the twenty-two Bolshevik old guards, *To Members of the International Conference of the Communist International*[16], drafted by Shliapnikov in 1922 and addressed to CI on lack of inner-party democracy was not even allowed to be an agenda of the Conference of CI. The convention of discussing internal affairs of communist parties in the meetings of CI was there except for the Russian section and slowly that became the rule.

To Trotsky all along, "socialism" essentially was a question of management of society, albeit for the physical betterment of the underprivileged and the exploited including the working class at the cost of the hitherto existing privileged sections of society. That *socialism* is self-rule of the underprivileged for the collective benefit of them, emancipation of the working class can be effected only by this self-rule through institutions created by the working class in their own revolutionary effort. The deeper and wider ideological roots of the *new* society were very quickly vanishing from his perspective along with the Bolsheviks at whose helm of leadership he was there in that period. Earlier we have seen Trotsky's reservation towards coalition of parties having the revolutionary objective to run the Soviet administration.

To Lenin, the sole meaning of bourgeoisie democracy was a charade only to hide the socio-economic reality of exploitation by capitalist production relations. This is absolutely true urging the need for replacing the bourgeois state apparatus with the new *quasi-state* that amalgamated the role of the executive and the legislature into a single elected body, i.e. the Soviets or the 'proletarian councils'. However, in Russia the totalitarian *obverse* became the unfortunate truth. In the charade of separation of authorities of the executive, legislature, judiciary, press, and army, the bourgeoisie society not only provides the veil of cover, the hideout of the capitalist class, it also provides the exploited "*masses*" the avenues to dissent, leaves the room for taking the battle of democracy from one pillar to the other of the state. The basic cornerstone of representative democracy that dictatorship of the proletariat inherited from the historic experience of bourgeois democracy is the forum of elected representatives while bringing in significant *new elements* in the institution. That is, the direct producers composing the electorate who preserved the right to recall the representatives. According to Lenin's and Trotsky's assertions these forums of representative democracy were to be subjugated to the authority of an ombudsman called *Party* having no institutional accountability to the electorate of these forums. For them, trade unions, Soviets, 'non-party Conferences', peasants', soldiers' "*mass*" organizations all had the same purpose existence—that is executing instructions of the infallible *Party*. In Russia, all authority after the October Revolution was first vested in only one forum, i.e. the Soviets. Minimizing the leading political role and authority of the Soviets and bringing in the *Party* as the sole arbitration authority made representative democracy a meaningless term in the society, the soul of the dictatorship of the proletariat was lost. When Lenin wrote of the 'new, epoch-making *type* of democracy namely, proletarian democracy,' first of all and above all it meant was the unmitigated right of dissent for the proletariat in the forums consisting of the elected representatives of the proletariat. Let us remember here Luxemburg's pointer to democracy in *socialism*, 'But this dictatorship must be the work of the class and not of a little leading minority in the name of the class—that is, it must proceed step by step out of the active participation of the masses; it must be under their direct influence, subjected to the control of complete public activity;'. In place of the elected representatives of the producers including the workers, the Soviets were constituted largely by the paid administrative staff that created the bloated bureaucracy [Pirani, 2008].

Lenin assured the delegates of CI in the First Congress in 1919, 'no impediments in the way of any workingman (or groups of workingmen, in any numbers) for enjoying and practising equal rights in the use of public printing press and public stocks of paper.' This commitment turned out to be a farce after the Tenth Congress in 1921, when even the old guard Bolsheviks opposing the party leadership had no legal opportunity, freedom to publish their views for general reading, let alone other opposing political parties and groups. It will be a hugely mistaken reading of history that these political tendencies, groups, parties had lost the following of workers with them. The wave of workers' strikes in the spring of

1921 had not only the support of rival political identities, in many places the factory workers loyal to the Bolshevik party refused to obey the orders of the *Party* hierarchy [Pirani, 2008]. By suppressing dissent of the workers, and divesting them of any participatory political forum the Bolshevik leadership prepared the ground for the totalitarian regime that followed particularly after Lenin's death.

One arena of society that suffered horribly from the absence of political rights of dissent and divergence in the Soviets was judicial freedom and laws of justice. While we make this statement we have to keep in account the extreme situations that the Russian revolution invited when social and political conflicts of ideas and programmes were settled by arms, by Civil War. "*Smashing*" the wings of old state structure and political authority that the bourgeoisie wielded in society necessarily needed call to arms by the revolting proletariat. This was a particular, grim reality after the WWI in all places wherever the proletariat attempted to usher in dictatorship of the proletariat in civil-war torn Europe. Historically, a true revolution does *not only* turn old laws and old strictures vacuous; it defeats old institutions of power by call to arms. At the same time, the proletariat cannot lay claim to the leadership of transition of society, to carry along the huge "*masses*" of the underprivileged and exploited if their aspirations for capitalist production relations are also settled by arms. For defeating old, sworn, known enemies, even an intelligent army for the tactical sake of warfare do not create new enemies in its backyard. The proletariat cannot win the 'battle of democracy' for themselves by throttling democracy of the other exploited sections of the society who were genuine participants in the revolution the other day just because their aspirations do not fit the programme of the proletariat. These *new* specific features of the *transitional society* actually turn the society an arena of tortuous *class struggle* where in the analysis of balance of class power it is quite likely the proletariat may find itself on the defensive on occasions. In this struggle for ideological domination equality before *new* and alternative laws of justice plays a crucial role to justify and legitimize the leadership of the proletariat in this *quasi-state*. Unfortunately, this was not at all the case before the justice system of Soviet Russia even in germination. As we have reviewed the few pages above, while the political opponents took up arms against the Russian revolution had only one course left—*death by shooting*.[17]

It may be said a revolution is a call for solution for "eyeball for an eyeball". Theoretically, this may go on till the proletariat ensures its victory over the bourgeoisie to the end, over the old masters although in practical terms of today's society it is necessary to have second thoughts for this interpretation of *class struggle*. By this principle violence becomes a credo for the revolutionary proletariat and that needs to be disapproved strongly. Nonetheless, Lenin himself did not subscribe to this belief of responding to the 'bourgeoisie war with the proletarian war' all pervasive as then the existence of the justice system was superfluous in itself. Lenin admitted the limitations of the Soviet justice system on several occasions as below:

> As the fundamental task of the government becomes, not military suppression, but administration, the typical manifestation of suppression and compulsion will be, not shooting on the spot, but trial by court. In this respect also the revolutionary people after October 25, 1917 took the right path and demonstrated the viability of the revolution by setting up their own workers' and peasants' courts, even before the decrees dissolving the bourgeois bureaucratic judiciary were passed. But our revolutionary and people's courts are extremely, incredibly weak. One feels that we have not yet done away with the people's attitude towards the courts as towards something official and alien, an attitude inherited from the yoke of the landowners and of the bourgeoisie. ....that the courts are an *organ of the power* of the proletariat and of the poor peasants, that the courts are an instrument *for inculcating discipline*. [Lenin, 1974b, p. 266]

Summary execution of the political opponents became the norm in the period of Civil War even though many of them were strenuous in their efforts to usher the October Revolution. Here, we must stress the Soviet institution as elected representatives of the producers had practically no role in dictating these summary executions. We quote here from the memoirs of Serge again.

> In the middle of January 1920, Dzerzhinsky, with the approval of Lenin and Trotsky, recommended the abolition of the death sentence throughout the country, except in districts where there were military operations. ...

> The death penalty was reintroduced and, under the stimulus of defeat, the Chekas were given enlarged powers. [Serge, 2012, pp. 116, 118]

It must be noted that Serge nowhere mentioned the role of the Soviets either in the promulgation or abolition of death penalties. Decisions on such fundamental and crucial principles of justice to the political opponents rested with a dozen Central Committee members of the Bolshevik party whom Trotsky and Lenin considered the fountainhead of wisdom. In fact, such methods were a direct consequence of the Blanquist principle of organization of society that we referred to earlier. Although Lenin admitted the weakness of such methods of secret killing the Bolsheviks themselves were prisoners of their own principle of centralization of authority in all aspects of society, and the "eyeball for an eyeball" solution with respect to the political opponents in defending the revolution. Serge wrote in his memoirs,

> I believe that the formation of the Chekas was one of the gravest and most impermissible errors that the Bolshevik leaders committed in 1918, when plots, blockades, and interventions made them lose their heads. All evidence indicates that revolutionary tribunals, functioning in the light of day (without excluding secret sessions in particular cases) and admitting the right of defence, would have attained the same efficiency with far less abuse and depravity. Was it so necessary to revert to the procedures of the Inquisition? By the beginning of 1919, the Chekas had little or no resistance against this psychological perversion and corruption. I know for a fact that Dzerzhinsky urged them to be "half-rotten," and saw no solution to the evil except in shooting the worst Chekists and abolishing the death penalty as quickly as possible. .. Meanwhile, the Terror went on, since the whole Party was living in the sure inner knowledge that they would be massacred in the event of defeat, and defeat remained possible from one week to the next. [Serge, 2012, p. 94]

We introduced our analysis in this subsection with a reference to Nazism as a pointer to the height of counterrevolution that followed the political and economic crises in Germany after the defeat of the repeated attempts to state-power by the revolutionary sections of the working class. Unless the revolution is able to usher living examples of qualitatively *new* ideas in the practices of society that embolden and catalyze *new* enthusiasm among the vast toiling "*masses*" in deciding their own course of administration of society as a whole, the nature of despair and exhaustion among the toiling "*masses*" make little or no distinction between *revolution* and *counterrevolution*. In the absence realizable and visible practices of democracy and accrued social benefits, 'the mood of the masses' do not take ages to swing from *revolution* to *counterrevolution*. In an underdeveloped country like Russia this was particularly true where in the absence of *liberty* in social life the tradition of medieval practices of settling conflicts by terror and instant justice by murder were the ingrained tradition of the state under the centuries-old Tsarist rule. While an exasperated Lenin scolded Sukhanov for his ignorance of the heroic sacrifice of the toiling "*masses*" in building "socialism" in an economically underdeveloped country like Russia[18], he actually had no mention of the very limited avenues that these toiling "*masses*" had access to express their dissent. Many such conflicts of interest, in logical terms, could be solved by the contest of political trends in institutional forms as usually happen in bourgeois parliamentary forums. Unfortunately, the proletariat was divested from the political authority in the strife-torn society during the Civil War; the initiative for carrying out the revolution did not rest with them. Their sacrifice and valour turned into labour conscription, forced labour under the authority of a state that became synonymous with control of an all pervasive ombudsman. The thin line of distinction between *revolution* and *counterrevolution* got obliterated in the process.

The glaring shifts in the political, ideological standpoints of Bolshevism first in matters between theory and practice, and later defending their practices as a new theory for the international working class invited notice and criticism. Even during the formative period of CI, Pannekoek as the foremost representative of the Dutch 'Left' group of Internationalists pointed out opportunism of the statist and despotic rule to which Bolshevism was being *metamorphosed*. Pannekoek in a hard hitting criticism of Bolshevism observed:

> Opportunism does not necessarily mean a pliant, conciliatory attitude and vocabulary, nor radicalism a more acerbic manner; on the contrary, lack of clear, principled tactics is all too often concealed in rabidly strident language; and indeed, in revolutionary situations, it

> is characteristic of opportunism to suddenly set all its hopes on the great revolutionary deed. Its essence lies in always considering the immediate questions, not what lies in the future, and to fix on the superficial aspects of phenomena rather than seeing the determinant deeper bases.
>
> ....
>
> For its goal is immediate success, and to that it sacrifices the conditions for lasting success in the future. It seeks justification in the fact that by forming alliances with other 'progressive' groups and by making concessions to outdated conceptions, it is often possible to gain power or at least split the enemy, the coalition of capitalist classes, and thus bring about conditions more favourable for the struggle. But power in such cases always turns out to be an illusion, personal power exercised by individual leaders and not the power of the proletarian class; this contradiction brings nothing but confusion, corruption and conflict in its wake. [Pannekoek, 1978]

Pannekoek's criticism of the Bolsheviks' practices that bore the 'characteristic of opportunism' was not without basis. While Lenin derived satisfaction before the domestic audience in letting Martov move out of the country, soon the representatives of the three international organizations of the working class including CI were meeting in Berlin at the initiative of the so-called Two-and-a-half International, the International Union of Socialist parties with its centre at Vienna.[19] The Conference was held in Berlin, on April 2, 1922 under the nose and eyes of the Weimar Republic in Germany, the government that was responsible for the murder of the German revolutionaries. Although the Conference could achieve only the minimum for the united action of the working class against capital, its resolution announced,

> The Conference, therefore, proposes that the Executives should agree to the setting up of an Organization Committee of Nine, which shall undertake preparations for further conferences of the three Executives, as well as conferences on a wider basis, to include parties which are not affiliated to either of the three international organizations. Each Executive is free to appoint as it thinks fit the three representatives to whom it is entitled. In this Organization Committee no majority resolutions will be allowed, its task will be to express the general point of view of the three Executives as far as this is declared." [Degras, 1971, p. 338]

Not only in platforms of the international working class organizations were the Bolsheviks found as representatives of the Soviet Government in the Genoa Conference of all governments held "from April 10 to May 12, 1922 to consider questions of European economic reconstruction.... It was the first general post-war conference to which Germany and Russia had been invited." [Degras, 1971, p. 342] This was the first international conference of European governments where the Soviet rule in Russia was accepted as the sovereign, legitimate government from Russia.[20-21] The approach of the Soviet government (definitely of the Bolsheviks also) was best summarized by Karl Radek, the main spokesperson of the Soviet government in the Conference. We quote from his article in [Black, 1975],

> The Soviet Government knows that the first wave of world revolution has subsided and that the next will mount only slowly. It knows that the Russian economy cannot be restored without the help of the European economy. It hoped that it would be the European workers who would supply the Russian workers with machines and the Russian peasants with ploughs.... . . .
>
> But the European workers are not yet masters in their own house. Therefore the Soviet Government declares: We need world capital and therefore we must give it profits. [Quote, p. 488]

All these references to the contemporary events definitely point to the expressed intention of the Soviet government and the ECCI for negotiating stability and earning so-called "recognition" for Soviet Russia in international trade and finances. However, the Bolsheviks were in no mood to reconcile or negotiate with their political opponents inside the country for running the domestic affairs of governance in Russia. We have made a detailed analysis in the subsequent Chapters that by their domestic programmes of economic reconstruction the Bolsheviks ended up only in national accumulation of state capital for which they had no room for allowing dissent of the workers involved in the arduous hardship of undergoing labour conscription. The Bolsheviks ended up in doing the job that any conscious national leadership will do, i.e. revival of the national economy at the cost of freedom of the people that constituted the nation—these are the reasons we found valid in Pannekoek's stinging observation on 'opportunism' of the Bolsheviks even in 1920.

## 2.4 Did Marx Envisage a *Transitional Society* to *Socialism*?

The above question brings us to the end phase of our arguments regarding Lenin's theses on dictatorship of the proletariat. Thus far our critique of the Bolshevik policies and theses before the Congress of CI are there to show the limitations, inconsistencies, and in fact gross divergence from Marx's idea of dictatorship of the proletariat. The idea of Marx was a transitional *state* towards communistic union of *free* producers based on voluntary association and exchange of social labour. Such divergence from theoretical postulation is quite likely and possible in actual development of the course of revolution. These divergences only make theories of development of human society more enriched in the light of actual experiences of revolution. In fact, with this conviction on possible divergence Lenin could quote Goethe in *Letters on Tactics*, "Theory, my friend, is grey, but green is the eternal tree of life." At the same time, as we reviewed earlier, the October Revolution cannot be explained as only a spontaneous outbreak of violence or a *putsch*, instantaneous fallout of the catastrophe of the WWI that was instrumental in setting the stages for the revolution. The political revolution of the working class could sail through the tortuous course of the Civil War period because of the deep conviction and determination among the Bolshevik leadership about the international significance of the revolution in ushering "socialism" as the international social order *vis-a-vis* capitalism. The October Revolution brought before the world the theory of *communism* as enunciated by Marx and Engels as a practical matter of foundation of the *new* order in society. Therefore, it was imperative for the communist revolutionaries of CI to review the social, political theory of Marx and Engels in the light of the experiences of the *transitional society* towards "socialism" in Russia. Lenin made a remark in his report before the Third Congress of CI that was significantly different from his assertions on dictatorship of the proletariat in the First Congress. He said,

> From the international standpoint, if we regard the international revolution as one process, the significance of the period into which we are now entering in Russia is, in essence, that we must now find a practical solution for the problem of the relations the proletariat should

> establish with this last capitalist class in Russia. All Marxists have a correct and ready solution for this problem in theory. But theory and practice are two different things, and the practical solution of this problem is by no means the same as the theoretical solution. [Lenin, 1972e, p. 112]

Here, Lenin was elaborating on the actual programme of class alliances 'with this last capitalist class in Russia', i.e. the peasantry under the hegemony of a *state*, albeit on behalf of the proletariat. Lenin assessed that such a 'practical solution' having direct implications to international revolution was quite divergent from the theoretical understanding of the "Marxists". That was rightly so as we have seen in the actual programmes of the political economy of Soviet Russia in the transition period under *War Communism*.

However, the vital questions that remained unanswered by Lenin and in the documents of CI were whether these divergences in the practical programmes made the theoretical postulates of Marx and Engels untenable. Did Lenin in any way question Marx's assertions on transition to *socialism* under dictatorship of the proletariat in the light of his practical programmes that he found 'by no means the same as the theoretical solution'? On the other hand, did Lenin substantiate that such divergence in practice from theory to be inevitable? Had he asserted that even though the practical policies did not follow such theoretical postulates, they were actually commensurate with the analysis of historical materialism by Marx and Engels? The problem with both Lenin and his contemporary critiques such as Pannekoek and Luxemburg was that their response to such fundamental questions of evolution of dictatorship of the proletariat was a big, resounding *silence*. During his very active seven-year period of involvement in the formation and evolution of CI, Lenin never shed any light on *The Critique of the Gotha Programme* that remained Marx's most unambiguous exposition of the political and social programmes of the proletariat during the transition to *socialism*. It is important to mention this *silence* as Lenin was abundantly clear that the actual programmes were bound to be different in *substance* from such theoretical assertions. On the other hand, while Luxemburg and Panekoek made cogent and timely interventions with their criticisms of the Bolshevik policies particularly with respect to self-governance, initiative of the working class *"masses"* for building *socialism*, their standpoint was self-contradictory when the actual programmes of transformation of production relations came into the picture (in subsequent Chapters these issues in the context of Lenin's other theses in CI are discussed). While criticizing the Bolshevik programme for "socialism" they had not introspected how such actual practices also put questions on Marx's theoretical assertions. The social conditions of Russia where the proletarian revolution could actually hold itself were not ripe for *socialism* as envisaged by Marx. Their silence about such theoretical problems of transition to *socialism* played havoc over the century-old international working class movement.

While Lenin was aware that the political economy of Soviet Russia was not *socialism* as envisaged by Marx, he was at the same time convinced that the Bolshevik programmes and practices were definitely stepping stones towards "socialism" of international significance. It led to canonization of these practices as *Leninism*, as novelty to "Marxism" after Lenin's death[22] when the Russian experience became the unquestionable edicts with CI. Without at all questioning how such statist policies of strengthening 'state capitalism' went hand in hand with Marx's critique of capitalism as the political economy of society, *Marxism-Leninism*[23] was put forward by CI as the theory of the international working class movement. On the other hand, those who criticized the foundation of the totalitarian state of Russia as the direct fall out of the *Leninist* policies did not investigate nor had the courage to ask whether the gigantic failures of the international working class in the aftermath of the WWI put serious question marks on the theoretical postulates and projections of Marx. While burying *Leninism* that modern history has already debunked as a dead milestone they canonized Marx. They did not ponder that by questioning Marx and later Engels' political postulation "Marxism" is actually enriched as the social science of historical materialism. Such discourse strengthens the theoretical weapon before the international working class in its war against capitalism.

### *2.4.1 Views of Marx and Engels on dictatorship of the proletariat*

We consider enquiry into such questions as vital to explain the *metamorphosis* of Bolshevism as the ideological outlook of the proponents of the *quasi-state* getting transformed into the votaries of the absolutist state as a theory of revolution. The Bolsheviks could possibly do so because of the major loopholes left by Marx in his understanding of *state* and society during the transition to *socialism*. As a concrete instance, let us look at Hal Draper's work in five volumes on *Karl Marx's Theory of Revolution* in which a full third volume was devoted to the viewpoint of Marx and Engels on dictatorship of the proletariat. In this third volume, Hal Draper made a detailed study of Marx's and Engels' interpretation and coinage of dictatorship of the proletariat in their entire body of literature (he counted twelve loci of references) spanning from 1850 to 1892. Hal Draper reviewed Marx's interpretation of *state* under dictatorship of the proletariat as the *class dictatorship*, "The dictatorship *of* the proletariat was his alternative to the dictatorship of the party *over* the proletariat."[Draper, 2011b] Although the review is of considerable historical value in understanding the conceptions of Marx and Engels about the subject, it is lamentable that Hal Draper never questioned why Marx and Engels always considered dictatorship of the proletariat as *a transitional form of state* and *not a transitional form of society* ('*the class dictatorship* of the proletariat as the necessary transit point to the *abolition of class distinctions generally'*—Marx). Historically, it is important to bring to focus that the twelve occasions of references by Marx and Engels on dictatorship of the proletariat were always in relation to the *transitional* state-power that is revolutionary in the sense it leads to dissolution of *state* as a social, political entity. Hal Draper emphasized,

> It is not problematical if we adopt the only meaning of the term that corresponds to the way Marx actually used it: a 'dictatorship of the proletariat' is a state in which the proletariat exercises dominant political power—a 'workers' state', the rule of the proletariat'. No more, no less. [Draper, 201b, p. 269]

Our statement should not be construed to mean that Marx did not have any projection regarding the transitional period of society to *socialism*. Indeed he had, that we have earlier referred to *The German*

*Ideology*. Similar projections on features of transition to alternative society may be found in other writings such as *The Holy Family*, *The Poverty of Philosophy*, and above all in *Capital, Volume Three.*[24] To justify our argument, let us look at the celebrated passage of Marx that is quoted endlessly in "Marxist" literature.

> The question then arises: What transformation will the state undergo in communist society? In other words, what social functions will remain in existence there that are analogous to present state functions?
>
> This question can only be answered scientifically, and one does not get a flea-hop nearer to the problem by a thousand-fold combination of the word 'people' with the word 'state'. Between capitalist and communist society there lies the period of the revolutionary transformation of the one into the other. Corresponding to this is also a political transition period in which the state can be nothing but *the revolutionary dictatorship of the proletariat*. [Marx, 1958a, p. 30]

There are two important pointers in this statement: first, of course Marx himself emphasized the transitional nature of *state* as the political instrument that the proletariat wields, '*the revolutionary dictatorship of the proletariat*'. Marx consciously emphasized the word '*revolutionary*', the word that is never found prefixed in Lenin's works while discussing dictatorship of the proletariat, nor in the works of his critiques, and of course not with Hal Draper. Dictatorship of the proletariat has to be revolutionary for the reasons we elaborated earlier, particularly to initiate the revolutionary transformation of existing production relations and to exercise *revolutionary democracy*, to usher the tortuous *class struggle* among the non-proletarian "*masses*" so as to draw them towards *socialist* society, in the sense of the permanence of revolution that Marx explained in [Marx, 1969a]. The transitional nature of society that Marx indicated in the sentence before is, "Between capitalist and communist society there lies the period of the revolutionary transformation of the one into the other." This is the second point: the 'period of the revolutionary transformation' corresponds to the transitional nature of *quasi-state*, but Marx did not find the society in this 'period' to represent a separate historical stage of development of human civilization. To Marx, society is to go through a temporary phase of evolution from capitalism to *communism* as like the transient, temporary nature of *state*, the organ of power under dictatorship of the proletariat. While this statement of Marx was made in 1875, similar socio-political contours of transition to *socialism* were drawn by Marx and Engels nearly twenty-eight years earlier in the *Communist Manifesto* in 1847. They wrote,

> The proletariat will use its political supremacy to wrest, by degrees, all capital from the bourgeoisie, to centralize all instruments of production in the hands of the State, i.e., of the proletariat organized as the ruling class; and to increase the total productive forces as rapidly as possible. [Engels, 1958a, p. 53]

We understand the *Leninists* will leap in the air (Lenin quoted exactly this passage in Chapter 2 of *The State and Revolution*) seeing this reference as Marx and Engels directly recommended centralization of all 'instruments of production in the hands of the state'. We have dealt with this issue earlier in Section 2.1 in relation to the revolutionary nature of the *socialist* mode of production. Secondly, we must keep in mind this state is also a *quasi-state*, 'i.e. of the proletariat organized as the ruling class.' We have seen the prominent features contrary to this dictum in the demise and decay of the Soviets in Russia as platforms of the proletariat's self-rule.

Here, we want to point to the transitional nature of *state* as indicated in the above statement, 'The proletariat will use its political supremacy to wrest, by degrees, all capital from the bourgeoisie'. These socio-economic programmes are the immediate tasks of the proletariat as the *ruling class*, and the *new state* is the organ for executing such programmes. Again, in Marx's and Engels' view, these programmes do not reflect a separate category for society. Let us use another reference from Engels as he visualized the objectives of dictatorship of the proletariat.

> Whilst the capitalist mode of production more and more completely transforms the great majority of the population into proletarians, it creates the power which, under penalty of its own destruction, is forced to accomplish this revolution. Whilst it forces on more and more of the transformation of the vast means of production, already socialized, into State property, it shows itself the way to accomplishing this revolution. *The proletariat seizes political power and turns the means of production into State property.*
>
> But, in doing this, it abolishes itself as proletariat, abolishes all class distinction and class antagonisms, abolishes also the State as

> State. Society, thus far, based upon class antagonisms, had need of the State. That is, of an organization of the particular class which was, pro tempore, the exploiting class, an organization for the purpose of preventing any interference from without with the existing conditions of production, and, therefore, especially, for the purpose of forcibly keeping the exploited classes in the condition of oppression corresponding with the given mode of production (slavery, serfdom, wage-labor). The State was the official representative of society as a whole; the gathering of it together into a visible embodiment....
>
> As soon as there is no longer any social class to be held in subjection; as soon as class rule, and the individual struggle for existence based upon our present anarchy in production, with the collisions and excesses arising from these, are removed, nothing more remains to be repressed, and a special repressive force, a State, is no longer necessary. The first act by virtue of which the State really constitutes itself the representative of the whole of society — the taking possession of the means of production in the name of society — this is, at the same time, its last independent act as a State. State interference in social relations becomes, in one domain after another, superfluous, and then dies out of itself; the government of persons is replaced by the administration of things, and by the conduct of processes of production. The State is not "abolished". *It dies out."* [Engels, 1958b, pp. 137-138]

One of the biggest problem with the generations of interpreters of Marx and Engels is the malady in the interpretation itself that often serves their own self-purpose in the half-quotes (the reason with all hesitation we are forced to provide long passages of references to avoid misquotes or wrongly quoting without context.) If one ceases to read Engels after the first passage one falls consciously in line with Trotsky and Lenin in their interpretation of "socialism" as 'state capitalism' with the state in command and control of all the means of production on behalf of the proletariat, as the political organ to suppress the erstwhile owners, the bourgeoisie. Unfortunately for them, Engels by all means went on to explain in the next passages why this act of *state* also sounds the death–knell to the institution called the state—the institution of class oppression that has attained huge sophistication of the methods of exploitation over the history of human civilization. 'The State is not "abolished". *It dies out'*—a startling revelation poignant with countless possibilities to be enacted by the hitherto exploited "*masses*" in their participation in the process of the dying out of *state*. This statement was made by Engels in 1880 without seeing any prospect of the process happening in reality. The reader is requested to contrast Engels' hypothetical reasoning with the arguments of Lenin countering Kautsky on the same subject in November 1918 [Lenin, 1974d] when the prospect of the state dying was supposed to happen in practice. Anyway, our lookout here is not counterpoising Lenin with Engels on the question of the state but to point out that Engels' observations were not regarding a *transitional society* that should preside over the dying out process of the institution state. Engels made the direct observation that the proletariat as the ruling class leverages the state, the institution of its authority to posses the instruments of production, and by that process the social classes with opposing, antagonistic interests also cease to exist.

Such reasoning in the above passage from Engels brings us face-to-face to the gulf of difference between theoretical projection and actual practice that history witnessed in Russia. Even though one does not agree with Lenin's interpretation of "socialism", one cannot ignore at all the fact that post-revolutionary society in Russia actually faced a tortuous transition, a transition whose dimensions were not only limited to the political, social turmoil of the Civil War. It was the transition where the *new* and the old production relations were competing in the society with opposing objectives. One, that was ushered by the proletariat by their revolutionary dictatorship for which the *Workers' Opposition group* were aspiring, that Kollantai found, 'This question is just as important as the question of seizure of political power by the proletariat..' Even with their misdirected demand to continue with the law of wage-labour, ('systematic implementation of the naturalization of wages'), the *group* led by Shliapnikov, Kollontai and others were aspiring for a 'workers' state', a rule where the workers were literally to be at the helm of control of political and economic affairs of *state*. On the other hand, there were Lenin and Bukharin, in their concern to keep the flow of grain supply to the urban proletariat intact, stood for the immediate demands of the sections of peasantry engaged in petty-commodity production. They became strong votaries of 'state capitalism' in industry and agriculture. Lenin was candid in his last appearance before CI in the Fourth Congress about this policy when he remarked,

> I repeat; it seems very strange to everyone that a non-socialist element [state capitalism] should be rated higher than, regarded as superior to, socialism in a republic which declares itself a socialist republic. But the fact will become intelligible if you recall that we definitely did not regard the economic system of Russia as something homogeneous and highly developed; we were fully aware that in Russia we had patriarchal agriculture, i.e. the most primitive form of agriculture alongside the socialist form. [Lenin, 1972d, p. 132]

In our understanding, Lenin's forthright admission is more enlightening in the sense that one cannot overlook nor ignore the reality of the challenges before the transition to *socialism*. At the same time, we must assert Lenin's and the Bolsheviks' policy actually drove the existing production relations much away from the *socialist* aim of diminishing the role of market and exchange of *values* in agricultural production. Nonetheless, the Russian experience revealed that wielding the political power from the erstwhile bourgeoisie may facilitate the proletariat to create the avenues, the open ground, the freedom to initiate the revolutionary transformation, overhauling of erstwhile production relations. Unlike the erstwhile production relations that humanity has gone through *socialist* production relations cannot be realized in society without the political power of *state* of the proletariat as *socialist* production relations are to end all social relations among humans based on alienation of labour from the direct producers. Only in a *socialist* society, independent of the form of the individual's participation in social labour, the producer finds a direct linkage to the collectiveness of ownership of the means of performing labour. There is no place for exchange of labour power as an abstract *value*, as a form of abstract labour alienated from its direct producer in the *socialist* mode of production and distribution. At the same time, seizure of the state power and even the new form of *state* that the Soviets represented did not preclude nor did they guarantee victory of *socialist* production relations in the society that the Russian experience has also taught us in its momentous failure. This is the loophole or void that Marx and Engels left to posterity that was met with deafening silence by their loyal interpreters. Their obligation towards the teachings of Marx and Engels did not permit them to muster courage so as to question the Masters about the inadequacy of their socio-political projections. Understanding the evolution of the competing and contradictory class interests that a revolution can only bring to sharp focus was of much more living interest to them than the critique of a political programme that was already dead in all its compromises as was the *Gotha Programme.*[25]

However, in the same breath, one cannot claim to enrich the understanding of the social process of transition to *socialism* in congruence with Marx's arguments by actually going in the reverse direction of the logic of Marx's views. Let us look at [Marx, 1958a] again for the precise view of Marx on the collective ownership of the means of production *vis-a-vis* an individual's contribution in the social labour process.

> Within the cooperative society based on common ownership of the means of production, the producers do not exchange their products; just as little does the labor employed on the products appear here as the *value* of these products, as a material quality possessed by them, since now, in contrast to capitalist society, individual labor no longer exists in an indirect fashion but directly as a component part of total labor. The phrase "proceeds of labor", objectionable also today on account of its ambiguity, thus loses all meaning. [Marx, 1958a, p. 21]

This is the *socialist* production relation that we justified above and such production relations *cannot* be expected to grow within the capitalist society. The objective basis of dictatorship of the proletariat arises not just to shift the reign of political-administrative state apparatus from one *class* to another *class* in the society, but to usher these fundamental changes in the production relations as explained above in reference to Marx. Just after the above quoted passage Marx had put forward his precise view on transition of society from capitalism to *communism* where he articulated for the two phases of *communism*. He defined the first phase of 'communist society' where the principle of 'each according to his ability' is executed in social exchanges.

> What we have to deal with here is a communist society, not as it has *developed* on its own foundations, but, on the contrary, just as it *emerges* from capitalist society; which is thus in every respect, economically, morally, and intellectually, still stamped with the birthmarks of the

> old society from whose womb it emerges. Accordingly, the individual producer receives back from society—after the deductions have been made—exactly what he gives to it. What he has given to it is his individual quantum of labor.... The same amount of labor which he has given to society in one form, he receives back in another.
>
> Here, obviously, the same principle prevails as that which regulates the exchange of commodities, as far as this is exchange of equal values. Content and form are changed, because under the altered circumstances no one can give anything except his labor, and because, on the other hand, nothing can pass to the ownership of individuals, except individual means of consumption. But as far as the distribution of the latter among the individual producers is concerned, the same principle prevails as in the exchange of commodity equivalents: a given amount of labor in one form is exchanged for an equal amount of labor in another form.
>
> Hence, *equal right* here is still in principle—*bourgeois right*, although principle and practice are no longer at loggerheads, while the exchange of equivalents in commodity exchange exists only on the average and not in the individual case. In spite of this advance, this equal right is still constantly stigmatized by a bourgeois limitation. The right of the producers is *proportional* to the labor they supply; the equality consists in the fact that measurement is made with an *equal standard*, labor....
>
> But these defects are inevitable in the first phase of communist society as it is when it has just emerged after prolonged birth pangs from capitalist society. Right can never be higher than the economic structure of society and its cultural development conditioned thereby. [Marx, 1958a, pp. 21-22]

There are several interesting pointers in this long passage from Marx. First, Marx defined the *new* society as a 'communist society' and not as a *transitional society*. This is understandable as Marx did not see the role of *state* in enforcing equality of the right of the individual to draw the 'individual means of consumption' from the social pool. At the same time, there is no exchange of *value* in the society, 'because under the altered circumstances no one can give anything except his labour, and because, on the other hand, nothing can pass to the ownership of individuals'. Therefore, such a society has been able to stand on its own feet surpassing the laws of commodity exchanges. Society has been able to claim to be a voluntary association of producers with equal opportunity to perform labour. Then, how are we to interpret the statement, 'What we have to deal with here is a communist society, not as it has *developed* on its own foundations, but, on the contrary, just as it *emerges* from capitalist society; which is thus in every respect, economically, morally, and intellectually, still stamped with the birthmarks of the old society from whose womb it emerges.'? By 'defects', Marx pointed to the law of exchange being still *in force* in society; equality being understood as equality of opportunity in performing labour. That results in inequality as performance of labour of any two individuals is different. In that sense *only*, the bourgeoisie law of inequality before equal standards of labour should prevail in this first phase of 'communist society', and *not* in the old, prevailing sense of equality of opportunity of any two producers before the market to exchange their products as abstract social labour in the form of *value*. Therefore, this is not yet the 'communist society' Marx looked for, 'the higher phase of communist society'. The society in the first phase of *communist* associations in his view is 'not as it has *developed* on its own foundations'. He made the distinction in the second or 'higher' phase as,

> In a higher phase of communist society, after the enslaving subordination of the individual to the division of labor, and therewith also the antithesis between mental and physical labor, has vanished; after labor has become not only a means of life but life's prime want; after the productive forces have also increased with the all-around development of the individual, and all the springs of co-operative wealth flow more abundantly—only then can the narrow horizon of bourgeois right be crossed in its entirety and society inscribe on its banners: From each according to his ability, to each according to his needs! [Marx, 1958a, p. 23]

It is important to mention that Marx did not see the two phases as two stages of 'communist society', nor did he visualize any qualitative change of production relations in the two phases. He only visualized the higher phase of 'communist society' where equality before the 'bourgeoisie right' for performing labour has attained irrelevance in the society. Society is able and prepared to shed this last vestige of inheritance of bourgeois law not as an economic law of exchange but as rigorous enforcement of the right and compulsion of performing labour.

This explanation is not to interpret the society in the 'higher phase' a conglomerate of idle thought mongers and day dreamers. On the contrary, it was projected to be an association of *free* individuals whose existence depends on the individual's freedom to perform labour not as to earn the rights of means of consumption but as the primary condition of freedom of existence, as 'life's prime want'. Nowhere in the two phases had Marx seen any role of exchange of *value*, nor the role of coercive instrument of *state* to enforce the rule of equality of right in performing labour and in its social exchanges. His comments on 'communist society as it is when it has just emerged after prolonged birth pangs from capitalist society' are not for a *transitional society* where the old capitalist law of exchange of wages prevail in the society side by side with the new rule of drawing 'individual means of consumption' according to the labour added in the social pool. To emphasize our argument on Marx's view of 'communist society' as an association of *free* individual producers of labour we also refer here to his analysis in *Capital*.

> In fact, the realm of freedom really begins only when labor determined by necessity and external expediency ends; it lies by its very nature beyond the sphere of material production proper.... Freedom in this sphere, can consist only in this, that socialized man, the associated producers, govern the human metabolism with nature in a rational way, bringing it under their collective control instead of being dominated by it as a blind power; accomplishing it with the least expenditure of energy and in conditions most worthy and appropriate of their human nature. But this always remains realm of necessity. The true realm of freedom, the development of human powers as an end in itself, begins beyond it, though it can only flourish with this realm of necessity as its basis. (Chapter 48) [Marx, 1959, p. 571]

It is evident in Marx's view there is no labour conscription in 'communist society' as such a society transcends the 'realm of necessity' of labour. At the same time, he did not negate the 'realm of necessity' as the basis and precondition for an association based on *free* labour. Such a society cannot be envisaged without a high level of self-regulation among the direct producers who are in a position to declare them as *free* to perform the labour of their choice and want such that the necessary access and opportunities of performing labour are present in the society that emanates from the governing rule of performing labour according to one's capacity. Nor does such a society, in anyway be envisaged as hegemony of a particular class of producers, the *erstwhile working class* that was in the forefront of the political revolution beforehand because such a demand negates the fundamental principle of *free association* of direct producers. That is why Engels wrote, 'But, in doing this, it abolishes itself as the proletariat, abolishes all class distinction and class antagonisms, abolishes also the State as State.' Only in this way the statement on progression of the two phases of *communism*—'only then can the narrow horizon of bourgeois right be crossed in its entirety and society inscribe on its banners: From each according to his ability, to each according to his needs!'—be understood in its context.

In reality, one cannot envisage such a society just by the event that the old rule of capital exploiting and controlling the exchange of abstract labour in the form of *valu*e in the market is unseated from political power. As we have seen from the Russian experience, unseating the bourgeoisie from political power brought the proletariat face-to-face to the teething questions of *class struggle* within the society of the erstwhile exploited and powerless people, 'with this last capitalist class—the rock bottom of capitalism—small private property, the small producer' [Lenin, 1972e, p. 112]. Marx did not envisage such a society between capitalism and *communism*. In his view (and also in Engels' view) transition is only effecting the lower phase of 'communist society' by enforcement of the socio-political programme by seizing and owning the means of production by *state* whose 'transient' role as dictatorship of the proletariat is finished as soon as society in the main enters the *communist* phase of production relations. By any means such visualization of Marx and Engels did not fit the abysmal reality that stared before Lenin and his comrades in Russia as the point of departure to their "socialism".[26] On the other hand, what Lenin was recommending as steps to combat the impending catastrophe before the working class in Russia had not much in common with Marx's vision of even the lower phase of 'communist society'.

### 2.4.2 *Interpretation of dictatorship of the proletariat by* **Leninism**

We have to limit our discussion on Marx's viewpoint of 'communist society' here as it will be only a realm of conjecture to further dwell on the features of 'communist society'. Secondly, this will stretch our focus on the *metamorphosis* of Bolshevism beyond the scope of the essay. The votaries of *Leninism* skipped the fundamental issues of society in transition as they subscribed to Lenin's treatise [Lenin, 1974e] with an uncritical devotion without pondering at the glaring inconsistency that is implied in the analysis.[27] Let us look again at Hal Draper's work [Draper, 2011b]. At the end of the book, in a special note, he reviewed the work of "Marxologists" as the interpreters of dictatorship of the proletariat. In the opening sentence of the survey Hal Draper wrote out of veneration,

> The first substantial effort to bring together Marx's and Engels' statements about the 'dictatorship of the proletariat' was Lenin's *State and Revolution* – a work that has rarely been given the credit for the innovation simply in the field of scholarship.[1] [Draper, 2011b, p. 329]

Hal Draper then went on to count the number of "Loci" Lenin mentioned in his work. It is true that Lenin's treatise was not respected in the academic circles of bourgeoisie society after the Soviet revolution. That was an expected reaction from the bourgeoisie given that people with sympathy towards Bolshevism were at the risk of physical liquidation in their world in that period. On the contrary, Lenin's work completed under immense hardship of hibernation was an article of faith not only with revolutionaries within CI but also with generations of *Leninists* in the later period. Did it really deserve that high pedestal of reverence among the revolutionaries?

Etienne Balibar, the renowned French philosopher and a central committee member of the French communist party (PCF) strongly reaffirmed Lenin's viewpoint in his work [Balibar, 2011] in 1976. Balibar condemned the decision of PCF to formally renounce dictatorship of the proletariat as the policy of the party. Most unfortunately, while advocating staunch support for Lenin's viewpoint, Balibar produced his own interpretation that was definitely *not* Marx's version. Writing even fifty years after the revolution he found dictatorship of the proletariat as understood and practised in Russia to be of universal significance. In his entire writing there is no mention of Rosa Luxemburg, an act of amazing omission considering that he belonged to the French school of modern "Marxism". Balibar acknowledged,

> Of course, there are powerful historical reasons for the direct identification of the concept of the dictatorship of the proletariat with Soviet history. They are related to the determinant place of the Soviet revolution and to its objective role in the history of the international labour movement. In a certain sense this identification is a fact, an irreversible fact, which binds us, for there is no theory whose meaning is independent of the conditions of its practical utilization. But if it is an irreversible fact, that does not mean that it is immutable. [Balibar, 2011, p. 44]

In defence of Lenin's articulation he brought out under the heading "Lenin's three theoretical arguments about the dictatorship of the proletariat" (Title of Chapter 2). He wrote,

> As far as Lenin is concerned, the reason is different: *for the first time, Lenin was confronted with the real experience of the dictatorship of the proletariat*. Now this experience was extraordinarily difficult and contradictory. *It is the contradictions of the dictatorship of the proletariat*, as it was beginning to develop in Russia, that form the object of Lenin's analysis and of his arguments. [Balibar, 2011, p. 58]

We have reviewed earlier in detail '*the real experience*', and Lenin's response to the grim reality of Russia. That should not have given licence to Balibar to defend Lenin's theoretical arguments in a way that even Lenin did not conclude from his '*real experience*'. For the first argument Balibar wrote,

> ...historically speaking, State power is always the political power of a single class, which holds it in its capacity as the ruling class in society.
>
> Let us be more precise: this argument implies that, in modern society, which is based on the antagonism between capitalist bourgeoisie and proletariat, State power is held in an absolute way by the bourgeoisie, which does not share it with any other class, nor does it divide it up among its own fractions. ....The first thesis has the following consequence: the only possible historical 'alternative' to the State power of the bourgeoisie is an equally absolute hold on State power by the proletariat, the class of wage-labourers exploited by capital. Just as the bourgeoisie. [Balibar, 2011, p. 59]

By all accounts, this was an ahistorical statement that is neither supported by the history of modern states that evolved in modern Europe with the consolidation of bourgeoisie civilization from the eighteenth century (for example the Prussian state in Germany, the Ottoman Empire that existed till the WWI, the Orange Republics of Europe), nor was the experience of Soviet rule that came into existence briefly in Germany and also in Russia. More important, Lenin's assessment of the Soviets as the organ of dictatorship of the proletariat hovered from an alliance of proletariat-soldiers-peasant deputies (*April Thesis*) to an alliance of the proletariat with the agricultural labourers, and then shifted to 'alliance between the proletariat and the peasantry' during the NEP-period. It is only as a matter of theory Lenin invoked the working class as the stake holder, but again he saw the soldiers as an important component of Soviet rule along with the workers. In fact, as we have seen at several times, Lenin and of course Trotsky in their assertion even replaced the working class by the ombudsman *Party*. It is only an idealist theory of state to be owned undivided by a *class* of ownership, even though Marx and Engels emphasized this interpretation in the *Communist Manifesto*. Second, we cannot explain the multiplicity of bourgeoisie parties in the arena of parliamentary politics in modern capitalist societies unless we recognize different factions among the bourgeoisie, their sectional interests, both in national and international terms, being crucial in the formulation of policies of governments in different periods of time.

More fantastic revelation waits for us in Balibar's third argument in support of Lenin's view on "socialism" and *communism*. He wrote,

> It is obviously no accident that Marx and Engels always presented their position as a communist position, and only explicitly adopted the term 'socialist' (and even more so the term 'social-democrat') as a concession. We can in fact say that in the absence of this position (and of the thesis which it implies) the theory of Marx and Engels would be unintelligible. But they were not in a position to develop it at length. This task fell to Lenin, and in carrying it out he based his work on the development of the class struggles of the period of the Russian revolution, of which his work is therefore the product, in the strong sense of the term....

> A first, very abstract formulation is sketched out by Marx in the *Communist Manifesto* and in the *Critique of the Gotha Programme* : it is that *only communism is a classless* society, a society from which all forms of exploitation have disappeared. And since capitalist relations constitute the last possible historical form of exploitation, this means that only communist social relations, in production and in the whole of social life, are really in antagonistic contradiction with capitalist relations, only they are really incompatible, irreconcilable with capitalist relations. Which implies a series of immensely important consequences, both from the theoretical and especially from the practical point of view. It implies that socialism is nothing other than the dictatorship of the proletariat. The dictatorship of the proletariat is not simply a form of 'transition to socialism', it is not a 'road of transition to socialism'—it is identical with socialism itself. ....
>
> The proletariat, the proletarian masses and the whole masses of the people whom the proletariat draws with it are not fighting for socialism as an independent aim. They are fighting for communism, to which socialism is only the means, of which it is an initial form. No other perspective can *interest* them, in the materialist sense of this term. They are fighting for socialism just because this is the way to arrive at communism. [Balibar, 2011, p. 62]

We have quoted extensively from Balibar's work in support of Lenin to show Balibar's explicit argument to demarcate "socialism" as some different stage of social evolution than *communism*, and that "socialism" to be identical with dictatorship of the proletariat. This was not only Balibar's argument, another renowned "Marxist" philosopher Graheme Lock supported this argument in the Introduction of Balibar's book by even providing graphical sketches of these stages of development marking "socialism" distinctly as dictatorship of the proletariat. (Diagram 1, [Balibar, 2011, p. 25]). Earlier we have seen Sweezy's views on 'socialist society' ('still less that a socialist society can hope to dispense with market relations in the near future').

Therefore, our precise query is what precipitated in all these modern "Marxist" thinkers' minds to understand dictatorship of the proletariat as "socialism"? More important, what were the implications of this change of nomenclature towards the vision of *communism*? We have explained above in detail that in the understanding of Marx there was no exchange of *value* in performing social labour in any phase of 'communist society'. Then how did the distinction between "socialism" and 'communist society' come into the picture?

It will not be out of context to show that Marx and Engels distinguished the nomenclature with a reference to the political *tendencies* within the working class movement in their time. Although Balibar conceded that to Marx and Engels "socialism" in the loose sense of the term was coincidental to 'communist society', he was actually quite off the mark there also. Marx and Engels did not distinguish the terms as separate historical stages of development of human civilization from capitalism to *communism* (*socialism*). Engels repeated this understanding as late as 1888 in the preface to the English edition of the *Communist Manifesto*. We give below a long reference to what they had in mind while differentiating between the contemporary political tendencies and the historical stages of development of human society.

> Yet, when it was written, we could not have called it a *socialist* manifesto. By Socialists, in 1847, were understood, on the one hand the adherents of the various Utopian systems: Owenites in England, Fourierists in France, both of them already reduced to the position of mere sects, and gradually dying out; on the other hand, the most multifarious social quacks who, by all manner of tinkering, professed to redress, without any danger to capital and profit, all sorts of social grievances, in both cases men outside the working-class movement, and looking rather to the "educated" classes for support. //Whatever portion of the working class had become convinced of the insufficiency of mere political revolutions, and had proclaimed the necessity of total social change, called itself Communist. It was a crude, rough-hewn, purely instinctive sort of communism; still, it touched the cardinal point and was powerful enough amongst the working class to produce the Utopian communism of Cabet in France, and of Weitling in Germany. Thus, in 1847, socialism was a middle-class movement, communism a working-class movement. Socialism was, on the Continent at least, "respectable"; communism was the very opposite. And as our notion, from the very beginning, was that "the emancipation of the workers must be the act of the working class itself," there could be no doubt as to which of the two names we must take. Moreover, we have, ever since, been far from repudiating it.
>
> The Manifesto being our joint production, I consider myself bound to state that the fundamental proposition which forms the

> nucleus belongs to Marx. That proposition is: That in every historical epoch, the prevailing mode of economic production and exchange, and the social organization necessarily following from it, form the basis upon which it is built up, and from that which alone can be explained the political and intellectual history of that epoch; that consequently the whole history of mankind (since the dissolution of primitive tribal society, holding land in common ownership) has been a history of class struggles, contests between exploiting and exploited, ruling and oppressed classes; That the history of these class struggles forms a series of evolutions in which, nowadays, a stage has been reached where the exploited and oppressed class—the proletariat—cannot attain its emancipation from the sway of the exploiting and ruling class—the bourgeoisie—without, at the same time, and once and for all, emancipating society at large from all exploitation, oppression, class distinction, and class struggles.
>
> This proposition, which, in my opinion, is destined to do for history what Darwin' s theory has done for biology we both of us, had been gradually approaching for some years before 1845. [Engels, 1958a, p. 31]

If the above elaborate explanation on adopting the 'communist' nomenclature in support of the revolutionary sections of working class in Europe, and explaining in the next paragraph the crux of Marx's argument on 'history of class struggles' being the essence of hitherto evolution of human society do not suffice, we may offer the blunt argument. Engels could have easily entitled his explanatory work [Engels, 1968b] in *Anti-Duhring* as "Communism: Utopian and Scientific" had he in mind that the nomenclature signify distinct and different stages of development of human society.

The answer to the above query on confusion over nomenclature therefore, cannot be found in the works of Marx and Engels. The answer to the query is to be found in Lenin's works as he was the source of the theoretical confusion and some deliberate misrepresentation that was carried over by generations to follow.

Lenin meant "socialism" and *communism* with different connotations in different places in the evolution of his ideas. For example, one work that he could not finish but was of enormous significance in its intent was [Lenin, 1974f] published in *Pravda*, November 1919. If completed, Lenin meant to provide in the article, "A summarized exposition, of course, possesses many disadvantages and shortcomings. Nevertheless, a short magazine article may perhaps achieve the modest aim in view, which is to present the problem and the groundwork for its discussion by the Communists of various countries." Lenin started the article with a statement,

> Theoretically, there can be no doubt that between capitalism and communism there lies a definite transition period which must combine the features and properties of both these forms of social economy. This transition period has to be a period of struggle between dying capitalism and nascent communism—or, in other words, between capitalism which has been defeated but not destroyed and communism which has been born but is still very feeble. [Lenin, 1974f, p. 107]

Then, he continued to more significant realizations,

> Socialism means the abolition of classes.
>
> In order to abolish classes it is necessary, first, to overthrow the landowners and capitalists. This part of our task has been accomplished, but it is only a part, and moreover, *not* the most difficult part. In order to abolish classes it is necessary, secondly, to abolish the difference between factory worker and peasant, to make *workers of all of them*. This cannot be done all at once. This task is incomparably more difficult and will of necessity take a long time. It is not a problem that can be solved by overthrowing a class. It can be solved only by the organizational reconstruction of the whole social economy, by a transition from individual, disunited, petty commodity production to large-scale social production. This transition must of necessity be extremely protracted. [Lenin, 1974f, p. 112]

From Lenin's incomplete treatise in 1919 there should not be any doubt that Lenin meant *communism* to be synonymous with *socialism* ('Socialism means the abolition of classes.'). He definitely realized the transition from capitalism to *communism* (*socialism*) is a historical stage of human society, ('This task is incomparably more difficult and will of necessity take a long time.'). Lenin carried over in 1921 the sense of this statement in his theses on the NEP while stating that practical solutions of transition are very different from theoretical postulates. The goal of revolution in the first *Manifesto* of CI that Lenin himself approved as 'classless communistic commonwealth' also carried this sense of synonymous understanding.[28]

However, Lenin made startlingly different observations in his works with more theoretical weight, particularly in the works completed on the eve of the revolution. Those observations were definitely not following the arguments of Marx that we elaborated above. We have cited while commemorating the Fourth anniversary of the October Revolution in 1921 Lenin wrote of different stages in the transition, 'It appears that a number of transitional stages were necessary—state capitalism and socialism—in order to *prepare*—to prepare by many years of effort—for the transition to communism.' Whether Lenin was aware of his profound shifts even in the domain of theoretical arguments will be a matter of conjecture, but his arguments on these separate stages of transition *seldom* explained the distinction in terms of production relations. In defence of the change of the name of the Bolshevik party in *April Thesis*, Lenin clearly made a distinction between "socialism" and *communism*.

> Mankind can pass directly from capitalism only into Socialism, i.e. into social ownership of the means of production and the distribution of products according to the work of the individual. Our party looks farther ahead than that: Socialism is bound sooner or later to ripen into Communism, whose banner bears the motto: "From each according to his ability, to each according to his needs ."
>
> That is the first reason.
>
> Here is my second: The second part of the term "Social-Democracy" is scientifically wrong. Democracy is only a form of state, while we Marxists are opposed to every form of state. [Lenin, 1974g, pp. 84-85]

Here, by 'Socialism' Lenin definitely meant the first phase of 'communist society' that Marx elaborated in his critique [Marx, 1058a]. Lenin's second argument is his own "discovery", and to that extent it followed Engels' interpretation as we have seen in our discussion on *revolutionary democracy*. He meant democracy *purely* as a political instrument, synonymous with the state, with class antagonisms and struggle being the prime mover of society. Therefore, he has no other dimensions of democracy to offer such as individual freedom, as *liberty*, as the right and voice to dissent. He stretched the *obverse* sense of this second argument when he made the bizarre statement by taking sanction from Engels' letter to Bebel.

> Only now can we fully appreciate the correctness of Engels' remarks mercilessly ridiculing the absurdity of combining the words "freedom" and "state". So long as the state exists there is no freedom. When there is freedom, there will be no state. [Lenin, 1974e, p. 473]

Here, Lenin made a clear *binary* negation between the existence of state and democracy. He was more emphatic in his theses in 1920 to distinguish the two paradigms that he drafted in the Second Congress of CI to outline the fundamental objectives of CI. Under the heading "The nature of proletarian dictatorship and soviet power" he wrote, "The victory of socialism (as the first stage of communism) over capitalism requires the proletariat, as the only truly revolutionary class, to carry out the following three tasks."

The 'three tasks' that he charted out are the basic premises of existence of revolutionary state power, i.e. dictatorship of the proletariat.

> First—overthrow the exploiters, and first and foremost the bourgeoisie, as their principal economic and political representatives; utterly rout them; crush their resistance; absolutely preclude any attempt on their part to restore the yoke of capital and wage-slavery.
>
> Second—win over and bring under the leadership of the Communist Party, the revolutionary vanguard of the proletariat, not only the entire proletariat, or its vast majority...
>
> Third—neutralize, or render harmless, the inevitable vacillation between the bourgeoisie and the proletariat, between bourgeoisie democracy and Soviet power. to be seen in the class of petty proprietors in agriculture, industry and commerce–" [Lenin, 1974h, pp. 185-186]

One cannot fail to notice the three primary tasks that Lenin outlined were the political objectives of dictatorship of the proletariat to win over particularly the 'class of small proprietors in agriculture' to ensure the victory of "socialism". The tasks outlined did not mention the socio-economic programmes of transition to such a stage of society. Nor had Lenin mentioned what would happen to the instrument of *state* as the tasks were completed. Lenin's arguments provided Balibar with the ammunition to declare, 'The dictatorship of the proletariat is not simply a form of 'transition to socialism', it is not a 'road of transition to socialism'—it is identical with socialism itself'. By all means, Balibar justified the historical stages of development of human society *only* as the events and phenomena fulfilling the political objectives.

Here, we must point out the dichotomy of Lenin's views within successive Chapters of his treatise *The State and Revolution* in the context of *state* representing the proletariat as the ruling class. While defending Marx's arguments to counter the reformists, Lenin emphatically wrote in Chapter 2,

> The proletariat needs the state—this is repeated by all the opportunists, social-chauvinists and Kautskyites, who assure us that this is what Marx taught. But they "forget" to add that, in the first place, according to Marx, the proletariat needs only a state which is withering away, i.e., a state so constituted that it begins to wither away immediately, and cannot but wither away. And, secondly, the working people need a "state, i.e., the proletariat organized as the ruling class. [Lenin, 1974e, p. 407]

Again in Chapter 4, to counter the anarchists on the same issue with the arguments of Marx, he wrote,

> To prevent the true meaning of his struggle against anarchism from being distorted, Marx expressly emphasized the "revolutionary and transient form" of the state which the proletariat needs. The proletariat needs the state only temporarily. We do not after all differ with the anarchists on the question of the abolition of the state as the aim. We maintain that, to achieve this aim, we must temporarily make use of the instruments, resources, and methods of state power against the exploiters, just as the temporary dictatorship of the oppressed class is necessary for the abolition of classes. [Lenin, 1974e, p. 441]

Undoubtedly, here Lenin was following in Marx's footsteps in strongly arguing for the 'transient', 'temporary' requirement of the instrument of suppression called *state*, and consequently in his argument that no *transitional society* came into the picture between capitalism and *communism*. Lenin was countering here the arguments from both ends of opportunism, one from the reformists, the other from the anarchists' quarter in stressing *state* being necessary but only to wither away, 'immediately, and cannot but wither away' during transition from capitalism to *communism*. However, Lenin created the fallacy in Chapter 5 of the same work while quoting the same passages from Marx's critique [Marx, 1958a] that we reviewed earlier in this section. Lenin commented on the first phase of *communism* as below:

> And so, in the first phase of communist society (usually called socialism) "bourgeois law" is not abolished in its entirety, but only in part, only in proportion to the economic revolution so far attained, i.e., only in respect of the means of production. "Bourgeois law" recognizes them as the private property of individuals. Socialism converts them into common property. To that extent—and to that extent alone—"bourgeois law" disappears. [Lenin, 1974e, p. 472]

It is as if by a sleight of hand Lenin found 'socialism' in common parlance to be synonymous with the first phase of *communism* '(usually called socialism)'. Who called?—Definitely not Marx and Engels, the claim does not bear scrutiny from the elaborate explanatory treatment by Engels [Engels, 1958b] that we quoted at length. This was actually the interpretation of the pandits of the Second International whose reformism Lenin fought tooth and nail during the formation of CI. Lenin's interpretation was extremely hazy and misrepresenting such as 'Socialism converts them into common property', 'common property' owned by whom? If it is not the direct producers, then is it owned by the state? Did he mean 'common property' owned by the state to be synonymous with ownership by the society? Next we see the statement, '"bourgeois law" is not abolished in its entirety, but only in part, only in proportion to the economic revolution so far attained,' signifying the capitalist production relations still play a considerable role in society. Therefore, a transition is still in progress, and the existence of the institution *state* is legitimized in the first phase of 'communist society' (as Sweezy and others also wrote later).

None of these presumptions were part of Marx's critique in [Marx, 1958a]. If we now read Lenin's interpretation on the second or higher phase of 'communist society', we cannot avoid drawing the above inferences. Lenin wrote in the next paragraph,

> That is why we are entitled to speak only of the inevitable withering away of the state, emphasizing the protracted nature of this process and its dependence upon the rapidity of development of the higher phase of communism, and leaving the question of the time required for, or the concrete forms of, the withering away quite open, because there is no material for answering these questions.
>
> Until the "higher" phase of communism arrives, the socialists

> demand the strictest control by society and by the state over the measure of labor and the measure of consumption; but this control must start with the expropriation of the capitalists, with the establishment of workers' control over the capitalists, and must be exercised not by a state of bureaucrats, but by a state of armed workers. [Lenin, 1974e, pp. 474-475]

The statement is bizarre on two counts: Lenin demanded emphatically the recognition of existence of the institution of the 'state' in "socialism" (the first phase of communism in Lenin's view). Second, the transition to the higher phase of communism where finally *state* may be allowed to 'wither away' is a distant possibility embedded in the mist of the future. How then did Lenin emphasize in Chapter 2 and 4 the '"revolutionary and transient form"' of *state* while society marches towards *socialism*? In that sense, all historical stages of development of human society are temporary and only the *class struggle* is permanent. Therefore, the existence of the 'state' is a permanent feature of society, withering away of the bourgeois institution of the state remains a hypothetical agenda, a goal existing only as an article in the programmes of *Party* and never in actual reality of society.

It is in this sense that we consider Bettelheim's statement '*historical tasks* that the proletariat must accomplish' to win over capitalism in society an obfuscation. It was Lenin, who asserted, 'while capitalism and socialism exist side by side, they cannot live in peace: one or the other will ultimately triumph'. If we do not consider the *transitional* nature of society under dictatorship of the proletariat, we actually belittle the need of *socialism* within the society in the sense that we belittle the need for *state* to dissolve among the "*mass*" organizations of society. Concurrently, we belittle the need to bring in complete domination of *free* labour in social exchanges in place of *value* as abstract labour power in social production.

We have to concede that Lenin's arguments and his followers cannot be construed to be interpreted in the historical sense of ages to pass. We have to reject the argument that a competition between capitalism and "socialism" simultaneously can coexist over ages together, that all major political streams emanating from the Third International forced entire generations of ardent and adamant "communist" revolutionaries to believe. Such misrepresentation of Marx's arguments created havoc among the ardent followers of Lenin in CI to whom he was *metamorphosed* as the ultimate theoretician, final authority in interpreting Marx's writings. Lenin accomplished that particular duty by taking recourse to miserable half-quotes from Engels' letters to the contemporaries. Legitimization of the punitive instrument of the state in "socialism" was theoretically sanctified by Lenin. Continuation of the state in the name of dictatorship of the proletariat not only when classes were actually existing in society but also when antagonistic classes were *claimed* to be not the main force of society, and abandonment of this instrument of subjugation a hypothetical question for a distant, unknown future—all such huge hypocrisy became the standard practice of CI in later parts of the twentieth century. There cannot be any doubt that the followers of *Leninism* made Lenin's arguments a matter of conviction, a credo establishing "communism" as a totalitarian regime before the working class, as a theory of the salvation army, and of course not a practice of *self-emancipation* as the prime activity of the proletariat in the *socialist* revolution. Sweezy and Bettelheim did not represent an exception to this general tradition of the Third International that continued till the 1970s decades all over the world.

## 2.5 Marx's Idea of "*Smashing*" the Bourgeoisie State Apparatus

We cannot conclude our critique of the theses that Lenin placed before the First Congress of CI without reviewing the concept of "*smashing*" the bourgeoisie state apparatus. The contribution of Marx to the international working class movement rests not only upon his unsparing criticism of bourgeoisie ideology or political economy, but above all, in his proposition of an advanced social theory before the proletariat as the principles of revolutionary practice. In that sense, Marx's contribution remained immensely political that his contemporaries riled contemptuously. The bourgeois ideologues later tried to bring out a harmless icon out of philosophic and socio-economic analysis later after shedding off his revolutionary appeal to politics. As Lenin wrote on the eve of the revolution that one of the fundamental convictions that Marx repeatedly tried to establish was,

> Marx basing himself on the experience of Paris Commune taught that the proletariat cannot simply lay hold of the readymade state-machine for its own purposes, that the proletariat must smash this machine and substitute a new one for it. This new state machine was created by Paris Commune. [Lenin, 1972c, p. 102]

Lenin was truthful here about Marx as 'the proletariat must smash this machine' was a major cornerstone of Marx's politics. Marx wrote to Dr. Kugelmann in April 1871 while the Communards were still putting up their valiant effort in Paris.

> If you look at the last chapter of my *Eighteenth Brumaire* you will find that I say that the next attempt of the French revolution will be no longer, as before, to transfer the bureaucratic-military machine from one hand to another, but to *smash* it, and this is essential for every real people's revolution on the Continent. And this is what our heroic Party comrades in Paris are attempting. [Marx, 1958b, p. 420]

One cannot overlook the stress Marx put on the word '*smash*'—he repeated this at a number of places. To Marx and Lenin (even for the German revolutionaries) arming the proletariat for seizure of political power was axiomatic with "*smashing*" the old state machine. Therefore, militarization of the exploited people was a necessary consequence for revolutionary effort. Lenin vigorously argued for the armed workers' militia as the *new* state apparatus. He wrote,

> The Soviets are a new state apparatus which, in the first place, provides an armed force of workers and peasants; and this force is not divorced from the people, as was the old standing army, but is very closely bound up with the people. From the military point of view this force is incomparably more powerful than previous forces; from the revolutionary point of view, it cannot be replaced by anything else. [Lenin, 1972c, p. 113]

In fact, in line with Engels' preface to the third edition of *The Civil War in France*, written in March 1891 on the lessons the proletariat learned from experience of the Paris Commune, Lenin stressed,

> The essence of the matter—among other things, on the question of the state (has the oppressed class arms?)— is here remarkably well-grasped. It is precisely this essence that is most often evaded by both professors influenced by bourgeois ideology, and by petty-bourgeois democrats. [Lenin, 1974e, p. 454]

However, several questions arise from this conviction of *state* being synonymous with armed people's militia, and as the means to smash 'the bureaucratic-military machine'. How does *socialism* being a society without any class exploitations and antagonisms compatible with arming of the population as a matter of principle? Of course, the counter question is well understood—how can a society that is an antithesis to bourgeois society can at all come into existence without defeating the state-power that the bourgeoisie represents? It can be strongly argued that in no phase of human history has the ruling class ever abdicated power without offering the stiffest resistance, particularly when a popular rule mandated by the huge support of the oppressed population is embroiled in the civil war.

If the strength of the revolution lies in the change of guard in the seat of power (it must be conceded that conquest of state-power till now remains the central theme of revolution) then the counter questions in themselves certainly contain the answer; armed conflict in the society between reigning state-power and the resistance of rising popular power is the inevitability. We hope we have made it abundantly clear in our discussion that *socialism* is much more than the quest of state-power (even in the sense of class war reflecting the acuteness of *class struggle*). The fundamental strength of *socialism* in contravention to bourgeoisie civilization lies in overhauling the production relations so that exchange of social labour as *value* becomes irrelevant in society. This can only happen when the "*mass*"-participation in social production becomes a voluntary affair, and not forced compulsion. The uncertainty and exploitation in the exchange of the commodity called labour power as the measure of abstract *value* becomes a matter of the past; just as slavery as a form of civilization that continued in history for many epochs is now a matter of antiquity.

*Socialism* is the fundamental transformation of understanding how we exchange our labour in society, and how we adjust ourselves as *free* individuals in a cooperative society as a collective of direct producers. The most active participation of the exploited "*masses*" in ushering such a transformation in production relations is a mandatory precondition that cannot be bypassed or substituted by the active participation of the population in armed conflict with the existing power structures. Nor can it be theoretically argued that unless the working class participate in the armed conflict with the reigning state-power of the bourgeoisie they do not and cannot realize the strength of their own *state* as this is tantamount to demanding sacrifice from the working class. Revolutionary transformation in capitalist production relations is a question of social necessity, fulfilling the yearning or anticipation of the working class is a byproduct of such revolution, and that is of course not *accidental*, nor *secondary* in the agenda of social revolution. Just as the fact that the locomotives that at one time served the necessity of society got replaced by huge transport aircrafts do not mean that society has sacrificed the locomotives but has only moved over to the new, modern versions of transportation. In a similar metaphor, *socialism* becomes imperative for the society to adopt as the civilization that truly affords to provide the joy of labour and the joy of living. Such a conjecture can be true as capitalism loses its worth before the society and the society yearns to move on, beyond capitalism. The prime motive force of capitalism to exist is exploitation of the producers of *value* and money being the ultimate in commodity fetishism that becomes irrelevant in *socialist* society. This understanding of *socialism* is not the outcome of the notions of sacrifice and salvation, but is the result of *transcendence* of an antiquated mode of production that guaranteed exploitation and uncertainty in living.

The essential feature of the revolutions ('has the oppressed class arms?') that the European proletariat faced in the civil wars at the end of the WWI was primarily the consequence of the war itself that was the handiwork of the bourgeoisie. The same was the fate of the working class who served as the fodder for the WWII that was only the attempts to force capitalism to survive as a social system. It is not a binding argument that capitalism will survive only by means of war among the nations; that last seventy years after the WWII the world has not seen war among the nations that are the biggest producers of war machineries. There are equally strong arguments to view the collapse of capitalism under the huge onslaught of popular resistance that galvanize the exploited population, particularly the working class to lay the foundation of *socialist* society on the basis of active participation in decision-making in huge numbers (we saw in the Lenin shipyard, Gdansk in the 1980s, in Tienanmen Square in 1989, in Tahrir Square in 2011). Such scale of "*mass*"-participation in decision-making may consciously affect the huge production apparatus and organizations by which the bourgeoisie survive to be idle and obsolete. One certainly cannot rule out the possibility of collapse of the bourgeoisie society in front of the wall of international "*mass*" uprisings that may be apparently silent and voiceless, but in actuality are decisive in bringing in the cooperative society, the only way the proletariat transcends its own existence in the capitalist society ('in ridding itself of all the muck of ages and become fitted to found society anew.'—Marx).

We do not satisfy ourselves by providing only the hypothetical arguments in support of *transcendence* as an alternative to the concept of '*smashing*'. The arguments of Marx and Lenin in support of '*smashing*' the state apparatus are counterproductive also to the objective of *socialism*. The "*mass*" appeal of *socialism* lies in the end of war as the means of resolving conflicts in human society. War industries can exist only in capitalist mode of production to serve the nationalist intent of the bourgeoisie, more importantly as the most unproductive pillars in society for the survival of capitalism. The huge anachronism of capitalism is best exemplified in the war industry that has minimal utility so far as social production and consumption are concerned but weighs heavily over society as the pillars of support for the absurdly exploitative production relations. Strangely, nowhere in the writings of the "Marxists" that we visited is the necessity of abolition of war industries in *socialism* discussed except only in one statement by Rosa Luxemburg. She wrote,

> Naturally, the entire *war and munitions industries* must be abolished since a socialist society does not need murder weapons and, instead, the valuable materials and human labour used in them must be employed for useful products. *Luxury industries* which make all kinds of frippery for the idle rich must also be abolished, along with personal servants. All the human labour tied up here will be found a more worthy and useful occupation. [Luxemburg, 2004b, p. 347]

Even if it was a brief statement, it clearly stated overhauling of the production relations is possible only when the divisions of labour associated with the war industry, luxury industry are also simultaneously abolished. Of course, these steps cannot be decided by decree of some ombudsman (in fact a single minority authority cannot affect abolition of war industry). These steps can only be effective as conscious decisions of the workers of the war industry and the soldiers to abrogate the profession with what they are known for the ages, as the members of the instruments of state-power to suppress all expressions of protest of the exploited in society. This argument on abolition of the war industry in effect also the poses question to the viability of armed militia, armed contingent of workers, etc. Secondly, as we have seen in Trotsky's arguments, naming an army as the "Red Army" did not necessarily dissolve the army within the population. Rather, Trotsky glorified the new Soviet state for strengthening the army and production for the armed forces that turned into a permanent fixture and a strong component of strength of the state. Hence, the argument of "*smashing*" the state by arming of the people turns counter-productive as the programmes of *socialism* are advanced as an immediate agenda before the society. The process of withering away of *state* is not augmented by distributing arms among the exploited "*masses*" of population in the society so as to encourage mutual cross-fire among the class-brethren as it happened in the Kronstadt uprisings against the Bolsheviks and their subsequent extermination. The dissolution of *state* becomes practical when such arms, ammunitions, weaponries, Goliath-like systems of *mass*-destruction are sent to the Museums as the examples of stupidity and cruelty of the bourgeoisie exhibiting their measures of annihilation of humanity.

We do not fail to notice in Lenin's observation even as he found the elements of bourgeois-democracy to be purposeful in augmenting the proletarian institutions of political power, 'it makes it possible to combine the advantages of the parliamentary system with those of immediate and direct democracy, i.e. to vest in the people's elected representatives both legislative *and executive* functions.' Of course, he made bizarre arguments of binary negation between democracy and *state* elsewhere that we have seen above. Significantly, Lenin recognized the strength of the Soviet-type of institutions in imbibing the principle of elected representatives inherited from the parliamentary system that only came into force in the bourgeois civilization. The noteworthy point here is the Lenin's realization that while old institutions of parliamentary democracy turn obsolete as Soviets of the elected representatives of producers become both executive and legislative authorities, they also inherit the elements that are historically conducive for the proletariat to implement the immediate programmes of ushering *socialism*. In that sense, the concept of "*smashing*" the state apparatus does not fit into the transition to *socialism*. *Transcendenc*e signifies the dialectical process of negation of bourgeois civilization in a more apt manner so that the *new* society in its journey knows what to accept and what to reject from the old society. Therefore, such a society has to decide on the fundamental principle of disbanding the war industry, and at the same time has to stick to election of representatives of direct producers while preserving the right to recall the representatives. "*Smashing*" the old state apparatus leaves only the rubble of the old institutions that a society of conscious producers cannot afford to execute.

We conclude here our detailed critique of Lenin's theses on bourgeois democracy and dictatorship of the proletariat. In the following Chapters, we review the other significant theses and discuss how they moulded CI in the formative years.

## NOTES

1. Lenin presented the "Theses and report on bourgeoisie democracy and dictatorship of the proletariat" on March 4, 1919 after the First Congress of Communist International (CI) was declared open on March 2, 1919. As Jane Degras wrote in introducing the documents of the First Congress of CI the thesis was accepted among the delegates present without any discussion. "Lenin expressed the belief, shared by the other delegates, that the capitalist world was rapidly approaching its end, and that the working class everywhere was moving towards revolution (he likened the shop stewards' movement in England to the Soviets)." [Degras, 1971, p. 7]
2. The article by Rosa Luxemburg first appeared under the heading "What Does the Spartacus League Want?" in *Die Rote Fahne*, December 14, 1918. "With insignificant changes, the text became the first party programme of the KPD, adopted at its founding congress." [Kuhn, 2012, p. 99].

   The *Kommunistische Partei Deutschlands* [Communist Party of Germany] (KPD) was formed by the Spartacus League and the

*Internationale Kommunisten Deutschlands* [International Communists of Germany] (IKD) in the founding Congress between 31 Dec. 1918 - January 1 1919. [Kuhn, 201, p. xii]

3. This has reference to Grahame Lock's English Introduction to Etienne Balibar's work *On the Dictatorship of the Proletariat*. Lock wrote,

   > Balibar spells out the reasons for this conclusion against the background of the 22nd Congress of the French Communist Party, which decided to 'drop' the aim of the dictatorship of the proletariat and to substitute the objective of a 'democratic' road to socialism. His concrete references are therefore usually to arguments put forward within the French Party. But it is quite obvious that the significance of the book is much wider, not least because, in spite of the important political and economic differences separating the nations of Western Europe, many of their Communist Parties are evolving in an apparently similar ideological direction, and indeed appear to be borrowing arguments from one another in support of their new positions. [Balibar, 2011, p. 8]

4. For example, the Italian communist party (PCI), the party with the largest membership in Europe founded on January 21, 1921, was officially dissolved in 1991 in Bologna, Italy. Other communist parties either changed their name or got transformed to minuscule existence.
5. This has reference to the eyewitness account of Maurice Brinton in his work *Paris: May 1968* about the march of the workers and students in Paris in May, 1968. Under the heading "Monday, May 13, 1.15 pm.", Brinton wrote,

   > The streets are crowded. The response to the call for a 24-hour general strike has exceeded the wildest hopes of the trade unions. Despite the short notice Paris is paralyzed. ....
   >
   > By about 4.30 pm the students' and teachers' contingent, perhaps 80,000 strong, finally leaves the Place de la Republique. Hundreds of thousands of demonstrators have preceded it, hundreds of thousands follow it, but the "left" contingent has been well and truly "bottled-in"....

   The main student contingent proceeds as a compact body. Now that we are past the bottleneck of the Place de la République the pace is quite rapid. The student group nevertheless takes at least half an hour to pass a given point. The slogans of the students contrast strikingly with those of the CGT. The students shout "*Le Pouvoir aux Owners*" (All Power to the Workers); "*Le Pouvoir est dans la rue*" (Power lies in the street); "*Libérez nos camarades*"... [Brinton, June 1968]
6. We want to put on record that this wider, societal interpretation of dictatorship of the proletariat was raised by Claudin in his work. [Claudin, 1975] Claudin wrote,

> Stalin's manipulation of Lenin's idea on this subject was facilitated by the very widespread confusion between two concepts which are formulated in the same terms: the concept of socialist revolution as a *social* revolution, as the socialist transformation of economic and social structures and of political and cultural superstructures; and the concept of the socialist revolution as a *political* revolution, marked with distinctive feature of the capture of power by the working class. The first content of the concept 'socialist revolution' *wholly* includes the second: every social revolution whether socialist or bourgeoisie, includes as a necessary stage a political revolution, the taking power by a new class. The second content, however, includes the first only *partly*: every political revolution—unless it is merely a *coup d' etat* that transfers power from one group to another in the same ruling stratum—has a more or less developed social content; and this is all the more so when the political revolution in question is the one implied by the capture of power by the working class. But this politico-social content is only the first stone of a building the construction of which is subject to laws and conditions different from those that made it possible to lay that first stone. In order to distinguish between the two contents of the concept 'revolution', Lenin brought in the expressions, 'revolution in the broad sense' and 'revolution in the narrow sense', and these I shall make use from now on. 4 [p. 47]

However, we also note Claudin did not elaborate the reasons behind such 'very widespread confusion between two concepts' among the followers of CI and the source of such confusion so that the 'idea' could be manipulated later.

7. This has reference to Lenin's work *The Immediate Tasks of the Soviet Government*. According to the end note of the Editor,

> In the manuscript, Lenin's work *The Immediate Tasks of the Soviet Government* was headed "Theses on the Tasks of the Soviet Government in the Present Situation". Lenin's theses were discussed at a meeting of the Party Central Committee on April 26, 1918.
>
> The Central Committee unanimously approved them and passed a decision to have them published as an article in *Pravda* and *Izvestia*, and also as a separate pamphlet. In 1918 the pamphlet went through more than ten editions, in Moscow, Petrograd, Saratov, Kazan, Tambov and other cities of Russia. It was published in the same year in English in New York, and in French in Geneva; an abridged version in German, edited by F. Platten, appeared in Zurich under the title *Am Tage nach der Revolution*.

The Central Committee instructed Lenin to give a report on the immediate tasks of the Soviet government at a meeting of the All-Russia CEC and to formulate the Theses briefly as a resolution (see this volume, pp. 314-17). [Endnote, Vol. 27, p. 581]

8. We take the cue from Charles Bettelheim's article, "On the transition between capitalism and socialism" in [Bettleheim, 1972d]. Bettelheim wrote,

   In my opinion, the *decisive factor*–i.e. the *dominant factor*—is not *economic* but *political*.

   This decisive political factor (the importance of which you unfortunately appear to deny in the last pages of your article) results from the fact that the proletariat (Soviet or Czech) *has lost its power to a new bourgeoisie*, with the result that the revisionist leadership of the Communist Party of the Soviet Union is today instrument of this new bourgeoisie. [p. 16]

9. This has reference to Hal Draper's analysis of the views of Marx and Engels on the course of bourgeoisie revolution. Under a subtitle "Marx poses the dilemma", Hal Draper wrote,

   Like Engels earlier in the year, Marx explained why the proletariat was not ready to take the place of the bourgeoisie in the overthrow of absolutism. He did this in a polemic against a democratic liberal named Heinzen, in October-November." Hal Draper later quoted Marx as

   "They [the workers] know that their own struggle with the bourgeoisie can only get started on the day the bourgeoisie has been victorious. For all that, they do not share Mr. Heinzen's bourgeoisie illusions. They can and must treat the *bourgeoisie revolution* as a condition for the *workers' revolution*. But not for a moment can they consider it their *final goal*.[53] [Draper, 2011a, p. 184]

   We note here, the idea of class alliances being floated from the side of the proletariat for the victory of the bourgeoisie revolution did not occur to Marx. May be, Engels went ahead taking the idea of class alliances as a logical step forward from what we have seen above as the unequivocal support from Marx towards the bourgeoisie revolution.

10. This has reference to the trial of forty-seven Social-Revolutionaries (SR) in June 1922 who were charged with the attempt on Lenin for assassination. Before the trial, the representatives of CI assured the Conference of the three Internationals held in Berlin, April 1922 that the accused "will be allowed any defenders they wish; that, as already announced in the Soviet press before the Conference, no death sentences will be inflicted in this trial; that, as the trial will be public,

representatives of all three Executives will be allowed to attend, to listen to the proceedings, and will be allowed to take stenographic reports for the information of their affiliated Parties." [Degras, 1971, p.35]

At another place, Rosmer quoted Trotsky's article,

> Once again the Russian Social-Revolutionary Party has become the object of general attention, but in a quite different way than during the February Revolution. ....But in the struggle against Tsarism and serfdom, this party played a revolutionary role. It incited the peasants to rebellion, called young students into political activity, and brought together under its flag a large number of workers who were linked morally and materially to the countryside, and who considered the revolution, not from a proletarian class standpoint, but from the point of view of the vague notion of "labour". [Rosmer, 1973, p. 166]

11. Our observation is based on Adam B. Ulam's work *The Bolsheviks* [Ulam, 1998] that is treated as one of the standard historiographies on the Russian revolution. Ulam wrote under the heading "The World of the Comintern",

> For Lenin the erection of the Third International was not only the fulfilment of the vow he had made in the summer of 1914 when he heard about the betrayal of the French and German Socialists. It was also in a way the settling of long-standing accounts with those elders of the Second International who for many years had been so infuriatingly patronizing toward the Russian Socialists. How many times did he himself have to wait upon German or Austrian comrades to ask them for help with funds, identification papers, or protection from the police? How many times did he have to listen to fatherly sermons about the Bolsheviks being too excitable, about the need to work together with the other Socialist and progressive forces in his country, to the taunts as to why the Russians could not settle their disputes in a civilized manner? [p. 495]

At another place, Ulam commented upon the formation of CI in most dismissive terms. Quoting Lenin, he wrote,

> The conquest of the majority in the soviets constitutes [our] main task in the countries where Soviet power has not as yet conquered."[45] To the vast majority of workers in other countries the sentence was hardly comprehensible. Where except in Germany and Hungary had there been soviets at all? The literal translation of the word was "council." Council power? What could it mean in Lyons or Birmingham? [p. 495]

12. The *Theses of the Workers' Opposition* drafted by Alexander Shliapnikov was published in *Pravda* as "Tasks of Trade Unions." January 25, 1921. This was presented as a platform of the trade unions before the Tenth Congress of the Bolshevik Party held on March 8-16, 1921. Shliapnikov signed the theses as Chairman of the Central Committee of All-Russian Union of Metalworkers. Along with Shliapnikov many of the Chair holding members of trade-unions such as Chairman, Central Board of Artillery Factories, Chief of Board of Aviation Factories, etc. were signatories in the theses. [Shliapnikov, 1921]
13. The Supreme Soviet of the National Economy, *Vesenkha* was formed by a decree of the Council of People's Commissars and All-Russian Central Executive Committee of Soviets on December 5, 1917. Its stated purpose was to "plan for the organization of the economic life of the country and the financial resources of the government". [Brinton, 1970]
14. This has reference to a footnote in Ulam's work [Ulam, 1998] regarding the voting pattern in the Tenth Party Congress on the theses submitted by the *Workers' Opposition group*, Trotsky's resolution on Trade Unions and Lenin's resolution. Ulam wrote,

    24 In the voting Lenin's resolution on the labor unions had 336 votes, Trotsky's 50, and that of the Workers' Opposition only 18. [Footnote, p. 474]

15. Here we take the cue from the summary drawn by Hal Draper on 'dictatorship of the proletariat'. Hal Draper wrote,

    The first period during which 'dictatorship of the proletariat' occurred in Marx was 1850-52, that is, the period following the revolution of 1848-49, a period of stock-taking and analysis. In this period Marx confronted the Blanquist tendency and similar tendencies of Jacobin-communism within the ranks of the Communist League; and, we have seen, as against their ideas of the revolutionary dictatorship of the party or communist band, he counterpoised the conception of a class dictatorship. The dictatorship *of* the proletariat was his alternative to the dictatorship of the party *over* the proletariat. [Draper, 2011b, Vol. 3, p. 264]

16. The appeal drafted by Shliapnikov and signed by 22 members of the Bolshevik Party (the oldest party membership was of Kollontai 1898, and the most recent was of G. Shokhanov, 1918) was to be presented before the ECCI on February 26, 1922. One recent research account has depicted the scene when Kollontai attempted to speak on the appeal before ECCI as,

    When Kollontai attempted to speak before the Comintern conference on February 26, 1922 on behalf of the views expressed in the appeal, Russian party leaders (most notably Trotsky and

Zinoviev) on the presidium 33 of the Comintern conference had her name removed from the list of orators. In a private meeting with Kollontai, they urged her not to speak. Zinoviev insisted that support for the united front was a party directive that the entire Russian delegation had to pursue without reservations. When Kollontai proved recalcitrant, Trotsky forbade her to speak and issued a decree, in the name of the CC, ordering all members of the Russian delegation to "obey the directives of the party."[34] Thus, both Trotsky and Zinoviev stifled criticism in the name of party discipline. [Barbara Allen, p. 31]

17. This is again in reference to the trial of forty-seven SRs charged with the attempt to assassinate Lenin. Rosmer recorded his observation about the defendants in the trial as,

    The accused defended themselves energetically throughout the trial and were given complete freedom to do so. Their capabilities might be disputed, and their political ideas are open to discussion, but no one would have dreamt of denying their personal courage, their spirit of self-sacrifice, nor of denying or even forgetting the heroic past of their Party. [Rosmer, 1973, p. 164]

    For the record of history, at the end of the trial, eleven of the accused were condemned to death.
18. This has the context to our earlier reference to Lenin in Chapter I, p. 24. The article in *Pravda* in May 1923 was a rebuttal to N. Sukhanov's (a Menshvik by conviction) memoirs *The Russian Revolution, 1917: Eyewitness Account*.
19. This Conference was held at the initiative of the International Union of Socialist Parties (the so-called Two-and-a-half International of Vienna). The note from the ECCI in the Conference read as,

    This is the first time since July 1914, when the last meeting of the International Bureau was held in Brussels and was followed by the world war and the collapse of the Second International, that representatives of all sections of the international labour movement, which once formed a single international association, are to deliberate together at one table. This event cannot be passed over in silence....

    That is why the Communist International issued the slogan of the united front for the struggle against the bourgeoisie, and welcomed the initiative of the Vienna Union in calling for an international workers' congress. It regards the proposed congress as a way of unifying the workers' struggles which are now opening. [Degras, 1971, pp. 333, 335]

20-21. Rosmer wrote about the Genoa Conference, "It was the first time since the war that representatives of all nations were gathered around one table. The classification into allies and enemies was finished with". [p. 161] The interesting fact that went unreported was the treaty between the Weimar Republic of Germany and Soviet Russia known as the Rapallo Treaty in the background of the Conference. Degras wrote,

> The only practical result of the Genoa Conference was the Rapallo treaty signed between Russia and Germany. This was rarely mentioned in the communist press....

At the subsequent world congress the only reference to the treaty—and that an oblique one—was made by Bukharin in his report on the Comintern programme.

> 'The revolutionary Soviet governments themselves are in a rather different position from the revolutionary parties.... The Commissar for Foreign Affairs who writes in the journal of the Third International must remember that he is bound by the position of his government, a position which is no longer that of a revolutionary party far removed from power".... [Degras, 1971, p. 344]

22. Here, we take the cue from Charles Bettelheim's work *Class Struggles in the USSR*. Regarding Stalin's authority in the Bolshevik party, Bettelheim observed,

> His authority was due to what almost the entire party, from the early 1930s onwards, saw as the exceptional twofold merit of Stalin —that he had not given up the idea of building socialism in the USSR, and that he had worked out a policy which, as the party saw it, would successfully bring about that result....

By proclaiming that the Soviet Union could advance to socialism, Stalin, contrary to Trotsky's claims, appeared as heir to Lenin's position, several of whose writings, especially the last, asserted this possibility. This was one of the sources of Stalin's authority, which was linked with the theses he propounded. [Bettelheim, 1977, p. 40]

23. We take the cue from Bettelheim's confident assertion at the conclusion of his debates with Paul Sweezy. He wrote under the heading, "Marxism-Leninism as the Theory of the Proletariat",

> Marxism-Leninism is the theory of the proletariat because *it is the theoretical expression of the existence of the proletariat in the capitalist mode of production*—Marxism developed by adopting the point of view of the proletariat, the only point of view from which the significance of proletarian struggles can be understood....

The proletarian ideology *corresponds to the position of the proletariat in the capitalist mode of production*; this ideology is Marxism-Leninism which, precisely, developed and continues to develop on the basis of an analysis of the objective position of the proletariat,... [Bettelheim, 1972d, p. 66]

For the record of history, neither Bettelheim nor Sweezy explained in their entire debate, what made *Leninism* distinguished as an extension of *"Marxism"*.

24. Peter Hudis discussed the contribution of Marx on post-capitalist society in a recent work [Hudis, 2016]. He observed,

 What is especially striking about the *Grundrisse* is its wealth of discussion of the alternative to capitalism. Indeed, it can be argued that no single work of Marx discusses a future post-capitalist society as directly or as comprehensively. [p. 101]

25. About the historical significance of Marx's critique on the *Gotha Program*, Sweezy wrote during his debate with Bettelheim,

 *The most important document of classical Marxism bearing on this process is Marx's *"Critique of the Gotha Program."* [Footnote, Sweezy, 1972, p. 50]

26. This limitation of Marx in overlooking or ignoring a transitional society under dictatorship of the proletariat was pointed out [Hudis, October 19, 2005] a decade ago although the authors did not elaborate on the subject. The authors wrote,

 To Marx the political transition period is brief. If the revolutionary transformation from capitalism to communism is not achieved the political transition—regardless of the particular form—is not sustainable. A political transition period is therefore not the same as a lengthy transitional society, which Marx does not discuss at all in his Critique—or anywhere else for that matter! [p. 6]

27. Certain strands of arguments and analysis in this subsection run in parallel with earlier analysis, notably:
 *i)* Paresh Chattopadhaya, Lenin Reads Marx on Socialism, *Economic and Political Weekly* (EPW), Vol. XLVII, No. 50, pp. 65-68, December 2012.
 *ii)* Goutam Sen, *Chirayata Marxbader Koyekti Moulik Shiksha* (Some Fundamental Lessons of Classical Marxism – free English translation of Bengali title), Sandhan, February 2013, pp. 7-38.

28. This has reference to the *Manifesto of the Communist International* adopted at the First Congress of CI.

## REFERENCES

Communist International. Manifesto and Governing Rules of the Communist International. Chicago Arbeiter-Zeitung Publishing Company, 1642 N. Halsted Street, Chicago, 1919.

V.I. Lenin. Theses and Report on Bourgeoisie Democracy and the Dictatorship of the Proletariat, March 4, 1919. In *Speeches at Congress of the Communist International*. Progress Publishers, Moscow, 1972a.

Rosa Luxemburg. What Does the Spartacus League Want? In Peter Hudis and Kevin B. Anderson, Editors, *The Rosa Luxemburg Reader*, Chapter 14. Monthly Review Press, New York, 2004a.0.

Gabriel Kuhn, Editor. *All Power to the Councils! A Documentary History of the German Revolution of 1918-1919*. The Merlin Press Ltd, Wales, 2012.

Anton Pannekoek. World Revolution and Communist Tactics. In D.A. Smart, Editor, *Pannekoek and Gorter's Marxism*. Pluto Press, UK, 1978.

Etienne Balibar. *On the Dictatorship of the Proletariat*. Verso Books, London, 2011.

Gwyn Williams. *Proletarian Order: Antonio Gramsci, Factory Councils and the Origins of Italian Communism*. Pluto Press, UK, 1975.

V.I. Lenin. Speech on the Italian Question. In *Speeches at Congress of the Communist International*. Progress Publishers, Moscow, 1972b.

Karl Marx. *The Poverty of Philosophy*. Progress Publisher, Moscow, 1955.

Karl Marx. The German Ideology. In David McLellan, Editor, *Karl Marx: Selected Writings*. Oxford University Press, 2000.

Karl Marx. *The Class Struggles in France: 1848-1850*. Selected Works, Volume I. Progress Publishers, Moscow, 1969a.

Rosa Luxemburg. The Socialization of Society. In Peter Hudis and Kevin B. Anderson, Editors, *The Rosa Luxemburg Reader*, Chapter 14. Monthly Review Press, New York, 2004b.

Charles Bettelheim. More on the Society of Transition. In Paul M. Sweezy, Editor, *On the Transition to Socialism*. Monthly Review Press, New York, 1972a.

V.I. Lenin. *Can the Bolsheviks Retain State Power*? Collected Works, Vol. 26, 2nd ed. Progress Publishers, Moscow, 1972c.

V.I. Lenin. The Impending Catastrophe and How to Combat It. *Collected Works*, Vol. 25, 4th Ed. Progress Publishers, Moscow, 1974a.

V.I. Lenin. The Immediate Tasks of the Soviet Government. *Collected Works*, Vol. 27, 4th Ed. Progress Publishers, Moscow, 1974b.

Leo Trotsky. *Terrorism and Communism: A Reply to Karl Kautsky*, 2006. URL: *http://www.marxists.org/archive/trotsky/1920/terrcomm*.

V.I. Lenin. Letters on Tactics. *Collected Works*, Vol. 24, 2nd Printing. Progress Publishers, Moscow, 1974c.

V.I. Lenin. Five Years of the Russian Revolution and the Prospects of the World Revolution. In *Speeches at Congress of the Communist International*. Progress Publishers, Moscow, 1972d.

Georg Gravy. *The Origin and Evolution of the Soviet Banking System: A Historical Perspective*. National Bureau of Economic Research Publication, 1977. URL: *http://www.nber.org/books/gravy77-1*.

Simon Pirani. *The Russian Revolution in Retreat, 1920-24*. Routledge, UK, 2008.

Victor Serge. Memoirs of a Revolutionary. English Translation. *The New York Review of Books*, USA, 2012.

Eric Hobsbawm. Marx and History. In *On History*. The Orion Publishing Group Ltd, London, 1997.

Hal Draper. *Karl Marx's Theory of Revolution: The Politics of Social Classes*. Vol. 2. Aakar Books, Delhi, 2011a.

V.I. Lenin. Fourth Anniversary of the October Revolution. *Collected Works*, Vol. 33, 2nd Printing. Progress Publishers, Moscow, 1973a.

Paul Sweezy. A Reply. In Paul M. Sweezy, Editor, *On the Transition to Socialism*. Monthly Review Press, New York, 1972.

V.I. Lenin. Report on the Tactics of the RCP. In *Speeches at Congress of the Communist International*. Progress Publishers, Moscow, 1972e.

Karl Liebknecht. To the Workers and Soldiers of the Allied Countries, 1919. URL: *https://www.marxists.org/archive/liebknecht-k/works/1918/misc/workers-soldiers-allied-countries.htm*.

Rosa Luxemburg. The Russian Revolution. In Peter Hudis and Kevin B. Anderson, Editors, *The Rosa Luxemburg Reader*, Chapter 14. Monthly Review Press, New York, 2004c.

Frederick Engels. The Peasant War in Germany, 1926, English translation. URL: *https://www.marxists.org/archive/marx/works/1850/peasant-war-germany/index.htm*.

V.I. Lenin. Theses for a Report on the Tactics of the RCP. In *Speeches at Congress of the Communist International*. Progress Publishers, Moscow, 1972f.

Karl Kautsky. Terrorism and Communism: A Contribution to the Natural History of Revolution, Chapter 8, 1919. URL: *http:// www.isn.ethz*.

Jane Degras, Editor. *The Communist International 1919-1943 Documents*. Volume I, Routledge, 1971.

Communist International. Manifesto of the Second Congress of the Third Communist International. United Communist Party of America, American Edition, Moscow, 1920. URL: *https://www.bannedthought.net/International/Comintern/index.htm*.

O. Piatnitsky. *The Twenty-One Conditions of Admission into the Communist International*. American Left Ephemera Collection.1894-2008, University of Pittsburgh, USA, February 1934. URL: *http://www.digital.library.pitt.edu/u/ulsmanuscripts/pdf/*.

Rosa Luxemburg. The Junius Pamphlet. In Peter Hudis and Kevin B. Anderson, Editors, *The Rosa Luxemburg Reader*, Chapter 13. Monthly Review Press, New York, 2004d.

Karl Marx. The Bourgeoisie and the Counterrevolution. *Selected Works*, Volume I, Progress Publisher, Moscow, 1969b.

Karl Marx. Theses On Feuerbach. *Selected Works*, Volume I. Progress Publisher, Moscow, 1969c.

Maurice Brinton. *The Bolsheviks and Workers' Control*, 1917-1921: *The State and Counterrevolution*. Solidarity, First Edition, London, 1970.

Goutam Sen. *Against Substitutionism*. SEARCH, Kolkata, India, 2000.

Alexander Shliapnikov. Theses of the Workers Opposition, 1921. URL: *https: //www.marxists.org/archive/shliapnikov/1921/workersopposi tion.htm.*

Alexandra Kollontai. The Workers' Opposition. Workers ' Dreadnought, UK, April 22 - August 19, 1921. URL:*https://libcom.org/files/The Workers' Opposition.*

V.I. Lenin. The Trade Unions, The Present Situation and Trotsky's Mistakes[1]. *Collected Works*, Vol. 32, 2nd Printing. Progress Publishers, Moscow, 1973b.

Charles Bettelheim. Dictatorship of the Proletariat, Social Classes, and Proletarian Ideology. In Paul M. Sweezy, Editor, *On the Transition to Socialism*. Monthly Review Press, New York, 1972b.

Charles Bettelheim. More on the Society of Transition. In Paul M. Sweezy, Editor, *On the Transition to Socialism*. Monthly Review Press, New York, 1972c.

Frederick Engels. On the 20th Anniversary of the Paris Commune: Introduction to Civil War in France, 1891, *Postscript*. URL: *https://www.marxists.org/archive/marx/works/1871/civil-war-france/postscript.htm.*

Leo Trotsky. "Trotskyism" and the PSOP. The New International [New York], Vol. 5, No. 10, October 1939. URL: *https://www.marxists.org/archive/trotsky/1939/07/psop02.*

V.I. Lenin. The Tax in Kind. *Collected Works*, Vol. 32, 2nd Printing. Progress Publishers, Moscow, 1973c.

Leo Trotsky. Speech on Comrade Zinoviev's Report on the Role of the Party. The First Five Years of the Communist International, Vol. 1, 1924. URL: *https://www.marxists.org/archive/trotsky/1924/ffyci-1/ch11.htm.*

V.I. Lenin. Political Parties in Russia and the Tasks of the Proletariat.[3] *Collected Works*, Vol. 24, First Printing. Progress Publishers, Moscow, 1964.

Robin Black. Fascism in Germany: How Hitler Destroyed the World's Most Powerful Labour Movement, 1975. URL : *https://www.marxists.org/subject/fascism/blick/ch22.htm.*

Hal Draper. *The Dictatorship of the Proletariat*. Vol. 3. Aakar Books, Delhi, 2011b.

Karl Marx. Critique of the Gotha program. *Selected Works,* Volume II. Foreign Language Publishing House, Moscow, 1958a.

Karl Marx , Frederick Engels. Manifesto of the Communist Party. *Selected*

*Works,* Volume I. Foreign Language Publishing House, Moscow, 1958a.

Frederick Engels. Socialism: Utopian and Scientific. *Selected Works,* Volume II. Foreign Language Publishing House, Moscow, 1958b.

V.I. Lenin. The Proletarian Revolution and the Renegade Kautsky. *Collected Works,* Vol. 28, 4th English Ed. Progress Publishers, Moscow, 1974d.

Karl Marx. *Capital,* Volume III. Institute of Marxism-Leninism, Moscow, 1959.

V.I. Lenin. The State and Revolution. *Collected Works,* Vol. 25, 2nd Printing. Progress Publishers, Moscow, 1974e.

V.I. Lenin. Economics and Politics in the Era of the Dictatorship of the Proletariat. *Collected Works,* Vol. 30, 4th English Ed. Progress Publishers, Moscow, 1974f.

V.I. Lenin. Tasks of the Proletariat in Our Revolution. *Collected Works,* Vol. 24, 4th English Ed. Progress Publishers, Moscow, 1974g.

V.I. Lenin. Theses on the Fundamental Tasks of the Second Congress of the Communist International. *Collected Works,* Vol. 31, 4th English Ed. Progress Publishers, Moscow, 1974h.

Karl Marx. Letter to Dr Kugelmann Concerning the Paris Commune, April 12, 1871. *Selected Works,* Volume II. Foreign Language Publishing House, Moscow, 1958b.

Maurice Brinton. Paris: May 1968, June 1968. URL: *https://www.marxists.org/archive/brinton/1968/06/may-68.htm.*

Fernando Claudin. *The Communist Movement: From Comintern to Cominform.* Monthly Review Press, New York, 1975. ISBN: 0-85345-366-7.

Charles Bettelheim. On the Transition Between Capitalism and Communism. In Paul M. Sweezy, Editor, *On the Transition to Socialism.* Monthly Review Press, New York, 1972d. ISBN: 978-0-853451-83-9

Alfred Rosmer. *Moscow Under Lenin.* Monthly Review Press, New York, 1973.

Adam B. Ulam. *The Bolsheviks.* Harvard University Press, Cambridge, 1998.

Barbara C. Allen. Early Dissent within the Party: Alexander Shliapnikov and the Letter of the Twenty-Two. *The NEP Era: Soviet Russia 1921-1928,* 1:21–54, 2007.

Peter Hudis. *Marx's Concept of the Alternative to Capitalism.* Aakar Books, New Delhi, 2016.

Arvind Ghosh, Peter Hudis. Can We Change the World without Taking Power? *The International Marxist-Humanist,* p. 7, October 19, 2005. URL: *https://www.internationalmarxisthumanist.org/articles.*

# 3

# Theses and Report on State Capitalism and the New Economic Policy (NEP)

Lenin dwelt at length on state capitalism and the New Economic Policy (NEP)[1] in his theses and reports while addressing the Third and Fourth Congresses of CI. These two topics represented the major milestones of the Bolshevik party's views on economic reorganization under dictatorship of the proletariat. Lenin consistently emphasized the need of state capitalism in several places before and after the October Revolution as the ladder towards "socialism". For example, before the revolution he reiterated the need for state capitalism as, "For socialism is merely the next step forward from state-capitalist monopoly." [Lenin, 1974a, p. 362] At other places, he stressed,

> "...because state-monopoly capitalism is a complete *material* preparation for socialism, the *threshold* of socialism, a rung on the ladder of history between which and the rung called socialism *there are no intermediate rungs*." [Lenin, 1974a, p. 363]

After the revolution, he was particularly assertive in defence of state capitalism to counter the arguments of the "*Left* Communists" both in Russia and within CI. Therefore, it is pertinent here to bring under discussion state capitalism and the NEP to understand the political economy of Soviet Russia under the Bolshevik rule.

As the revolution in Russia progressed towards more peaceful times it was amply clear before Lenin that Marx and following him Engels did not envisage a *transitional society* towards *socialism* as a separate entity between the capitalist and *communist* societies. While presenting the political report in the Eleventh Congress of the Bolshevik Party in March-April 1922, Lenin emphatically defended 'state capitalism' under the Bolshevik rule as an original approach to *communism*.

> Not a single book has been written about state capitalism under communism. It did not occur even to Marx to write a word on this subject; and he died without leaving a single precise statement or definite instruction on it. That is why we must overcome the difficulty entirely by ourselves. And if we make a general mental survey of our press and see what has been written about state capitalism, as I tried to do when I was preparing this report, we shall be convinced that it is missing the target, that it is looking in an entirely wrong direction.
>
> The state capitalism discussed in all books on economics is that which exists under the capitalist system, where the state brings under its direct control certain capitalist enterprises. But ours is a proletarian state it rests on the proletariat; it gives the proletariat all political privileges; and through the medium of the proletariat it attracts to itself the lower ranks of the peasantry (you remember that we began this work through the Poor Peasants Committees). That is why very many people are misled by the term state capitalism. To avoid this we must remember the fundamental thing that state capitalism in the form we have here is not dealt with in any theory, or in any books, for the simple reason that all the usual concepts connected with this term are associated with bourgeois rule in capitalist society. Our society is one which has left the rails of capitalism, but has not yet got on to new rails. The state in this society is not ruled by the bourgeoisie, but by the proletariat. We refuse to understand that when we say "state" we mean ourselves, the proletariat, the vanguard of the working class. State capitalism is capitalism which we shall be able to restrain, and the limits of which we shall be able to fix. This state capitalism is connected with the state, and the state is the workers, the advanced section of the workers, the vanguard. We are the state." [Lenin, 1973a, p. 278]

Of course, Lenin was boisterous in his bizarre simplification above to declare, 'This state capitalism is connected with the state, and the state is the workers, the advanced section of the workers, the vanguard. We are the state.'—equating the rule of the Bolshevik party as *synonymous* with dictatorship of the proletariat. However, our focus here is the more probing observation on the *transitional society*, 'Our society is one which has left the rails of capitalism, but has not yet got on to new rails. The state in this society is not ruled by the bourgeoisie, but by the proletariat.' It was such a *transitional society* the Bolsheviks encountered in Russia after the revolution that Marx did not envisage or anticipate. Here, we bring under review the supposed originality of the Bolsheviks in the sphere of political economy in Soviet Russia that had these two integral components: state capitalism and the NEP.

### 3.1 State Capitalism Under the Bolshevik Rule in Soviet Russia

Lenin had a peculiar interpretation of capitalism under state control. He considered the Soviet state with the proletariat as the *ruling class* would provide a completely different interpretation of capitalism. According to Lenin, this form of capitalism necessarily would lead to "socialism" ('a rung on the ladder of history between which and the rung called socialism *there are no intermediate rungs' - Lenin).* A clear exposition of the nature of state capitalism can be found below in Lenin's arguments against the "Left Communists".[2]

> To make things even clearer, let us first of all take the most concrete example of state capitalism. Everybody knows what this example is. It is Germany. Here we have "the last word" in modern large-scale capitalist engineering and planned organization, *subordinated to Junker-bourgeois imperialism.* Cross out the words in italics, and in place of the militarist, Junker, bourgeois, imperialist *state* put *also a state*, but of a different social type, of a different class content—a *Soviet* state, that is, a proletarian state, and you will have the *sum total* of the conditions necessary for socialism.
>
> Socialism is inconceivable without large-scale capitalist engineering based on the latest discoveries of modern science. It is inconceivable without planned state organization, which keeps tens of millions of people to the strictest observance of a unified standard in production and distribution. We Marxists have always spoken of this, and it is not worth while wasting two seconds talking to people who do not understand *even* this (anarchists and a good half of the Left Socialist-Revolutionaries).
>
> At the same time socialism is inconceivable unless the proletariat is the ruler of the state. This also is ABC. And history (which nobody, except Menshevik blockheads of the first order, ever expected to bring about "complete" socialism smoothly, gently, easily and simply) has taken such a peculiar course that it *has given birth* in 1918 to two unconnected halves of socialism existing side by side like two future chickens in the single shell of international imperialism. In 1918 Germany and Russia have become the most striking embodiment of

> the material realization of the economic, the productive and the socio-economic conditions for socialism, on the one hand, and the political conditions, on the other. [Lenin, 1974b, p. 339]

Lenin's explanation of state capitalism sounds quixotic—('Cross out the words in italics, and in place of the militarist, Junker, bourgeois, imperialist *state* put *also a state*, but of a different social type, of a different class content—a *Soviet* state, that is, a proletarian state, and you will have the *sum total* of the conditions necessary for socialism.') How can the existence and supremacy of the Soviet *state* be interpreted and equated to capitalism of any variety? We have seen earlier the interpretation of such a *state* by Engels as the instrument that would place the monopoly of the means of production at the disposal of the society. ('the taking possession of the means of production in the name of society—this is, at the same time, its last independent act as a State.'–Engels). However, the actual social practices to follow from the possession of the means of production were somewhat different to Lenin. Nowhere is it mentioned that *socialism* is inconceivable with simultaneous existence and recognition of the economy based on regulations of market and exchange of social productions based on the law of *value*. The pre-eminence of the Soviet *state* with 'different class content' could only be recognized if it was able to minimize the influence of market-laws in the economy, and not the reverse—that is promotion of capitalism in deciding the laws of exchange in both national and international spheres of the economy. It did not occur to Lenin that the essential and primary pivots of capitalism are production relations based on exchange of *value,* and control over accumulation of abstract labour for further production of *value* in the society. Private profiteering *alone* does not constitute capitalism, as the "profit" in absolute terms is the component of surplus labour extracted in the society that may be appropriated by a state enjoying the monopoly right over all productive forces including deployment of human labour. Administrative rule by a certain political party or a group of parties having access and control over the means of production and with huge support of the toiling "*masses*" do not necessarily obviate or transcend these laws of exchange and accumulation in society, although they certainly create facilitating conditions for abolition of such production relations.

Lenin's fundamental argument was to interpret Russian political economy as a peculiar variety of state capitalism with the hegemony of the proletarian party at the helm of political power. He envisaged that the world revolution 'has taken such a peculiar course that it *has given birth* in 1918 to two unconnected halves of socialism existing side by side like two future chickens in the single shell of international imperialism'. According to Lenin, large-scale organized industrial production inherited from the German model of capitalist growth accompanied by the so-called "will" of the proletariat embodied in a political party (as was the experience of the Russian revolution) together were to constitute "socialism". The fallacy however remains starkly present that these two conditions, *de jure in themselves*, do not make existence of domestic market, circulation of *currency* in domestic and international business, building up the reserve of foreign exchange, establishment of international trade relations with the capitalist states, concessions to foreign investments operating in the national trade and manufacturing sphere, etc.—i.e. all the elements and facets of capitalist production relations by any means *irrelevant*. At best, the presence of large-scale industrial enterprises with a disciplined and dedicated workforce is the precondition to regulate the size and volume of the national market, and prioritize the volume of production according to the needs of the regulated market. At worst, they are the preconditions of labour conscription and forced labour camps with strictest discipline and uniformity in enactment of harsh wage-laws at the mercy of meagre social benefits from the benevolent state.

Lenin's advocacy of state capitalism as a peculiar development of capitalism that was suited to dictatorship of the proletariat in post-revolution Russia was best demonstrated by the support that Lenin received from Bukharin later. Bukharin wrote,

> In the system of state capitalism the economic subject is the *capitalist state*, the collective capitalist. In the dictatorship of the proletariat, the economic subject is the *proletarian* state, the collectively organized working class, "The proletariat organized as state power." Under state capitalism, the production process is that of the production of surplus value which falls into the hands of a capitalist class, which tries to transform this value into surplus products. Under the dictatorship of

> the proletariat the production process is a means for the planned satisfaction of social needs. The system of state capitalism is the most complete form of exploitation of the masses by a handful of oligarchs. The dictatorship of the proletariat makes any exploitation whatsoever altogether unthinkable, as it transforms collective capitalist property and its private capitalist form into collective-proletarian "property". Notwithstanding their formal similarity, these are diametrical opposites in content. This antagonism determines also the antagonism of all parts of the systems under discussion, even if formally they are similar. [Bukharin, 2003, p. 134]

It is really surprising that even Tony Cliff, the acknowledged author of the detailed analysis of state capitalism in Russia, later in the decades of the 1940s supported Bukharin's peculiar argument on 'state capitalism' that hinged on the postulate 'The dictatorship of the proletariat makes any exploitation whatsoever altogether unthinkable, as it transforms collective capitalist property and its private capitalist form into collective-proletarian "property".' While analysing the virtues of state capitalism, Tony Cliff wrote,

> Whereas under state capitalism wage labour is partially negated in that the worker is not free to choose his employer, under the dictatorship of the proletariat, wage labour is partially negated in that the workers as a collective cease to be "free" of the means of production. At the same time, in a workers' state, wage labour ceases to be a commodity. The "sale" of labour power is different from the sale of labour power under capitalism, because under a workers' state the workers as individuals do not sell their labour power but put it at their own service in their role of a collective. Labour power ceases really to be a commodity, as here the exchange takes place between the workers as individuals, and these same workers as a collective, and not between two entities which are totally independent of one another except in their exchange. Whereas state capitalism brings about the fusion of the unions with the state until they are ultimately annulled as unions, the workers' state raises the influence of the trade unions to the maximum. Whereas state capitalism signifies historically the totalitarianism of the state, a workers' state brings the highest degree of democracy society has ever known. State capitalism signifies the extreme subjegation of the working class by a capitalist class in control of the means of production. A workers' state means the suppression of the capitalists by a working class in control of the means of production. (Chapter 5) [Cliff, 1974]

We wonder, if at all 'Labour power ceases really to be a commodity, as here the exchange takes place between the workers as individuals,' in a 'workers' state', then how did the production relations still represented state capitalism with the state as the owner of the means of production and the wage-giver? Was it from some endowment of the benevolent state that the social service of 'wage' was distributed among the volunteering proletariat? *Or*, was 'wage' still the component of *value* the proletariat as a socio-economic category continued to raise? Only the exchange laws were regulated in the new labour market where the state represented the new owner and the *sole* arbitrator of the market exchanges, and *only in that way* 'state capitalism' got enshrined in the new political economy of Soviet Russia. If there is any difference in the two passages referred from these two luminaries who stood separated by the two decades, it was the substitution of the paradigm 'dictatorship of the proletariat' in Bukharin's work by 'workers' state' in Tony Cliff's work. By the 1940s, Tony Cliff must have been aware that the 'workers' state' did not exist in Russia, particularly after the Tenth Congress of the Bolshevik party and the trouncing defeat of the *Workers' Opposition group*. We wonder whether Cliff was aware of the theses of the *group* before the Tenth Congress that demanded the very rights of the 'workers' state', whose virtues such as 'a workers' state brings the highest degree of democracy society has ever known' the world has hardly ever seen even in the tumultuous period of post-revolution Russia. In that sense, the arguments of both Bukharin and Tony Cliff in support of Lenin's peculiar advocacy for state capitalism remained a pious, political wish—a mishmash of vocabulary to justify *Party* control over regimentation of the working class. Bukharin and Tony Cliff in the passages quoted above did not pose a single argument how 'state capitalism' under dictatorship of the proletariat was going to regulate market prices of commodities, distribution of processed goods, procurement of raw material for production, investment from state, and fix wage-laws given the fact these were the central issues over which the *Workers' Opposition group* wanted to assert the right of the central trade unions of Russia after the revolution.

Lenin's actual steps and exhortations, on the other hand, were far more clear than his supporters in articulating his actual expectation from 'state capitalism' in Russia. His foremost priority was rapid industrialization and growth of heavy industry in the aftermath of the Civil War. For that, his priority was to broker peace and trading with the capitalist world at large. Soviet Russia got the opportunity to speed up development of the industrial productive forces as the prospect of actual war started receding, and consequently the social basis of a new working class was strengthened. He emphasized in the same pamphlet against the "*Left* Communists",

> It has not occurred to them [*Left* Communists] that state capitalism would be a *step forward* as compared with the present state of affairs in our Soviet Republic. If in approximately six months' time state capitalism became established in our Republic, this would be a great success and a sure guarantee that within year socialism will have gained a permanently firm hold and will have become invincible in our country. [Lenin, 1974b, pp. 334-335]

Lenin and the Bolsheviks were acutely conscious of the fact that the post-revolution Russian economy was devastated. It was generally agreed among the Bolsheviks also that post-revolution Russia did not possess the material basis for "socialism". That is why Lenin repeatedly compared the economic situation of Russia with Western Europe. We have seen that he compared post-revolution Russia's economic situation with the French bourgeois revolution of 1793. At another place, he compared post-revolution Russia as "*certain* conditions prevail which correspond to those which might have existed in Britain half a century ago" [Lenin, 1974c]. Soviet Russia needed peace and stabilization of its *currency* in the international financial market to leapfrog progress in the material basis of "socialism" in the shortest possible time. Lenin had a time target of one year so that 'socialism will have gained a permanently firm hold' in Russia. We have already seen Lenin's assertion before the Fourth Congress of CI regarding stabilization of the ruble after five years of completion of Soviet rule in Russia. From the time of the Third Congress of CI in June 1921 in the opening remarks of reports and theses Lenin always dealt with the "relative equilibrium, which although extremely unstable" in the international scenario. Soviet Russia did not have to bear the human and material cost of military aggression on its frontiers after 1920. As Premier of Soviet Russia, he actively pursued diplomatic recognition of the governments of the capitalist world right from the beginning, and took an active role in commercial negotiations with the capitalists who invested in Russia in lieu of the "concessions".[3]

One major point of debate and apprehension within the ranks of the Bolsheviks was regarding the "concessions" offered to the foreign governments and industry owners in allowing investment of capital in Soviet Russia. Lenin had to offer a series of replies at different forums of the Bolsheviks and Soviet Congress to allay their fear that the Soviet government was succumbing to the pressure of the Western capitalists by allowing them "concessions" in lieu of their offer to invest in Soviet Russia. Lenin's principal arguments were twofold: the possibility of war with the Western capitalists was avoided by allowing them to invest in Russia as the diplomatic recognition of Soviet Russia by the enemy governments was axiomatic with their investments. Second, their investments in the core sectors such as in the energy sector, particularly in exploration of oil were going to catalyze manifold improvement of the instruments of production, particularly in heavy industry and for electrification. We provide below a few passages of Lenin's reply in two different forums in 1920 regarding the issue of "concession" to foreign capitalists.

Lenin delivered a report before the meeting of the Bolshevik activists in Moscow on December 6, 1920 as a form of his reply to the concerns of the activists. First, he had to reveal some sombre truths regarding the downturn of the international proletarian revolution. He said,

> Since the Second Congress of the Third International we have secured a firm foothold in the imperialist countries, not only in the sphere of ideology but also in that of organization. In all countries there are groups which are carrying on independent work and will continue to do so. That has been accomplished. But the rate, the tempo of development of the revolution in the capitalist countries is far slower than in our country. It was evident that the revolutionary movement would inevitably slow down when the nations secured peace. Therefore, without surmising as to the future, we cannot now rely on this tempo becoming rapid. We have to decide what we are to do at

> the present time. Every people lives in a state, and every state belongs to a system of states, which are in a certain system of political equilibrium in relation to one another. [Lenin, 1974d, pp. 441-442]

Then, he focused on the political significance of the "concession" that Soviet Russia could barter with the enemy governments who very recently were involved in military engagement with Soviet Russia.

> While capitalism and socialism exist side by side, they cannot live in peace: one or the other will ultimately triumph—the last obsequies will be observed either for the Soviet Republic or for world capitalism. This is some respite from war. The capitalists will seek pretexts for going to war. If they accept our proposal and agree to concessions, that will be harder for them. On the one hand, we shall have the best conditions in the event of war; on the other hand, those who want to go to war will not agree to take concessions. The existence of concessions is an economic and political argument against war. States that might go to war with us will not be able to do so if they take concessions. This will bind them. We set such a high value by this that we shall not be afraid to pay, the more so that we shall be paying from the means of production that we cannot develop. For Kamchatka we shall pay in terms of 100,000 poods of oil, taking only 2 per cent for ourselves. If we do not pay up we shall not get even two poods. This is an exorbitant price, but while capitalism exists we cannot expect a fair price from it. Yet the advantages are beyond doubt. From the angle of the danger of a collision between capitalism and Bolshevism, it can be said that concessions are a continuation of the war, but in a different sphere. [Lenin, 1974d, p. 457]

Surely, Lenin was trying to present a brave front before the activists in terming a raw barter deal of a very weak state as 'war, but in a different sphere' with much stronger enemy states those were mortally hostile to the existence of Soviet Russia. Reading this passage along with the first passage above there is no room for doubt that the hefty "concessions" was the only route available for an internationally isolated Soviet Russia to buy peace so as to strengthen its own economy. Next, we refer to Lenin's report to the Bolshevik group in the Eighth Congress of Soviets held in the same month on December 20, 1920. Here, he stressed the desperate needs of material resources for survival of Soviet Russia's economy.

> If we want to trade with foreign countries—and we do want to,

> because we realize its necessity—our chief interest is in obtaining as quickly as possible, from the capitalist countries, the means of production (locomotives, machinery, and electrical equipment) without which we cannot more or less seriously rehabilitate our industry, or perhaps may even be unable to do so at all, because the machinery needed by our factories cannot be made available. It is with the motive of extra profit that we must attract the capitalist. He will get surplus profit—well, let him have that surplus profit; we shall obtain the fundamentals that will help strengthen us; we shall stand firmly on our own feet, and shall win in the economic field. We shall have to pay up if we want to get the best machinery, etc. What are we to pay with? We still dispose of gold reserves totalling several millions. You will see from the special plan for the electrification of Russia, drawn up for several decades, that this plan, together with the additional work for the rehabilitation of industry, will involve an approximate expenditure of something like 17,000 million gold rubles. Electrification alone will require the direct expenditure of more than 1,000 million rubles in gold. We cannot cover this with our gold reserves; it is extremely undesirable and dangerous for us to export foodstuffs because we have not got sufficient for our own industry, and yet this need has to be met. In this case there is no concession project economically more suitable for us than the forests of the Far North which cover an enormous area, and where the timber is rotting away and a total loss because we are economically unable to exploit these timber reserves. Timber, however, is of tremendous value on the world market. Besides, the Far North is also convenient politically because it is an outlying border area. This concession is convenient to us both politically and economically, and we must make the best possible use of it. [Lenin, 1974e, p. 480]

While reading these passages nearly after a century has passed one must admit and bow our heads in respect before the heroic and stupendous efforts the Bolsheviks were forced to make to salvage "their socialism" in Russia in the absence of international support of the working class from the developed capitalist countries of the world. At the same time, one must be clear and put across the tragic truth this was a case of "state socialism" that Lenin was exhorting, that had very little in common with the vision of Marx and Engels about the role of *state* under dictatorship of the proletariat. We can elaborate here more on such "concessions" which the Soviet government offered to the British and American capitalists but they would now appear as dated annals from a tragic history. The Russian government could afford to offer these "concessions" to the foreign capitalists as Soviet Russia had an abundance of mineral treasure and natural resources at its disposal. It could allow these resources to be plundered by the Western capitalists in order to gain their diplomatic recognition, to buy peace with them so as to devote attention to rapid electrification, heavy industry on a large scale. This "state socialism" was the essence of Lenin's peculiar version of state capitalism with the Bolshevik party at the helm of affairs of an egalitarian state. The new working class that came out of these efforts of rapid, large-scale industrialization was a recipient, a beneficiary of the state-funded and monitored wage-laws and social services in lieu of labour conscription. We have seen in the previous Chapter how wage-laws were manipulated to the advantage of experts, the role of the trade unions were relegated to the "school for bringing up the masses"; even discriminations were introduced in regard to food rations among the workers to keep the working class under strictest control for raising labour-productivity.

The biggest fallacy here was Lenin's defence of this primitive accumulation of Russian state capital that was dictated by the needs of a weak state and underdeveloped capitalism as an original practice of "socialism" before the gatherings of CI. Lenin defended the agricultural policy of *tax in kind* as the major policy shift of Soviet Russia. He clearly admitted in his *Report on the Tactics of the RCP* [Lenin, 1972a], before the Third Congress of CI the features of 'state capitalism' in Soviet Russia and their necessity.

> Freedom to trade means freedom for capitalism, but it also means a new form of capitalism. It means that, to a certain extent we are re-creating capitalism. We are doing this quite openly. It is state capitalism. But state capitalism in a society where power belongs to capital, and state capitalism in a proletarian state, are two different concepts. In a capitalist state, state capitalism means that it is recognized by the state and controlled by it for the benefit of the bourgeoisie, and to the detriment of the proletariat. In the proletarian state, the same thing is done for the benefit of the working class, for the purpose of withstanding the as yet strong bourgeoisie, and of fighting it. It goes without saying that we must grant concessions to the foreign bourgeoisie, to foreign capital. Without the slightest

> denationalization, we shall lease mines, forests and oilfields to foreign capitalists, and receive in exchange manufactured goods, machinery, etc. And thus restore our own industry. ....
>
> We have been so ruined by seven years of war that it will take many years to restore our industry. We must pay for our backwardness and weakness, and for the lessons we are learning and must learn. Those who want to learn must pay for the tuition. ....
>
> We admit quite openly, and do not conceal the fact that concessions in the system of state capitalism mean paying tribute to capitalism. But we gain time, and gaining time means gaining everything, particularly in the period of equilibrium, when our foreign comrades are preparing thoroughly for their revolution. [Lenin, 1972a, p. 118]

It is starkly apparent from the above reference that Lenin was much more clearheaded about the role of 'state capitalism' under the Bolshevik rule than his ardent supporter Bukharin or his apologist Tony Cliff two decades later. Lenin did not mince words. One of the most important reasons that he was held in high esteem among the contemporary revolutionaries across the nations was his capacity for plain speaking, not concealing bitter facts, and objectivity in the analysis of situations that suited him for the purpose at hand. However, the problem that remains is his glaring shifts in the theoretical formulation and claims that everything he was exhorting was an original contribution to Marx's vision since his formulations were not to be found in Marx. In 1918, he was supremely confident that 'state capitalism' was going to usher "socialism" in Russia within a year provided strictest accounting and control were maintained in the production system, banks were nationalized, and industrialists were allowed to form trusts with workers in the management bodies. In 1921, he was candid before the Congress of CI regarding the fact that all the Bolsheviks were doing in the name of 'state capitalism' was to adjust to the conditions of foreign capitalists in international trade. Soviet Russia bargained hard for capital, instruments of production, technology with a blind hope that the working class in those foreign countries will rise one day against "their capitalists" so as to relieve Soviet Russia of these discriminatory and exploitative practices of international capital. For Lenin, the *only* and the fundamental difference between 'state capitalism' in Germany and Russia was his conviction that the working class was holding the state-power in Russia although all the features of capitalism were present in the contemporary reality of Russia. The macroeconomics of Soviet Russia was a controlled regime of market and exchanges operated by an artificially stabilized *currency* that was supported and incubated by the reserved gold rubles in the central bank inherited from the Tsarist regime. In fact, Lenin's formulation of "state socialism" made a crude irony of *socialism* when he found the nationalized German postal service system of the late nineteenth century to be a true example of the "socialist" economic system.[4]

It may be argued that the Bolsheviks' helplessness in adjusting to the might of international capital was borne out of isolation of Soviet Russia in the world economic system. Parallels may be drawn with the compromise and the adjustment that sections of the working class are forced to sign with their owners in countless occasions of bargains through their trade union in their isolated struggles. Sections of the working class stand defeated temporarily in their disjointed, isolated struggles against the industrialists by these numerous humiliating agreements but certainly they do not stand vanquished as a *class* so as not to measure up the strength later. We need to say and stress now forcefully when the bitter results of defeat in the guise of "victory" are so apparent that such parallels can never be drawn. Here, Lenin was justifying 'state capitalism' as the course towards "socialism", whereas in effect the Bolsheviks were laying the foundation of the edifice of bureaucratic state monopoly of capital only. He was advancing the objectives of modern industrialized nation-building that was ruined by the war. His motto was to force Soviet Russia rushing in competition with the advancement of technology in developed capitalist countries. It would be pertinent here to read what Eugen Verga, the acknowledged economist of CI in its formative years, had to say in his book *Economic Problems of the Proletarian Dictatorship*, published by CI in1921. Paul Mattick[5] quoted several times the following passage from Verga,

> The danger exists that Russia may be cut out as the motive power of the international revolution... There are Communists in Russia who have grown tired of waiting for the European revolution and wish to make the best of their national isolation... With a Russia which would

> regard the social revolution of the other countries as a matter with which it had no concern, the capitalist countries would at any rate be able to live in peaceful neighbourliness. I am far from believing that such a bottling up of revolutionary Russia would be able to stop the progress of the world revolution. But that progress would be slowed down. [Mattick, 1935]

The most important instance of this nation-building exercise was the general electrification plan of Soviet Russia. Lenin devoted huge attention to this plan and to him the future of "socialism" in Russia was mortally bound to this plan. So much so, he devoted considerable space of his reports in the Third Congress of CI to this electrification plan as the "material basis of socialism". He wrote,

> A large-scale machine industry capable of reorganizing agriculture is the only material basis that is possible for socialism. But we cannot confine ourselves to this general thesis. It must be made more concrete. Large-scale industry based on the latest achievements of technology and capable of reorganizing agriculture implies electrification of the whole country. We had to undertake the scientific work of drawing up such a plan for the electrification of the R.S.F.S.R. [Russian Soviet Federative Socialist Republic] and we have accomplished it. With the cooperation of over two hundred of the best scientists, engineers and agronomists in Russia, this work has now been completed; it was published in a large volume and, as a whole, endorsed by the Eighth All-Russia Congress of Soviets in December 1920. Arrangements have now been made to convene an all-Russia congress of electrical engineers in August 1921 to examine this plan in detail, before it is given final government endorsement.[34] The execution of the first part of the electrification scheme is estimated to take ten years, and will require about 370 million man days.
>
> In 1918, we had eight newly erected power stations (with a total capacity of 4,757 kw); in 1919, the figures rose to 36 (total capacity of 1,648 kw), and in 1920, it rose to 100 (total capacity of 8,669 kw). [Lenin, 1972b, p. 87]

We quoted the above passage at length to show the feverish pitch, the superhuman effort that was made in Soviet Russia to achieve hundred per cent increase in the installed capacity of electricity generation in a span of only three years (the figure in the bracket corresponding to the year 1919 is obviously wrong), very near to achieve Lenin's previous prediction of 'sure guarantee' to "socialism" within a year.

One can always argue in pointing out what was wrong in it? Nobody can possibly dispute the imperative need of intensive planning for harmonious existence of direct producers' cooperative society on a countrywide scale. *Socialism* cannot be conceived as a society like the Brownian motion of gaseous molecules in a test tube. Even the organic composition of beehives represents a highly organized, disciplined conglomeration of the honey bees. The collective of migrant birds cross thousands of miles from one continent to another in a disciplined, focused direction of guidance. Here, we are considering building of a *new* human society from scratch with very little material basis at hand, and limited material resources from their class brethren in the more developed and organized nations. Was Lenin not citing the highly democratic manner of collective decision-making as the electrification plan was endorsed 'by the Eighth All-Russia Congress of Soviets' and in the later years by the 'all-Russia congress of electrical engineers'?

Of course, all these arguments are right in their places. In fact, all these arguments pose the poignant problems underlying the conscious effort towards a *new* civilization called *socialism or communism*. There still remain great challenges before the international proletariat and the teeming millions of working people of the world who are searching for a just, equitable, and humane society other than, and alternative to the modern *barbarism* in the name of civilization that capitalism continues to offer for centuries. At this juncture, we can only say and repeat with conviction that all these superhuman efforts of the Bolsheviks and the Soviets were involuntarily (one may even say against the wishes of many of them) meant to augment primitive accumulation of bureaucratic state capital.

As the years progressed, Lenin's reports brought out clearly the fact that all the macroeconomic features of 'state capitalism' in Russia were nothing other than state-sponsored capitalism. His review after five years of completion of Soviet power in Russia at the Fourth Congress of CI retained the words "the prospects of the world revolution" in the title, but the whole report contained nothing of that sort. Rather, he dwelt at length on the urgent need of accumulation for subsidizing the heavy industry from the state reserve in Soviet Russia. He wrote,

> At the present moment, however, our heavy industry is still in great difficulties. But I think that the decisive circumstance is that we are already in a position to save a little. And we shall go on saving. We must economise now though it is often at the expense of the population. We are trying to reduce the state budget, to reduce staff in our government offices.... We are economising in all things, even in schools. We must do this because we know that unless we save heavy industry, unless we restore it, we shall not be able to build up an industry at all; and without an industry we shall go under as an independent country. We realize this very well....
>
> Heavy industry needs state subsidies. If we are not able to provide them, we shall be doomed as a civilized state, let alone as a socialist state. In this respect we have taken a determined step. We have began to accumulate the funds that we need to put heavy industry on its feet. True, the sum we have obtained so far barely exceeds twenty million gold rubles; but at any rate this sum is available, and it is earmarked exclusively for the purpose of reviving our heavy industry. [Lenin, 1972c, p. 139]

In this Section, our aim was to critically review the Bolshevik attempts to reorganize industrial production while standing alone and isolated over the ruins of economy after the WWI. The Bolsheviks were compelled to offer huge "concessions" to the foreign capital for primary accumulation of capital in terms of heavy industry. These actual, concrete practices revealed the programme of national reconstruction for reviving the industrial economy. Lenin interpreted this practice of 'state capitalism' under the rule of the Bolshevik party as equivalent to dictatorship of the proletariat and transition to "socialism". The programme of industrial reorganization was actually congruent with his justification of the existence of the state in "socialism" in *The State and Revolution* that we discussed in detail in Section 2.4. We are now going to discuss the NEP, and show how together with the NEP the post-revolution Russian economy was made to fit for a totalitarian interpretation of "socialism" that never occurred in Marx's vision. On the other hand, we are going to show subsequently in this Chapter that the interpretation of 'state capitalism' as the immediate step to the 'rung called socialism' was never challenged even by Lenin's contemporary critics. On the contrary, 'state capitalism' was accepted as the political economy of transition to "socialism"; it remained the professed theory of "socialism" among the leading theorists of all varieties of strands of *Leninism* till the decade of the 1970s.

### 3.2 The NEP and State Capitalism

The other important (probably the most important) argument of Lenin in favour of 'state capitalism' was the new Soviet agricultural policy, the NEP adopted after February 1921. It was named "New" as this was *not* the economic policy of the Bolsheviks on the eve of the revolution, rather the results of an afterthought that Lenin offered facing the concrete reality of rural Russia. We have seen earlier Lenin harping before the delegates of CI, 'But theory and practice are two different things,'—in the aftermath of Civil War, typhus and famine that ravaged the Russian countryside in 1919-1921. Lenin articulated before the Fourth Congress of CI,

> In the spring of that year [1921] we decide unanimously—I did not observe any considerable disagreement among us on the question—to adopt the New Economic Policy. [Lenin, 1972c, p. 135]

However, Lenin's broad explanation on the background of the NEP was in the Third Congress of CI. While introducing the reasons of the NEP in his *Report on the Tactics of RCP* before the delegates of CI in the Third Congress, Lenin admitted,

> I have already said that in the spring of 1921 the most appalling want caused by the fodder shortage prevailed among peasantry, which constitutes the majority of our population. .... The condition of the working class is extremely hard. It is suffering horribly. Those who have more political understanding, however, realize that in the interest of the dictatorship of the working class we must make tremendous effort to help the peasants at any price. The vanguard of the working class has realized this, but in that vanguard there are still people who cannot understand it, and who are too weary to understand it." [Lenin, 1972a, p. 117]

The candidness of Lenin's observation regarding the sufferings of the working class in Soviet power centres like Moscow, Petrograd and other major cities cannot be overlooked here. We may also note in passing that this candidness and honesty in acknowledging the facts of life became rarer and rarer in the discourses of CI after these formative years when posing questions about the Russian Section of CI became an anathema.[6]

During the Fourth Congress of CI, Lenin enumerated five categories of production relations in Russian agriculture. These categories came straight out from his counter to "*Left* Communists" in May 1918 [Lenin, 1974b]. He wrote,

> Let us enumerate these elements:
> 1. patriarchal, i.e. to a considerable extent natural, peasant farming.
> 2. small commodity production (this includes the majority of those peasants who sell their grain).
> 3. private capitalism.
> 4. state capitalism.
> 5. socialism. [pp. 335-336]

Here, we cannot but note here that 'socialism' in agriculture was the least significant component to Lenin even after five years of the revolution. In fact, we have seen during his review at the Fourth Congress while defending the NEP he mentioned, 'we were fully aware that in Russia we had patriarchal agriculture, i.e. the most primitive form of agriculture alongside the socialist form.' The first three elements of production relations, in any case, were carried over from the pre-revolutionary period of semi-feudal estate-based agricultural society. Lenin considered small commodity production as the principal and dominant form of agricultural production among the five elements cited above. ("The question arises: what elements predominate? Clearly, in a small-peasant country, the petty bourgeoisie element predominates, for the great majority of those working in the land are small commodity producers." [Lenin, 1974b, p. 336]) However, considering the prevailing situation in Russia, the bulwark that Lenin proposed against this preponderance of small commodity production in agriculture was not 'socialism' but 'state capitalism'. He explained in 1918,

> It is not state capitalism that is at war with socialism, but the petty bourgeoisie plus private capitalism fighting together against both state capitalism and socialism. The petty bourgeoisie oppose *every* kind of state interference, accounting and control, whether it be state capitalist or state socialist. This is an absolutely fact of reality, and the root of the economic mistakes of the "Left Communists" is that they have failed to understand it. [Lenin, 1974b, p. 336]

This was the first time as early as 1918 after the revolution we find Lenin falling back on the paradigm 'state socialist'. The open question here is how Lenin was differentiating the impact and influence of the two paradigms 'state capitalist' *or* 'state socialist' in agricultural production relations? Lenin openly concluded before the international delegates of CI on completion of five years of the revolution,

> What gave rise to this peculiar, and for us, of course, very unpleasant, situation? The reason for it was that in our economic offensive we had run too far ahead, that we have not provided ourselves with adequate resources, that the masses sensed what we ourselves were not then able to formulate consciously but what we admitted soon after, a few weeks later, namely that the direct transition to purely socialist forms, to purely socialist distribution, was beyond our available strength, and that if we were unable to effect a retreat so as to confine ourselves to easier tasks, we would face disaster. [Lenin, 1972c, p. 134]

Not only in one place, during the Third Congress of CI where he explained the NEP, Lenin's reasoning highlighted the dire necessity to revive capitalism in agriculture by state intervention.

> And so, *our economic policy was changed*; the tax in kind superseded the requisitions. This was not invented in one stroke. ....The important thing is that we changed our economic policy, yielding to exclusively practical considerations and impelled by necessity. A bad harvest, fodder shortage and lack of fuel—all, of course, have a decisive influence on the economy as a whole, including the peasant economy. If the peasantry goes on strike, we get no firewood, and if we get no firewood, the factories will have to be idle. [Lenin, 1972a, p. 115]

Lenin's own analysis and admissions presented above by all means show 'socialism' was of minuscule existence in Russian agriculture after the NEP, and the fifth element in his enumeration was cited *only* for consolation of the Bolsheviks and the delegates assembled in the Congress of CI. Still the question remains what mode of exchange this 'socialism' element actually was that Lenin found running 'too far ahead'? To be *honest* to history, it was forcible seizure of grains by the state in the name of cementing the alliance between the proletariat and the peasantry.

In the first phase of revolution during the seizure of power in

October 1917 to the spring of 1918 when the peasant "*masses*" by virtue of the Second Decree of the first Soviet Government[7] got the first right of the land they tilled, Lenin referred to this mode of exchange as "the military alliance between the proletariat in the R.S.F.S.R." [Lenin, 1972b]. The basis of the alliance was

> The peasants received from the workers' state all the land and were given protection against the landowners and the kulaks; the workers have been receiving from the peasants loans of food supplies until large-scale industry is restored. [pp. 84-85]

It is interesting that Lenin took the confidence of the peasantry to the Soviet Government as 'loans of food supplies' granted. In reality, large-scale seizure of grains was the need of the hour for the columns of the Red Army whose formations moved in floating encounters with the white army raised by 'the landowners and the kulaks' in Russia's countryside. At another place in the same Third Congress of CI, Lenin wrote categorically about large-scale seizure of grains under the pretext of the primitive military alliance of the proletariat and the peasantry.

> The peasants gave their produce to the Red Army and received from the latter assistance in protecting their possessions. This is always forgotten by the heroes of the Second International, who like Otto Bauer, totally fail to understand the actual situation. [Lenin, 1972b, p. 114]

Although Otto Bauer, the prominent leader of the Austrian SDP and 'hero of the Second International' failed 'to understand the actual situation' his comrade-in arms Karl Kautsky, the failed authority of German "Marxism" could realize the gravity of the situation. In his criticism of the Bolshevik terror tactics in rural Russia, Kautsky had to concede to the huge, fiery, revolutionary appetite of the Russian landless, poor peasantry that devoured the centuries-old property relations in the Russian countryside in the flames of the agrarian revolution. In fact, that was the primary reason the Bolsheviks and Soviet Russia in their initial days of holding state-power could withstand the military onslaught of the white army that was aided by the armed intervention of fourteen capitalist governments of Europe. Kautsky wrote,

> The Bolsheviks won the peasants over to their side, by introducing

> anarchy in the country, and by allowing every community to have a free hand; so that the destruction of these estates went on in the most primitive fashion, with technical loss and the destruction of many means of production. In return, however, the peasants allowed the Bolsheviks a completely free hand in the towns in which they had already likewise won over the working classes. [Kautsky, 1919, p. 82]

Such a military alliance in any case could not last long; in fact it cannot be said to be a proper economic relation of social exchange although Lenin harped on those contemporary revolutionary events as 'loans' from the peasantry.

The second phase was from May 1918 when the Soviet government introduced the terms of "socialist" exchange for agricultural production. That was in Lenin's parlance, "the surplus appropriation system" [Lenin, 1972b]. In actuality, it was the monopoly right of the state over the surplus grain production. While formally retreating from this policy of grain monopoly of the state in his text [Lenin, 1972a], Lenin provided the broad contours of this policy during the period of *War Communism*.

> Under this peculiar War Communism we actually took from the peasant all his surpluses—and sometimes even a part of his necessaries —to meet the requirements of the army and sustain the workers. Most of it we took on loan, for paper money. [Lenin, 1973b, p. 342]

We have already seen that Lenin admitted such market-less exchange was beyond the strength of the Soviet economy. As the facts stood in history, he was very soon advocating retreat from this 'suicidal' policy in the form of the *tax in kind* that was the basis of the new agricultural policy (NEP) of Soviet Russia. Considering the alternatives before the Soviet government he wrote,

> One way is to try to prohibit entirely, to put the lock on all development of private, non-state exchange, i.e. trade, i.e. capitalism, which is inevitable with millions of small producers. But such a policy will be foolish and suicidal for the party that tried to apply it. It would be foolish because it is economically impossible. It would be suicidal because the party that tried to apply it would meet the inevitable disaster....
>
> The alternative (and this is the only sensible and the last *possible* policy) is not to try to prohibit or put the lock on the development of capitalism, but to channel it into *state capitalism*. This is economically

> possible, for state capitalism exists—in varying form or degree - wherever there are elements of unrestricted trade and capitalism in general. [Lenin, 1973b, p. 344]

To make matters more comprehensible to the readers, we quote below a few passages from a recent work that gives a graphic picture of the details about the reality of economic transactions in rural Russia during this period of *War Communism*.

> War communism began with a grain monopoly. But it broadened to include a comprehensive range of state controls on the economy. It aimed to abolish private trade, to nationalize all large-scale industry, to militarize labour in essential industries, and at its height, in 1920, to replace money with universal rationing by the state. Because it was a model for the Stalinist economy it is important to explain its origins and decide where it fits into the revolution's history. ....
>
> The root of the crisis was the peasantry's reluctance to sell foodstuffs for paper money where there was nothing they could buy with it. The peasants reduced production, stored their surpluses, used their grain to fatten up their cattle, or sold it to black-market traders from the towns. Townsmen travelled to the countryside to trade with the peasants. They left with bags of clothes and household goods to sell or exchange in the rural markets and returned with bags of food. Workers traded tools they had stolen from factories, or manufactured simple items, such as axes, ploughs, primus stoves or cigarette lighters to barter with the peasants. The railways were paralysed these armies of 'bagmen'. The Orel station, a major junction between Moscow and the agricultural south, had 3,000 bagmen pass through it every day. Many of them travelled in armed brigades with hijacked trains.
>
> The Bolsheviks announced their grain monopoly on 9 May. All the peasants' surplus harvest became state property. Armed brigades went into villages to requisition grain. When they found none (because there was no surpluses) they assumed it was being hidden by the 'kulaks'—the phantom class of 'capitalist' peasants invented by the Bolsheviks—and a 'war for grain' began." [Figes, 2014]

It would not be out of context here to refer to Bettelheim, the staunch *Leninist* who was aware of the actual status of the economy under *War Communism* in 1919-20 in Moscow, the capital of Soviet Russia. He wrote (some fifty years before the above reference),

> It is necessary indeed, to emphasize that even during "war communism" the disappearance of commodity exchanges was more

> formal than real. In every town there were in fact places where illegal traffic was carried on almost openly, since it was tolerated by police. An example was Sukharevka Square in Moscow, a name which even became the word commonly used in Russian to mean "black market". The scale of this illegal traffic was such that in 1919-1920 the official distribution of foodstuff in the towns covered, generally speaking, no more than 25-40 per cent of the calories needed by the inhabitants.[16] [Bettelheim, 1977, p. 462]

By all means, it will be highly naive to consider that the Bolsheviks were unaware of all these features of most unscrupulous norms of commodity exchange under the "socialist" rule. The actual reality of economic exchanges in the domestic markets of Russia was in sharp contrast with the vision of *socialist* exchanges that Lenin had in mind even though it was primitive and wishy-washy. Lenin's specific vision on the ideal *socialist* agrarian economy was of course out of place in the then Soviet Russia considering the fact that the very material basis of *socialism* was missing there. We bring here this contrast more so as to understand what distinction he made between these "state socialist" measures with 'state capitalism' in agriculture. Lenin delivered a report on *tax in kind* among the closed quarters of the Bolshevik activists in Moscow just after the Tenth Congress of the Bolshevik party in April 1920 where he had much more distinctive appreciation of the two paradigms. He mentioned,

> In the event of a workers' revolution in a country with a predominantly peasant population, with the factories, works and railways taken over by the working class, what, in essence, should be the economic relations between the working class and the peasantry? They should obviously be the following: the workers producing in the factories and works, which now belong to them, all that is necessary for the country—and that means also for the peasants, who constitute the majority of the population—should transport all these things on their railroads and river vessels and deliver them to the peasants, in return for the surplus agricultural produce. This is absolutely obvious and hardly requires detailed explanation although it is constantly forgotten in the tax discussions. But it should be borne in mind, because if we are to explain the significance of the tax in kind, which is only a transitional measure, we must have a clear understanding of what we want to achieve. What I have said makes it clear that we do not want the peasants' products to be delivered to the workers' state as appropriations of surplus grain, or a tax. We want them in exchange

> for all the goods the peasants need delivered to them by our transport system. We must have such an arrangement. It is a basis for the economy of a country which has adopted socialism. [Lenin, 1973c, pp. 287-288]

Clearly this vision of 'socialism' did not fit at all in 'the surplus-appropriation system' that was carried on, ruthlessly fought for by the Soviet power throughout the *War Communism* period. The important point we want to highlight here is these measures of grain monopoly, forceful seizure by the state in lieu of 'paper money' were for the dire need of feeding the urban working "*masses*" and the Red Army; they were *not* meant to be 'socialism' even for the poor peasants (leave alone the middle peasants, the most predominant constituent of agricultural producers who were Lenin's main concern for Soviet power in rural society). It will not be out of place to record from the Editors' note at the end of the said report [Lenin,1973c] about the fate of the *poor peasants' committees* that were formed to usher 'socialism' in Russian rural society.

> [91]*The Poor Peasants' Committees* were set up under the June 11, 1918 decree of the All-Russia Central Executive Committee, "On the Organization and Supply of Poor Peasants". They were to take stock of the food stored on peasant farms; to uncover surplus food on kulak farms, and to help the Soviet food supply bodies in requisitioning such surpluses and distributing them among the poor peasants. They were also to distribute farming machines, manufactured goods, etc. The committees actually became organs of the proletarian dictatorship in the villages. Their activity embraced all spheres of work and signified the further development of the socialist revolution in the countryside. At the end of 1918, after they had fulfilled their tasks, the committees were merged with volost and village Soviets." [Lenin, 1973c, p. 551]

We record in jest that this English edition of *Lenin's Collected Works* (LCW) was first published in 1965 from Soviet Russia. Therefore, it was innocuously observed, 'At the end of 1918, after they had fulfilled their tasks, the committees were merged with volost and village Soviets.' In actuality, these committees were dissolved as we have seen from Lenin's confession above, while beating a hasty retreat after facing the peasant uprisings against the policy of monopoly right of the state over surplus grain. Lenin admitted in pithy terms, 'It would be foolish because it is economically impossible. It would be suicidal because the party that tried to apply it would meet with inevitable disaster.'

If 'socialism' was a rare presence in Soviet agriculture, then how are we to understand the paradigm 'state capitalism' in Russian agriculture that was the *pin-hole camera* for Lenin to reach "socialism", '(and this is the only sensible and the last *possible* policy)'? We must say here that Lenin's interpretation of 'state capitalism' in agriculture, the cornerstone of the NEP was the worst case of *self-deception*, a case of relentlessly running after the ghost of capitalism to drive it out of rural Russia while at the same time professing the necessity of reviving capitalism in the agricultural economy.

While addressing the Third Congress of CI Lenin declared on July 5, 1921,

> Freedom to trade means freedom for capitalism, but it also means a new form of capitalism. It means that, to a certain extent we are re-creating capitalism. We are doing this quite openly. It is state capitalism. [Lenin, 1972a, p. 118]

Nearly at the same time, on April 21, 1921 his pamphlet *Tax in Kind* was published.[8] Lenin concluded the pamphlet by saying,

> The tax in kind is a transition from War Communism to a regular socialist exchange of products....
>
> The extreme ruin rendered more acute by the crop failure in 1920 has made this transition urgently necessary owing to the fact that it was impossible to restore large-scale industry rapidly. Hence, the first thing to do is to improve the condition of the peasants. The means are the tax in kind, the development of exchange between agriculture and industry, and the development of small industry.
>
> Exchange is freedom of trade; it is capitalism. It is useful to us inasmuch as it will help us overcome the dispersal of the small producer, and to a certain degree combat the evils of bureaucracy; to what extent this can be done will be determined by practical experience. The proletarian power is in no danger, as long as the proletariat firmly holds power in its hands, and has full control of transport and large-scale industry. [Lenin, 1973b, p. 364]

It is strange that in the same breath, in the same paragraph quoted above, Lenin justified both 'state capitalism' and "socialism" together by the policy of *tax in kind*. It requires now no more explanation that during the *War Communism* period the exchange of products between the agricultural producers and the Soviet state was no *communism* at all. Even if someone insists on stressing this to be a "communist" production relation it was posing social and economic disaster threatening the very existence of the Soviet state. Therefore, according to Lenin, for the agricultural society to ascend to "regular socialist exchange of products", it required revival of capitalist production relations between agriculture and industry. He mentioned, 'The means are the tax in kind, the development of exchange between agriculture and industry', and these exchanges were to be determined by norms of capitalist production relations. There was absolutely no meaning in the statement, 'The tax in kind is a transition from *War Communism* to a regular socialist exchange of products.' Eventually if we do not want to reduce the paradigms into plain and simple demagogy.

Our question here is regarding Lenin's second assertion in the above paragraph ('Exchange is freedom of trade'): what were the attributes of these capitalist exchanges under the NEP? What were the attributes of the state capitalist exchanges, that is between the proletarian state and the agricultural producers that distinguished the production relations as capitalist, and not 'socialist'? It is extremely surprising that in the whole pamphlet [Lenin, 1973b], or, in his report [Lenin, 1973c] Lenin never mentioned any of the attributes of capitalism, such as "market", "price", "circulation of money", "wage", "profit" for the agriculturalists who were permitted to 'trade' or 'exchange' their products to the state after deducting the 'tax in kind'. Rather, Lenin insisted on writing of the 'concession' and 'surplus' as economic categories of exchange. Even a man posing to be blind with eyes awake will not agree that Lenin did not understand the fundamental basis of capitalist trade is exchange of commodities at "prices" fixed by the market. That "profit" is the part of surplus *value* that the owner of the commodity derives from the market in case he is not free from any other means of production other than his labour. Not only did Lenin maintain complete silence about the capitalist attributes of exchanges in trade, he was actually advocating barter exchanges in the name of 'state capitalism'. Let us see the instructions from Lenin about the operative part of 'state capitalism' to the cooperative societies of small commodity producers. He wrote,

> The cooperatives are also a form of state capitalism, but a less simple one; its outline is less distinct, it is more intricate and therefore creates greater practical difficulties for the government. The small commodity producers' cooperatives (and it is these, and not the workers' co-operatives, that we are discussing as the predominant and typical form in a small-peasant country) inevitably give rise to petty-bourgeois, capitalist relations, facilitate their development, push the small capitalists into the foreground and benefit them most. It cannot be otherwise, since the small proprietors predominate, and exchange is necessary and possible. In Russia's present conditions, freedom and rights for the cooperative societies mean freedom and rights for capitalism. It would be stupid or criminal to close our eyes to this obvious truth.
>
> But, unlike private capitalism, "cooperative" capitalism under the Soviet system is a variety of state capitalism, and as such it is advantageous and useful for us at the present time—in certain measure, of course. Since the tax in kind means the free sale of surplus grain (over and above that taken in the form of the tax), we must exert every effort to direct this development of capitalism—for a free market is development of capitalism—into the channels of co-operative capitalism. [Lenin, 1973b, p. 347]

So, the cooperatives of the small peasants were not free to sell their 'surplus grain' in the market with free movement of 'prices', rather they were supposed to exchange this produce in a barter deal with 'food workers' of the Soviet state. Lenin had to write the following concrete directives regarding exchanges 'between industry and agriculture',

> Hitherto the food supply worker has known only one fundamental instruction: collect 100 per cent of the grain appropriations. Now he has another instruction: collect 100 per cent of the tax in the shortest possible time and then collect another 100 per cent in exchange for the goods of large-scale and small industry. Those who collect 75 per cent of the tax and 75 per cent (of the second hundred) in exchange for the goods of large-scale *and small* industry will be doing more useful work of national importance than those who collect 100 per cent of the tax and 55 per cent (of the second hundred) by means of exchange....
>
> It should be the primary task of every regional economic centre

> and economic conference of the gubernia executive committees immediately to organize various experiments, or systems of "exchange" for the surplus stocks remaining after the tax in kind has been paid. In a few months' time practical results must be obtained for comparison and study. Local or imported salt; paraffin oil from the nearest town; the handicraft wood-working industry; handicrafts using local raw materials and producing certain, perhaps not very important, but necessary and useful, articles for the peasants; "green coal" (the utilization of small local water power resources for electrification), and so on and so forth—all this must be brought into play in order to stimulate exchange between industry and agriculture at all costs. [Lenin, 1973b, pp. 353-354]

We are now perplexed to ask where is 'trade'? Lenin was advocating for taxing the agricultural producer in the form of grain without compensation, and also at the same time, he was demanding the rest of the grain to be in state possession in exchange for the articles the peasants required to be provided by the 'food workers' of the state. Where was the "profit" of the cooperative societies of the 'middle peasants' that they may reinvest further in agricultural production? What was to be understood by Lenin's statement before the delegates of CI, 'It means that, to a certain extent we are re-creating capitalism.'? Was there at all any money circulation in these capitalist exchanges, was there any aspect of loans that these cooperative societies of 'middle peasants' took from banks even with nominal interest to augment production? Who decided the rates for exchange of these items and how? After all, we cannot say what Lenin had in mind was the medieval barter economy prevalent at that time between the traders of Samarkand with the traders of Bukhara in Uzbekistan! He was writing about the trading of grains from the 'middle peasants' of Ukraine, the granary of R.S.F.S.R. to the Soviet state. In the report to the Bolshevik activists [Lenin, 1973c] he mentioned this aspect very clearly regarding the analysis of class forces in Ukraine.

> Now, in conclusion, let me explain how this policy can be reconciled with the communist standpoint and how it has come about that the communist Soviet power is promoting a free market.
>
> Is it good from the standpoint of communism? To answer this question we must make a careful examination of the changes that have taken place in peasant farming. First, we witnessed the assault

> of the whole of the peasantry on the rule of the landowners, who were fought both by the poor peasants and the kulaks, although, of course, their motives were different: the kulaks wanted to take the land away from the landowners to develop their own farms. That was when it became clear that the kulaks and the poor peasants had divergent interests and aims. In the Ukraine, this divergence of interests is still much more in evidence than it is over here. The poor peasants could derive very little direct benefit from the transfer of land from the landowners to themselves, because they had neither the materials nor the implements. We find the poor peasants organizing to prevent the kulaks from seizing the land taken away from the landowners. The Soviet government helped the Poor Peasants' Committees that sprang up in Russia and in the Ukraine.[2] As a result, the middle peasants have become the predominant element in the rural areas. We know this from statistics, and everyone who lives in the country knows it from his own observations. The extremes of kulak and poor have been rounded off, and the majority of the population have come closer to the status of the middle peasant. If we want to raise the productivity of our peasant farming we must reckon chiefly with the middle peasant. The Communist Party has had to shape its policy accordingly. [Lenin, 1973c, pp. 294-295]

If one looks into the above analysis of the strength of the class forces in the agricultural society of Ukraine the *self-deception* in Lenin is very apparent. Lenin clearly understood that revival of the agricultural economy depended upon 'the middle peasants' given the fact the Soviet state could not leverage the rich peasants or the kulaks towards 'socialism'. At the same time, he could not allow a market-based economy to be the driving force for this revival even though he talked of 'free market', 'freedom of trade', etc. Lenin always stressed that agricultural tax to be paid in *kind*, and not in rubles, the abstract medium of money circulation. He was actually not meaning it to be a *tax* in the economic sense of the category, it was in reality a *levy*, the 'middle peasant's tribute to the state in lieu of the freedom to produce grains or other items of agricultural products. On the other hand, by the *Decrees* of the Second and Third All-Russia Congress of Soviets[9] land was not a *commodity*; it could not be rented, nor could land or any rural pastures such as forests, water bodies, etc. be sold or purchased after the landowners' estates were demolished in the revolutionary storm. The idea of the NEP finally boiled down to foreclosing the avenues of capital formation and expansion in the rural economy while simultaneously advocating barter exchanges of the agricultural products to the state.

To buttress our above argument of *self-deception* we may conclude this discussion on the nature of political economy of the NEP by commenting on Lenin's appreciation of agricultural *tax*. Lenin wrote,

> What, then, is the tax in kind? It is a measure in which we see something of the past and something of the future. A tax is something the state takes from the population without compensation. If it is fixed at approximately one half of last year's rate of surplus-grain appropriations it alone will not suffice for the workers' state to maintain its Red Army, the whole of industry, and the whole of the non-agricultural population, and to develop production and relations with foreign countries, whose assistance in the way of machinery and equipment we need. On the one hand, the workers' state wants to rely on the tax at approximately one-half the surplus-grain appropriations rate, and on the other, on the exchange of manufactured goods for the surplus products of peasant farming. Hence, the tax contains a moiety of the old appropriation system and a moiety of that which is the only correct system, namely, the exchange of the manufactures of big socialist factories for the products of peasant farming through the medium of food supply organizations of the working-class state and workers' and peasants' cooperative societies. [Lenin, 1973c, pp. 288-289]

There were strong reasons behind such glaring inconsistency and misrepresentation of 'free trade' in Lenin's formulation of 'state capitalism'. Lenin's proposition actually meant very controlled and regulated exchanges of agricultural products with industry-produced items, often being advised to the extent of barter exchanges with the state. The state held the monopoly right of deciding all the rules of such exchanges between urban and rural social needs. While Lenin was writing about barter exchanges between the agricultural producers and the Soviet state he was clear headed enough to bring in the issue of support prices of grain as early as August 2, 1918 in his *theses* on the food question. In the *Decree* on *tax in kind* from the Council of People's Commissars issued on October 26, 1918[10], Lenin clearly mentioned the support prices to be offered to the 'middle peasants' for grain procurement, and the *tax in kind* to be imposed on rich peasants, the prices to be fixed on industrial items which were to be exchanged against surplus grain and agricultural products.

> (2) I suggest raising the grain prices to 30 rubles a pood, and correspondingly (and even more) to raise prices on manufactured and other goods.
>
> (4) To enact several very urgent measures for *requisitioning all* the products of urban industry for exchange (and put up their prices after requisitioning to a *greater* extent than the rise in grain prices).
>
> (5)To preface the decree on grain price rise with a popular elucidation of the measure connected with the trade exchange and the establishment of the correct correlation between the prices of grain, manufactured and other goods.
>
> (8) To impose a tax *in kind,* in grain, on the rich peasants. This category could include those whose amount of grain (including the new harvest) is double or more than double their own consumption (taking into account needs for their family, lives to and sowing).

This is to be designated as an *income* and property tax and made progressive. [Lenin, 1974f, pp. 45-46]

Even though the *Decree* was issued by the Soviet government in the winter of 1918 it was not made effective for two principal reasons. The first was the dire need to seize and confiscate all grain production in the name of *War Communism,* and to check the rampant black marketing and profiteering in the absence of any stable *currency* for economic transactions. The second reason was more related to the internal strife within the Bolsheviks; there was staunch opposition from the "*Left* Communists" that Lenin and his supporters faced in their effort to bring in money circulation in the agrarian economy. The opposition of the "*Left* Communists" was a deterrent as they were looking for the abolition of the market-based economy in 'socialism'. Therefore, Lenin had to resort to do some fine act of balancing between the two contradictory pulls in his pamphlets [Lenin, 1974b], [Lenin, 1973b]. He could not openly bring the market categories of 'free trade' so as not to antagonise the "*Left* Communists" beyond a point. At the same time, he was determined to revive small peasant farming that had no other option but to pursue the capitalist economy under the regulations of the Soviet government. Therefore, he had to couch his formulations in such a way that was neither "socialism" nor capitalism in their classical understanding of the paradigms. Lenin wrote in his pamphlet [Lenin, 1973b],

> Can the Soviet state and the dictatorship of the proletariat be combined with state capitalism? Are they compatible?
>
> Of course they are. This is exactly what I argued in May 1918. I hope I had proved it then. I had also proved that state capitalism is a step forward compared with the small proprietor (both small-patriarchal and petty-bourgeois) element. Those who compare state capitalism only with socialism commit a host of mistakes, for in the present political and economic circumstances it is essential to compare state capitalism also with petty-bourgeois production.
>
> The whole problem—in theoretical and practical terms—is to find the correct methods of directing the development of capitalism (which is to some extent and for some time inevitable) into the channels of state capitalism, and to determine how we are to hedge it about with conditions to ensure its transformation into socialism in the near future. [p. 345]

We have discussed the issue of *tax in kind* along with 'state capitalism' for the Soviet agricultural policies in somewhat detail to show that it remained a particular, vexed question of profound importance that Lenin and the Bolsheviks refused to recognize and realize in their self–deceptory masking of the problem. At one point Lenin realized, 'In order to abolish classes it is necessary, to abolish the difference between factory worker and peasant, to make *workers of all of them*. This cannot be done all at once. This task is incomparably more difficult and will of necessity take a long time.'—but that was an incomplete, unfinished writing. On the other hand, he was asserting 'Those who compare state capitalism only with socialism commit a host of mistakes,' although his arguments themselves represented a bundle of confusion over the degree and necessity of commodity exchanges under the dictatorship of the proletariat. Neither were the Bolsheviks admitting capitalism to have free play, yet they were looking for rapid development of the productive forces for both agriculture and industry within the controlled boundaries of capitalist production relations. On the one hand, the "*Left* Communists" were not prepared to realize the reality of the absence of 'material basis' to usher *socialism*, nor was Lenin prepared to concede that 'state capitalism' is *no barter economy*. That he expected 'state capitalism' to 'hedge it about with conditions to ensure its transformation into socialism in the near future' [Lenin, 1973b] meant nothing in terms of concrete economic or production relations, and created only more confusion among the Bolshevik ranks.

It is also interesting to note that in all these documents on 'state capitalism' produced by Lenin [Lenin, 1974b], [Lenin, 1973b], [Lenin, 1973c] there was no more mention of *class struggle* in agriculture. There was no mention of the 'wage' component at all in these agrarian exchanges. The poor peasants with no land, and no instruments of production in possession were simply absent in the discourse. We have seen before that Lenin repeatedly mentioned the importance of *class struggle* in the sphere of agricultural production relations before the delegates of CI. During our review of the class alliances under the Bolshevik regime in Section 2.2, we have seen Lenin's analysis of the rural classes and their alliances with the urban proletariat hovered and shifted over many positions. He started with the argument of 'split' within the alliance between the proletariat and the peasantry before the revolution, and ended up to firming 'alliance, close alliance' with the entire of peasantry during the Civil War.

The last mention of *class struggle* among the rural "*masses*" was in August 1918, at the height of *War Communism* that was against the kulaks, the rich peasants. They resisted parting with the surplus gain, and insisted on hoarding and black marketeering. "About three million must be regarded as middle peasants, while barely two million consist of kulaks, rich peasants, grain profiteers. These bloodsuckers have grown rich on the want suffered by the people in the war; they have raked in thousands and hundreds of thousands of rubles by raising the price of grain and other products."[Lenin, 1974g] This writing was not published before January 1925[11]. While calling for waging war against the kulaks, ("Ruthless war on the kulaks! Death to them!" was the heading of the article), Lenin was careful in accommodating the concerns of 'middle peasants'. He wrote,

> But there is no reason why the working class should quarrel with the middle peasant. The workers cannot come to terms with the kulak,

> but they may seek, and are seeking, an *agreement* with the middle peasant. The workers' government, the Bolshevik government, *has proved* that in deed....
>
> We proved it (the other day) by *trebling* grain prices; for we fully realize that the earnings of the middle peasant are often disproportionate to present-day prices for manufactured goods and *must* be raised.
>
> The class-conscious worker's programme is the closest alliance and complete unity with the poor peasants; concessions to and agreement with the middle peasants; ruthless suppression of the kulaks, those bloodsuckers, vampires, plunderers of the people and profiteers, who batten on famine. That is the policy of the working class. [Lenin, 1974g, p. 57]

In the above paragraph, Lenin openly conceded to the market needs of the 'middle peasants' while defining the policy of class-alliances among the rural "*masses*". This policy was no more relevant to him in 1921 while the NEP was enforced as the 'middle peasants' themselves were now part of the new economy of 'state capitalism'. There were no more *poor peasants committees*, and therefore the rich peasants were dealt directly by the punitive measures of the state authorities. Possibly, it became very difficult for Lenin to defend the cooperative societies of 'middle peasants' as forums of *class struggle*, and now therefore in his view the 'Soviet state and the dictatorship of the proletariat' became compatible with 'state capitalism'. By April 1921, every aspect of rural economy was under the hegemony of the state apparatus that was increasingly getting alienated from the rural "*masses*". The measures of the state towards "forced collectivization", i.e. driving first the so-called kulaks and then increasingly the 'middle peasants' to the collective farms by dispossessing them from private ownership of their means of production in a "*mass*"-scale started from 1925.

## 3.3 Contemporary Critique of the Bolshevik Agricultural Policy

Not only did Lenin and the Bolsheviks in Russia represent complete muddle-headedness while confronting the question of organizing "socialist" agricultural economy in a *transitional society*, their contemporary critics were equally confused. They had no clue in facing the practical reality of workers' revolution in a country where most of the rural populace were engaged in relatively undeveloped agrarian capitalist production relations.

We have seen earlier several illuminating observations of Luxemburg in [Luxemburg, 2004] regarding the international perspective of the October Revolution in Russia, her hugely valiant criticisms to the leaders of Second International in her own country, her precise criticisms on the Bolshevik understanding of dictatorship of the proletariat and their practices. Unfortunately, when she reviewed "The Bolshevik Land Policy" she was hugely away from the concrete reality of rural Russia. In the whole Section of her review she had written not a single word on 'state capitalism' that was the cornerstone of Soviet agrarian policy. Although her writing was in 1918 from the prison cell, the period of *War Communism*, it is highly unlikely she was not aware of Lenin's formulation of 'state capitalism'. Lenin advocated this policy as transition to "socialism" even before the October Revolution, and as we have seen also after in several places. Rather her criticisms posed highly abstract recommendations that actually were glaring in the failure to understand the fundamental issues of the agrarian revolution. She first admitted,

> Surely the solution of the problem by the direct, immediate seizure and distribution of the land by the peasants was the shortest, simplest, most cleancut formula to achieve two diverse things: to break down large land-ownership, and immediately to bind the peasants to the revolutionary government. As a political measure to fortify the proletarian socialist government, it was an excellent tactical move. Unfortunately, however, it had two sides to it; and the reverse side consisted in the fact that the direct seizure of the land by the peasants has in general nothing at all in common with socialist economy." [Luxemburg, 2004, p. 290]

There was grave omission and commission in the above statement. Land was never 'distributed' among the peasants after the revolution, particularly among the poor peasants, in the sense the *Decrees on Land* of the Soviet government from the very beginning made it clear that the land rights ceased to be private. The tilling rights and capacity of employing the means of production were distributed by the Decree based on other factors of agricultural resources that Lenin categorized as, 'poor peasants', 'middle peasants, 'rich peasants', etc.. The fundamental issue of conflict between the Soviet government and the 'rich peasants' was due to the prevention of commercial sale and purchase of land, and prevention of selling grains in the open market that resulted in proliferation of black marketeering and profiteering in a large-scale underground economy.

The grave commission was to interpret the policy as 'an excellent tactical move'. In fact, unlike Lenin, many Bolsheviks also saw dismantling of the rights of feudal landed estates by the *poor peasants' committees* and also by the 'middle peasants' as a 'tactical move'. It was Lenin's huge political acumen (being a die-hard communist too!) to declare the transfer of land rights to the landless peasantry in the very second *Decree* of the Soviet government. There would have been no other meaning of agrarian revolution in the Russian countryside given that the most prevalent agrarian production relations till the provisional government ruled Russia from February to October 1917 were deeply feudal, patriarchal in nature. Later in the passages Luxemburg wrote,

> Now the slogan launched by the Bolsheviks, immediate seizure and distribution of the land by the peasants, necessarily tended in the opposite direction [to socialism]. Not only is it not a socialist measure; it even cuts off the way to such measures; it piles up insurmountable obstacles to the socialist transformation of agrarian relations.,
>
> The seizure of the landed estates by the peasants according to the short and precise slogan of Lenin and his friends-*"Go and take the land for your selves"* -simply led to the sudden, chaotic conversion of large land ownership into peasant land ownership. What was created is not social property but a new form of private property, namely, the breaking up of large estates into medium and small estates, or relatively advanced large units of production into primitive small units which operate with technical means from the time of the Pharaohs. [Luxemburg, 2004, p. 292]

Did Luxemburg not sound here like Otto Bauer who 'totally fails to understand the actual situation'? Can widespread revolutionary events ever happen without 'chaotic conversion of large land ownership into peasant land ownership'? Did not her argument here echo Kautsky's lamentation for the Bolshevik's support of the spontaneous peasant revolt against the landed gentry? Could any Red Army be formed at all to fight the heavily armed white guards without this policy of transfer of land rights to the rural poor? We have pointed out above that no new private ownership of land was created by the *Decree*. Lenin's assertion during this phase that he termed 'military alliance between the proletariat and peasantry' also confirms this fact. Luxemburg opined while criticizing Bolshevik land policy as,

> Lenin's own agrarian program before the revolution was different. The slogan taken over from the much condemned Socialist-Revolutionaries, or rather, from the spontaneous peasant movement..
>
> The Leninist agrarian reform has created a new and powerful layer of popular enemies of socialism in the countryside, enemies whose resistance will be much more dangerous and stubborn than that of the noble large landowners. [Luxemburg, 2004, p. 293]

It is true that Lenin advocated, "We must demand the nationalization of all lands, i.e. the passing of all land ownership in the state to the central state power." in the *April Thesis* before the revolution. To avoid misconception regarding the nature of distribution of land, we reproduce here two pertinent clauses from the *Decree on Land* issued from the Second Congress of the Soviets under the heading "Peasant Mandate in the Land".

> (6) The right to use the land shall be accorded to all citizens of the Russian state (without distinction of sex) desiring to cultivate it by their own labour, with the help of their families, or in partnership, but only as long as they are able to cultivate it. The employment of hired labour is not permitted....
>
> (7) Land tenure shall be on equality basis, i.e. land shall be distributed among the working people in conformity with a labour standard or a subsistence standard, depending on local conditions.
>
> There shall be absolutely no restrictions on the forms of land tenure, household farm, communal, or cooperative as shall be decided in each individual village and settlement. [Lenin, 1917]

To ensure the nature of land rights established by the Soviet government after the revolution we quote from a recent encyclopaedia.

> The October 1917 land decree was followed by legislation in January 1918 that forbade the selling, renting, or mortgaging of land. Nationalized land became the possession of "all the people" and could be used only by those who cultivated it. Although all land was nationalized, individuals or families could obtain allotment of land

> for small-scale agricultural activities, assuming that they themselves used the land and did not employ hired labour. [Wegren, 2004]

The question of 'nationalization of land' was settled effectively by ruling out land of any agricultural or industrial use to be *commodity*; land was in the possession of the state by *Decree*. Luxemburg's criticism was redundant and misleading when she wrote, "Here the property right must first of all be turned over to the nation, or to the state, which, with a socialist government, amounts to the same thing." [Luxemburg, 2004, p. 293] This was enforced by the very second act of the new Soviet state. What she did dwell upon in her critique (and that was pertinent) was the Bolshevik policy of granting freedom to the peasants to own the agricultural produce. When Luxemburg was criticizing 'The Leninist agrarian reform has created a new and powerful layer of popular enemies of socialism in the countryside,' she was unmindful of the concrete ground reality of post-revolution Russian rural economy that was *very different* from her assessment. As the peasant uprisings of February 1921 had shown, the new proletarian regime would have been on a 'suicidal path' without admitting this freedom or right to the 'middle peasants' to approach the market with their grain products.

Our discussion above has revealed repeatedly that agriculture in post-revolution Russia was not suffering from the want of *socialism*, but from the want of basic revival of the economy. It sounds an empty theory when Luxemburg recommended, 'A socialist government which has come to power must in any event do one thing: it must take measures which lead in the direction of that fundamental prerequisite for a later socialist reform of agriculture.' The Russian agricultural society was crying for social production relations that would have engaged the rural population on a large-scale as the major form of the prevailing economy was based on petty-commodity production. On the other hand, the ground reality was that the new proletarian state was not in a position to afford or implement large-scale socialization of agricultural production. The primary want *after* the revolution was *not* the access to land rights, but the huge lack of the material basis of social production. The new 'workers' state' in Soviet Russia urgently required a huge raise in the quantum of grain production for the urban working class, but the agricultural economy was not in a position to support this requirement. It was perishing from acute scarcity in the supply of the means of production for augmenting grain production. This wide gap in the demand and supply from both the ends, i.e. from the state and the agricultural producers' community could not be mitigated by dismantling the market economy, a path that the "*Left* Communists" wanted to pursue. Nor was there any brotherly support of the resources of grain (food) assistance from any other country when all of Russia was starving in the famine of 1920-21.

On the other hand, Lenin could not advocate giving a free hand to the capitalist mode of exchange of commodities, allowing the freedom of the market-price based economy to flourish as that would have brought existence of the conflicting interests of agrarian social classes to be more violent, more open. He could not afford the invitation of another spring of 1921 ('I hope the last time in the history of Soviet Russia that feeling ran against us among large masses of peasants, not consciously but instinctively'—Lenin) that would have been 'suicidal' for the Bolsheviks to continue their hold on state power. Yet like Luxemburg, Lenin also vouched for 'later socialist reform of agriculture', by introducing the NEP, 'state capitalism' that in his view was 'the only sensible and the last *possible* policy' in Soviet Russia. It will be not out of context here to mention how Lenin concluded his report on the agricultural policy in the Third Congress of CI.

> We tell the peasants quite openly that they must choose between the rule of the bourgeoisie and the rule of the Bolsheviks—in which case we shall make every possible concession within the limits of retaining power, and later shall lead them to socialism....Our point of view is : for the time being—big concessions and the greatest caution, precisely because a certain equilibrium has set in, precisely because we are weaker than our combined enemies, and because our economic basis is too weak and we need a stronger one. [Lenin, 1972a, p. 123]

Clearly, this intricate, profoundly complex dilemma the Bolsheviks actually faced was not present in Luxemburg's criticisms. The just quoted passage above shows Lenin's clear perception that "socialism" was not the immediate objective of the peasantry unlike the case for the workers of Russia, who participated actively in the revolution anticipating "socialism"—*abolition of private property* in the society. She understood the gravity posed by the conflicting class interests in the agrarian relations of Russia when she wrote, "we can safely say, the most difficult task of the socialist transformation of society!"; but understood them through the alien, distant viewing glasses of an abstract theory of "European socialism". Probably, that is why Lenin remarked, 'But theory and practice are two different things.' as the Bolsheviks trudged through the bloodied soils and woods of Russia along with their Red Army to protect the lonely, isolated ownership of "socialism" throughout the Civil War (*War Communism*) period.

The tragic fact of the political economy of post-revolution Russia was that neither the Bolsheviks nor their European critiques (here we have in mind names like Paul Mattick, Anton Pannekoek, Herman Gorter and Karl Korsch) viewed *socialism* as the need and aspirations of the rural "*masses*" whose interests could be closely tied, could be associated with the urban proletariat. At best, their view was to tag and trolley the rural "*masses*" as appendages to the class interests of the urban proletariat. Today, when a century has elapsed after the debacle of the "socialist" experiment in Russia, Luxemburg sounded prophetic when she wrote, 'In Russia the problem could only be posed. It could not be solved in Russia.' The important general lesson we can draw from the experience of the NEP is that the Russian agricultural economy, and for that matter any economy with predominantly small commodity production relations was not prepared for *socialism* in the period following the WWI. The most significant challenge that the Russian revolution brought before the world was whether without sufficient material development of the agricultural society (that could *only* be the outcome of capitalist production relations), there could at all be a *transitional society* towards *socialism*. The bitter lesson the international working class received by passing through the history of huge human tragedy in the name of "forced collectivization" in Soviet Russia is that the working class in such an isolated *transitional society* was bound to face the defeat when the objective of revolution was to *transcend* to a society of *free* direct producers without capitalism. *Socialist* production relations could never win over the pre-capitalist economy or arrest their gravitation towards full-fledged capitalist production relations in a revolution where the interests of the working class remain isolated against the predominant interests of the petty-commodity producers.

We will have more to say on this topic as we move on to Chapter 5 to review the famous "Colonial Thesis". We will find what started as a self-deception in the NEP, and a tragedy out of very limited understanding of the forces of capitalism within the society became a theory in these theses. The false conviction that emanated out of this contrived theory of transition to "socialism" proved to be the nemesis for the international working class movement, particularly in the colonies under the banner of the Third International.

## NOTES

1. Lenin's theses and report on "The Tactics of RCP" delivered in the Third Congress of CI, June 22-July 12, 1921, and Lenin's review titled "Five years of the Russian revolution and the prospects of the world revolution" delivered in the Fourth Congress of CI during November 5 - December 5, 1922 form the *basic material* for this Chapter. Lenin broadly explained the international and nation perspectives of state capitalism, and the programme outlines for the NEP in all these documents presented in the sessions of the two Congresses of CI.
2. The trend of criticism of Lenin's domestic policies in Soviet Russia by the so-called"*Left* Communists" *group* within the Bolshevik party started with the debate in the Central Committee regarding the Brest-Litovsk Peace Treaty. Several members of the Central Committee (prominent among them was Bukharin) were bitterly opposed to it. This *group* publicly started their opposition through the journal *Kommunist* (No. 1, April 20, 1918) that Lenin referred in his work [Lenin, 1974b].
3. Lenin actively took part in the commercial negotiations as the Premier of R.S.F.S.R. with the capitalists from the USA who invested in Russia in lieu of the "concessions" from the Soviet government. In particular, Lenin devoted particular attention to the negotiations with Washington Vanderlip, the US businessman concerning the "concessions" offered by the Soviet government for oil and coal prospecting and extraction in Kamchatka, with Armand Hammer and B. Mishell of the American Allied Drug and Chemical Corporation concerning the asbestos mines in the Alapayevsk district in the Urals, etc. [Lenin, 1983, p. 16]

4. This has reference to Lenin's following observation in *The State and Revolution*, (*LCW*, Vol. 25)
A witty German Social-Democrat of the seventies of the last century called the *postal service* an example of the socialist economic system. This is very true. At the present the postal service is a business organized on the lines of state-*capitalist* monopoly. [p. 431]
5. Paul Mattick, an active participant in the German revolutions of 1919-1921 was a member of the *Spartacus League* from the early age of fourteen. He was an active proponent of "Council Communism" along with Pannekoek, Karl Korsch. Mattick referred to the passage from Eugen Verga's book on *Economic Problems of the Proletarian Dictatorship*, published by CI (1921) in his articles such as "The Lenin Legend" (1935).
6. This refers to the historically well established confrontation between Amadeo Bordiga, from the Italian Communist Left faction and Stalin during the Sixth Enlarged Executive of the Communist International held between February 17 and March 15, 1926 in Moscow. During the sessions, Bordiga openly denounced the Russian tactics of 'Bolshevization' of CI, hunting down of factions within the Russian communist party, and stressed "the necessity for the International as a whole to discuss what was happening to the Russian Revolution". [Bordiga, 1926]
7. *The Decree on Land* was drafted by Lenin. It was the second *Decree* (the first being the *Decree on Peace*) that was passed on October 26, 1917 by the Second Congress of the Soviets of Workers', Soldiers' and Peasants' Deputies. The *Decree* legalized seizure of the landed estates by the peasantry but prohibited private ownership of land. A few salient features of the *Decree on Land* were
   - Landlord ownership of land is immediately abolished without compensation.
   - Private ownership of land shall be abolished forever; land shall not be sold, purchased, leased, mortgaged, or otherwise alienated. All land, whether state, crown, monastery, church, factory, entailed, private, public, peasant, etc., shall be confiscated without compensation and become the property of the whole people, and pass into the use of all those who cultivate it. [Lenin, 1917]
8. [102] Lenin began to work on *The Tax in Kind* pamphlet at the end of March 1921, just after the Tenth Party Congress, and finished it on April 1921. He attached great importance to its earliest publication and distribution, because it explained the necessity of transition to the New Economic Policy. – Editors Note, [Lenin, 1973b, p. 554]
9. The provisions of the *Decree on Land* are referred to in item [5] above,

and again on p. 155 of this Chapter. The Third Congress of the Soviets of Workers', Soldiers' and Peasants' Deputies that was held during January 23-31, 1918 ratified the provisions of the *Decree on Land* promulgated in the Second Congress.

10. Lenin's *Theses on the Food Question* provided the basis for the six *Decrees* on the food question which were discussed and adopted at the sessions of the Council of People's Commissars on August 3 - 6, 1918. They were the basis for the *Decree on Tax in Kind* that was drafted later, and adopted by the Council of People's Commissars on October 26, 1918. – Editor's Note [Lenin, 1974f, p. 496].
11. The article of Lenin referred here was titled "Comrade Workers, Forward to the Last, Decisive Fight". Although the article was written in August 1918, it was first published in *Rabochaya Moahva* No. 14, January 17, 1925 when the call of *class struggle* among the rural "masses" was virtually abandoned. This article, after publication may have served the purpose of a distant *alibi* for "forced collectivization" policy. By that time, it was understood by the state administration that the policies of the NEP had failed to deliver the dual objectives of raising the quantum of food production and accumulation of grain stock by the state.

## REFERENCES

V.I. Lenin. The Impending Catastrophe and How to Combat It. *Collected Works*, Vol. 25, 4th Ed. Progress Publishers, Moscow, 1974a.

V.I. Lenin. Political Report of the Central Committee of the RCP(B), March 27, 1922. *Collected Works,* Vol. 33, 2nd Printing. Progress Publishers, Moscow, 1973a.

V.I. Lenin. "Left Wing" Childishness and the Petty-Bourgeoisie Mentality. *Collected Works*, Vol. 27, 2nd Printing. Progress Publishers, Moscow, 1974b.

Nikolai Bukharin. The Politics and Economics of the Transition Period. In Kenneth J. Tarbuck, Editor, Vol. 3. Routledge, Oxon, UK, 2003.

Tony Cliff. State Capitalism in Russia, 1974. URL: *https://www.marxists.org/archive/cliff/works/1955/statecap/ch05.htm*.

V.I. Lenin. The Immediate Tasks of the Soviet Government. *Collected Works,* Vol. 27, 4th Ed. Progress Publishers, Moscow, 1974c.

V.I. Lenin. Speech Delivered at a Meeting of the Activists of the Moscow Organisation of the RCP(B). *Collected Works,* Vol. 31, 2nd Printing. Progress Publishers, Moscow, 1974d.

V.I. Lenin. Report on Concessions Delivered to the RCP(B) Group at the Eighth Congress of Soviets. *Collected Works,* Vol. 31, 2nd Printing. Progress Publishers, Moscow, 1974e.

V.I. Lenin. Report on the Tactics of the R.C.P. In *Speeches at Congress of the Communist International*. Progress Publishers, Moscow, 1972a.

Paul Mattick. The Lenin Legend, 1935. URL: *https://www.marxists.org/archive/mattick-paul/1935/lenin-legend.htm.*

V.I. Lenin. Theses for a Report on the Tactics of the RCP. In *Speeches at Congress of the Communist International*. Progress Publishers, Moscow, 1972b.

V.I. Lenin. Five Years of the Russian Revolution and the Prospects of the World Revolution. In *Speeches at Congress of the Communist International*. Progress Publishers, Moscow, 1972c.

Karl Kautsky. Terrorism and Communism: A Contribution to the Natural History of Revolution, Chapter 8, 1919. URL: *http:// www.isn.ethz.ch/.*

V.I. Lenin. The Tax in Kind. *Collected Works*, Vol. 32, 2nd Printing. Progress Publishers,Moscow, 1973b.

Orlando Figes. *Revolutionary Russia, 1891-1991*: A Pelican Introduction. Penguin UK, 2014.

Charles Bettelheim. *Class Struggle in the USSR, First Period: 1917-1923*. Part I. Monthly Review Press, New York, 1977.

V.I. Lenin. Report on the Tax in Kind Delivered at a Meeting of Secretaries... of Moscow and Moscow Gubernia, April 9, 1921. *Collected Works*, Vol. 32, 4th Ed. Progress Publishers, Moscow, 1973c.

V.I. Lenin. Theses on the Food Question. *Collected Works*, Vol. 28, 4th Ed. Progress Publishers, Moscow, 1974f.

V.I. Lenin. Comrade Workers, Forward To The Last, Decisive Fight! *Collected Works*, Vol. 28, 2nd Printing. Progress Publishers, Moscow, 1974g.

Rosa Luxemburg. The Russian Revolution. In Peter Hudis and Kevin B. Anderson, Editors, *The Rosa Luxemburg Reader*, Chapter 14. Monthly Review Press, New York, 2004.

V.I. Lenin. Report on Land, October 26 (November 8), 1917. URL: *https://www.marxists.org/online/lenin/works/1917/oct/25-26/26d.htm*.

Stephen K. Wegren. Decree on Land, Encyclopedia of Russian History, 2004. URL: *https://www.encyclopedia.com*.

V.I. Lenin. On State Capitalism During the Transition to Socialism. Lenin *Collected Works* (*Edited*). Progress Publishers, Moscow, 1983.

Amadeo Bordiga. The Communist Left in the Third International, 1926. URL:*https://www.marxists.org/archive/bordiga/works/1926/comintern.htm*.

# 4

# Report on the International Situation and the Fundamental Tasks of the Communist International

Lenin delivered the report at the opening session of the Second Congress of CI in Moscow on July 19, 1920[1]. The report was a survey of the crisis of capitalism and post-WWI bourgeoisie society. The report dealt with the issues and challenges before the working class while preparing for the ensuing world revolution.

The Second Congress was much more representative in character compared to the First Congress, and was held with high expectations and ambitions towards the prospect of the international Soviet movement. Apart from the delegates of the newly formed communist parties of Europe, the Congress was attended by the delegates of the workers' organizations like the Shop Stewards Committee of England (elected representative of workers from the factories and workshops in England), IWW representatives from Australia, Britain and Ireland, and the delegates representing the oppressed peoples of the colonies. At the conclusion of the Congress on August 7, 1920, speaking before a joint meeting of the Congress delegates, the Central Executive Committee of the Soviets, and other representative of the Soviet bodies, Zinoviev as the President of ECCI remarked, "I am deeply convinced that the second world congress of the CI is the precursor of another world congress, the world congress of Soviet republics." [Degras, 1973, p. 109] Rosmer recorded, "This Second Congress, on the other hand, was remarkably representative. Delegates came from all corners of the world, and the agenda contained all the problems of socialism and revolution." [Rosmer, 1973, p. 66] While the Congress was in session the delegates were expecting a new revolutionary situation in Germany from the advance of the Red Army in Poland leaving behind the past memories of the defeated German revolution in January 1919. Riddell quoted Trotsky in his work as, "You will recall, the Red Army was advancing on Warsaw and it was possible to calculate that because of the revolutionary situation in Germany, Italy, and other countries, the military impulse...might bring on the landslide of revolution, then temporarily at a dead point. That did not happen. We were beaten back."[12] [Riddell, 2016, p. 6] It was another matter that the military offensive ended in a fiasco as noted by Trotsky, with no substantial support from the Polish workers and peasants in support of the Soviet Red Army's intervention in Poland. Preparations were afoot to convene the First Congress of the Eastern peoples in September 1920 at Baku, the oilfield town drawing the border between Europe and Asia. The people's Congress was targeted to bring the oppressed people of the East, suffering under the yoke of colonialism, towards the Soviet movement of the working class in Europe.

The Second Congress of CI was therefore viewed as the Congress for organizing revolutions, a meeting to chart the course for organizing the proletariat towards the impending revolution in the countries around the capitalist world. The expectations were genuine to a certain extent as Lenin recorded in his report on the international situation,

> He [Ramsay Macdonald, the British leader of Independent Labour Party and the first Prime Minister from Labour Party] admits that there is a revolutionary crisis and that revolutionary sentiments are growing, that the sympathies of the workers are with the Soviets and the dictatorship of the proletariat (note that this refers to Britain) and that the dictatorship of the proletariat is better than the present dictatorship of the British bourgeoisie. [Lenin, 1972a, p. 43]

Lenin intervened several times on the issues regarding organizing the proletariat towards the impending revolution. His theses on the *Basic Tasks of the Communist International* laid the ground work for organizing the proletariat in the forum of revolutionary political parties (communist parties). He responded to the issues such as political participation in the bourgeoisie establishments such as parliaments, trade unions, etc. He wrote,

> From the standpoint of the international proletarian movement, therefore, the chief task of the communist parties at the present moment is to rally the scattered communist forces, to create a united communist party in each country (or the consolidation and regeneration of the parties already in existence), to multiply tenfold the work of preparing the proletariat for the conquest of State power in the form of the dictatorship of the proletariat. [Degras, 1971, p. 118]

The Second Congress adopted the "Twenty-one conditions of admission into Communist International" [Piatnitsky, 1934] that was drafted by Lenin and Zinoviev.[2] This document occupied a very high pedestal among the communist parties the world over. It was treated like the manual of principles for organizing the revolutionary sections of the international working class. The document was resisted by a considerable section of the delegates representing the syndicalists, the shop stewards, particularly those who did not subscribe to the idea of organizing the proletariat in the forum of political parties. Lenin spoke on these aspects, such as in his "Speech on the role of the communist party", "Speech on parliamentarism", "Speech on affiliation to the British Labour party", etc. [Lenin, 1972a] The Second Congress witnessed a lively debate between the followers of anarchism, the German-Dutch "*Left* Communists" represented by KAPD[3] and the Bolsheviks represented by Lenin and Trotsky on the questions of communist participation in the bourgeoisie institutions. Lenin took the cudgel in attacking these groups in his famous pamphlet *Left Wing Communism*: *An Infantile Disorder*, published just before the Congress in June 1920. This pamphlet was Lenin's rebuttal to the "*Left* Communists" who apart from in his own country were posing challenges to the Bolshevik strategy of coexistence with the capitalist world in the international scenario, and imposition of the so-called 'Russian model' in the revolutions of the European countries. Lenin was conscious to say at the very introduction of the work,

> It would also be erroneous to lose sight of the fact that, soon after the victory of the proletarian revolution in at least one of the advanced countries, a sharp change will probably come about: Russia will cease

> to be the model and will once again become a backward country (in the "Soviet" and the socialist sense).
>
> At the present moment in history, however, it is the Russian model that reveals to *all* countries something—and something highly significant—of their near and inevitable future. [Lenin, 1974, p. 22]

After saying 'Russia will cease to be the model' once proletarian revolution erupts 'in at least one of the advanced countries', Lenin fell back on his pet topic that he found of universal significance ('to *all* countries'). The first principle he found worth emulation from the Russian experience was the necessary existence of a highly disciplined, centralized political party of the proletariat. He articulated under the heading "An essential condition of the Bolshevik success" as,

> It is, I think, almost universally realized at present that the Bolsheviks could not have retained power for two and a half months, let alone two and a half years, without the most rigorous and truly iron discipline in our Party, or without the fullest and unreserved support from the entire mass of the working class, that is, from all thinking, honest, devoted and influential elements in it, capable of leading the backward strata or carrying the latter along with them....
>
> I repeat: the experience of the victorious dictatorship of the proletariat in Russia has clearly shown even to those who are incapable of thinking or have had no occasion to give thought to the matter that absolute centralization and rigorous discipline of the proletariat are an essential condition of victory over the bourgeoisie. [Lenin, 1974, pp. 23-24]

Here, in our review of Lenin's report, we purposefully disengage from the critique on these policies that were indispensable in Lenin's view; the policies directed to organize the proletariat as conscious, centralized, and resolute force to execute the revolution. These policies stood for the indispensability of the *vanguard party* ('capable of leading the backward strata or carrying the latter along with them'.) These policies have remained largely the theme and focus of the numerous criticisms of the Russian revolution in the literature, either from academic researchers or from the laborious documents of the "communist" militants, parties, groups and tendencies frittered across the world.

We are not at all refusing to concede that the question of the leading forum of the working class for an international proletarian revolution is a principal issue; of course it is. However, as we pointed out in the introduction of this essay the questions of the organizational effort of the proletariat for a *communist* (*socialist*) revolution are not the substitution nor can be posited to counter the problems of the political economy of transition to the *socialist* society from the capitalist society. Unfortunately, these challenges in the domain of political economy do not generally come under the agenda of discourse. These challenges were earlier treated as solved questions like the resolution of the debates between Bettelheim and Sweezy in the decades of the 1970s. On the other hand, these issues of transition are treated usually as distant questions of the unforeseeable future having little relevance to the present-day issues and problems confronting the working class in particular, and society in general. We cannot but remember Luxemburg's wise, fulsome praise of the Bolsheviks, 'Thereby they won for themselves the imperishable historic distinction of having for the first time proclaimed the final aim of socialism as the direct programme of practical politics.' [Luxemburg, 2004] Our purpose here is to pose the issues of 'final aim of socialism' that remained as unsolved questions of reality in the deliberation of CI. We attempt to reason why they remained as unsolved questions over the past century keeping this context in mind.

### 4.1 Analysis of Lenin on the Post-WWI Crisis of International Capitalism

In his report, Lenin brought out the consequences of economic instability under capitalism. He pointed out that the accumulation of wealth among a few monopolies as the reasons behind the mayhem of humanity in the WWI. Simultaneously, he had shown the end of war did not mitigate the instability inherent in capitalism. The treaty at Versailles was signed on June 28, 1919 following the armistice among the warring nations of Europe and USA. The treaty further compounded the crisis of "imperialism", the world capitalist system as was understood by Lenin. In broad terms of the mechanisms of international economics, Lenin's outlines were crystal clear in showing how the war benefited the capitalist class of the world as a whole, and how as a nation state, the United

States of America (USA) being the last entrant in the mutual genocide harvested maximum benefit from the war. The war resulted in the redistribution of private property among the monopolies, redistribution of the sources of raw materials, and repartitioning of the privileges to rule and dominate over the vast majority of humanity in the colonies among the few nations. As the fundamental reasons for the war Lenin wrote,

> Thus, the entire branches of industry, not only in single countries, but all over the world, have been taken over by monopolists in the field of finance, property rights, and partly of production. This has formed the basis for the unprecedented domination exercised by an insignificant number of very big banks, financial tycoons, financial magnates who have, in fact, transformed even the freest republics into financial monarchies. Before the war this was publicly recognized by such far from revolutionary writers as, for example, Lysis in France....
>
> The first imperialist war of 1914-18 was the inevitable outcome of this partition of the whole world, of this domination by the capitalist monopolies, of this great power wielded by an insignificant number of very big banks—two, three, four or five in each country. This war was waged for the repartitioning of the whole world. [Lenin, 1972a, p. 32]

As far as the summary of the net debt-credit relationship at the end of the war was concerned, Lenin estimated in the report some gross figures that showed the USA as "the only full beneficiary from the war, a country which, from a heavy debtor, has become a general creditor". His calculation was as follows:

> What are the debtor-creditor relations that have developed between the principal powers? I shall convert pound sterling into gold rubles, at a rate of ten gold rubles to one pound. Here is what we get: the United States has assets amounting to 19,000 million, its liabilities are nil. Before the war, it was in Britain's debt.... All the other powers in the world are debtors. Britain has been reduced to a position in which her assets total 17,000 million, and her liabilities 8,000 million. She is already half-way to becoming a debtor nation....In regard to France, Keynes quotes the following figures: her assets amount to 3,500 million, and her liabilities to 10,500 million! And this is a country which the French themselves called the world's moneylender, because her "savings" were enormous. [Lenin, 1972a, pp. 35-36]

Lenin banked heavily in his analysis on the classic work of John Maynard Keynes, the British negotiator at the Paris Conference on "peace" and the author of the book *The Economic Consequences of the Peace*, published in December 1919.[4] Keynes was so disgusted with the terms of "peace" that the four victor states, England, France, USA and Italy inflicted on Germany that he branded the terms as "Carthaginian peace" drawing a parallel to the most punitive conditions of "peace" the ancient Roman rulers imposed on the belligerent city of Carthage at the end of the second Punic war in 146 BC. Keynes resigned on June 5, 1919 from the British treasury after writing to Llyod George, the British prime minister and chief negotiator from the British side at the "peace meeting" that was convened in January 1919 in Versailles, near Paris.

### *4.1.1 Analysis by Keynes of the terms of "peace"*

What made Lenin so enthusiastic about Keynes that he profusely quoted economic statistics from Keynes's work in his report? Keynes made a detailed and cold estimate of the balance sheet of the liabilities that the cost of war imposed upon the belligerent nations, particularly the cost dictated by the countries that got directly affected by the German invasion such as Belgium and France. He had shown out of his calculations that the conditions imposed by the victor powers upon vanquished Germany were not only going to ruin the German economy for good, those would effectively turn Europe into an economic graveyard. Keynes quoted from the report of the German economic commission that was responsible to study the effect of the "peace" terms on the economic activities of the German population. He quoted Count Brockdorff-Rantzau, the first foreign minister of the Weimar Republic and the German representative, who addressed the meeting at Paris on May 13, 1919.

> Before the war a total of 15 million persons in Germany provided for their existence by foreign trade, navigation, and the use, directly or indirectly, of foreign raw material. After rehearsing the main relevant provisions of the peace treaty the report continues: 'After this diminution of her products, after the economic depression resulting from the loss of her colonies, her merchant fleet and her foreign investments, Germany will not be in a position to import from abroad an adequate quantity of raw material. An enormous part of German

> industry will, therefore, be condemned inevitably to destruction. The need of importing foodstuffs will increase considerably at the same time that the possibility of satisfying this demand is as greatly diminished. In a very short time, therefore, Germany will not be in a position to give bread and work to her numerous millions of inhabitants, who are prevented from earning their livelihood by navigation and trade....
>
> The Report concludes, "whether the delegates of the Allied and Associated Powers realize the inevitable consequences which will take place if Germany, an industrial state, very thickly populated, closely bound up with the economic system of the world, and under the necessity of importing enormous quantities of raw material and foodstuffs suddenly finds herself pushed back to the phase of her development to the phase of her development which corresponds to her economic conditions and the number of her population as they were half a century ago. Those who sign this treaty will sign the death sentence of many millions of German men, women and children." [Keynes, 1920, pp. 109-110]

The Treaty at Versailles was not only an abject national humiliation for Germany, it was literally back-breaking for her economy. To give an example, we quote here the renowned (cited in the *Encyclopaedia Britannica*) contemporary German economist and professor of the then Munich University, Lujo Brentano whose article on the quantum of German reparations can be found in the nationalist German website.

> M. Poincaré [the then Prime Minister of France], in particular, has during the past two years neglected no opportunity of declaring, with well-feigned indignation, that Germany has made no payments whatever and that she is endeavouring by all means at her command to escape her obligations. Yet day after day between September 1919 and January 11, 1923 a coal train[1] of 50 trucks crossed the German frontier every quarter of an hour all for the purpose of supplying French, Belgian and Italian industries without any consideration in return. This was hardly an indication of bad faith on the part of Germany.
>
> And these coal deliveries, which amounted in round figures to a total of 54,000,000 tons with a value of 2,424 million gold marks (£ 121,000,000) are only a small part of the vast tribute that Germany has paid to her former enemies from the conclusion of the Armistice down to December 31, 1922. The total of this tribute has been variously estimated as follows:

> **1.** According to the official figures of the Reparation Commission at 7,940,426,000 gold marks (about £ 397,000,000)...." [Brentano, 1923]

It is not very difficult to understand that such severe harsh conditions from the victors' side particularly by the French government were imposed not only to satisfy national vengeance and retaliation, there were also deep and immediate economic reasons. The Allied powers wanted to clear their war-debt repayments from these German reparations, and of course, they wanted the monopoly capitalists of German origin to be permanently out of competition in the race of the accumulation of "profit". Keynes suggested a blanket waive of these war-related loans and debts as "settlement of inter-ally indebtedness"; he appealed to "the generosity", "farseeing statesmanship "of Great Britain, and USA. [Keynes, 1920, pp. 130-131] Even if such an arrangement of loan-waiver among the Allied states were agreed upon, Keynes offered no consolation in his analysis that would have solved the international monetary crisis, the crisis of devaluation of *currency*, and the inflation in the economy that the capitalist world including revolutionary Russia was plagued with. We give below his prognosis over the terminal illness from which the post-WWI European economy suffered out of the monetary crisis, and the inflationary pressure over *currency* as the governments resorted to arbitrary paper-note circulation to run their economy.

> The inflationism of the currency system of Europe has proceeded to extraordinary length. The various belligerent governments, unable or too timid or too short-sighted to secure from loans or taxes the resources they required, have printed notes for the balance. In Russia and Austria-Hungary this process has reached a point where for the purpose of foreign trade the currency is practically valueless....
>
> But while these currencies enjoy a precarious value abroad, they have never entirely lost, not even in Russia, their purchasing power at home. A sentiment of trust in the legal money of the state is so deeply implanted in the citizens of all countries that they cannot but believe that someday this money must recover a part at least of its former value. To their minds it appears that value is inherent in money as such, and they do not apprehend that the real wealth that this money might have stood for has been dissipated once and for all. This sentiment is supported by the various legal regulations with

which the governments endeavour to control internal prices, and so as to preserve some purchasing power for their legal tender....

The preservation of a spurious value for the currency, by the force of law expressed in the regulation of prices, contains in itself, however, the seeds of final economic decay, and soon dries up the sources of ultimate supply. If a man is compelled to exchange the fruits of his labours for paper which, as experience soon teaches him, he cannot use to purchase what he requires at a price comparable to that which he has received for his own products, he will keep his produce for himself, dispose of it to his friends and neighbours as a favour, or relax his efforts in producing it. A system of compelling the exchange of commodities at what is not their real relative value not only relaxes production, but leads finally to the waste and inefficiency of barter. If, however, a government refrains from regulation and allows matters to take their course, essential commodities soon attain a level of price out of the reach of all but the rich, the worthlessness of the money becomes apparent, and the fraud upon the public can be concealed no longer....

The note circulation of Germany is about ten times[2] of what it was before the war. The value of the mark in terms of gold is about one-eighth of its former value. As world prices in terms of gold are more than double what they were, it follows that mark prices inside Germany ought to be from sixteen times to twenty times their pre-war level if they are to be in adjustment and proper conformity with prices outside Germany.[3] ....

The note circulation of France is more than six times of its prewar level. The exchange value of the franc in terms of gold is a little less than its two thirds its former value; that is to say, the value of the franc has not fallen in proportion to the increased volume of the currency. This apparently superior situation of France is due to the fact that until recently a very great part of her imports have not been paid for, but have been covered by loans from the governments of Great Britain and the United States....

The situation in Italy is not very different. There the note circulation is five or six times its pre-war level, and the exchange value of the lira in terms of gold about half its former value. Thus the adjustment of the exchange to the volume of the note circulation has proceeded further in Italy than in France." [Keynes, 1920, pp. 113-117]

We have given above a lengthy reference to Keynes's analysis of inflation in post-war Europe for two reasons. First, to familiarize the reader with the original writing of Keynes, his lucid explanation of the factors that pushed devaluation of the paper-*currency* all over Europe (including Russia), destabilizing the very confidence of the people in monetary circulation itself. Second, we want to make the reader aware from his interpretation of the facts that the civil war-like situation in almost all states of Europe after the war had a strong economic basis. The WWI was fought on the basis of loans and sureties that even the victor states could not guarantee to pay. The economic misery of Germany out of the Versailles Treaty would have made the very basis of the capitalist economic system untenable in Europe. These were not mere exhortations of Lenin during his review of the international capitalist crisis before the delegates of CI in the Second Congress. We provide below a few facts of daily life in Germany from the reports of a Spanish journalist Eugeni Xammar stationed in Berlin in the winter of 1922. The news reports vividly reflected the havoc caused by hyperinflation of German *currency* upon the national socio-economic fabric.

> In December 1922, the dollar was still worth 2,000 marks. Within four months this had jumped to 20,000 marks, and by August 1923 it stood at more than a million....
>
> Take for example the family that sold its house to emigrate to America. On arrival at the port of Hamburg, they found that the money wasn't enough to pay for their crossing—in fact, it didn't even pay for their tickets back home. Then there was the man who drank two cups of coffee at 5,000 marks each, only to be presented with a bill for 14,000. When he asked why this was he was told he should have ordered the coffees at the same time because the price had gone up in between. And then there's the story about the couple that took a few hundred million marks to the theater box office hoping to see a show, but discovered it wasn't nearly enough. Tickets were now a billion marks each. ....
>
> At the Junkers plant in Dessau the company gave its workers the equivalent of the day's price of three-and-a-half loaves of bread at 9 am every morning. Their wives, who were waiting at the factory gates, took the money and dashed off to the shops before the new dollar exchange rate was published at around midday. Many doctors insisted on being paid not in cash but sausages, eggs, coal, and the like. Because of the constant increase in prices, shops stopped displaying them in their windows. And when the Prussian authorities forced them to do so nonetheless, it drove prices even higher because

> traders simply took prospective increases into account." [Jung, August 14, 2009]

These macabre dances of anarchy in the name of "civilization" were caused in Germany not by any epidemic or natural disaster such as an earthquake; they were the consequences of reparation and the terms of treaty that other "civilized" nations imposed upon her. Germany was barely able to import any foodstuff that caused breakdown of trading in Europe as a consequence.

Keynes was a huge minority when he published his work [Keynes, 1920], but such was the impact of his work that the economic theories of capitalism can only be broadly divided into two categories: theories before Keynes, and theories after Keynes. A century after his celebrated work was published the world will remember him as the person who being a huge minority among his class brethren could see through working of the very inner cycle of *barbarism* that capitalism represents. According to Keynes, the fundamental features of modern capitalism are to focus on accumulation leading to the frenzy for "profit" that is of private interest to a minority class of people. When the rate of "profit" goes down these monopoly interests and proprietors of capital will force war or war efforts on the population by investing heavily in armament manufacturing and foisting any local issue to whip up chauvinism among people. At the cost of human genocide, capitalism will make room for future investments by providing long-term structural loans, and would run the cycle of "profit" again.

Lenin could find an echo of his words in Keynes when he reported,

> This fact shows that the "mechanism" of the world capitalist economy is falling apart. The trade relations on which the acquisition of raw materials and the sale of commodities hinge under capitalism cannot go on; they cannot continue to be based on the subordination of a number of countries to a single country—the reason the change in the value of money. No wealthy country can exist or trade unless it sells its goods and obtains raw materials.
>
> Thus we have a situation in which America, a wealthy country that all countries are subordinate to, cannot buy or sell. And the selfsame Keynes who went through the entire gamut of the Versailles

> negotiations has been compelled to acknowledge this impossibility despite his unyielding determination to defend capitalism and all his hatred of Bolshevism. Incidentally, I do not think any communist manifesto, or one that is revolutionary in general could compare in forcefulness with those pages of Keynes's book which depict Wilson [the US President] and "Wilsonism" in action. [Lenin, 1972a, p. 38]

We now wonder why Lenin missed the left handed recognition that he and 'Bolshevism' earned from Keynes while he was busy in heaping such fulsome praise on Keynes. It is highly unlikely that an objective and voracious reader as Lenin would have missed the pages to read that he did not mention in his report or theses. However, we need to mention here that Keynes, being the devoted and vigilant spokesman of international capitalism could sense the historical significance of the possible alliance of 'Bolshevism' and 'Spartacism' in Russia and Germany respectively. Therefore Keynes warned,

> From the military point of view an ultimate union of forces between Russia and Germany is greatly feared in some quarters. This would be much more likely to take place in the event of reactionary movements being successful in each of the two countries, whereas an effective unity of purpose between Lenin and the present essentially middle class government of Germany is unthinkable. On the other hand, the same people who fear such a union are even more afraid of the success of Bolshevism; and yet they have to recognise that the only efficient forces for fighting it are, inside Russia , the reactionaries, and outside Russia, the established forces of order and authority in Germany. Thus the advocates of intervention in Russia, whether direct or indirect, are at cross-purposes with themselves.
>
> They do not know what they want; or, rather they want what they cannot help seeing to be incompatibles. This is one of the reasons why their policy is so inconstant and so exceedingly futile.
>
> The same conflict of purpose is apparent in the attitude of the council of the Allies at Paris towards the present government of Germany. A victory of Spartacism in Germany might well be the prelude to revolution everywhere: it would renew the forces of Bolshevism in Russia, and precipitate the dreaded union of Germany and Russia; it would certainly put an end to any expectations which have been built on the financial and economic clauses of the treaty of peace. Therefore Paris does not love Spartacus." [Keynes, 1920, p. 138]

We are surprised that Lenin failed to comment on this passage of Keynes above in the gathering of the revolutionaries across the world in July 1920 while presenting his report on the international situation in the Second Congress of CI. We request the reader to keep in mind that these observations of Keynes were made in December 1919. The Civil War supported by the fourteen "civilized states" and the so-called "reactionaries" was in full swing in the Russian countryside against the Red Army whose might had become formidable even in the eyes of Keynes by that time. Of course, while pointing out the scare of his class brethren bundled here as 'the reactionaries' he was unable to define the class nature of themselves, he being part of the reaction itself. His commentary is significant as he saw the real, ominous threat the revolutions posed to the fate of capitalism. The meticulous planning and calculations behind 'the financial and economic clauses of the treaty of peace' might vanish into thin air in the wake of an alliance between 'Spartacism in Germany' and 'Bolshevism in Russia'. Everybody in the Congress of CI was looking for such an alliance. On the other hand, it was a distinct possibility of ominous proportions for Keynes and the class he represented.

Keynes' observations should also serve as the rebuttal to the trend of criticism that the October Revolution was a *putsch* by a minority (possibly a bigger one than the counter revolutionary *Kapp Putsch* in Germany in 1922), and not a revolution by the proletariat of Russia directed against capitalism. It would be a poor logic to argue that Keynes was objective in assessing the miserable conditions of capitalism in post-war Europe but was subjective in assessing the threat to international capitalism from the Russian and German revolutions. *Or*, to argue that Keynes had the revolting working class in mind while writing about 'Spartacism in Germany', but only meant a band of dedicated revolutionaries while writing about 'Bolshevism in Russia'. We also record here the impact 'Spartacism in Germany' created upon Keynes even when the revolution was conclusively defeated in March 1921 after the failure of the March general strike[5] to arouse the working class in Germany. The Spartacists were a minority political force among the working class in Germany in the January 1919 revolt, the majority of their illustrious leaders were assassinated 'by the present essentially middle class government of Germany'. The flame of the revolution created piercing fear in Keynes's heart that was reflected in his cautionary remarks to his class brethren.

Lenin may have missed this significant appraisal of the anti-capitalist revolutions in Germany and Russia, but he definitely ignored the other profound inferences of Keynes that were particularly directed to Lenin in the book. There was the well known commentary of Keynes as below:

> Lenin is said to have declared that the best way to destroy the capitalist system was to debauch the currency. By a continuing process of inflation, governments can confiscate, secretly and unobserved, an important part of the wealth of their citizens. By this method they not only confiscate, but they confiscate *arbitrarily*; and while the process impoverishes many, it actually enriches some. .... As the inflation proceeds and the value of the currency fluctuates wildly from month to month, all permanent relations between debtors and creditors, which form the ultimate foundation of capitalism, become so utterly disordered as to be almost meaningless; and the process of wealth-getting degenerates into a gamble and a lottery.
>
> Lenin was certainly right. There is no subtler, no surer means of overturning the existing basis of society than to debauch the currency. The process engages all the hidden forces of economic law on the side of destruction, and it does it in a manner which not one man in a million is able to diagnose.
>
> In the latter stages of the war all the belligerent governments practised from necessity or incompetence, what a Bolshevist might have done from design. Even now, when the war is over, most of them continue out of weakness the same malpractices. [Keynes, 1920, p. 113]

The first sentence in the reference from Keynes is wide in circulation among the economic historians, among the bankers, and other policy makers, etc. Although there is no authentic verification of this statement purported to Lenin except an unsigned interview said to be given by Lenin and "published on April 23, 1919, by the *Daily Chronicle* in London and the *New York Times*[2] dated April 22 and cabled from Geneva." [White and Schuler, 2009] The said interview is not part of the English version of *LCW* published in Soviet Russia in 1965. It was concluded that "Fetter [Frank W. Fetter, the US historian who searched for Lenin's aforesaid comment] doubted, however, that Keynes was really quoting Lenin. After extensive inquiries, Fetter reported that no such statement could be found in Lenin's published writings and that the "first attribution in English, and probably in any language," was by Keynes." [White and Schuler, 2009, p. 213]

Even if we doubt the authenticity of the said interview of Lenin, the fact remains it was part of Keynes's long commentary on the Bolshevik monetary policy in post-revolution Russia. Lenin could have easily repudiated Keynes's observation with his characteristic pithiness and contempt instead of unusually heaping praise upon Keynes. In any case, we have already seen in Lenin's own admission before the Fourth Congress of CI how the ruble, the *currency* in Soviet Russia, was reeling under inflationary pressure.

> But what is really important is the problem of stabilizing the ruble. We are now grappling with this problem, our best forces are working on it. If we succeed in stabilizing the ruble for a long period and then for all time, it will prove that we have won. [Lenin, 1972b, p. 135]

However, the more important issue to consider here is whether the *socialist* aim of abolition of monetary exchanges can be made equivalent to making the *currency* worthless by printing an endless number of handbills and issuing them from banks. We have just highlighted how people in Germany soon found such paper form of *currency* exchanges useless due to hyperinflation of the mark, or the case of the peasants in Russia who refused to accept paper-note circulation from the Soviet government in exchange of grains. Can *socialism* be made equivalent to the effort of building a grand edifice upon the graveyard of economic destruction that 'all the belligerent governments practised from necessity or incompetence'? This is the sense we get from the above observation of Keynes when he equated the Bolshevik motto of "socialism" to the violent misdeeds of the bourgeoisie governments of Europe in the name of printing crates of *currency*-notes that lost the trust and confidence of the people under their rule. Throughout his book, Keynes candidly bemoaned the misfortune of Europe being under the rule of the capitalist class.

> We are thus faced in Europe with the spectacle of an extraordinary weakness on the part of the great capitalist class, which has emerged

> from the industrial triumphs of the nineteenth century, and seemed a very few years ago our all-powerful master. The terror and personal timidity of the individuals of this class is now so great, their confidence in their place and in their necessity to the social organism so diminished, that they are easy victims of intimidation." [Keynes, 1920, p. 114]

May be these reasons of incapacity, of diffidence prompted the bourgeoisie in some places of Europe to reconcile with the belligerent proletariat. History witnessed the bloodless coup in the name of revolutionary state-power in Hungary that was soon defeated by the armed invasion from Rumania and Germany. Similar brief capitulation of the bourgeoisie before the revolutionary sections of the proletariat were also there in the temporary formation of revolutionary Soviet governments in Austria, in Finland, in Bavaria just after the October Revolution. On the other hand, the SDP-led Weimar Republic in Germany while kneeling before the reparation conditions of the Allies did the yeoman service to the international bourgeoisie by committing atrocious bloodshed of the belligerent workers and sailors in Berlin during January 1919. In spite of the subsequent political reverses for the proletariat out of these eventful historical tragedies the fact remains that *socialism* is *not* the helpless cry of the wounded proletariat. *Socialism* is not the hysterical response of a mortally weak proletariat bewildered under the tyranny of the uncertainty of life and social existence that was forced upon the people by the incapacity and ruin under capitalism.

We may contrast here Keynes's observation on "socialism" by debauching the *currency* with Marx's vision of 'the material conditions necessary' for *socialism*. While countering Proudhon in his seminal work *The Poverty of Philosophy*, Marx wrote,

> So long as the proletariat is not yet sufficiently developed to constitute itself as a class, and consequently so long as the struggle itself of the proletariat with the bourgeoisie has not assumed a political character, and the productive forces are not yet sufficiently developed in the bosom of the bourgeoisie itself to enable us to catch a glimpse of the material conditions necessary for the emancipation of the proletariat and for the formation of a new society, these theoreticians are merely Utopians who, to meet the wants of the oppressed classes, improvise systems and go in search of regenerating science. [Marx, 1955, p. 56]

We have quoted this reference to show Marx's clear understanding about *socialism* where the proletariat is sufficiently prepared to usher and transcend to the *new* society not only through its political struggles but also as and when 'the material conditions necessary for the emancipation of the proletariat and for the formation of a new society,' are visible and comprehensible. This understanding of Marx proves the interpretation of "socialism" by Keynes as equivalent to a bankrupt society possessing no worthwhile medium to exchange the produce of labour an utterly false figment of imagination. We have seen that Lenin retreated very soon from the money-less exchanges in the rural economy of Russia as he found such policies to be 'suicidal' in the absence of the material conditions that Marx concluded as necessary for *socialism* to be viable and realizable. We do not know what would have happened provided 'Bolshevik Russia' and 'Spartacists Germany' could come together to usher the economic resurgence of Europe without holding on to the *currency* being the medium of social exchanges, and without the mandatory requirement of the monopoly financial institutions as the custodians of *currency* and money circulation. That would be a conjecture of a historical non-factual setting. But we can definitely say about Keynes's analysis of post-WWI European economic crisis that debauching the *currency* as the means of commercial and economic exchanges by the European states was a huge conspiracy with the economically devastated population. It was invocation of the spectre of uncertainty in the social life that had nothing in common with the holistic reasoning of Marx towards *socialism*.

While concluding this part of our review on Lenin's analysis of the post-WWI crisis of the world capitalist order, we can certainly say that Lenin hugely missed to comment or critique the forecast on the "socialist" world order by Keynes while otherwise praising the analysis of the European economic crisis by Keynes. We now turn our attention to the other important aspect of Lenin's report where he dealt with the challenges in organizing the working class for the ensuing revolution. He found 'opportunism' to be the principal weakness of the European working class movement against capitalism.

## 4.2 The Challenges Faced by the European Working Class Post-WWI *within* its Own Formation

At the beginning of this Chapter we offered the clarification that we would refrain from discussing the issues of political organization of the working class as was formulated by the Third International in the "twenty-one conditions". Not only because of the reasons we cited above, but *above all*, we openly admit that we face the toughest challenge, the biggest dilemma while commenting on this issue. The principal focus of the Second Congress of CI was to provide the guidelines for organizing the proletariat towards ensuring the world revolution, particularly in the developed countries. Nothing like that happened, even though the possibilities came and went by, between the interval of the two World Wars. Yet, the fundamental issues that Lenin identified *within* the working class of the developed nations for establishing political organizations with strong roots among the workers was seldom put under closer scrutiny in later discussions. On the other hand, we cannot simply remain silent on this question of the *real practice* of the revolutionary sections of the working class particularly while we are discussing the formative years of CI and the programmes adopted during the period. Therein lies our dilemma in confronting this vital issue before *socialism* on which very little critique exists, an issue we do not want to confront in an elaborate way either, yet we cannot avoid the issue without deliberation. Therefore, we take the approach of reviewing the general course of action as suggested in Lenin's report and the theses in the Second Congress of CI in the light of the actual developments of the revolutionary initiative of the working class, particularly in Germany. Simultaneously, we assess such programmes for organizing communist parties in the light of the vision of the 'final aim of socialism' as outlined in different works of Marx.

We cannot ignore Lenin's assessment regarding the actual development of communist parties in Europe in his theses under the heading "preparation for the dictatorship of the proletariat". He wrote,

> It is a distinguishing feature of the present moment in the development of the international communist movement that in the great majority

> of capitalist countries the preparations of the proletariat to bring its dictatorship into being have not been completed, indeed in many cases have not even been systematically begun. It does not follow that the proletarian revolution is impossible in the immediate future. It is quite possible, for the entire economic and political situation is unusually rich in inflammable material and in reasons for its suddenly catching fire. A further prerequisite of revolution, apart from the preparation of the proletariat, namely, a general state of crisis in all ruling and all bourgeois parties, is also present. But from what has been said it follows that for the communist parties the immediate task is to accelerate the revolution, taking care not to provoke it artificially before adequate preparations have been made. The preparation of the proletariat for the revolution must be promoted by action. On the other hand the history of many socialist parties, previously referred to, makes it essential to see that recognition of the dictatorship of the proletariat does not remain an empty word. [Degras, 1971, pp. 118-119]

When we look at Lenin's above analysis and directives, we face the contradiction. Lenin observed, 'in the great majority of capitalist countries the preparations of the proletariat to bring its dictatorship into being have not been completed, indeed in many cases have not even been systematically begun.' At the same time, his proposition was to see the communist parties as the catalysts of revolution, 'for the communist parties the immediate task is to accelerate the revolution, taking care not to provoke it artificially before adequate preparations have been made'. *Prima facie*, Lenin's assessment was not wrong. Ralf Hoffrogge, author of the seminal biography on Richard Müller and the working class politics in Germany, recounted Antonio Gramsci on this issue as,

> The Italian Communist, Antonio Gramsci, famously asked why the revolution had failed in the West and succeeded in the East, precisely the opposite of the predictions of Marxism as it was commonly understood by European Social Democracy until the Bolshevik Revolution. The German Revolution should have been at the centre of the various answers to that question, but was not. [Hoffrogge, 2014, p. 2]

It was not only Gramsci in the much later period, a very contemporary Pannekoek in his rebuttal to Lenin's criticism of "*Left*wing communism" posed this very intriguing question in 1920 that was particularly present before the West European communists.

> Western European social democrats often expressed derisive astonishment that the 'ignorant' Russians could claim to be the vanguard of the new world of labour. Referring to these social democrats, an English delegate at the communist conference in Amsterdam[4] pointed up the difference quite correctly: the Russians may be more ignorant, but the English workers are stuffed so full of prejudices that it is harder to propagate communism among them. (Chapter 3) [Pannekoek, 1978]

So, the dilemma is not only of us, it was in the minds of the most prominent protagonists of the working class revolutions in Europe —the *central question* was what made the working class of the developed countries hesitant and diffident in marching forward with the banner of revolution under the leadership of the "communist" parties that were only nascent and emerging on the political scene? In later times, the question continued to be ringing among the dissidents of CI. For example, Claudin in his work posed the question as,

> The defeat suffered by the attempts made at the proletarian revolution in Western Europe after the war of 1914-1918 was due to a highly complex set of factors and circumstances; but from this diversity it is possible to select one incontestable fact which was of fundamental importance, namely, that the majority of the European working class, even where the crisis went farthest, as in Germany, continued to follow their traditional political and trade-union organizations and not the new revolutionary party.[29] In one way or another this is acknowledged in all the analyses made by Lenin and the Comintern, when they alleged that the basic factor in the defeat was 'betrayal' by the reformist leaders. This explanation calls out for another to be given: why did the workers follow these 'traitor' leaders?" [Claudin, 1975, p. 56]

Claudin's above observation on the assessment of Lenin and the leadership of CI about the failure of the European working class to rally firmly behind the banner revolution was not without basis. Lenin, in his report before the delegates of CI in the Second Congress, dealt in considerable detail on the 'Opportunism in the upper ranks of the working class movement'. He wrote,

> Opportunism is our principal enemy. Opportunism in the upper ranks

> of the working class movement is bourgeoisie socialism, not proletarian socialism. It has been shown in practice that working class activists who follow the opportunist trend are better defenders of the bourgeoisie than the bourgeoisie themselves. [Lenin, 1972a, p. 46]

Lenin had an explanation for the 'persistence' of the phenomenon of 'opportunism' among the European working class. Lenin wrote beforehand in the same report,

> Here we must ask: how is the persistence of such trends in Europe to be explained? Why is this opportunism stronger in Western Europe than in our own country? It is because the culture of the advanced countries has been, and still is, the result of their being able to live at the expense of a thousand million oppressed people. It is because the capitalists of these countries obtain a great deal more in this way than they could obtain as profits by plundering the workers in their own countries.
>
> Before the war, it was calculated that the three richest countries —Britain, France and Germany—got between eight to ten thousand million francs a year from the export of capital alone, apart from other sources.
>
> It goes without saying that, out of this tidy sum, at least five hundred millions can be spent as a sop to the labour, the labour leaders and the labour aristocracy, i.e. on all sorts of bribes. The whole thing boils down to nothing but bribery. It is done in a thousand different ways: by increasing cultural facilities in the largest centres, by creating educational institutions, and by providing cooperative, trade union and parliamentary leaders with thousands of cushy jobs. This is done whenever present-day civilized capitalist relations exist....In America, Britain and France we see a far greater persistence of the opportunist leaders, of the upper crust of the working class, the labour aristocracy; they offer stronger resistance to the communist movement. [Lenin, 1972a, pp. 45-46]

To Lenin, the reason behind 'this opportunism' of the working class in the developed capitalist economies was their being part of the loot of the colonies, 'It is because the culture of the advanced countries has been, and still is, the result of their being able to live at the expense of a thousand million oppressed people.' Immediately the question arises how could he advise the "communist" parties to prepare the ground for revolution; ('the preparation of the proletariat for the revolution must be promoted by action') in case the loot of the colonies continued, and the socio-economic basis, 'the culture' remained unaltered in these countries? Although Lenin talked of the 'general state of crisis in all ruling and all bourgeois parties' as a pre-condition for a revolutionary situation, he had declared, 'Opportunism is our principal enemy'. Lenin's exhortation for engineering the revolution by the working class of the developed countries remained challenged by his own analysis. The challenge was the socio-economic bondage of the working class to the capitalist production relations as being the receptor of the loot of "imperialism" in the colonies, as being the receptor of 'all sorts of bribes'—the stumbling block of resistance before 'the communist movement'.

The confusion grows as Marx's vision on the preparation for revolution was quite *different* from Lenin's recommendation of engineering the revolution. The issue before both Marx and Lenin in the referred passages is the same: how the proletariat readies to be *socialist* as a *class*, prepares themselves for unseating the hitherto state-power of the bourgeoisie, for an alternative society where the rights and assertion of the *new class* in power are promised to reign to the fullest. In the following we present a brief elucidation of the difference in approach of Marx and Lenin towards building revolutionary political organizations of the working class in Europe.

### *4.2.1 Towards revolutionary political organization of the working class—the approach of Lenin* **vis-a-vis** *the vision of Marx*

For Marx, revolution is a social necessity, a social imperative for the proletariat that of course required political education, political consciousness that the proletariat gathers in the *class struggle*. Marx was very keen to emphasize in the two places of the passage we quoted above (p. 166) about the sufficient development of the productive forces that necessitates the political revolution as the bourgeoisie is incapacitated to justify the rule of "profit" before the political awareness of the proletariat. Continuing his critique against Proudhon on the social basis for "*combination*" of the workers against the capitalists, Marx wrote,

> This mass [the workers] is thus already a class as against capital, but not yet for itself. In the struggle, of which we have noted only a few

> phases, this mass becomes united, and constitutes itself as a class for itself. The interests it defends becomes *class interests*. But the struggle of class against class is a political struggle. [Marx, 1955, p. 79]

The emphasis of Marx on '*class interests*' and 'struggle of class against class' for the advance of the class consciousness of the working class is worth noting. To Marx, the *socialist* consciousness is ingrained in the measure of the advance of *class struggle* which is the political education for the *new class* to aspire for state-power. This theme of self-education for the working class by means of *class struggle* is repeated again in the same work when Marx wrote,

> Meanwhile the antagonism between the proletariat and the bourgeoisie is a struggle of class against class, a struggle which carried to its highest expression is a total revolution. Indeed, is it at all surprising that a society founded on the opposition of classes should culminate in brutal *contradiction*, the shock of body against body, as its final *denouement*?
>
> Do not say that social movement excludes political movement. There is never a political movement which is not at the same time social.
>
> It is only in an order of things in which there are no more classes and class antagonisms that *social evolutions* will cease to be *political revolutions*. Till then, on the eve of every general reshuffling of society, the last word of social science will always be:
>
> "Le combat on la mort; la lutte sanguinaire ou le neant. C'est ainsi que la question est invinciblement posee." ["Combat or Death: bloody struggle or extinction. It is thus that the question is inexorably put."] [Marx, 1955, p. 80]

A few points become clear from the above observations of Marx. In no way, did Marx abandon or undermine the idea of intense political struggle, 'bloody struggle or extinction' as the manifestation of *class struggle*. Along with the direct participation of the broad "*masses*" of the proletariat in defending their 'class interests', these political forms of struggle also become social struggle paving the way where the proletariat 'constitutes itself as a class for itself'. With the intensity of *class struggle* reaching its peak, the political and social nature of the struggle get interwoven as the political demand of dictatorship of the proletariat becomes increasingly evident and apparent in society.

In this process of self-education through the class activity, is there any separate need for educators? Interestingly, Marx did not deny the need and place of the educators in the progress of *class struggle*, but at the same time he visualized progressive irrelevance of the role of the specialized educators for the proletariat as their self-awareness grows. In the same passage from Marx we quoted in the context of Keynes's interpretation of "socialism", there were a few observations that will not be out of context here to repeat for elaboration of our discussion.

> Just as the *economists* are the scientific representatives of the bourgeois class, so the *Socialists* and *Communists* are the theoreticians of the proletarian class.... these theoreticians are merely utopians who, to meet the wants of the oppressed classes, improvise systems and go in search of a regenerating science. But in the measure that history moves forward, and with it the struggle of the proletariat assumes clearer outlines, they no longer need to seek science in their minds; they have only to take note of what is happening before their eyes and to become its mouthpiece. So long as they look for science and merely make systems, so long as they are at the beginning of the struggle, they see in poverty nothing but poverty, without seeing in it the revolutionary, subversive side, which will overthrow the old society. From this moment, science, which is a product of the historical movement, has associated itself consciously with it, has ceased to be doctrinaire and has become revolutionary. [Marx, 1955, p. 56]

Evidently, Marx included himself also in the club of 'the theoreticians of the proletarian class' whose social necessity as a 'doctrinaire' diminishes as the momentum of revolution peaks up, when there would be no need to conjecture 'science' (modelling "socialism"). Jest apart, in Marx's vision the proletarian revolution unfolds an immense creative response of the "*masses*" in their self-governance, self-sustenance as a cooperative society of *free*, emancipated labour rendering the political theorists and their conjectures irrelevant and out of place in the society. In that sense, with the withering character of *class struggle* in the *new* society, the political nature of struggle among contradictory 'class interests' lose their relevance, '*social evolutions* will cease to be *political revolutions*.' The role of 'the *Socialists* and *Communists*' remain limited to conjecture '*socialism*' as a doctrine till the "*masses*" grasp the theory in their own firm hands, *and* 'become its mouthpiece.'

Therefore, according to Marx the role of the educators is limited to bring in the theory of *socialism* before the proletariat. They remain 'Utopians' 'so long as the struggle itself of the proletariat with the bourgeoisie has not yet assumed a political character.' The existence of the political-ideological mouthpiece of the proletariat, the '*Socialists* and *Communists*' theoreticians serve the role of raising this class consciousness of the proletariat by baring open the political economy of capitalism, and the oppressive nature of the instrument of power – the state. Their modelling, their doctrinaire approach to revolution could be put aside by the "*mass*" awareness, creative participation of the proletarian "*masses*" generated in the social nature of class struggle. Till such events become reality in society, as Marx puts it, '*so long as they are at the beginning of the struggle*', the political '*mouthpieces*' serve and contribute to the class interests, class struggle of the proletariat. If the political spokespersons are represented by a resolute, consistent and class conscious minority among the working class, the communist party, as it happens in the concrete reality of class struggle, going by the above argument of Marx nobody can possibly object to it.

The vision and interpretation of Marx about the role of the communists is substantially different from Lenin's assertion when he wrote [Lenin, 1974], 'absolute centralization and rigorous discipline of the proletariat are an essential condition of victory over the bourgeoisie.' Whereas Marx visualized the *communists* more as educators and publicists among the working class, Lenin and Trotsky looked for active practitioners of revolution among them who would always be at the head of revolution, resolute and epitome of self-sacrifice to see through that revolution is accomplished.[6] In that sense, Lenin viewed the "communists" and the proletariat to be always engaged in physical street battle, if not in a bigger and wider scale with the army of the bourgeoisie. To them, the role of the "communists" was not limited to only being ideological, political educators. As the practitioners of revolution their argument was at the end of the day, wresting of the political authority of state-power that mattered decisively, as it happened in Petrograd and in Moscow in the tumultuous days of revolution in Russia in October 1917.

The difference in the approach of Marx and Lenin for preparation of revolution stemmed from the difference of their perspective about the nature of the build up of revolution. To Marx, proletarian revolution is accentuation of *class struggle*, 'a struggle which carried to its highest expression is a total revolution,' that actually surpasses the role of the educators, 'the theoreticians'. To Lenin, going by his interpretation of the October Revolution and events after, victory of the revolution rested crucially on the leadership of the "communist" party that moulded and regimented the social *class* of people, the proletariat into a disciplined army.

We cannot doubt our understanding of Marx given that the communists in the very midst of revolution faced the same dilemma. The basis of our dilemma is if we go by the arguments of Marx, on both the counts of material progress of the productive forces and awakening within the working class about their class interests, Western Europe was far more advanced than in Russia. Lenin also repeated this fact in agreement in several places. Yet, it was in Russia where the proletariat could retain the state-power for a brief period, went through the sharp and decisive turns of political struggle and education, even though Russia was in far underdeveloped conditions in terms of capitalist economy than Western Europe.

We believe the answer lies in refuting and rejecting the mechanistic reading of Marx, understanding Marx *only* as his argument flows. It is futile and erroneous to believe the dynamics of social unrest, conflicts, even revolutions are to follow textbook style, neat structural logic of a doctrinaire. Marx was certainly objective in bringing out *class struggle* as the political expression of the class antagonisms in production relations in society. A vast majority of the workers in Europe understood and sensed that very well in the post WW-I period while reeling under the torture of inflation, seeing profiteering, black marketeering, speculative trading ascending to dizzy heights, facing acute unemployment and uncertainty in daily life, seeing military conscription of the protestors. On the other hand, the workers of Europe also witnessed the spontaneous and unusual fraternization of the German and Russian soldiers facing opposite sides of the barbed fences in the war trenches. However, even if Marx himself understood that such inflammable material of revolution in the society will in linear progression of steps lead to the confidence of the proletariat to claim their own dictatorship, for being prepared for the Civil War, for demolishing the age-old, near-superstitious submission to the proprietors of capital—we have solemnly to say Marx was not reasoning in materialist dialectics in which he was the first Master. We cannot ignore the fact that while Marx was confident of the interrelations between the development of productive forces and class awakening along the route of *class struggle* he was tentative; he was hemming the analysis with characteristic fluidity of the phenomenon. His observations always encompassed the multidimensional events that influence social evolution and associated political awareness. As Marx stated, 'So long as the proletariat is not yet sufficiently developed to constitute itself as a class,' 'and the productive forces are not yet sufficiently developed in the bosom of the bourgeoisie itself to be enable us to catch a glimpse of the material conditions necessary for the emancipation of the proletariat'—can anybody provide metrics, units of measurements for optimum growth of the attributes 'sufficiently developed', 'glimpse of the material conditions necessary', 'emancipation of the proletariat', etc.? Can the attainments of any revolution right from the time of Spartacus against the Roman Empire to the insurrection of the Communards in the Paris Commune at the time of Marx be predicted with finality while the flames of revolution were raging?

Conversely, are we to understand these profound realizations of Marx in pointing out the poverty of thought of Monsieur Proudhon were only academic exercises, were only conjectures as it happens in theoretical argumentation between two philosophers? The German revolution that raised the spectre of the *Judgement Day* in Keynes about the fate of capitalism ('Therefore Paris does not love Spartacus') was a strong rebuttal to this perception of imaginative argumentation between Marx and Proudhon. In the same work [Hoffrogge, 2014], the author notes in the introduction,

> By contrast, the working class was the principal protagonist of the German Revolution of 1918. The revolution started with a mutiny of sailors and soldiers, but it came to be driven by workers and their organizations. [Hoffrogge, 2014, p. 1]

We will have occasion in this Section to comment on the momentous events of the workers' insurrection in Germany; before that we want to focus our attention to Lenin's analysis of 'opportunism', of 'the upper crust of the working class, the labour aristocracy'. Compared with Marx the features like immediacy, urgency, and drive for action as it happens with the practitioner of politics were very apparent in Lenin's directive in his theses and the rebuttal to the "*Left* Communists". However, his analysis of the hurdles confronting the proletarian revolution remained at best superficial, at worst it was paraphrasing of jargons. We can only wonder in dismay to find in Lenin's writing, 'Opportunism in the upper ranks of the working class movement is bourgeoisie socialism, not proletarian socialism.' Can *socialism* be made equivalent to any variety of bourgeoisie civilization? Is *socialism* a kind of dress material found hanging for window shopping, either of the bourgeoisie variety or of proletarian origin, and, as if, one is free to choose any one of them? This is like branding some social phenomenon, political tendencies with jargon as we have seen earlier in reference to 'state socialism' by Lenin.

Next, we find Lenin denigrating the welfare facilities that the workers enjoyed in Europe from the capitalist class as bribes. 'The whole thing boils down to nothing but bribery. It is done in a thousand different ways: by increasing cultural facilities in the largest centres, by creating educational institutions, and by providing co-operative, trade union and parliamentary leaders with thousands of cushy jobs. This is done whenever present-day civilized capitalist relations exist.' It is one thing to condemn purchase of the individual leaders and parliamentary deputies, or even organizations officially recognized by the state such as 'trade unions, parliamentary' establishments by the bourgeoisie possessing all the money bags. It is completely different in meaning when Lenin painted with the same brush the welfare facilities the workers with better wages enjoy as bribe. Not only in one place, did Lenin repeat and stress the capacity of the bourgeoisie in purchasing a sizeable stratum of the working class as 'labour aristocracy', ironically while he was speaking on the necessity of the participation of the communists in the trade unions affiliated to the British Labour Party.

> After all, the labour aristocracy has existed in Britain, not for decades but for centuries. The British bourgeoisie, which has had far more

> experience—democratic experience—than that of any other country, has been able to buy workers over and to create among them a sizable stratum, greater than in any other country, but one that is not so great compared with the masses of the workers. [Lenin, 1972a, p. 76]

Lenin was not unaware that capitalism thrives by competition among the divisions of labour, among the wage earners. The hegemony of ownership of capital in the industries that enjoy the monopoly over the market offer even stiffer competition within the same discipline of division of labour. The welfare facilities that Lenin alleged to be 'bribes' were earned by the workers through long-standing struggle, by their wage negotiations through the trade unions only. In a broader perspective, these welfare facilities were part of the *surplus value* the workers themselves generated that the bourgeoisie had to part with to keep the class antagonisms within a limit so that their production cycles remain effectively secured, undisturbed. After the WWI, many of these facilities to the workers were wiped off from the industrial scenario in which Lenin made this report. Even in Great Britain there was large-scale unemployment after the war. The workers in Britain, in Italy (we have quoted earlier the factory occupation movement by the workers in Italy) were restive because of the huge loss in real wages after the war, the primary reason that attracted them to the Soviet form of government. Lenin's analysis about the living standard of the workers in the countries that enjoyed a larger share of net "profit" in the capitalist world ('It is done in a thousand different ways') actually ran in contradiction with Marx's argument for the conditions ripening into revolution. It is those workers who enjoy a better wage structure under capitalism are also related to the more advanced production processes, and therefore are more aware of their class position in the capitalist cycle of "profit" generation. It is true that the existence of the different strata among the wage earners in general and among the industrial workers in particular is a great challenge before the working class unity, towards *class struggle* taking the shape of political struggle. The challenge will remain to be grave in the understanding of the working class till their average class-consciousness remains tied to the wage-slavery of existing production relations. However, the challenge cannot be confronted, let alone be overcome by designating the workers attached to the most advanced production centres as the recipient of 'bribes' by the capitalist class. Saying that is tantamount to seeking the abolition of the modern large-scale production machinery, the industries, the technologies that are in many cases forerunners of *socialism* in an industrialized society.

In fact, if Keynes portrayed "socialism" as a graveyard of economic transactions in society, "communism" to Lenin was a society of the ascetics, a society practising only frugality, a society where poverty is redistributed in an egalitarian manner as in Russia the Bolsheviks were forced to do. On the other hand, to Marx *communism* is a society of joy, a society of abundance, of freedom where individuals pursue labour of their own choice. Emma Goldman, the well known anarchist[7] who was deported to Russia in 1919 after being released from prison in the USA for her revolutionary activities, famously stated after witnessing revolutionary Russia, "If I can't dance, I don't want to be part of your revolution." By *socialism*, Marx envisaged such a society with freedom to harness the joy of life requiring no license from the state. This society was progressing in Europe where the productive forces were developing 'in the bosom of the bourgeoisie itself to enable us to catch a glimpse of the material conditions necessary for the emancipation of the proletariat and for the formation of a new society.' By branding the workers engaged in more developed production process as recipients of 'bribes', Lenin questioned this very fundamental needs of 'the material conditions necessary for the emancipation of the proletariat', for *communism* to exist. In terms of the real, concrete features of the workers' politics, Lenin's analysis divided the working class (instead of uniting them on the higher plane of knowledge, realization and self-awareness) into two broad categories. One category was the elite workers with better wages who were supposed to be disinterested in "communism". The other category was the average, downtrodden workers ruthlessly exploited by capital who would be more outrageous in their expressions of class hatred towards the capitalist class. The implication of such categorization among the working class is admission of the status quo of existence of the working class *as they are* under capitalism, not preparing the ground for unity on an alternative higher plane where the working class can exist without, and independent of the bourgeoisie. Such categorization and blaming the workers engaged in the modern, advanced production process for their social status in the capitalist society actually strengthened the influence of the 'opportunist' leadership among them.

While we are critical about Lenin's assessment of the constitution of the working class in terms of the political economy of European capitalism we do share the opinion that no two revolutions have to follow the single course, either the Russian or the German variety. The question of leadership in revolution that Lenin and Trotsky wanted to project with all sincerity (their intention of international revolution was never in doubt even among their fiercest critics during the period) can never be ignored. What they meant with absolute conviction was the leadership of the "communists" will be indispensable in every revolution of the working class. Their conviction was borne out of the historical fact that one principal reason behind the terrible defeat of the German revolution was the lack of resolute, determined centre at the head of revolution. The absence of a resolute, unified leadership did not only cost the working class in Germany alone, it made the Russian revolution vulnerable to all the inherent features of weakness that we have elaborated earlier. The bulwark against the European capitalist society, the modern form of *barbarism* of wanton destruction of civilization, was decimated in the bloodied jails and streets of Berlin. Saying this, we should also ask what did the German revolution achieved? In the following subsection, we briefly retrace the achievements of the working class revolution in Germany in January 1919 so as to put the views of Marx and Engels on political organization of the working class in the context of practical history of the revolt of the modern working class under the developed form of capitalism.

### *4.2.2. The January 1919 Revolt of the working class in Germany*

It is true that the leaders of social-democracy in Europe, particularly the political parties and leaders affiliated to the Second International, deserted the class interests of the proletariat all over Europe that was most apparent in their support of the war efforts of the belligerent states. Particularly in Germany, the overwhelming support of the leadership of SPD to the war efforts of Kaiser Germany was revealed by the fact that only one parliamentary deputy raised the flag of internationalism (Karl Liebknecht). But what was the response of the Berlin workers whom Lenin found to constitute the 'upper crust of working class'? We quote from [Hoffrogge, 2014],

> The German working class in 1914 did not oppose the war with enthusiasm, but they did not cheer it either. Especially the skilled workers were in a position to develop their own opinion. As Müller pointed out, the Berlin lathe operators were a group that was organizationally firm and indispensable to production. In a way, they represented the heart of heavy industry. The companies paid them better and they worked under better conditions than other sections. This group rebelled entirely against the companies' war provisions [including an effective wage freeze], demanded higher wages, and got them ... But the lathe operators not only protected their own interests. They also supported other weaker groups, particularly female workers, in disagreements with their companies.[17]....
>
> The first political mass strike of June 1916 is widely associated with Karl Liebknecht and Rosa Luxemburg's Spartacist group, founded in January of the same year.[2] However, while the dramatic arrest of Karl Liebknecht on May Day 1916, immediately after he condemned the war and the government before a massed meeting the Spartacists had called in Potsdamer Platz, provided the occasion, and while the Spartacists were indeed involved, the strike was in fact organized by the Revolutionary Shop Stewards. The two groups worked as allies, but not without tensions. They also had different spheres of mobilization: while the Shop Stewards organized workers on the shop floor, the Spartacists wanted to take them to the streets....
>
> It started with Berlin's large companies—Borsig, AEG, Löwe, and Schwartzkopff—and grew from there. News that 'The lathe operators are striking for Liebknecht!' spread by word of mouth, activated other divisions in their respective companies, and led to a complete walkout on many job sites.[6] The action turned a demonstration of state power into a show of strength for the anti-war movement and showcased the new opposition group's potential. Although the Shop Stewards were at first confined to the Berlin lathe operators employed in large companies, they were soon able to draw out enormous masses of workers from throughout the metal industry wherever their calls fit the mood of the workforce. [pp. 26, 37]

The leading role of the Berlin shop stewards, in Lenin's words, a part of the 'labour aristocracy' in organizing the revolution later in January 1919 is now appearing well documented in recent publications [Kuhn, 2012], [Broue, 2005]. Their contribution in the making of revolution was deliberately obliterated in the last century by defacing the accounts of revolutionary movements of the working class. Historical accounts were narrated by observing the events only through the looking glass of the history of political groups, be it the 'Spartacists' or the Bolsheviks. The most significant event in the above passage was 'News that 'The lathe operators are striking for Liebknecht!' spread by word of mouth, activated other divisions in their respective companies, and led to a complete walkout on many job sites'.[6] The highly paid workers in war-torn Germany could find their wavelength instantly in the anti-war political standpoint of Liebknecht as their own class interest that galvanized them in immediate strike action. Their leader, Richard Müller, himself a lathe operator with no formal education "beyond the eight years of primary school that was common at the time.[5]" [Hoffrogge, 2014], was elected the Chairman of First General Congress of the Workers' and Soldiers' Councils of Germany in Berlin during the January days of revolution in 1919. Lenin, the devoted enthusiast of the workers' insurrection in Germany, was completely at variance in his analysis before the gathering of international revolutionaries in CI with the actual events of the German revolution. His 'Utopia' of the leading role of the "communist" party in the execution of revolution was overwhelmingly challenged by the experience of the workers' participation as decision-makers. The workers on their own became leaders of the "*masses*" of the workers, and most significantly in many cases, without being in direct association with any of the political streams, be it the Spartacus group that later became the KPD, or other larger parties like USPD or SPD, when the workers were asserting for the alternative rule in the form of Workers' and Soldiers' Council.

We again take the reference from [Hoffrogge, 2014] that shows how the workers in Berlin involved in the modern, scientific process of production prepared themselves for the general strike of January 1918, the prelude to the impending revolution.

> On the morning of January 28, 1918, the lathe operators and Shop Stewards signalled the beginning of the strike by striking the oxygen tanks used for welding with hammers.[45] Within a few hours Berlin's entire armament industry came to a standstill. By the afternoon of the first day, 414 delegates representing 400,000 workers gathered for a meeting in the Berlin union hall. Richard Müller led the assembly and received their demands. By unanimous decision, the demand for peace without annexations or indemnities as well as consultation with labour representatives from every nation at the peace negotiations was set. Domestic demands included better food supply, an end to the state of siege, restoration of freedom of the press, an end to military interference in union affairs, and a 'drastic democratization of the entire state apparatus', beginning with universal suffrage—including women's suffrage—for the Prussian Landtag or state parliament....
>
> Although their demands were not yet council-democratic, workers' council practices pervaded the strike: rank-and-file delegates directly determined demands and actions, the Action Committee received its mandate from them and its legitimacy was not mediated by parties or unions. Indeed, many of the councils that spontaneously emerged throughout Germany during the Revolution later that year followed the example of the January Strike leadership in Berlin.[47] [pp. 49-50]

We now proceed to a more definitive account of the history of the German working class revolution to get a vivid portrayal of the tensions and contradictions among the workers. They inevitably were part of the momentous political, social events enacted in the revolution of January 1919 alongside the resoluteness of the workers to accomplish the revolution. Dual power existed in Germany from November 1918 to January 1919 when both the Weimar Republic and the Workers' and Soldiers' Council vied for supremacy of political and state-power in German society. Comparing the accomplishment of the Russian revolution with the German case in the Chapter on "The period of dual power", Pierre Broue inferred,

> But it would be a mistake to go on to compare the German councils in November 1918 to the Russian soviets in November 1917. We need to compare them first to the soviets in February 1917; both had emerged from largely spontaneous activity before the great political debate about power had developed. Despite the weakness of their organization, the German revolutionaries played a more important role in the formation of the councils than the Bolsheviks did in the

> formation of the soviets. Moreover, the bourgeoisie recognized this factor, both in Germany and in the countries of the Entente.
>
> In reality, the chances of a German soviet revolution appeared on 9 November 1918 to be more serious than those of a Russian soviet revolution in February 1917. To be sure, the councils in all the workers' centres were divided between the two influences of the SPD and the USPD. In Russia, the Mensheviks and the Socialist Revolutionaries were in the majority across the country, including on the Petrograd Soviet. In Germany, on the contrary, the revolutionaries, left Independents, International Communists and Spartacists, partisans of the dictatorship of the proletariat, led some of the most important councils. Müller in Berlin, Kurt Eisner in Munich, Rück in Stuttgart, Heckert in Chemnitz, Lipinski in Leipzig, Merges in Brunswick, Laufenberg in Hamburg, all were chairmen of councils of workers and soldiers, the authority of which spread over whole regions." [Broue, 2005, p. 187]

Broue wrote in detail about the programmes of state-power these revolutionary councils took upon themselves as immediate programmes of action in the next few pages of his work,

> An important development which signified the will of the revolutionaries to create an alternative centre of power was the formation by the councils of their own armed force or police.[16] There were workers' guards in Frankfurtam-Main and Hildenburghausen,[17] workers' volunteers in Düsseldorf,[18] a security force in Hamburg[19] and, most often, red guards, the nuclei of which were formed by mutinous sailors, for example, under the leadership of the non-commissioned officer Lunsmann[20] in Bremen, in Halle the 'security regiment', led by the former officer Fritz Ferchlandt and the 'red sailor' Karl Meseberg,[21] and in Brunswick, a guard numbering a thousand.[22]
>
> Lastly, in the councils led by revolutionaries, the Executives provided themselves with structures suited to the tasks of government, with individual commissions responsible for finance, public security, food supplies, labour problems, and so on. They took upon themselves powers at every level, those of the judiciary as well as of the legislature or the executive, in accordance with the very character of soviet power. [Broue, 2005, p. 192]

The workers followed direct election of the executives so far as the constitution of these bodies are there as the organs of revolution. The elected representatives reflected the influences of the political parties, groups or tendencies among the workers. Broue wrote on the formation of "The councils of workers and soldiers" as,

> Whatever confusion existed amongst the revolutionaries over the precise definition of councils, all agreed that they had to be democratic, and this bluntly contradicted any idea of rigged elections or votes by acclamation. Most of the time, the working people wanted an elected council. The Social Democrats, ever loyal to their 'democratic principle', wanted elections on a territorial basis, by districts; suffrage was 'universal', and public figures, such as members of the apparatus, could, as in ordinary elections, defeat candidates known for their class positions. ....
>
> Elsewhere, the elections were held in the factories according to the principle of the dictatorship of the proletariat, where the right to vote was organized on the basis of units of production. In Berlin, the workers elected one delegate per thousand votes in the big factories, and one delegate per part of a thousand elsewhere.[7] In Frankfurt-am-Main, the figure was one per 400, in Hamburg and Leipzig it was one per 600, in Stuttgart one per 300, and in Bremen one per 180.[8]
>
> In the pyramid of councils from the workplace to the locality, the influence of the SPD and the trade-union apparatus became stronger the closer to the summit. They therefore worked hard in the weeks which followed the establishment of the councils to form regional councils in which they kept a majority, simply by adding the councils which they controlled, or in which they enjoyed parity. .... [Broue, 2005, p. 159]

We provide long references of the workers' participation in the agitations in Germany right from May 1916 to the revolution in January 1919 to strengthen a few points that we argued in this Section with respect to the preparation of the proletariat for *socialism*, for dictatorship of the proletariat. First, the glorious history of the German working class in their attempt to usher their own, independent rule over society showed Marx was no 'Utopian', he was not engaged in mere academic argumentation with Proudhon. The fact that he could visualize and argue for an intense, life-and-death competition from the workers for building the society based on the alternative narrative of *abolition of private property* is itself the mark of a genius. Second, the records from history that we placed above clearly show the revolution started in November 1918 by the sailors at Kiel was not a one-off event; it was indeed preceded by continuous, militant, active and spontaneous participation of the workers in the political milieu, who asserted their rights to elect their political representatives and chart out the course of action. Third, although the October Revolution of the Russian workers was the precedent, the German revolution grew on its own feet, was more mature in content towards dictatorship of the proletariat. It drew inspiration from the feat the Russian workers had accomplished, but had developed its own course that showed clearly the attainments in its victory and defeat. Fourth, the historical records of the events in revolutionary Germany put Lenin's analysis in a poor light that the awareness, consciousness, assertion in the political domain by the working class necessarily need guidance, mentoring by a leading minority that was understood to be an *elite* grown within the working class in the *obverse* sense of Lenin's definition of 'labour aristocracy' under capitalism. His directive in the theses for the Second Congress of CI, 'to create a united communist party in each country.... to multiply tenfold the work of preparing the proletariat for the conquest of State power in the form of the dictatorship of the proletariat.' carried this sense of tutoring the working class. The pitfall of this directive was as it happened in Russia, the tutor turned to be the "Master" of the working class.

In this context, we would like to remember Herman Gorter[8], the Dutch communist whom Lenin considered as one of the targets of Lenin in his attack against "*Left*-wing communism". Gorter wrote the *Open Letter to Comrade Lenin* in 1920 as the rebuttal to Lenin's attack where he made the following critical comments,

> And nowhere, at least as far as I have read, is there a clear and outspoken recognition of the immense difference which prevails in the matter between Russia (and a few other countries in Eastern Europe) and Western Europe (that is to say Germany, France, England, Belgium, Holland, Switzerland, and the Scandinavian countries, and perhaps even Italy). And yet, in my opinion, the fundamental difference between your conception of the tactics concerning Trade Unionism and Parliamentarism, and that of the so-called Left Wing in Western Europe, lies mainly in this point.
>
> ....
>
> Have you not observed, Comrade Lenin, that in Germany there are no great leaders? They are all quite ordinary men. This points to the fact that this revolution must in the first place be the work of the masses, not of the leaders.

> And as it is in Germany, it is in all Western Europe, for everywhere the proletariat stands alone.
>
> The revolution of the masses, of the workers—of the masses of workers alone, for the first time in the world. [Gorter, 1920]

Beautiful words from Gorter whose primary accomplishment was his mastery over Greek and Latin poetry.

However, we want to point out although the theses of Marx enumerating *class struggle* as the political struggle between the bourgeoisie and the proletariat paved the general course of this alternate narrative of the proletariat, he did not mention or comment on the huge challenge that comes from *within* the working class to build the narrative. Marx could visualize the generality, 'Meanwhile the antagonism between the proletariat and the bourgeoisie is a struggle of class against class, a struggle which carried to its highest expression is a total revolution.' In the same chapter of *The Poverty of Philosophy*, Marx identified four schools of bourgeoisie economists, "the scientific representatives of bourgeois production" namely, *i*) fatalists, *ii*) romantics, *iii*) humanitarian, *iv*) philanthropic. These schools attempted to interpret the class antagonisms and the class interests of 'bourgeoisie production' in their own ways, substantially different from Marx. Consequent to these different interpretations of the political economy of capitalist production relations there were different political parties as characterized in England in Lenin's time such as the Fabians, the Liberals, the Torys, and of course the Labour party with considerable political influence among the working class. Their different political programmes and internal strife among them did not inhibit them to serve the class interests of the bourgeoisie society as a whole representing the commonness among the different political programmes. Likewise, in Germany as well as in Russia, there were different political programmes and interpretations of the socio-economy existing in the general interest of the working class. In Germany, the original party of social democracy founded on the basis of the Erfurt programme in 1891 with the "blessings" from Engels was the Social Democratic Party (SPD) of Germany that carried and continued the tradition of the Second International. This was the party with the largest parliamentary vote share and trade union affiliation following among the working class, and was the principal political party of the Weimar Republic.

Apart from SPD there were the following major political parties and groups among the working class that actively took part in the revolution and in the revolutionary councils' executive formation:

1. The communists, first organized in the *Spartakusbund* [Spartacus League] and the *Internationale Kommunisten Deutschlands* [International Communists of Germany] (IKD), then in the *Kommunistische Partei Deutschlands* [Communist Party of Germany] (KPD), founded by the Spartacus League and the IKD on January 1, 1919.
2. The *Unabhängige Sozialdemokratische Partei Deutschlands* [Independent Social Democratic Party of Germany] (USPD), founded in 1917, when the left wing of the *Sozialdemokratische Partei Deutschlands* [Social Democratic Party of Germany] (SPD) split from the mother party in protest against the SPD's continued support of the war. All Spartacus League members were part of the USPD before the founding of the KPD.
3. Radical labor organizers, most notably the *Revolutionäre Obleute* [Revolutionary Stewards], who were predominantly factory workers with long experience in union struggles and strong trust among the radical proletariat.
4. The *anarchists*, most notably Gustav Landauer and Erich Mühsam. [Kuhn, 2012]

There were several counter currents of fluxes inside these political formations as, "In 1917, both Eduard Bernstein and Karl Kautsky became members of the independent social democratic party of Germany (USPD), a party that also included Karl Liebknecht, Rosa Luxemburg, and their Spartacus League." [Hoffrogge, 2014, p. 3] Again, soon after the defeat of the revolution, KPD could not keep its ranks together when the party ousted "ultra-left ranks" among them as early as in September 1919. The communist workers' party of Germany (KAPD) constituting the so-called "Left-Wing" ranks of KPD was formed in April 1920 where both Gorter and Pannekoek played the principal role of theoretical mentors. It is interesting to note that in the Second Congress of CI representation of the German working class came from USPD, KPD, and KAPD, signifying all these political currents then stood on the same platform of dictatorship of the proletariat. The principal proponents of "Left-wing Communism" were found all over Europe. They were in direct disagreement with the Bolshevik standpoints in the Second Congress of CI regarding the policies of communist organizations after the defeat of revolutions in Europe in 1919-20, particularly in Europe as reflected in Gorter's response to Lenin's attack in [Lenin, 1974]. The following paragraph from a recent research account [Bourrinet, 2008] may be cited as a pointer to these developments during the time of the Second Congress of CI.

> It was during 1919 that a communist current of the left, with a political, rather than a Unionist basis, was really formed in the developed countries. The electoral question was the key question for the left in some countries. In March 1918, the polish Communist Party – which was the descendant of the SDKPiL of Rosa Luxemburg and Leo Jogisches—boycotted the elections. In Italy, the Naples *Il Soviet* was published on December 22, 1918, edited by Amadeo Bordiga. In contrast with Gramsci and his syndicalist current, which defended participation in elections, Bordiga's current defended communist abstentionism with a view to eliminating the reformists in the Italian socialist party and in order to form a "pure communist party".[406] Formally the abstentionist communist fraction of the PSI was formed in October 1919. In Britain Sylvia Pankhurst's Workers' Socialist Federation declared itself against "revolutionary" parliamentarism in order to avoid "wasting energy".[407] In Belgium the 'De Internationale' group of Flanders and War van Overstraeten's group were against electoralism.[408] The situation was the same in the more 'peripheral' countries. At the Congress of the Bulgarian Communist Party in May 1919 a strong minority distinguished itself in condemning parliamentary action in principle.[409] [p. 118]

We provide these details of the historical currents of political formations all over Europe (not to mention the "*Left* Communists" in Russia whom Lenin attacked in May 1918) to show even among the revolutionary sections of the workers who were united on the common platform of dictatorship of the proletariat, Soviet rule, and formation of communist party there were strong disagreements, that soon splintered into a number of different formations. One cannot ignore the fact these debates were not among the idealists, but among the revolutionists who were active participants and played a crucial role in organizing the militant revolts of the European working class. Such disagreements among the revolutionists were one principal reason for the defeat of the

German revolution that could not find a focused, resolute direction when it was most wanted. We quote from [Broue, 2005] to substantiate this argument.

> The drama and the historic weakness of the German workers' and soldiers' councils is ultimately bound up with the fact that there did not exist a real 'conciliar party', to encourage and invigorate them, and to take part in the struggle for conciliar power, which the Bolsheviks were able to do between February and October 1917. On the decisive problem of 'constituent assembly or councils', the leaders of the right wing of the USPD, Haase, Dittmann, and so on, adopted, with a few fine differences, the positions of the SPD. The leftwing Independents, organized separately, generally shared the conception of the leading Spartacists. The Spartacists themselves were divided between the leading nucleus, which worked within the perspective that it was necessary to win the masses, and the impatient elements who gave up the task of convincing the masses. This confusion and the absence of a revolutionary organization to lead a consistent struggle for winning the majority in the councils and for the seizure of state power by the councils, left the field clear for the enemies of the councils who were at work within them. [p. 196]

All these developments at the peak of revolutionary stride of the working class in Europe show clearly the limitation of Marx in conceiving political struggle as the sole representation and manifestation of *class struggle* between *the entire bourgeoisie interests with the whole proletariat.* That is why revolutionary "*mass*" actions are far more educative, far more piercing in bringing the hard truth of historical materialism surpassing the genius of the philosophers. In revolutionary times, the froth of every political current and interest in the society spill over the cauldron of upheaval in the society. The oppressed and exploited classes get more excited in sensing a nearing victory that probably for generations together they could not imagine, and the contradictions amongst their sectional interests often cloud their general class interests. More than resolution of *class struggle,* manifestations of the political demands of the society attain a certain degree of prominence. The immediate demands and rallying calls of the political parties take the priority over redressing the salient features of exploitations from the bourgeois society that the revolution confronts. Therefore, the political questions turn out to be imminent before the society that requires immediate resolution in the period of the revolution. It was the hallmark of the brilliant political leadership of Lenin, Trotsky and the Bolsheviks who even with strong currents of disagreements and dissidence among themselves could steer the Russian revolution towards their immediate resolution, towards peace on the war-front even if it was humiliating to the core of Russian national honour. They could remain united under tremendous stress and anticipation of losing the revolution (perhaps as every week passed by). They played the role of effective leadership among the Russian workers, soldiers and peasants in the initial days of Soviet rule, so that even after a hundred years have passed we have the opportunity and luxury of animated discussions and debates, both among the circles of academics and political activists, on whether at all dictatorship of the proletariat was ever practised on the earth.

At the same time, it is now beyond doubt that Lenin and Trotsky stretched the differences among the heterogeneous, varied strata of the working class to the extent of class contradiction, as if the *class struggle* between the bourgeoisie and proletariat were first to be finished within the ranks of the proletariat itself. Their egalitarian perspective about the working class, particularly their irrational approach towards the strata related to more advanced production process actually was detrimental to understand the contradictions and dynamism *within* the working class. On the converse side, the Bolsheviks themselves were playing the most ardent role in making Russia a developed nation-state along the path of 'state capitalism'. With the passage of time, their approach towards the international working class revolution became dependent on the sole interests of this new nation-state where the state-power was under the hegemony of the *vanguard* party in place of the working class. The social class that promoted the revolution was compelled to undergo 'absolute centralization and rigorous discipline' by the immediate needs of nation building. This inward bound outlook to defend and protect the national interests of the war-ravaged Russian economy compelled the Bolsheviks to insist on the 'Russian model' of revolution to be the standard bearer of the Third International. The tragic turn of history was such that the model that could have challenged the 'Russian model' as the signboard for rule under the control of the *vanguard* party in lieu of dictatorship of the proletariat was crushed to defeat owing to the lack of a unified command of revolution.

### 4.3 Ideological Outlook of the European Working Class During the Post-WWI Social Crisis

Another important aspect behind the failure of the working class in putting up decisive efforts for a *new*, alternative society in civil war-torn Europe was seldom discussed in the documents of CI onwards the Second Congress. That is the question of ideological preparation of the European proletariat towards *socialism*. We have dealt with the cardinal importance of revolutionary ideology in ushering a social revolution in Section 2.3 of this essay. We have specifically addressed the ideological moorings of Bolshevism there while we discussed the assertion of the workers' rights in the production process, and the juridical rights of the people under the Soviet state. The role of CI even in the formative years got restricted to a political platform with an immediate goal of seizing the state-power as it was understood to be the core issue of the *class struggle*. Marx analysed long back, "The ideas of the ruling class are in every epoch the ruling ideas, i.e. the class which is the ruling material force of society, is at the same time its ruling intellectual force." [Marx, 1968] The question of ideological preparation of the working class in this huge, arduous battle against the 'ruling intellectual force' of bourgeoisie society was given short shrift. By ideological preparation, it was understood to be the political education the proletariat derives in their daily, hourly eking out existence for self, of family against the bourgeoisie. While discussing the contribution of Rosa Luxemburg before the international proletariat, Tony Cliff in his article on Rosa Luxemburg's place in history had to say the following:

> In Central and Western Europe conservative reformism had much deeper roots, a much more embracing influence on the thoughts and moods of the workers. The arguments of the reformists had to be answered by superior ones, and here Rosa Luxemburg excelled. In these countries her scalpel is a much more useful weapon than Lenin's sledgehammer. ...
>
> Rosa Luxemburg's blend of revolutionary spirit and clear

> understanding of the nature of the labour movement in Western and Central Europe is in some way connected with her particular background of birth in the Tsarist Empire, long residence in Germany, and full activity in both the Polish and German labour movements. Anyone of smaller stature would have been assimilated into one of the two environments, but not Rosa Luxemburg. To Germany she brought the "Russian" spirit, the spirit of revolutionary action. To Poland and Russia she brought the "Western" spirit of workers' self-reliance, democracy and self-emancipation. [Cliff, 1959]

As the writing was in the form of personal tribute to an illuminating, departed personality the flowery pattern of language in the above passage is understandable. Equally understandable is Tony Cliff's realization why the working class in Europe over the ages did not confront the questions of state- power in a forceful, decisive manner. By referring to the 'conservative reformism had much deeper roots, a much more embracing influence on the thoughts and moods of the workers' of Europe, Tony Cliff pointed to the strong influence the currents of reformism, economism had over the workers even in their destitute condition after the war. These deep roots of submission before the supremacy of the established order of the bourgeoisie society were not confronted daily, hourly in the process of eking out the life of an ordinary worker. These deep roots of submission of the exploited people, commonly referred to as "*mass*", to the established order is the most crucial sign of subjugation as an ideological, cultural process of every class-divided society. It was not that the workers of post-WWI Europe did not fear the prospects of violent confrontation with the organs of state-power, the element of "fear" definitely would have been there as the *class struggle* remained at a low ebb. More than the "fear" element there were a thousand questions in the mind of an average worker that played a crucial role in making them diffident before the central query —"what next"?

It is often meant that the Russian workers were far less prepared to hold on to dictatorship of the proletariat once they ushered the revolution between February to October, 1917. In fact, that was the principal line of argument of Kautsky, Plekhanov, and the Menshevik streams of political thought process. Plekhanov wrote an *Open Letter* to the revolutionary workers of Petrograd on October 28, 1917 where he mentioned,

> The class-conscious elements of our proletariat must ask themselves the question: Is our proletariat ready to proclaim a dictatorship? Everyone who has even a partial understanding as to what economic conditions are necessary for the dictatorship of the proletariat will unhesitatingly answer no to this question.
>
> No, our working class is far from ready to grasp political power with any advantage to itself and the country at large. To foist such a power upon it means to push it towards a great historical calamity which will prove the greatest tragedy for all Russia. [Plekhanov, 1917]

Even a large section within the Bolsheviks did not anticipate that revolution and seizing of state-power was practically possible till the July action of firing over the workers' demonstration happened on July 4-5, 1917. This incident created the inflammable situation where the "*mass*" action of the workers swept all the inhibition among the Bolsheviks to prepare for insurrection. Paul Frölich[9], in his biography *Rosa Luxemburg*, wrote about the significant difference between the February and October revolution of Russia in 1917.

> The February uprising of 1917 was also a completely spontaneous action of the St Petersburg workers and soldiers. In contrast, the uprising of 7th November 1917 was systematically prepared and laid down according to a definite plan. It was carried out almost exclusively by regular army troops; this was possible because a significant part of the ordinary soldiers—in Petrograd the preponderant part by far—already stood by the side of the revolution and pressed for action, and the rest of the soldiers were wavering in their support of the old regime. We can see a similar development also in the great French revolution: a spontaneous action on 14th July 1789 which shook absolutism to its foundations, and a systematically planned action on 10th August 1792 which brought the decisive victory. [Frölich, 2010, p. 108]

A time line of the days of Russian revolution available at *www.marxists.org* reads the events of July 4, 1917 in Petrograd as,

> At 3 am, 80,000 workers and soldiers reach the Tauride Palace. Junkers meet the demonstrators, and tear up placards. A shot is fired, but disaster is averted. The Bolsheviks spend the early hours of morning figuring out how to organize the demonstrators.

> By 11 am the demonstrators assemble yet again. Now, entire Regiments arrive, but they are no longer at the front of the demonstrations: the workers have taken the lead by shear mass of numbers. Even in factories where Mensheviks and SRs hold influence, four out of five workers join the demonstrations. The nation witnesses a massive General Strike. Lenin speaks to the demonstrators, encouraging their slogan of *All power to the Soviets!*
>
> Over 500,000 people attend the demonstrations in Petrograd. The first of the soldiers from the front arrive ready to support the Provisional Government, and frightened that a revolution is imminent, are ordered to launch ambushes against the masses. 400 people are killed and wounded. The Mensheviks, hands covered in blood, eventually "convince" the demonstrators to go home. [Baggins, 2005]

We have quoted these references to show how the energetic "*mass*" actions swept over the doubts, inhibitions, vacillations of the more circumspective elements involved in the process. They are the hallmarks of every genuine revolution aspiring for a *new* society. Be it in Paris in August 1792, *or* in Petrograd in October 1917, one characteristic feature remained unaltered in the two revolutions led by the general class interests of the bourgeoisie and the proletariat respectively. The "*masses*" of the oppressed classes invade the seats and citadels of power with determined grit on the eve of revolution, even when the class interests of the leading sections of the two revolutions turned violently opposite of each other in the span of two centuries. If for an argument's sake, we consider that the later course of history possibly supported the cautionary argument of Plekhanov ('a great historical calamity which will prove the greatest tragedy for all Russia'), it would have been a case of foretelling the future. By all accounts of history, October 1917 in Petrograd sparked off the revolutionary zeal and imagination of the working class over the entire industrialized Europe. We could have given similar accounts of the days of January 1919 in Berlin, but since they are now available in a greater number of well-researched accounts (we have given elaborate references from a few of them), we refrain from that exercise.

In spite of the bravery of the working class in the post-WWI historical setting of Russia and Germany, the question we formulated earlier in this subsection remained unanswered that was in the mind of an average industrial worker in Europe. Defeat of the German revolution and the setback of the repeated efforts of the revolutionary sections there, the actual living standards of the Russian workers, their very limited access and freedom to exercise authority in the decision-making process definitely made the workers of Western Europe to wonder why for the revolution was enacted. The question that definitely haunted the working class of the industrialized nations was why such a high price of sacrifice was to be paid and for whose benefit? Paul Mattick, who later became a bitter critic of the Bolshevik practices, wrote while comparing Luxemburg's contribution with Lenin in 1935,

> Lenin was a practical politician. It was essentially only as a tactician that he distinguished himself from the theoreticians of the Second International. What they sought to attain along democratic ways, he attempted to win by revolutionary means. Not with speeches in parliament, but with force on the real field of the class struggle, he wanted to realize socialism for the workers. [Mattick, 1935]

One may disagree with Mattick's sweeping contention here. His significant remark quoted here, 'Not with speeches in parliament, but with force on the real field of the class struggle', that Lenin wanted to realize "socialism" for the workers' echoed in the reflection of thoughts among the workers of Europe. They were at the cross roads in choosing the future of serving *capitalism* either under the charade of parliamentary democracy, *or* under the labour conscription forced by the state in lieu of a certain degree of security in receiving food, lodging, education, health care—that too under the severe restrictions of movement, and after making all the sacrifices for the revolution. Today, we may have the luxury of hindsight of analysing the events that were past more than ninety years ago. What Mattick stated was the reality before the class-conscious workers suffering under the Great Depression of 1929 in Europe and USA, seeing the horror of hectic war preparation of Nazi Germany, and witnessing what for "socialism" stood in the regimentation of society in Russia. This was particularly true in Europe where freedom of the individual in choosing a profession was still a sacrosanct moral edict in the society as the preparations for the WWII were set in when military conscription was again enforced in the "free societies" of Europe.

By ideological preparation we mean the tough, challenging and tortuous task of bringing before the working class the true character of *socialism* as a society based on high degree of libertarian principles. Unfortunately, the Third International soon ceased to be the platform to wage this ideological battle not only within the secured precincts of the bourgeoisie, but much beyond and above the prevailing affairs of the society. Responding to Lenin's attack on "*Left* Wing Communism", Pannekoek brought out the significance of ideological preparation much to the focus in the context of defeat of the German revolution.

> But in November 1918, state power slipped from the nerveless grasp of the bourgeoisie in Germany and Austria, the coercive apparatus of the state was completely paralyzed, the masses were in control; and the bourgeoisie was nevertheless able to build this state power up again and once more subjugate the workers. This proves that the bourgeoisie possessed another hidden source of power which had remained intact and which permitted it to re-establish its hegemony when everything seemed shattered. This hidden power is the bourgeoisie's ideological hold over the proletariat. Because the proletarian masses were still completely governed by a bourgeois mentality, they restored the hegemony of the bourgeoisie with their own hands after it had collapsed. [3]....
>
> With its centuries of material and intellectual commerce, its literature and art, bourgeois culture has embedded itself in the proletarian masses, and generates a feeling of national solidarity, anchored deeper in the unconscious than external indifference or superficial internationalism suggest; this can potentially express itself in national class solidarity, and greatly hinders international action....
>
> The bourgeois past thus also survives in the proletariat as an organisational tradition that stands in the way of the class unity necessary for the creation of the new world; in these archaic organizations the workers make up the followers and adherents of a bourgeois vanguard. It is the intelligentsia which supplies the leaders in these ideological struggles. (Chapter 3) [Pannekoek, 1978]

Among all Pannekoek's criticisms we found the above passage most significant (as was Tony Cliff's realization some two decades later) where he pointed out the strength of the 'hidden power', 'bourgeoisie's ideological hold over the proletariat.' The 'hidden power' of bourgeois ideology was not a self-concocted ghost seated over the shoulder of the exploited "*masses*" that cannot be explained by science. Rather, it is the superstitious belief in the usual practices of bourgeois society as normal, moral activity. It is the habit of not questioning one's daily existence, and above all, it is the conformity and allegiance to the pillars of "profit" as the most dependable form of society. It acts through the proletarian "*masses*'" consent to the existing principles of governance, culture, science, justice system, social nature of distribution of all the amenities, social security, i.e. consent to all the components of a modern society under the production relations of capitalism that holds appropriation of the private property as the supreme law of reproduction and existence of society. Not only that, even when the proletariat prepares for the fight against these pillars of bourgeois society, the organization principles that were followed in the struggle were inherited from these same pillars, 'these archaic organizations the workers make up the followers and adherents of a bourgeois vanguard'—Pannekoek ('The tradition of all dead generations weighs like an nightmare on the brains of the living.'-Marx). Therefore, the bourgeois state and society are not only the embodiment of the class antagonisms in production relations, they represent the *social contract* also between the bourgeoisie as a *whole*, and the general class interests of the proletariat and other petty-commodity producers.

Rosa Luxemburg as early as in 1903 pointed out these features of a capitalist society and subjugation of the working class to the ideological strength of the bourgeoisie. She argued in a short essay on the reasons behind the intellectual stagnation of "Marxism" beyond Marx,

> In every class society, intellectual culture (science and art) is created by the ruling class; and the aim of this culture is in part to ensure the direct satisfaction of the needs of the social process, and in part to satisfy the mental needs of the members of the governing class. [Luxemburg, 2008, p. 95]

It is to be noted this passage is very close in meaning to Marx's celebrated statement that we referred earlier [Marx, 1968]. Luxemburg was more specific in the above passage as she acceded to the phenomenon of *social contract* when she mentioned, 'this culture is in part to ensure the direct satisfaction of the needs of the social process'. They are not 'bribes' that Lenin found the bourgeoisie are constrained to offer in a 'thousand different ways' to the 'labour aristocracy', but are the mainstay of ideological strength of the bourgeoisie society that encompass *all* including the proletariat as 'the needs of the social process'.

The fundamental question is how to breach this *social contract*? This was precisely the question where the European working class fumbled, vacillated in their post-war revolutionary initiative against the capitalist production relations. They could identify the political representatives of the bourgeoisie in the Weimar Republic in Germany, in the provisional government of Kerensky in Russia, in the coalition government of Count Michael Karloyi in Hungary and elsewhere as the enemy, so as to breach the contract in the political domain. They very rightly asserted their freedom to replace these moribund governments by the elected Soviets of the workers, soldiers, and in rural Russia in the beginning with the Soviets of poor peasants also. However, when it came to identify the ideological representatives of counter-revolution as in Russia, they could identify only the clergy and their religious practices those actually were the relics of the medieval past, a tradition that historically the bourgeoisie has crossed way back in 1648 in England and in 1789 in France as Marx pointed out in his statement, 'they were revolutions in the European fashion.' As for ideological superiority of the *new* proletarian power over the bourgeoisie, dictatorship of the proletariat had little to offer except the efforts to make education, health care and housing universally available to the working "*masses*". These programmes of social necessity and benefits were implemented in the bourgeoisie society of Europe also in due course of time with more scientific approaches to the social needs, particularly after the WWII under the Marshall Plan.[10] Therefore, comparing the degree and quantum of availability of social amenities to the working "*masses*" between the West European countries and Russia was not the correct parameter to judge the social requirement of *socialism* as an alternative to capitalism.

In the same essay, Luxemburg made another significant observation regarding the contribution of Marx to this question of ideological preparation.

> But Marx's creation, which as a scientific achievement is a titanic whole, transcends the plain demands of the proletarian class struggle for whose purpose it was created. Both in his detailed and comprehensive analysis of capitalist economy, and in his method of historical research with its immeasurable field of application, Marx has offered much more than was directly essential for the practical conduct of class war. [Luxemburg, 2008, p. 96]

What specifically Luxemburg meant here that 'Marx has offered much more than was directly essential for the practical conduct of class war' in his analysis of 'capitalist economy'? Was it the three volumes of *Capital* that was the topic of principal attention here in Luxemburg's essay? Was it the detailed analysis of the ascent of bourgeoisie classes in Europe to political power that was counterpoised by the rebellious working class? What had Marx himself to say about his own contribution to the social sciences? We quote here the celebrated passage from the letter of Marx to Joseph Weydemeyer in 1852 as far as his own contribution to the social sciences.

> And now as to myself, no credit is due to me for discovering the existence of classes in modern society or the struggle between them. Long before me bourgeois historians had described the historical development of this class struggle and bourgeois economists, the economic anatomy of classes. What I did that was new was to prove:
> (1) that the existence of classes is only bound up with the particular, historical phases in the development of production,
> (2) that the class struggle necessarily leads to the dictatorship of the proletariat,
> (3) that this dictatorship itself only constitutes the transition to the abolition of all classes and to a classless society. [Marx, 1969a, p. 410]

Marx was extremely modest in not taking credit for the significant contribution he made in the materialist interpretation of philosophy, in the materialist interpretation of the progress of human history. It was Marx who can undoubtedly be credited to bring dialectics in the materialist conception of philosophy, to bring philosophy down to earth as principles of social practice. It was the eleventh theses of Marx to declare, "The philosophers have only interpreted the world, in various ways; the point is to change it." [Marx, 1969b]. To Marx, this process of 'change' was in the third theses on Feuerbach, 'can be conceived and rationally understood only as *revolutionary practice*.'

Karl Marx provided the materialist philosophical strength to the concept of *class struggle* to interpret self-activity as changing one's own environment, as principles of '*revolutionary practice*.' The significance of this philosophical strength was in Luxemburg's mind when she recalled Marx's contribution as 'more than was directly essential for the practical conduct of class war', that goes much beyond the political nature of victory in the *class struggle* that Marx named as dictatorship of the proletariat. The proletariat in Europe failed to attain this ideological strength in their revolutionary practices while confronting the bourgeoisie society, while accomplishing the political programmes of revolution in October 1917 and in January 1919 both in Russia and Germany respectively.

There are, of course, two caveats from us to the passage we referred from Marx's letter [Marx, 1969a]. History of the proletarian revolutions over the last two centuries (including the Paris Commune) did not prove that the 'class struggle necessarily leads to the dictatorship of the proletariat'. The word 'necessarily' lead to mechanistic and wilful misinterpretation of wresting political power by the proletariat from the *whole* bourgeoisie as we have highlighted earlier. There were several attributes that worked behind achieving state-power by the proletariat in revolutionary Russia, the pivotal among them is the presence of revolutionary leadership that cannot be directly and solely related to the 'class struggle'. Second, we note that Marx did not qualify here dictatorship of the proletariat as *revolutionary* that he inscribed in italics in his critique to the *Gotha Programme* [Marx, 1858]. We have argued earlier this *state* has to be revolutionary in nature not only because it has to wrest power from the bourgeoisie, but more important this *state* has to devise the mechanisms to dissolve in the society, among the societal organs of administration. The *state* has to '*wither away*' within the society of *free* producers. If it is argued that this sense of revolutionary nature of dictatorship of the proletariat is embodied in the third point of Marx's letter, we may humbly say that the argument does not stand up to the materialist outlook of the history of revolutionary Russia. Dictatorship of the proletariat is only a transitional *state* that is the political organ of a *transitional society*. This *society* has both the components of production relations, *socialism* and *capitalism* competing with each other. Existence of the *state* as dictatorship of the proletariat does not (history shows it did not) itself guarantee 'the abolition of all classes and to a classless society'.

We are apprehensive our discussion on Lenin's theses on the international situation has long crossed the page limit that the most liberal editor will allow to the author of an essay. So we stop here and proceed on to the critique of the "Colonial Theses" next in Chapter 5 where we will try to be brief as most of what we wanted to say in this long essay has already been told.

## NOTES

1. This report on the post-war international situation and the *Theses on the Basic Tasks of the Communist International* were introduced by Lenin on the opening day of the Second Congress of CI. The opening session was held in Petrograd on July 19, 1920. Later the Congress was moved to Moscow where it was held till August 7, 1920. This report and the theses outlined Lenin's basic analysis regarding the crisis of international capitalism and the role of the communists in preparing the working class for dictatorship of the proletariat in the countries whose political economies were run under developed form of capitalism.
2. The draft theses on the conditions for inclusion in the Third International was introduced by Zinoviev under the heading *Theses on the Role of the Communist Party in the Proletarian Revolution* on July 24, 1920. His theses contained nineteen points. After discussion in the commission for framing the rules of inclusion in CI the draft theses was revised and two more points were included by Lenin. Degras wrote,

   > Among the most outspoken critics of this attitude was Tanner (shop stewards), who suggested that Russia had something to learn from the West as well as something to teach. The parties should agree on all basic questions, but for the rest might be left to act on their own. The Second International had been too formless and characterless, but the Third was going to the opposite extreme and being too dogmatic. He questioned whether the dictatorship of the communist party and the dictatorship of the proletariat were identical. Wijnkoop (Holland) also suggested a less dogmatic approach, since conditions varied so widely. Lenin reacted sharply

> to the charge of dogmatism; if each party were allowed to do as it pleased, the International was unnecessary. [Degras, 1971, p. 127]

3. The communist workers' party of Germany (KAPD) was the offshoot from the communist party of Germany (KPD) constituted at a conference of the "Left Communists" militants in April 4-5, 1920, in Berlin. Degras wrote,

   > Lenin regretted the split in the KPD which led to the formation of the KAPD, but had been unable to prevent it (communication between the two countries was slow and difficult). In a letter to the German central committee of October 20, 1919 he said he had learnt of the split from the official German news broadcast. [Degras, 1971, p. 105]

   As a glimpse of activities of the KAPD militants we provide the following passage from a historical sketch of the KAPD:

   > The delegates to the KAPD's founding Congress (April 4-5) represented 38,000 militants; other regions would join the party after the Congress. At that time the KAPD embraced almost the entire membership of the former KPD, and its social background was similar to that of its predecessor (derived from every layer of the working class, with a heavy representation of youth and the unemployed). (Chapter 14) [Dauvé, 1976]

   It goes without saying, the KAPD leadership was steadfast in their criticism of Lenin's advocacy of participation in bourgeoisie institutions like parliaments by the constituents of the Third International. At the same time they were too hasty and too optimistic in assessing the revolutionary aspirations of the international working class. Soon after the formation of KAPD, the "Left Communists" streams of the "Dutch Left" and KAPD, etc. went on to form a new International, a Communist Workers' International (KAI) in 1921 after these currents were expelled from CI in the Third Congress. A recent Ph.D. thesis on the "Dutch Left" currents found out,

   > The joint work between the left communists and the Komintern was of short duration. It did not survive the March 1921 action in central Germany. The international environment was becoming more and more unfavourable, not only with the very clear retreat of the world revolution, but above all in relation to the politics of the Russian state. The foreign policy of this state, the events at Kronstadt and finally the politics of the Komintern in Germany were to be signposts towards the final break which happened at the 3rd Congress of the Komintern. Preceded by the expulsion of the minority from the CPH, even before the 3rd Congress, that of the KAPD in September 1921 sounded the death knell of an

international opposition in the Komintern. [Bourrinet, 2008, p. 145]

4. John Maynard Keynes, author of the book *The Economic Consequences of the Peace*, and member of the British delegation at the Paris Peace Conference had severe warning for the future of capitalism in Europe based on the terms of peace in the Treaty of Versailles. He wrote,

   For one who has spent in Paris the greater part of the six months which succeeded the armistice an occasional visit to London was a strange experience. England still stands outside Europe. Europe's voiceless tremors do not reach her. Europe is apart and England is not her flesh and body. But Europe is solid with herself. France, Germany, Italy, Austria, and Holland, Russia and Romania, and Poland throb together, and their structure and civilization are essentially one. They flourished together, they have rocked together in a war which we, in spite of our enormous contributions and sacrifices (like though in a lesser degree than America), economically stood outside, and they may fall together. In this lies the destructive significance of the Peace of Paris. If the European Civil War is to end with France and Italy abusing their momentary victorious powers to destroy Germany and Austria-Hungary now prostrate, they invite their own destruction also, being so deeply involved and inextricably intertwined with the victims by hidden physic and economic bonds. [Keynes, 1920, p. 3]

5. This refers to the failure of the General Strike in March 1921 called by the factions of KPD, namely VKPD and KAPD. The strike was the one last attempt in the sequel of the defeated German revolution in January 1919 to rouse the revolutionary efforts of the German working class. From all definitive accounts the involvement of the working class in the "March Action" of 1921 was a far distant shade away from the spontaneity of participation in the January days of 1919. The strike was planned as more of instigation from the representative of ECCI to the Central Committee of VKPD, and the call abysmally fell short from the expectations of them. We refer to the same PhD Thesis [Bourrinet, 2008] below:

   However, faced with the government offensive, the strike call launched by the KAPD and the VKPD in the whole of Germany got little response. In the whole country about 300,000 workers followed the call. The strike met with very little response in Berlin despite the attempt to occupy the factories by surprise and prevent the workers from going to work. The common demonstration of the two parties, the KAPD and the VKPD, attracted 4,000 people, and that only with great difficulty. In the majority of cases the workers remained very suspicious, if not hostile, towards this type of action. [p. 151]

6. To corroborate this statement, we give below the following reference from Trotsky who delivered the concluding speech after the closing session in the Second Congress of CI.

   In all his work—whether as leader of a revolutionary strike, or as organizer of underground groups, or as secretary of a trade union, or as agitator at mass meetings, whether as deputy, cooperative member or fighter on the barricades—the communist always remains true to himself as a disciplined member of the communist party, a zealous fighter, a mortal enemy of capitalist society, its economic foundations, its state forms, its democratic lies, its religion and its morality. He is a self-sacrificing soldier of the proletarian revolution and an indefatigable herald of the new society." [Rosmer, 1973, p. 79]
7. Emma Goldman (1869-1940), born out of Jewish parents of Russian origin stands as a major figure in the history of American radicalism and feminism. She migrated to the USA early in her life along with her elder sister. An influential and well-known anarchist of her day, Goldman was an early advocate of free speech, birth control, women's equality and independence, and union organization. Her criticism of mandatory conscription of young men in the military during the WWI led to a two-year imprisonment, followed by deportation to Soviet Russia in 1919. For the rest of her life until her death in 1940, she continued to participate in the social and political movements of her age, for the Russian Revolution to the Spanish Civil War. [Berkeley Library Introduction]
8. Herman Gorter was one of the leading figures of the "Dutch-Left" group, one of the most influential groups in Western Europe working for proletarian internationalism throughout the period of the WWI. For a political biography of Gorter please visit *http://www.marxists.org/glossary/people/g/o.htm*.
9. Paul Frölich (1884-1953), was a journalist by profession. He was a member of the SPD from 1902, was a staunch supporter of Karl Liebknecht for his voting against war in the Reichstag. Frölich joined the KPD Central Committee in the Congress of 1920. In December 1928, Frölich was expelled as a result of the Stalinist purge in KPD. Frölich migrated to France in 1934 in the wake of Nazi aggression. There in hibernation he completed the first political biography of Rosa Luxemburg, *Rosa Luxemburg: Her Life and Works* in 1938-39 and was published in 1940.
10. The Marshall Plan, also known as the Economic Recovery Programme, was channelled for spending of 13 billion USD to finance the economic recovery of Europe between 1948 and 1951. Economic rejuvenation of war-ravaged Europe after the WWII was the principal objective of

spending through the plan. Another salient objective was to keep the nation-states of Western Europe outside the ambit of political influence of Soviet Russia. The plan was named after the Secretary of State of USA, George C. Marshall, who announced the oulines of the plan in a commencement speech at Harvard University on June 5, 1947.

## REFERENCES


Jane Degras, Editor. *The Communist International 1919-1943 Documents*. Volume I. Routledge, 1971.

Alfred Rosmer. *Moscow Under Lenin*. Monthly Review Press, New York, 1973.

John Riddell. *To the Masses: Proceedings of the Third Congress of the Communist International, 1921*. Haymarket Books, Chicago, 2016.

V.I. Lenin. Report on the International Situation and the Fundamental Tasks of the Communist International. In *Speeches at Congress of the Communist International*. Progress Publishers, Moscow, 1972a.

O. Piatnitsky. The Twenty-One Conditions of Admission into the Communist International. American Left Ephemera Collection.1894-2008, University of Pittsburgh, USA, February 1934. URL: *http://www.digital.library.pitt.edu/u/ulsmanuscripts/pdf/*.

V.I. Lenin. "Left Wing" Communism—An Infantile Disorder. *Collected Works*, Vol. 31, 2nd Ed. Progress Publishers, Moscow, 1974.

Rosa Luxemburg. The Russian Revolution. In Peter Hudis and Kevin B. Anderson, Editors, *The Rosa Luxemburg Reader*, Chapter 14. Monthly Review Press, New York, 2004.

John Myrad Keynes. *The Economic Consequences of the Peace*. Harcourt, Brace and Howe, New York, 1920.

Lujo (Ludwig Joseph) Brentano. What Germany Has Paid Under the Treaty of Versailles, 1923. URL:*http://www.wintersonnenwende.com/scriptorium/english/archives/reparations/wgptv00.html*.

Alexander Jung. Millions, Billions, Trillions: Germany in the Era of Hyperinflation, Part 1 and 2, August 14, 2009. URL: *http://www.spiegel.de/international/germany/millions-billions-trillions-germany-in-the-era-of-hyperinflation-a-641758.html*.

Michael V. White and Kurt Schuler. Who Said "Debauch the Currency": Keynes or Lenin? *Journal of Economic Perspectives*, 23(2):213–222, 2009.

V.I. Lenin. Five Years of the Russian Revolution and the Prospects of the World Revolution. In *Speeches at Congress of the Communist International*. Progress Publishers, Moscow, 1972b.

Karl Marx. *The Poverty of Philosophy*. Progress Publishers, Moscow, 1955.

Ralf Hoffrogge. *Working Class Politics in the German Revolution*. Historical Materialism Book Series. Brill, Boston, 2014.

Anton Pannekoek. World Revolution and Communist Tactics. In D.A. Smart, Editor, *Pannekoek and Gorter's Marxism*. Pluto Press, UK, 1978.

Fernando Claudin. *The Communist Movement: From Comintern to Cominform*. Monthly Review Press, New York, 1975.

Gabriel Kuhn, Editor. *All Power to the Councils. A Documentary History of the German Revolution of 1918-1919*. The Merlin Press Ltd, Wales, 2012.

Pierre Broue. *The German Revolution 1917-1923*. Brill, Netherlands, 2005.

Herman Gorter. Open Letter to Comrade Lenin, 1920. URL: *https://www.marxists.org/archive/gorter/1920/open-letter/*.

Philippe Bourrinet. The Dutch and German Communist Left (1900–68), 2008. URL: *https://libcom.org/history/german-dutch-communist-left-philippe-bourrinet*.

Karl Marx. *The German Ideology*. Progress Publishers, Moscow, 1968.

Tony Cliff. Rosa Luxemburg, 1959. URL : *https://www.marxists.org/archive/cliff/works/1959/rosalux/9-history.htm*.

George Plekhanov. Open Letter to the Petrograd Workers (October 28, 1917), 1917. URL: *https://prezi.com/hbaay1oavor1/october-revolution-george-plekhanovs-open-letter/*.

Paul Frölich. *Rosa Luxemburg*. Haymarket Books, Chicago, 2010.

Brian Baggins. Timeline of the Russian Revolution (1917), 2005. URL:*https://www.marxists.org/history/ussr/events/timeline/1917.htm*.

Paul Mattick. Luxemburg versus Lenin, 1935. URL: *https://www.marxists.org/archive/mattick-paul/1935/luxemburg-lenin.htm*.

Rosa Luxemburg. Stagnation and Progress of Marxism. In *Rosa Luxemburg: Selected Writings*. SEARCH, Kolkata, 2008.

Gilles Dauvé and Denis Arthur. The Communists Left in Germany, 1918-1921. URL: *https://www.marxists.org/subject/germany-1918-23/dauve-authier/index.htm*.

Karl Marx. Letter to J. Weydemeyer. *Selected Works*, Volume II. Progress Publishers, Moscow, 1969a.

Karl Marx. Theses On Feuerbach. *Selected Works*, Volume I. Progress Publishers, Moscow, 1969b.

Karl Marx. Critique of the Gotha Programme. *Selected Works*, Volume II. Foreign Language Publishing House, Moscow, 1958.

# 5

# Report of the Commission on the National and Colonial Questions

The theses and report by Lenin on the above subject, loosely known as "Colonial Theses", were landmark events in the Second Congress of CI. In later periods, the theses turned out to provide the guidelines, the general directions of "communist" movements in a number of countries in Asia and Africa irrespective of the imperialist powers ruling over the destiny of the millions of people there. Down the ages, several political parties espousing the objectives of "communism" flourished in many countries of Asia, Africa, and East Europe for a considerable period of the twentieth century. In many of these countries, "communist" parties came to state-power leading the "*mass*" insurgencies and revolutions of the poor by drawing on the strength of their allegiance to Soviet Russia. A vast majority of the poor in these countries under the yoke of colonial rule was the peasantry who raised their head against the most oppressive feudal, pre-capitalist agrarian production relations. In most of these countries before the peasants' revolution there was no state-power in the proper sense of the term as was understood in Europe. Judicial redressal for even elementary grievances of the population was in many cases, simply out of the question. The population in these countries were hard pressed under the yoke of absolutist landlordism, clergydom, and above all by the administration of their imperialist "Masters". The so-called civil administrations in the emerging urban centres were essentially police-states. Millions of the peasant "*masses*" literally starved and continued their impoverished existence under slavery in many forms and traditions.

Towards the end of the WWII, the world witnessed a role reversal of the post-WWI workers' revolutionary efforts that we discussed at length in the preceding Chapters. Led by the most significant peasant revolution in China, many countries earned sovereign rule after the WWII. The struggle of the peoples of Asia and Africa against the crudest forms of colonial rule continued till late 1960-70s witnessing the rise of the so-called bipolar world. The governments of large parts of Asia and Africa including India declared themselves either to be "socialist", or were keen to follow "socialist" planning policies of Soviet Russia. Nations in East Europe through which the Red Army of Soviet Russia marched towards Berlin, one and all, turned out to be "socialist" after the war. Unlike the formative period of the Soviet state in Russia, there were no meaningful tensions, strife within these societies of East Europe regarding transition to the so-called "socialist" economy, or, declaration of the affairs of the state-policies as a period of dictatorship of the proletariat. The political economy of these countries was in direct control of the powerful "Masters" in Moscow whose "aids" and contracts were pushing these underdeveloped economies routinely to declare as "socialist" production relations. Many of the histories of the socio-economy of these countries are now well-known and well understood after the demise and dismantling of the so-called "socialist" state organizations of these societies of East Europe.

Here, we narrated very briefly the general course of the march of history between the two World Wars in the context of the "Colonial Theses". The deliberations in and around the period of the Second Congress of CI dwelt upon these theses that provided the ideological grounding, conviction and confidence among the peerless revolutionaries in many of the countries of Asia, Africa and Eastern Europe. Their doggedness, self-sacrifice, and volunteerism in raising the peasant army and the peasant revolutions in their national territories were part of the folklore of valour and self-sufferings. However, as we will soon see, their ideological grounding for "socialism" whose genesis can be found in the deliberations around the "Colonial Theses" was also the basis of untold suffering of the millions of population later in these erstwhile colonies or semi-colonies when their "revolutionary

Masters" started their "socialist" experiments. There was another no less significant milestone to the "Colonial Theses". This was the only theses in the history of CI that Lenin and the ECCI invited and accepted supplementary theses, from M.N. Roy the revolutionary of Indian origin, and together were known as the "Theses on Colonial Questions."[1] [Haithcox, November 1963]

The leadership of the newly formed CI were very keen, and energetic to form the alliance between the revolutionary workers of Europe and the growing revolutionary peasant movements, particularly in China, India, and West Asia—the land of the Arab populations. Following adoption of the "Colonial Theses" at the Second Congress of CI, ECCI organized a large Congress of the Eastern peoples at Baku on September 1, 1920 that germinated the "communist" parties in India, Persia, and elsewhere. "Reporting at the ECCI meeting of September 20, 1920, Zinoviev stated that the Baku Congress, called on the initiative of the ECCI, had been attended by 1,891 representatives of 32 nationalities. They came largely from the Caucasus and the Central Asian territories of Russia, but included also many Turks and Persians." [Degras, 1971, p. 105] Rosmer recorded in his memoirs, "The Executive Committee decided, as a logical follow-up and necessary complement to the work of the Second Congress, to convene the representatives of all the enslaved peoples to a vast conference. The place chosen was Baku, on the border between Europe and Asia. Zinoviev, Radek and Bela Kun were to represent the Communist International, and they were to be accompanied by delegates from countries with colonies." [Rosmer, 1973, p. 86]

### 5.1 Points of Lenin's Departure in the "Colonial Theses"

There were several significant points of departure in Lenin's theses and reports regarding the development of political economy in the colonies compared with the traditional "Marxist" understanding in Western Europe. We will see here the criticisms of Rosa Luxemburg and the "*Left* Communists" towards Lenin's understanding of the 'National Question', and the revolutionary struggle of the peasantry against the imperialist rule reflected this traditional viewpoint of the "Western Marxists". These viewpoints of the contemporary critiques were at variance with the reality, the precise development of the liberation struggles in the colonies. Lenin could correctly gauge the essence, the principal feature of national liberation movements of the colonies, "the freedom struggles". Lenin declared that the world population is divided in two broad categories: "being divided into a large number of oppressed nations, and an insignificant number of oppressor nations, the latter possessing colossal wealth and powerful armed forces." [Lenin, 1972a, p. 55] By bringing in the paradigm of 'nation' in the "Marxist" discourse of policies towards the colonies, Lenin digressed from the traditional viewpoint of interpreting political economy only through existing class relations as it happens under capitalism. The attributes of "nationhood" and "sovereignty" are always understood in the traditional "Marxist" view point as prominent features of 'bourgeoisie democracy'. Historically, this viewpoint was also cogent in expression as we have shown earlier how Marx understood the European revolutions as the ascent of a *new* civilization under the hegemony of the emerging bourgeoisie class. The problem came sharply into focus before CI while interpreting the role of the national bourgeoisie who were at the head of the "freedom struggles" in the colonies, whose primary agenda was to declare nationhood by seceding from the rule of the imperialist sovereign states of the West. Lenin wrote in his report after due consideration of Roy's supplementary theses as,

> As a result of our discussion, we have arrived at the unanimous decision to speak of the national-revolutionary movement rather than of the "bourgeoisie-democratic" movement. It is beyond doubt that any national movement can only be a bourgeoisie-democratic movement, since the overwhelming mass of the population in the backward countries consists of peasants who represent bourgeoisie–capitalist relationships. It would be utopian to believe that proletarian parties in these backward countries, if indeed they can emerge in them, can pursue communist tactics and a communist policy, without establishing definite relations with the peasant movement and without giving effective support. However, the objections have been raised that, if we speak of the bourgeoisie-democratic movement, we shall be obliterating all distinctions between the reformist and the revolutionary movements. Yet that distinction has been very clearly revealed of late in the backward and colonial countries, since the imperialist bourgeoisie is doing everything in its power to implant a

> reformist movement among the oppressed nations too. There has been a certain *rapprochement* between the bourgeoisie of the exploiting countries and that of the colonies, so that very often—perhaps even in most cases—the bourgeoisie of the oppressed countries, while it does support the national movement, is in full accord with the imperialist bourgeoisie, i.e. joins forces with it against all revolutionary movements and revolutionary classes." [Lenin, 1972a, p. 56]

It becomes clear how the motive forces of politics surged forward over the logic and reasoning of the political economy. Lenin was in full accord, 'It is beyond doubt that any national movement can only be a bourgeoisie-democratic movement, since the overwhelming mass of the population in the backward countries consists of peasants who represent bourgeoisie—capitalist relationships'. Here, his statements corroborated the cold, bitter logic of historical materialism that national liberation movements, either in the hands of the reformist bourgeoisie aspiring for independence, sovereignty from direct imperialists' rule, or the revolutionary peasant movements with which the "communists" of the colonial countries were advised to be inseparably connected were to be of 'bourgeoisie-democratic' in nature in its social, economic content. This precise assessment of the essential features of revolutionary peasants' movements was made abundantly clear in Roy's supplementary theses where he mentioned,

> 7. Two movements can be discerned which are growing further and further apart with every day that passes. One of them is the bourgeois democratic nationalist movement, which pursues the programme of political liberation with the conservation of the capitalist order; the other is the struggle of the propertyless peasants for their liberation from every kind of exploitation. The first movement attempts, often with success, to control the second; the Communist International must however fight against any such control, and the development of the class consciousness of the working masses of the colonies must consequently be directed towards the overthrow of foreign capitalism. The most important and necessary task however is the creation of Communist organizations of peasants and workers in order to lead them to the revolution and the setting up of the Soviet Republic. In this way the masses of the people in the backward countries will be brought to communism not by capitalist development but by the development of class consciousness under the leadership of the

> proletariat of the advanced countries. ....
> 9. In the first period the revolution in the colonies will not be communist; if however from the very start the communist vanguard emerges at its head the revolutionary masses will be brought on to the correct path along which, through the gradual gathering of revolutionary experience, they will reach the hidden goal. It would be a mistake to try to solve the agrarian question straight away according to purely communist principles. In the first stage of its development the revolution in the colonies must be carried out according to the programme of purely petty-bourgeois demands, such as distribution of the land and so on. But from this it must not be concluded that the leadership in the colonies can be allowed to fall into the hands of the bourgeois democrats. On the contrary, the proletarian parties must carry out an intensive propaganda of communist ideas and found workers' and peasants' councils at the first opportunity. These councils must work in the same way as the Soviet Republics in the advanced capitalist countries in order to bring about the final overthrow of the capitalist order throughout the whole world. [Roy, 1920]

Roy's supplementary theses really brought out the problematic cat out of the bag in the discourse within the delegates of CI that otherwise contained political reasoning *only* (possibly a reason the actual supplementary theses by him was seldom brought under discussion other than mentioning his contribution in the footnote of history). He clearly mentioned that even if the peasant revolutions in the colonies marched ahead of the nationalist movement of the 'reformist' bourgeoisie by dint of the sheer strength of revolutionary dedication and volunteerism of the "communists" to lead the peasant struggles, they will not result in a *communist* organization of production in the society. He repeated, 'It would be a mistake to try to solve the agrarian question straight away according to purely communist principles. In the first stage of its development the revolution in the colonies must be carried out according to the programme of purely petty-bourgeois demands, such as distribution of the land and so on.' Here, Roy stretched the boundaries of 'concessions' further ahead of the Bolsheviks while they espoused the cause of 'middle peasants' in Russia. Even in the period of the NEP the Bolsheviks did not advocate the policy of private proprietorship of 'land' for the 'middle peasants'. By championing the demand of 'division of land' Roy only asserted the class interests of those sections of the agrarian population whom Lenin found elsewhere as 'the rock bottom of capitalism', but who at the same time were of considerable priority to Lenin as a segment of agrarian population in Soviet Russia.

These vital issues of political economy of agrarian revolutions under the "communist" leadership were not at all discussed in Lenin's theses (probably the need for a supplementary thesis arose from such limitation). On the other hand, Lenin dealt squarely on the political imperative of supporting the peasants' struggle by CI from the viewpoint of weakening imperialists' rule over the colonies. That was, of course, the objective of the nationalist bourgeoisie also in the colonies. He wrote,

> 11. In regard to the more backward States and nations, primarily feudal or patriarchal or patriarchal-peasant in character, the following considerations must be kept specially in mind:
>
> d. It is particularly important to support the peasant movement in the backward countries against the landlords and all forms and survivals of feudalism. Above all, efforts must be made to give the peasant movement as revolutionary a character as possible, organizing the peasants and all the exploited wherever possible in Soviets, and thus establish as close a tie as possible between the West European communist proletariat and the revolutionary peasant movement in the East, in the colonies and backward countries.
>
> 12. The centuries-old enslavement of the colonial and weak peoples by the great imperialist Powers has left behind among the working masses of the enslaved countries not only feelings of bitterness but also feelings of distrust of the oppressing nations as a whole, including the proletariat of these nations....
>
> From this it follows that it is the duty of the class-conscious communist proletariat of all countries to be especially cautious and particularly attentive to the national feelings, in themselves out of date, in countries and peoples that have been long enslaved; it is also their duty to make concessions in order to remove this distrust and prejudice the more quickly. unless the proletariat, and all the working masses of all countries and nations of the entire world, themselves strive towards alliance, and unite as one, the victory over capitalism cannot be pursued to a completely successful end."[Degras, 1971, p. 143]

The pivot of Lenin's argument for supporting the 'national' struggle of the proletariat and peasantry among the oppressed nations is evident in the above passage of the theses. Lenin's argument was to weaken the economic exploitation of the imperialist nations that was sustained not only by the terms of balance of trade that hugely favoured the capitalist class of these exploiting nations, but also he stressed to ending the exploitation by taking advantage of 'national' prejudices. The imperialist nations enforced among the subjugated population of the colonies a deep sense of being 'backward' in civilization; they mandated military conscription among the people of the colonies to engage in a war that had minimal relevance to the people of the colonies. Lenin was unequivocal in supporting 'the peasant movement in the backward countries against the landlords and all forms and survivals of feudalism.'

The question that immediately would have confronted him was what would be the programmes of political economy of these revolutionary peasant movements, and what would be the nature of the forum for executing such revolutionary programmes? Lenin did not answer these teething questions in his theses that was entirely devoted to the political purposes of supporting the peasant movements against absolutist landlordism in the colonies. Nonetheless, he attempted to confront such questions in his report where he wrote,

> The question was posed as follows: are we to consider as correct the assertion that the capitalist stage of economic development is inevitable for backward nations now on the road to emancipation and among whom a certain advance towards progress is to be seen since the war? We replied in the negative. If the victorious revolutionary proletariat conducts systematic propaganda among them, and the Soviet governments come to the aid with all the means at their disposal—in that event it will be mistaken to assume that the backward peoples must inevitably go through the capitalist stage of development. .... but the Communist International should advance the proposition, with the appropriate theoretical grounding, that with the aid of the proletariat of the advanced countries, backward countries can go over to the Soviet system and , through certain stages of development, to communism, without having to pass through the capitalist stage. [Lenin, 1972a, p. 59]

This passage from Lenin's report was the cornerstone of the *cardinal* argument of the thousands of devoted "communists" in the colonies and semi-colonies of Asia and Africa, in the East European countries that *capitalism could be sidetracked;* society could move directly from pre-capitalist, patriarchal, feudal production relations to "communist" society provided the riders that Lenin cautioned in the above theses were present or taken into account.[2] It was paradoxical that in the same supplementary theses where Roy argued for the 'division of land' that was confiscated from the landlords by the revolutionary peasant movements for distribution among the landless, he also argued in the same line of reasoning as from Lenin, 'In this way the masses of the people in the backward countries will be brought to communism not by capitalist development but by the development of class consciousness under the leadership of the proletariat of the advanced countries.'

It is to be noted that Lenin was not at his confident, convinced best in the above passage that usually he was in his approaches to other policy questions such as regarding the NEP, regarding 'state capitalism', regarding 'opportunism' among the working class of West Europe, etc. He enmeshed his assertion with several riders such as, 'If the victorious revolutionary proletariat conducts systematic propaganda among them, and the Soviet governments come to the aid with all the means at their disposal', 'but the Communist International should advance the proposition, with the appropriate theoretical grounding....', etc. Lenin concluded just a few passages above in the same report,

> The preponderance of pre-capitalist relationships is still the main determining features in these countries, so that there can be no question of a purely proletarian movement in them. There is practically no industrial proletariat in these countries. Nevertheless, we have assumed, we must assume, the role of leaders even there. [Lenin, 1972, p. 57]

Elsewhere he remarked,

> In the general and world-historical sense, it is true that in a backward country like China, the coolie cannot bring about a proletarian revolution; however, to tell the workers in the handful of rich countries where life is easier, thanks to imperialist pillage, that they must be afraid of "too great" impoverishment, is counter-revolutionary. [Lenin, 1972b, p. 63]

Fortunately for Lenin, there was no delegate in the Second Congress of CI of mainland Chinese origin. He could get away with such a derogatory remark about the hugely underprivileged, impoverished Chinese bonded labour (Pearl S. Buck has made them immortal in *The Good Earth*!) by castigating them as 'coolie'. This also shows how even communists with such unblemished integrity as Lenin suffered from the 'national', European, bourgeois prejudices by considering five thousand-year-old civilizations such as in India, China, the Mesopotamia as 'backward' compared to 'civilized' countries of Europe. That apart, we find from the above passages, Lenin was doubly unsure of the role of the "communists" in such pre-capitalist economies where *socialism* could not be the agenda of the society. The concrete reality of development of the working class as a social force precluded them to play the role of leadership in the national liberation struggles against imperialism.

Moreover, we want to draw attention to a point that is never discussed in the discourses on national "freedom struggles". Even if for argument's sake, we agree that the revolutionary peasant movements would surpass the nationalist, 'reformist' bourgeoisie in ushering regimes that would banish absolutist landlordism (we have no doubt that happened in China under the leadership of the "communist" party) from society, the vital issue that remained unchallenged was such states could only have survived as national, capitalist economy under the umbrella of existing world capitalism. In fact, such states could only have invigorated, re-energized world capitalism as China and other such "socialist" states have effectively shown us over the years in the later parts of the twentieth century. These states could only have declared themselves as the *new* nations by attaining sovereignty, seceding from their status as erstwhile colonies or semi-colonies, and by joining the comity of the nation-states over the world.

Lenin himself had charted five categories of production relations in Russian agrarian economy that we have seen before, and he found it would have been 'suicidal' policy for existence of Bolshevism to pursue 'socialist' exchanges in rural Russia. The reality would have been *no different* in these newly formed nation-states where "communist" parties could attain state-power at the head of the peasant revolutions against patriarchal, feudal production relations. Historically, the political economy of these new sovereign states could not have been other than 'bourgeoisie democratic' in nature. Therefore, the political economy of these new nations would not have any other option but to pursue 'state capitalism' in *one or the other form* as the Bolsheviks had pursued under the garb of *tax in kind*— a form of *levy* from the middle and rich peasants. Such bureaucratic methods of regulating market, finance, banking, and accumulation of capital for heavy industry would have failed at one or the other time. So, even if Lenin fervently wished to weaken the hold of imperialism by encircling the developed capitalist economies by a ring of underdeveloped state-capitalist economies they could never have fulfilled his wishes otherwise. These nation-states had to be the lands of new capitalist investments, new capitalist ventures, new openings for multinational financial institutions starting with the International Monetary Fund (IMF) and the World Bank, and vice-versa. These new, sovereign states may have brought "their" national balance of trade towards "their" favour to an extent by asserting their new "nationhood". They may have earned deeper pockets of foreign exchanges for balance of payments in their export-import related trading. These developments of international trade and exchanges only provided deeper sustaining capability for world capitalism by expanding the outreach of the capitalist economies and production relations in the *new* nation-states. Thereby, such *new* states have only opened the avenues of rejuvenation of world capitalism in a *new* form by joining the orbit of international financial system as new "free" societies after attaining "freedom" from the colony status to pursue 'state capitalism' under the garb of "socialism".

Our above argument that the inherent course of the peasants' revolutions was meant to strengthen world capitalism gets doubly buttressed by Lenin's following reasoning favouring peasants' Soviets in the colonies. As forms of revolutionary organs of administration in the colonies Lenin advocated in the report as,

> However, the debate in the commission, in which several representatives from colonial countries participated, demonstrated convincingly that the Communist International's theses should point out that peasants' Soviets, Soviets of the exploited, are a weapon which

> can be employed, not only in capitalist countries but also in countries with pre-capitalist relations, and that it is the absolute duty of Communist Parties and of elements prepared to form Communist Parties, everywhere to conduct propaganda in favour of peasants' Soviets or of working people's Soviets, this to include backward and colonial countries. Wherever conditions permit, they should at once make attempts to set up Soviets of working people. [Lenin, 1972, p. 58]

Lenin and the commission on the "Colonial question" unanimously agreed for 'peasants' Soviets' as the organs of revolutionary power. Surprisingly, there was no mention of the agrarian economic programme of these germinating revolutionary organs of state-power. It had been the uniform experience among all countries where the "communist" movement flourished (inevitably in the colonies) that the slogans of the "communist" parties for the peasants have been "land to the tillers". Across all the lands in the colonies, the peasant "*masses*" found this slogan to be the most revolutionary appealing call against their immediate social enemies of feudal landlordism. Surprisingly, there was no mention in the theses regarding what the peasants would have done with the 'land' once they could succeed in removing this age-old obstacle that sustained exploitation for ages, for generations together.

Another significant point of departure is Lenin's imprecise definition of the class composition of the people under Soviet rule in the colonies. We have seen on the eve of the October Revolution, Lenin was very specific in identifying association of the political parties with the social classes among the agrarian population of Russia (see Chapter 3). Unlike that stated position, Lenin was so ambiguous here in defining the affiliation of the social classes to the 'peasant Soviets' in the colonies that he identified them as either 'peasants' Soviets or as 'working people's Soviets'. The reason being his understanding that these peasant societies might have represented production relations that were even less developed than pre-revolution agrarian relations in European Russia. He was convinced that 'The preponderance of pre-capitalist relationships is still the main determining features in these countries'.

The issue before us is what relations of production the 'peasants' Soviets' were to harness after overhauling the age-old 'pre-capitalist' production relations by revolutionary means, if they were not 'socialism' that Lenin had ruled out even in comparatively developed agriculture in Soviet Russia? Lenin could not simply hold the firmness to postulate that these 'peasants' Soviets' were only to practise some form of 'state capitalism' once their revolutionary power was established, even in some quarters where 'land' was in their possession, as was initially started in the Hunan province of China (Hunan Report)[3]. The ground-reality was the peasants had already celebrated the proprietorship of 'land' as the landmark achievement of the revolution; in fact this very call for possession of a parcel of the mother earth made them join the revolutionary army. Why would they allow some revolutionary government later to usurp this parcel of 'land', however small, from them to convert into collective property of the state? This very crucial issue of *possession* of 'land' by small land holders dominated the political economy of post-revolution agrarian policy that was the root cause behind the saga of untold sufferings of the millions of peasantry in all these erstwhile colonies. During the collectivization campaign of the "communist" parties holding state-power that failed miserably, the agricultural fields were turned into graveyards of the millions as was in the period of the "Great Famine" in China from 1959-61 [Meng, 2015]. It was repetition of the story of unmitigated sufferings and torture of the peasants by the state authorities as it happened during the "forced collectivization" campaign in Russia after the failure of the NEP. That story is now kept aside for some later time to recount. Here, we would only point out that such ambiguous, misleading political slogan for initiation of 'peasants' Soviets' without specific agrarian program in Lenin's reports, and loosely talking of revolutionary power without specifying the social basis of the class interests comprising such Soviet institutions left the most undesirable consequences for the international communist movement, particularly in the colonies.

There would have been possibly only one window of opportunity for such underdeveloped economies to bypass capitalist production relations that too we can mention only in the domain of conjectures. That was the rider from Lenin, 'the Soviet governments come to the aid with all the means at their disposal', 'with the aid of the proletariat of the advanced countries, backward countries can go over to the Soviet system and, through certain stages of development, to communism, without having to pass through the capitalist stage.' In his proposition, Lenin relied on the hope that proletarian revolutions in Europe would be able to be victorious over capitalism, so that the working class of the developed nations would able to provide the material basis of *socialism* to these underdeveloped economies of the colonies.[4] That would have been, in one sense, paying back the *tribute* that these colonial "Master nations" looted, sucked out from the colonies for centuries together starting with the mass-deportation of human beings as slaves to unhindered exploitation of natural resources. It is to be noted that Lenin suggested this prospective option in plural terms, i.e. under the condition of victory of the proletariat in a number of developed countries. He did not anticipate that such onerous responsibility of providing 'aid' to the underdeveloped economies to bypass capitalism would fall upon the proletariat of a unique country that was Soviet Russia. In that case, the population of post-revolution Russia were asked to undergo immeasurable sacrifices for the humankind of the world. Firstly, they had to continue sacrifices in terms of the very limited access to the basic needs of society being predominantly an underdeveloped agrarian economy. They had to wait for the victory of the working class in Europe to happen that never occurred. Moreover, the people of Soviet Russia would be asked to make sacrifices for the peasant revolutions in the underdeveloped colonies so as to provide 'aid' to them for being guided to the blessed lands of 'socialism'. We understand the reader will now be tired of listening to the fairy tales of salvation of the Russian people bearing the proverbial *cross of sacrifices* for the poor and exploited of all the nations in the world.

Even if we conjecture Lenin's prospective guidelines to have been realized in actuality, it is doubtful whether such *guided* 'socialism' could really lead to a society where labour turns out to be 'life's prime want'. We can reaffirm and reiterate the two fundamental conditions of 'material basis of socialism', and social consciousness of the proletariat as achieved by *class struggle* to be the essential conditions of *socialism* with universal appeal irrespective of the stage of development of capitalism in the colonies. In any case, that prospective future in Lenin's argument was really consigned to the realm of "non-factual" in the history of *class struggle* for the working class in the colonies and semi-colonies as later history proved. What the "communist" parties were mandated as guidelines from CI was to generate a set of 'leaders' who will be untiring in their volunteerism and sacrifices to arouse the "*masses*" of workers and peasants against the imperialist "Masters" and the landlordism of the estate owners, to usher a rule of these 'leaders' as future "socialism" ('Nevertheless, we have assumed, or must assume, the role of leaders even there'- Lenin). In that sense, Mattick's words were more fitting to the destiny of the "communist" parties of the colonies and semi-colonies, that 'What they [the 'reformist' bourgeoisie] sought to attain along democratic ways, he [the communist parties] attempted to win by revolutionary means.'

Our aim in the above passages is to explain how the points of departure in the "Colonial theses" became the fountainhead of the "revision of Marxism" from what was traditionally understood in the practices of revolutionaries who assembled in the Second Congress of CI. Till the German revolution was advancing and there were strong Soviet movements in the adjacent regions near Russia such as in Austria, Hungary, Finland, everybody could see and understand Bolshevism as the uprising of the workers and soldiers against existing state-powers. It appeared that Soviet rule was tantamount to the end of capitalism. Keynes or an average worker on the street in any European city would have no confusion or disagreement that Bolshevism was to end capitalism, and therefore they were sworn enemies of each other. From 1920, as the prospects of such European revolutions receded, the bourgeoisie of all the European countries heaved a sigh of relief for their prayers being heeded by some invisible force, churches rang bells for success of their prayers. The workers for another time got defeated in winning the challenge (this time the breadth and depth of the challenge was much more significant than the Paris Commune of 1871) they had put before the bourgeoisie. Leaving all theoretical arguments in the above passages aside, this was the simple, essential, and motive force of "Marxism" before the class-conscious workers of Europe.

We must say here, this is not our wild surmises and conjectures.

The above interpretation was also from Lenin while he was standing in the midst of actions and events that later are recounted endlessly in the textbooks of modern political history. Speaking before the assembly of Bolsheviks in Moscow after the Second Congress of CI, Lenin emphatically spoke about this revision of "Marxism".

> A journal of the Communist International recently appeared under the title of *Narody Vostoka* 158. It carries the following slogan issued by the Communist International for the peoples of the East: "Workers of all countries and all oppressed peoples, unite!" "When did the Executive Committee give orders for slogans to be modified?" one of the comrades asked. Indeed, I do not remember that it ever did. Of course, the modification is wrong from the standpoint of the *Communist Manifesto*, but then the *Communist Manifesto* was written under entirely different conditions. From the point of view of present-day politics, however, the change is correct. Relations have become tense. All Germany is seething; so is all of Asia. You have read how the revolutionary movement is developing in India. In China there is a fierce hatred of the Japanese, and also of the Americans. In Germany there is such seething hatred of the Entente as can only be understood by those who have seen the hatred of the German workers for their own capitalists. As a result, they have made Russia the immediate representative of the entire mass of the oppressed population of the earth; the events are teaching the peoples to regard Russia as a centre of attraction. [Lenin, 1974, p. 453]

After the "Colonial Theses", there were two varieties of "Marxism" —one for the workers of Europe to end capitalism, the other for the peasants from colonies to 'regenerate' capitalism as was happening in Russia after the NEP. At the end of the day, after all deliberations among the pandits, the crux of the dilemma, the *central query* might have been posed in such blunt terms before the delegates of CI in the Second Congress. The *central query* was whether in the name of pursing and advancing militant peasant revolutions in Asia and Africa for liberation from the clutch of imperialism the revolutionaries of CI were mandated to pursue aggressively the charter of 'state capitalism'. Such a charter, in reality as modern history has brutally proved, went against the prospect of weakening capitalism in the developed countries. In contrast to the stated aim, the policies of the "communist leadership" in the peasant revolutions only confirmed their avowed resolve to pursue 'state capitalism' that in turn re-energized world capitalism to survive. Lenin's above emphasis about the need to revisit the tenets of the *Communist Manifesto*, in fact, helped involuntarily to re-energize world capitalism by bringing the erstwhile colonies into its orbit.

## 5.2 Contemporary Critiques of the "Colonial Theses"

The criticisms of the "*Left* Communists" towards Lenin and the Bolshevik's policy regarding the Eastern people's liberation struggle under the rule of the imperialist nations may be summarized in the statement from Gorter. Considering the class position of the poor peasants and workers in Germany Gorter wrote in his retort to Lenin's attack as,

> Unless, therefore, there should come a crisis far more terrible than the present one in Germany, a crisis, indeed, far exceeding the horrors of any other crises that ever were before, the poor peasants in Western Europe will side with Capitalism, as long as it has any life left....
>
> The revolution in Russia was victorious with the help of the poor peasants. This should always be borne in mind here in Western Europe and all the world over. But the workers in Western Europe stand alone: this should never be forgotten in Russia. [Gorter, 1920]

"*Left* Communists" such as Gorter were soon found incompatible with the focus and objectives of CI. By the Third Congress of CI in 1921, KAPD of Germany and the Dutch "*Left* Communists" were expelled from CI. Gorter's *group* and KAPD in Germany announced formation of a new International as Communist Workers' International as early as in 1923 [Bourrinet, 2008]. Gorter drafted the charter of the new International where he wrote,

> In forming the Communist Workers' International, it is important to explain clearly the revolutionary battle of the proletariat, which is revealed in quite a new light by the Russian and German revolutions....
>
> The establishment of peasants' soviets on the other hand was bourgeois capitalistic, for it was certain that the peasants would fight for private property and against communism.
>
> A proletarian revolution in Germany and England will never give the peasants political rights till they have shown that they are really communists.

> The partition of the big estates, and of the land generally, was bourgeois, for this distribution made enemies of communism the peasants, that is almost the entire population of Russia. Through its seizure of the land, the peasantry, now enormously swollen in numbers, became the enemy of every kind of socialist agricultural society. A genuine proletarian revolution will never admit of the partition of the soil. On the contrary, it will allow all large landed properties to pass into communist management....
>
> A genuine proletarian revolution will not have peasants in its army, for its army must be wholly Communist. [Gorter, 1923]

A pathological distaste for the 'peasants' is self-evident in Gorter's announcement of the new International in the above passage. He and his International would have refused 'the peasants political rights till they have shown that they are really communists' had they the opportunity in Germany and England. It appears that Gorter would have liked to arrange mass-graves for the 'peasants' in Europe as was arranged three decades later in China's countryside for the millions of rural population! Nevertheless, he could grasp and made pointed criticism of the agrarian policy of CI when he wrote, 'it was certain that the peasants would fight for private property and against communism'.

On the other hand, Gorter was proud to announce before the world, 'But the workers in Western Europe stand alone: this should never be forgotten in Russia.' It appears from Gorter's statements that the workers of Western Europe were so unfortunate, or were so selfish otherwise that they had nobody else to share the bounty of their victory as well as the misery of the revolution with any other exploited sections in society! Jest apart, Gorter's statement showed in very crude and plain terms the essence of the traditional understanding of "Marxism" among the so-called "*Left* Communists" sections of the revolutionaries: that is "socialism" is for the workers and for the *workers alone*. That brings us to the limitation of the interpretation of dictatorship of the proletariat *only* as a 'workers' state', where other sections of the society who actually are further downtrodden, further exploited, who existed at the lowest layers of social prosperity had *no choice* but to be subjugated under this new 'workers' state' as they cannot claim to be part of the working class under capitalist production relations. In an *obverse* way, Gorter's statement also amplifies our previous assertion that Marx had no visualization of a *transitional society* under dictatorship of the proletariat, where capitalism at the 'rock bottom' of society actually competes with the new, revolutionary *socialist* production relations that the proletariat exercises in bringing in *new socialist* society as the freedom, as the fundamental right to be emancipated from the slavery of wage-labour. The huge majority of the exploited "*masses*" under the pre-capitalist, semi-feudal, or underdeveloped capitalist modes of agricultural production were simply kept out of the analysis during the transition from capitalism to *communism* by these critiques of Lenin.

We have seen similar critical views of Luxemburg regarding the "Bolshevik Land Policy" [Luxemburg, 2004] previously in Chapter 3, particularly regarding the question of 'land distribution'. If those comments were rather mild in nature, Luxemburg was virulent in her criticism regarding Lenin's emphasis on the 'right of self-determination to the point of separation,' of the nationalities under the Tsarist regime. The criticism of Luxemburg on the "national question" of course could be extended to the criticism of the "Colonial Thesis", where Lenin brought forward the paradigm of 'nation' by dividing the world population into two groups: 'being divided into a large number of oppressed nations, and an insignificant number of oppressor nations'. Under the heading "The Nationalities Question" Luxemburg wrote,

> The formula of the right of the various nationalities of the Russian Empire to determine their fate independently "even to the point of the right of governmental separation from Russia," was proclaimed again with doctrinaire obstinacy as a special battle cry of Lenin and his comrades during their opposition against Miliukovist, and then Kerenskyan imperialism.[10] ....
>
> Lenin and his comrades clearly calculated that there was no surer method of binding the many foreign peoples within the Russian Empire to the cause of the revolution, to the cause of the socialist proletariat, than that of offering them, in the name of the revolution and of socialism, the most extreme and most unlimited freedom to determine their own fate. This was analogous to the policy of the Bolsheviks towards the Russian peasants, whose land-hunger was satisfied by the slogan of direct seizure of the noble estates and who were supposed to be bound thereby to the banner of the revolution

> and the proletarian government. In both cases, unfortunately, the calculation was entirely wrong....
>
> The Bolsheviks were to be taught, to their own great hurt and that of the revolution, that under the rule of capitalism there is no self-determination of peoples, that in a class society each class of the nation strives to "determine itself" in a different fashion, and that, for the bourgeois classes, the standpoint of national freedom is fully subordinated to that of class rule.... The hope of transforming these actual class relationships somehow into their opposite and of getting a majority vote for union with the Russian Revolution by depending on the revolutionary masses—if it was seriously meant by Lenin and Trotsky—represented an incomprehensible degree of optimism....
>
> Instead of acting in the same spirit of genuine international class policy which they represented in other matters, instead of working for the most compact union of the revolutionary forces throughout the area of the Empire, instead of defending tooth and nail the integrity of the Russian Empire as an area of revolution and opposing to all forms of separatism the solidarity and inseparability of the proletarians in all lands within the sphere of the Russian Revolution as the highest command of politics, the Bolsheviks, by their hollow nationalistic phraseology concerning the "right of self-determination to the point of separation," have accomplished quite the contrary and supplied the bourgeoisie in all border states with the finest, the most desirable pretext, the very banner of the counter-revolutionary efforts. [Luxemburg, 2004, pp. 293-294]

We are forced to introduce discontinuities within the reference above as otherwise the quotation would have been too long. We hope the reader will find continuity of Luxemburg's arguments in the above reference. Luxemburg's criticism had a direct context to the then prevailing revolutionary situation, particularly in Finland and Ukraine where she assessed the defeat of the revolutionary forces was a direct result of this policy of the Bolsheviks to offer 'right of self-determination to the point of separation' to the nationalities under erstwhile Tsarist rule.

Here again, Luxemburg interpreted the policy of 'self-determination' as a 'tactical move' of the Bolsheviks as like their agrarian policy towards the peasants. In all these statements she was clearly tied to the traditional views of the "Western Marxists" that production relations *alone* guide the development of a bourgeoisie society. She asserted that 'under the rule of capitalism there is no self-determination of peoples, that in a class society each class of the nation strives to "determine itself" in a different fashion, and that, for the bourgeois classes, the standpoint of national freedom is fully subordinated to that of class rule.' By the continuity of her arguments the working class in Britain, in France, or even in Holland had emphatically rejected the demands of self-determination, the right to cessation of the people of India, China, vast areas of Southeast Asia to name a few, from the British, French or Dutch imperialism respectively that was the writ of destiny over their miserable existence. That we are not extrapolating from her arguments is clearly evident in her statements, 'instead of defending tooth and nail the integrity of the Russian Empire as an area of revolution and opposing to all forms of separatism the solidarity and inseparability of the proletarians in all lands within the sphere of the Russian Revolution as the highest command of politics, the Bolsheviks...' Her statement could have no other meaning but to align the class interests of the revolutionary proletariat of the developed countries with the interest of the monopoly capitalists of their own 'nations' so far as the colonial exploitation was to be continued. This was a terrible, mechanistic, unilinear interpretation of the progress of bourgeoisie civilization for the countries where the proletariat had a weak social basis, where the pre-capitalist production relations in the national economy were predominant. More significantly, these statements reflected a crude and haughty indifference to the struggle and cry of the millions of peasant population ('if it was seriously meant by Lenin and Trotsky-represented an incomprehensible degree of optimism,'-Luxemburg) who were denuded and were starved by their imperialist "Masters". Their aspiration to raise their voice for self dignity, for earning the respect of their civilization that is as old as nature were ignored in Luxemburg's statements when those aspirations for nationhood continued to be trampled under the boots of colonial savagery for centuries.

It is extremely ironical that the same Luxemburg who was arguing for an "iron fist" policy towards the nationalities erstwhile under the Tsarist Empire and those seeking "freedom" from Russia (and as good as from Bolshevik rule) was, on the other hand, found criticising the Bolsheviks for not allowing a conducive political atmosphere in Russia. She was criticising the Bolsheviks for 'destruction of the most important democratic guarantees of a healthy public life and of the political activity of the labouring masses: freedom of the press, the rights of association and assembly, which have been outlawed for all opponents of the Soviet regime.' Regarding disbanding of the Constituent Assembly and for not bringing in Suffrage Law in elections, Luxemburg had to write about the Bolsheviks in Russia as below:

> But when it comes to a suffrage law which provides for the general disfranchisement of broad sections of society, whom it places politically outside the framework of society and, at the same time, is not in a position to make any place for them even economically within that framework, when it involves a deprivation of rights not as a concrete measure for a concrete purpose but as a general rule of long-standing effect, then it is not a necessity of dictatorship but a makeshift, incapable of being carried out in life. This applies alike to the soviets as the foundation, and to the Constituent Assembly and the general suffrage law. [Luxemburg, 2004, p. 304]

Just because such demands and necessities of exercising franchise were championed by the 'nationalist' bourgeoisie of Finland and Ukraine, as the Soviet movement amongst the "*masses*" there could not reign over the influences of the bourgeoisie representatives, therefore it was wrong to support the demands of Constituent Assembly in Ukraine and was right for Russia where the Soviet movement was reigning over society—such contradiction would have portrayed even Luxemburg too farcical in her augments. If Lenin and Trotsky were to be held responsible for vanishing "democracy" from the public life of Soviet Russia, then Luxemburg would also be held responsible for advocating disenfranchisement in the public life of Ukraine and Finland.

If Luxemburg sounded weighty with her "Marxist" phraseology here, Gorter resonated this very mechanistic understanding of the progress of bourgeois society in the colonies in more crude and plain terms in his manifesto.

> The proclamation by the Bolshevists of the right to self-determination of all nations caused the detaching from Soviet Russia of Finland, the Baltic Provinces, Poland, the Ukraine, and the Caucasus. This resulted in the downfall of the proletarian revolution in most of these countries....

> The self-determination slogan was a bourgeois-capitalist one. Either the Bolshevists proclaimed it from weakness in the fear that if they did not give these States their freedom they could not smash up Czarism, or, as it appears now, they wanted, even then, a national Russian State. The doubts both as to the power of Communism to triumph and the necessity of nationalism were inspired by the peasants. [Gorter, 1923]

Essentially, it is fact that the ideological inspiration for the peasant population was 'nationalism' and not *socialism* (also true for the urban, enlightened petty bourgeoisie being conscious of degradation of their 'national' values and culture under imperialism). That can be no reason to ignore and vilify the existence of the peasantry and their aspirations. By ignoring and abstaining from the tortuous issues of *class struggle* among the peasantry no dictatorship of the proletariat could hold forth as the experience of the period of *War Communism* had established in Soviet Russia. On the converse side, by exhorting the "communists" to lead national liberation from the clutches of the imperialists by armed revolutionary uprisings of the peasantry and recommending 'peasants' Soviets' as the organs of revolutionary power, Lenin and the leadership of CI were at a loss to find ways ahead for "socialism" before the brute reality of political economy in the colonies.

In comparison to the above statements of Gorter and Luxemburg, Pannekoek was more circumspective in his rebuttal of Lenin's attack [Pannekoek, 1978]. Pannekoek could realize the impact of anti-colonial, liberation struggles on the economies of the developed countries. However, he also could not make out how the agrarian struggles of the liberation movements of the colonies could be part of the anti-capitalist struggles of the proletariat in the developed countries except that he wished those might happen. Pannekoek wrote,

> The call for freedom and for the self-determination of all peoples and for struggle against European capital throughout Asia is going out from Moscow, where delegations from Asiatic tribes are arriving one after another.
>
> [*7] The threads lead from the Soviet republic of Turan to India and the Moslem countries; in Southern China the revolutionaries have sought to follow the example of government by soviets; the pan-

> Islamic movement developing in the Middle East under the leadership of Turkey is trying to connect with Russia....
>
> The question may be raised as to whether purely nationalist movements seeking a national capitalist order in Asia should be supported, since they will be hostile to their own proletarian liberation movements; but development will clearly not take this course. It is true that until now the rising intelligentsia has orientated itself in terms of European nationalism and, as the ideologues of the developing indigenous bourgeoisie advocated a national bourgeois government on Western lines; but this idea is paling with the decline of Europe, and they will doubtless come strongly under the intellectual sway of Russian bolshevism and find in it the means to fuse with the proletarian strike-movements and uprisings. [Pannekoek, 1978]

We find Pannekoek drawing the same assessments as Lenin about the nature of "freedom struggle" in the colonies; but he left without signing comments upon the issues those were other raised by other "*Left* Communists" in their analysis of the political economy that would be the outcome of these "freedom struggle". Even leaving aside the isolation of Soviet Russia after the defeat of the European working class struggling for state-power we can surely see Pannekoek's misplaced optimism when he wrote, 'they will doubtless come strongly under the intellectual sway of Russian bolshevism and find in it the means to fuse with the proletarian strike-movements and uprisings.' At other places, Pannekoek openly criticized the national aspirations of the Bolsheviks as they stabilized their hegemony over Russia. We have seen these national aspirations in Chapter 3 in Lenin's clear admissions regarding the developments of 'state capitalism' in Soviet Russia. We have highlighted in Chapter 2 the international overtures of the Soviet government to the comity of capitalist states in Genoa, and in executing the "Rapallo Treaty" with the Weimar Republic of Germany. Yet Pannekoek found the virtues of 'intellectual sway of Russian bolshevism' over the leaders of peasant revolutions in the colonies.

For the sake of history we may record here two developments: first, although the criticisms of Rosa Luxemburg [Luxemburg, 2004] were hushed up among the proceedings of CI right from the time of the Third Congress in stony silence (when it got published by Paul Levi in Germany[5]), it was known to the European revolutionaries, particularly to the "*Left* Communists". Gorter even quoted from Luxemburg's work in his charter for the new International [Gorter, 1923]. Second, while Gorter was effusive in praising Luxemburg for her strident criticisms of Russia's new polity, the Bolsheviks *in metamorphosis*, they could not live together within one party even for a short while as the history of KPD and KAPD in Germany had shown us.

Before we end this discussion on the "Colonial Theses", we want to highlight one most tragic, unfortunate implication of the policy of the Third International. As the "communist" leadership hovered between the "reformist" bourgeoisie and the revolutionary peasantry in the political spectrum of the colonies and semi-colonies, the germinating working class in these countries remained the most cheated and the most confused lot. In lending an extra hand and going an extra mile to organize the peasant revolution and the 'peasants' Soviets' in these countries, the independent class outlook and interests of the urban proletariat that stood against both the 'national' and imperialist bourgeoisie were the primary victim of the policy of CI in these countries. Possibly the last independent show of strength of the working class in the colonies and semi-colonies together was the Shanghai Insurrection of February 1927, and the massacre that followed the uprising.[6] As the policy of CI became riveted to the interests of Soviet Russia, every independent political action of the working class was seen only to promote the international interests of Soviet Russia. The role of the working class was at best promoted in organizing them in trade unions with strong links to the parent political party, the question of *socialism* and dictatorship of the proletariat were never posed before the practices of trade union struggle of the working class at any stage of *class struggle*. In a complimentary sense, the working class never could raise its spontaneity in class actions, were always confined to their goal as tutored by the 'leaders' before them. We, therefore, conclude this discussion by referring to Pannekoek's observations about the Third International. Reflecting on Lenin's philosophical contribution much later in 1938, Pannekoek wrote,

> The Third International aims at a world revolution after the model of the Russian revolution and with the same goal. The Russian economic

> system is state capitalism, there called state-socialism or even communism, with production directed by a state bureaucracy under the leadership of the Communist Party....
>
> According to Communist Party ideas, a similar revolution is needed in the capitalist countries, with the working class again as the active power, leading to the overthrow of the bourgeoisie and the organization of production by a state bureaucracy. The Russian revolution could be victorious only because a well-disciplined united Bolshevist party led the masses, and because in the party the clear insight and the unyielding assurance of Lenin and his friends showed the right way. Thus, in the same way, in world revolution the workers have to follow the Communist Party, leave to it the lead and afterwards the government; and the party members have to obey their leaders in rigid discipline. Essential are the qualified capable party leaders, the proficient, experienced revolutionaries; what is necessary for the masses is the belief that the party and its leaders are right....
>
> In reality, for the working class in the countries of developed capitalism, in Western Europe and America, matters are entirely different. Its task is not the overthrow of a backward absolutist monarchy. Its task is to vanquish a ruling class commanding the mightiest material and spiritual forces the world ever knew. ... Such an aim cannot be attained by an ignorant mass, confident followers of a party presenting itself as an expert leadership. It can be attained only if the workers themselves, the entire class, understand the conditions, ways and means of their fight; when every man knows from his own judgment, what to do. They must, every man of them, act themselves, decide themselves, hence think out and know for themselves. Only in this way will a real class organization be built up from below, having the form of something like workers' councils. (Chapter 8) [Pannekok, 2003]

Pannekoek's emphatic focus on the independent class initiative of the workers in the developed countries is self-evident above, when he wrote, 'Such an aim cannot be attained by an ignorant mass, confident followers of a party presenting itself as an expert leadership. It can be attained only if the workers themselves, the entire class, understand the conditions, ways and means of their fight; when every man knows from his own judgment, what to do.'

Unfortunately, in their rush to compete with the bourgeoisie in the colonies to finish the bourgeois democratic revolution, the "communists" left the working class as an amorphous 'ignorant mass, confident followers of a party presenting itself as an expert leadership'. They were tied to the national interest of independence from imperialism, and at the same time were tied to the interests of regenerating capitalism in the new sovereign states. Essentially, the working class after attainment of nationhood in the colonies and in the semi-colonies was never near to class-power that the working class in Russia exercised in the prelude and immediately after the October Revolution, during the initial heydays of enthusiasm of the formation of the Third International. Even at the best of times their exercise of authority were confined to the trade-union interests under 'state capitalism'. It was a monotonic repetition of the affairs of the working class being controlled and tutored by the interests of a bureaucratic state apparatus pursuing 'state capitalism' nearing nowhere to the revolutionary authority to dictate the norms and terms of *socialist* production relations, the "self-activation" that Pannekoek highlighted in the context of the workers in societies under the rule of the developed forms of capitalism.

By these arguments, we end our critique and review of the major theses and propositions put forward and pursued avowedly during the living, animated discussions in the formative period of the Third International. In the next Chapter, we offer some salient concluding points that may have emerged out of this discussion.

## NOTES

1. Here we draw reference from [Haithcox, November, 1963] as,

   > Before the opening of the Second World Congress of the Communist International (July 19 - August 7, 1920) [which met on the first day in Petrograd but subsequently in Moscow], Lenin prepared a draft thesis on the national and colonial question. M.N. Roy, a young Bengali attending his first international Communist gathering, eagerly responded to Lenin's request for criticisms. As a result, Lenin invited him to write an alternative thesis. Both theses were modified as a result of discussions within the National and Colonial Commission, and both were subsequently adopted by the Congress. [p. 93]

2. This refers to the widespread belief among the "Marxists" that the postulate European working class revolutions can be connected to

the peasants' revolutions in Asia was not originally from Lenin and CI. The origin of the postulate can be drawn to Marx, in his response in March 1881 to the queries of Vera Zasulich, a prominent member of the early socialists in Russia. To be fair to history, even after correcting four drafts of the response, Marx was equivocal over the theoretical possibility of the peasants' communal property relationship in Russia being elevated to *communist* society. He wrote,

> The analysis in Capital therefore provides no reasons either for or against the vitality of the Russian commune. But the special study I have made of it, including a search for original source material, has convinced me that the commune is the fulcrum for social regeneration in Russia. But in order that it might function as such, the harmful influences assailing it on all sides must first be eliminated, and it must then be assured the normal conditions for spontaneous development. [Marx, 1983]

Even if we consider Marx's hypothetical conjecture 'commune is the fulcrum for social regeneration in Russia' it is to be noted that his final response was meant to be a social upliftment and qualitative transformation without the connotations of the proletarian revolution. The 'harmful influences assailing it on all sides' as mentioned in Marx's response can be related to the capitalist production relations emanating from the industrial revolution in Europe although we note that Marx was quite heuristic in description of these hypothetical projections.

3. This refers to the investigative report on the peasant struggles in Hunan province of China titled "Report on an investigation of the peasant movement in Hunan" by Mao-Tse-Tung, written in March 1927, popularly known as the "Hunan Report". Mao Tse-Tung spent thirty-two days in Hunan Province in January-February, 1927 making direct interaction with the activities of the peasant struggles, and prepared this report that played a crucial role in changing the course of the "communist" party of China.

   Regarding the nature of land-distribution activities under the peasant Soviets in Kiangsi province (1931-1934) we reproduce below the following excerpts:

> Subsequent to the preliminary survey of land and population carried out by the confiscation committee, the task of distributing land was usually turned over to the land committee....Each committee included the chairman of the local Soviet government, the leaders of the poor peasant corps and the farm-labor unions, and family representatives of the Red Army. This emphasis on representation involving many people in a local mass organization

aimed to create a sense of popular participation....

The central task of the land committee was to supervise and manage all aspects of distribution in the land-reform program. It was also responsible for land improvement. ....

The methods of land distribution varied. One of the simplest procedures was that established by the O-yu-wan (Honan-Huphe-Anhewei) soviet government, which is described in a booklet entitled "How to Distribute Land". According to the booklet, land distribution in the soviet area at that time followed the principle of " all land to the peasants based on the number of individuals (per capita) and the strength of labor force (working ability) of each household."12 [Kim, 1973, pp. 123-124]

4. Lenin drew the hope and belief in this postulate from the comments and projections of Marx and Engels, in the Russian preface of the *Communist Manifesto* in January 1882, the last preface that Marx and Engels signed jointly.

   Now the question is: can the Russian obshchina, though greatly undermined, yet a form of primeval common ownership of land, pass directly to the higher form of Communist common ownership? Or, on the contrary, must it first pass through the same process of dissolution such as constitutes the historical evolution of the West?

   The only answer to that possible today is this: If the Russian Revolution becomes the signal for a proletarian revolution in the West, so that both complement each other, the present Russian common ownership of land may serve as the starting point for a communist development. [Marx and Engels, 1958, p.24]

   Although it is true that the above hypothesis of Marx and Engels can be related to the prevailing international situation after the post-WWI Soviet revolutions in Russia and Germany, the hypothesis became a non-factual as we have already discussed during the sessions of the Second Congress of CI in 1920.

5. Rosa Luxemburg's work *The Russian Revolution* was published by Paul Levi before the Fourth Congress of CI in 1922 when Levi himself was departing (or "expelled") from CI although her work was known beforehand to the revolutionists. The following reference is a pointer to this statement.

   In early 1921, nevertheless, Levi and the Bolsheviks came to a parting of the ways. The immediate occasion was a bungled split in Italy, when Comintern representatives alienated the great majority of Italian socialists by attacking a leadership that (whatever its faults) identified with communism. When a majority of the KPD central committee sided with the Comintern leadership against Levi on the issue, Levi resigned in February as chair....

From 1922 on Levi gave up not only on the KPD and short-term revolutionary possibilities, but also on the Russian revolution. By publishing Rosa Luxemburg's 1918 critique of the Bolsheviks, he rightly reaffirmed her intransigent defense of democracy... [Drucker, Summer 2012]

6. This refers to the glorious "Shanghai Commune"—the workers' insurrection against the Northern Expedition of Chaing Kai-Shek at the head of the Kuomintang regime.

   Shanghai with its ports and industry contained the flower of the Chinese proletariat. It was under the control of the war-lords and the workers' bitter struggles against their local rulers was portrayed by the Kuomintang and the CCP as a prelude to the triumph of the 'national revolution'. As the Kuomintang army advanced towards the city, the CCP-led General Labour Union issued a call for a general strike to overthrow the city's ruling clique and so "support the Northern Expeditionary Army" and "hail Chiang Kai-shek". This initial attempt was brutally beaten back after fierce street-fighting. The city authorities unleashed a grim reign of terror against the working population, but its spirit remained unbroken. On March 21, the workers rose again, better organized this time, with a 5,000-strong workers' militia and between 500,000 and 800,000 workers actively taking part in the general strike and insurrection. Police stations and army garrisons were attacked and seized, and arms distributed to the workers' forces. By the next morning the whole city, except for the foreign concession, was in the hands of the proletariat. [ICC Online, February 7, 2007]

   The rest of the story of the Shanghai Commune is now history as after the defeat of the Shanghai insurrection of the Chinese workers the "communist" party of China completely changed track by founding the peasant guerrilla army in Hunan province.

## REFERENCES

John P. Haithcox. The Roy-Lenin Debate on Colonial Policy: A New Interpretation.

*The Journal of Asian Studies*, 23(1):93–101, November, 1963. doi: 10.2307/2050635.

Jane Degras, Editor. *The Communist International 1919-1943 Documents*. Volume I. Routledge, 1971.

Alfred Rosmer. *Moscow Under Lenin*. Monthly Review Press, New York, 1973.

V.I. Lenin. Report of the Commission on the National and the Colonial questons. In *Speeches at Congress of the Communist International.* Progress Publishers, Moscow, 1972a.

M.N. Roy. Supplementary Theses on the National and Colonial Question, 1920. *URL :https://www.marxists.org/history/international/comintern/2nd-congress/ch04.htm.*

V.I. Lenin. Speech on the Terms of Admission into the Communist International. In *Speeches at Congress of the Communist International.* Progress Publishers, Moscow, 1972b.

Xi Meng, Nancy Qian, Pierre Yared. The Institutional Causes of China's Great Famine, 1959-1961. The National Bureau of Economic Research, USA, September, 2010. URL: *http://www.nber.org/papers/w16361.*

V.I. Lenin. Speech Delivered at a Meeting of the Activists of the Moscow Organization of the RCP(B). *Collected Works*, Vol. 31, 2nd Printing. Progress Publishers, Moscow, 1974.

Herman Gorter. Open Letter to Comrade Lenin, 1920. URL: *https://www.marxists.org/archive/gorter/1920/open-letter/ch01.htm.*

Philippe Bourrinet. The Dutch and German Communist Left (1900–68), 2008. URL: *https://libcom.org/history/german-dutch-communist-left-philippe-bourrinet.*

Herman Gorter. The World Revolution, 1923. URL: *https://www.marxists.org/archive/gorter/1923/world-revolution.htm.*

Rosa Luxemburg. The Russian Revolution. In Peter Hudis and Kevin B. Anderson, Editors, *The Rosa Luxemburg Reader*, Chapter 14. Monthly Review Press, New York, 2004.

Anton Pannekoek. World Revolution and Communist Tactics. In D.A. Smart, Editor, *Pannekoek and Gorter's Marxism*. Pluto Press, UK, 1978.

Anton Pannekoek. *Lenin as Philosopher: A Critical Examination of the Philosophical Basis of Leninism*. Lance Byron Richey, Editor. Marquette University Press, 2003.

Karl Marx. The Reply to Zasulich In *Late Marx and the Russian Road, Marx and the Peripheries of Capitalism*. Teodor Shanin. Monthly Review Press, January, 1983.

Karl Marx and Frederick Engels. Preface to The Russian Edition. *Selected Works*, Vol. I. Progress Publisher, Moscow, 1958.

Ilpyong J. Kim. *The Politics of Chinese Communism: Kiangsi Under the Soviets*. University of California Press, 1973.

Peter Drucker. Paul Levi: A Luxemburgist Alternative? in *New Politics*, Summer 2012. URL: *http://newpol.org/content/paul-levi-luxemburgist-alternative.*

ICC (International Communist Current) Online. China 1927: Last Gasp of the World Revolution, February 7, 2007. URL: *http://en.internationalism.org/icconline/2007/china-march-1927.*

# 6

# Conclusions

At the end of the day, certain conclusions of this long essay are surely to be expected.

The celebrated Bengali poet Sudhindranath Nath Dutta wrote in 1937, "Aaj digante marichikao je nei, nirbak nil, nirmam mahakash" (translated by the poet himself the lines stand for '*While dead horizons cannot hold the quick mirage, and, never near, the cruel sky is mute and blue.*' [Ghose, 1972, p. 31]). We found the lines from his poem *Utpakhi* (*Camel-bird*) most appropriate to begin the conclusion of this essay. There is no denying the fact today the international working class movement is at its lowest ebb. This situation is not due to revitalization and reinforcement of world capitalism in the twenty-first century that could finally show off as the irresistible socio-economic system—rather far from it. Beginning with the infamous burst of the bubble "Y2K" the world capitalist system is hovering from one terminal crisis to another cycling over every four years. The fragile nature of the international financial institutions is covered up by keeping the war machines of capitalism alive and operational. The first two decades of the twenty-first century have witnessed constant military engagements and theatres of operation in the Middle East region, and Afghanistan in Asia. However, such crisis of capitalism is not being responded internationally by the class initiative of the workers. One phenomenon in which the votaries of capitalism can relish and find relief is that instead of class solidarity in confronting the crisis of world capitalism the international working class itself is in crisis to proclaim its own place in society, its class aspirations and objectives. Leave aside the feebleness of the voice of the working class in the society, questions and doubts are vehemently and regularly being raised about the separate social, political identity of the working class.

Reams of paper have already been written and many animated discussions are already there on the fate of the October Revolution in Russia. Endless number of dissections of the Bolshevik leadership of revolution has been done in the literature. More insights into the history of the revolution are expected to appear given the fact that this year is going to see the centenary of the revolution. It is natural to be sceptical about what new perspective and material this present essay is able to provide in the present scenario of ambivalence and confusion.

Our conscious effort here is *not* to attempt a comprehensive evaluation of the Russian political economy after the October Revolution. Several authoritative works on the subject exist in the literature and more will follow given the indelible impact the October Revolution has left over human civilization that are prominent both in their glare of illumination and in the deep depth of darkness. Rather, we concentrate on the theoretical and objective basis of the programmes of CI, and on the *dynamic* nature of transformation of the institution. All we wanted to bring into focus is how the process of *metamorphosis* of Bolshevism from being champions of world revolution to votaries of 'state-socialism' left its deep imprints over the programmes of CI. It is beyond reasonable limits of doubt that the Third International remained a major motive force of the international working class movement between the two World Wars. It was not only in Europe that CI remained the source of both theoretical and practical guidance for the peasant revolutions in the colonies in Asia and Africa. Even when CI was formally dissolved in May 1943 and several offshoots came into existence (the most prominent being the Fourth International constituted by the followers of Trotsky in New York, October 1938), the core programmes for "socialism" and dictatorship of the proletariat formulated during the formative period of CI remained intact in all these forums of international working class. Therefore, we felt it necessary to review these core programmes in the light of "socialist" reorganization initiated in Soviet Russia in right earnest after the Civil War was brought to an end.

# I

The issue of foremost importance before this essay is the international character of workers' rebellion in the post-WWI European society that has long been lost and forgotten in the discourse. The international character of the workers' revolt was present as a natural, living process before the revolutionaries who assembled under the banner of the Third International in the First Congress, Moscow in March 1919 and in the subsequent annual sessions of CI. We have seen Lenin analysed in 1918 the immediate consequence of the the WWI as history 'has taken such a peculiar course that it *has given birth* in 1918 to two unconnected halves of socialism existing side by side like two future chickens in the single shell of international imperialism.' These 'two unconnected halves of socialism', in Lenin's interpretation, were the revolutions in Germany and Russia those marked *socialism* as an immediate practical agenda before the international working class. The practical agenda before the working class in both the revolutions was to organize society in a qualitatively *newer* plane, launching the final struggle to end capitalism and exploitation of the human race by fellow humans.

We steadfastly avoid to conjecture in this essay about the historical non-factual, the hypothetical consequence of 'two future chickens' growing and bursting aside the 'single shell of international imperialism', as it would be an analysis of imagined history. Without surmising over something that did not fructify into reality, we can only say the genuine nature of the impact of the revolutions on world capitalist system cannot be doubted. We have seen in Keynes's anticipated fear about the fate of capitalism in Europe in the event of stabilization of Bolshevism in Russia and Spartacism in Germany. The spontaneous spread of the message of the revolutions among the industrial working class in post-WWI Europe needed no strenuous prodding and efforts to cobble up the revolution. Direct exercise of social governance by the elected councils of the workers and the soldiers were the hallmarks of the revolutions in spite of the distinctly chaotic administration that resulted as direct fallout of the revolutions; but historically every revolution worth the name invited that disorder in the society. The political postulates of Marx and Engels about 'the *class dictatorship* of the proletariat as the necessary transit point to the *abolition of class distinctions generally*' appeared too close to reality in the immediate post-revolutionary situation in Russia and Germany.

Yet, the bitter reality was the revolutions failed to live up to the expectation of the international working class. The defeat of the January Revolution in 1919 of Germany was visibly apparent in the merciless crushing of the workers' and soldiers' insurrection by the prevailing state-power in the custody of German social-democracy that proved worth its salt by offering steadfast allegiance and protection to capitalism. On the other hand, the defeat of the October Revolution of Russia was more surreal in nature. It happened over a period of time when everybody wanted to believe Soviet Russia as the fortress of "socialism". The Russian revolution could salvage itself from the attack of the armies of fourteen invader nation-states of Europe those actively supported the white army in the Civil War, could survive itself through the extremely tortuous journey during the period of *War Communism*, but got defeated in its isolation, in its singularly primitive attempts to usher *socialism* in a largely pre-capitalist economy. The tragedy of momentous proportion is that the defeat of the working class in being divested of *class power* was proclaimed as its antithesis - the *victory* of the working class against capitalism in Russia despite its isolation, and the series of defeats of the attempts of the working *class power* in the developed, industrialized countries of Europe.

It may sound incredible today, but the belief and confidence of the leaders of revolutionary sections of the working class upon the Bolsheviks in Russia was of enormous proportion. The Third International (CI) which was formed with the declared objective to usher an association of governance by the *workers' councils* in the industrialized countries got transformed into the mouthpiece of Soviet Russia to the external world along with this *metamorphosis* of Bolshevism with few resistance from inside. We have seen in Pannekoek's reflection in 1938,

> The Third International aims at a world revolution after the model of the Russian revolution and with the same goal. The Russian economic system is state capitalism, there called state-socialism or even communism, with production directed by a state bureaucracy under the leadership of the Communist Party....

In this essay, one principal objective of us is to stress that both these phenomena, i.e., transformation of CI as an extension of foreign policy of the then Soviet government of Russia and the attempts of Soviet Russia to join the comity of nation-states after the failure of initial sparks of revolution in the early days of CI were complimenting each other. In retrospect, we can say both the 'future chickens' of international *socialism* were lost before the strength of world capitalism. It took years of huge sacrifice and enormous defeats between the two World Wars to understand and realize the nature of 'state-capitalism', and consequently the hegemony of the Russian nation-state in international affairs that was falsifying itself as "socialism" before the international working class.

This process of transformation of CI was most prominent in the theses and reports of Lenin those he placed before the four Congresses of CI for deliberation among the delegates. Therefore, the review of the material took most of the space of this essay. The most apparent contradiction in Lenin's reports and theses was while he was cautioning against *russification* of CI in the Fourth Congress, he himself strongly suggested in the Second Congress the revolutionaries from other countries to emulate 'the Russian model that reveals to *all* countries something—and something highly significant—of their near and inevitable future.' In that sense, the tragedy of the international working class movement was enacted by Lenin, Trotsky and their fellow Bolsheviks, who in spite of their utmost sincerity to world revolution undertook the Herculean effort to make the Russian economy self-sufficient in the face of international isolation. Since no other model of working class revolution could come forward from the developed, industrialized world, the Russian experience of consolidating a nation-state under planned economic growth and "forced collectivization" of the farmers and rural population were projected to be the flagships of "socialism" before the international working class. The most significant loss in these overtures from Soviet Russia was the international class brethren-ship among the workers that was instinctively present in the fraternization across the borders immediately after the WWI. The mood among the revolutionary sections of the working class can be gauged as Lenin forced the misadventure in 1920, the invasion of the Red Army to Poland, with the false hope to rekindle the flames of revolution in industrialized Europe.

Like every revolutionary upheaval, the prospects that the October Revolution heralded in society had also faced severe criticisms from the contemporaries within the ranks of the working class; like Plekhanov and Kautsky on one side, Luxemburg and Pannekoek on the other. We have seen Kautsky, Plekhanov and other leaders of the Second International were bitter critiques of the Bolshevik strategy of seizing state-power ahead of the Second Congress of the Soviets in Russia. However, their central argument that the proletariat in Russia was ill-prepared to lead the society in a revolutionary upheaval was simply beside the context of history. Plekhanov wrote in his *Open Letter to the Petrograd Workers* on the eve of the insurrection 'no, our working class is far from ready to grasp political power with any advantage to itself and the country at large'. This was the central thread of their arguments.According to the same logic, the February Revolution of 1917 in Russia, *or*, the November Revolution of 1918 in Germany were also misadventures enacted by the revolutionary workers in Petrograd and Berlin respectively. If the initiative of the working class and the soldiers to bring an end to the monarchy cannot be refuted as remarkable events of history, the advances and initiatives for seizing the state-power by instituting dictatorship of the proletariat in similar veins cannot be condemned simply because it affected the bourgeoisie, simply because such initiatives had shaken the fundamental basis of class exploitation in existing production relations. In hindsight, compared to contemporary Germany in the socio-economic context the relative underdevelopment of Russia was a fact of life. Yet, revolution flared in both places overthrowing the existing rule by centuries-old monarchy. Both Kautsky and Plekhanov could not deny the initiative of the working class in these historic events of unseating the monarchy by revolution in both the countries.

We have shown in this essay by several references that the leadership in a revolution is essentially seizing the moment of opportunity that cannot be predicted or cannot be foretold by quoting copious textual references. Therein centres the magnificence, the ingenuity, the brilliance of the leaders of revolution that created history over which reams of paper can only be expended later analysing the merits and demerits of the upheaval. It is in this historical sense, Plekhanov, Kautsky and the European leaders of the Second International like them were trailing behind the "*masses*" of the workers and soldiers in igniting and celebrating the flames of revolution. They remained the wisecrackers of the bourgeoisie rule that was decadent and falling apart, they were unprepared to seize the call of the moment.

On the other hand, even though Luxemburg could sense the dangers of 'the rule of the Jacobins' in Russia in the name of dictatorship of the proletariat while she was imprisoned in Germany, she embraced the revolution with uninhibited support. Even when she was criticizing the Bolsheviks' efforts to *metamorphose* dictatorship of the proletariat as the handiwork of a clever and wise leadership of the revolution she was unequivocal to write,

> This is the essential and enduring in Bolshevik policy. In this sense theirs is the immortal historical service of having marched at the head of the international proletariat with the conquest of political power and the practical placing of the problem of the realization of socialism, and of having advanced mightily the settlement of the score between capital and labor in the entire world.

Luxemburg was hugely sagacious to read the October Revolution not as a misadventure of the unprepared working class, nor as a coup or *putsch* of disgruntled retinues of the Russian naval fleet, who were part and parcel of the insurrection. Rather she was in continuum with Engels, who remarked about the Paris Commune as,

> Of late, the Social-Democrat philistine has once more been filled with wholesome terror at the words: Dictatorship of the Proletariat. Well and good, gentlemen, do you want to know what this dictatorship looks like? Look at the Paris Commune. That was the Dictatorship of the Proletariat. [Engels, 2012]

In this essay, we look for inheriting this legacy of Engels and Luxemburg while we review the programmes of CI. Our aim is to reason for the revolutionary *class identity* of the proletariat against world capitalism even though we recognise the failure of the heroic attempts of the working class immediately after the WWI.

We concur with Luxemburg who wrote right after the above quoted passage, 'In Russia the problem could only be posed. It could not be solved in Russia.' The issue of a *transitional society* progressing towards *socialism* could only be posed in an underdeveloped economy like Russia (with petty-commodity production being the dominant feature in agriculture). It could never have been resolved there in the absence of the working class revolutions in Europe. In that sense, the Russian revolution could possibly have played only a role of curtain raiser to the expected European revolutions of the working class. Revolution in Russia could succeed due to several conflicting reasons (we elaborated the reasons in our critique), the most important among them being the WWI and the determined resolve of the Bolsheviks to carry forward the revolution that was helped by the circumstantial presence of a weak bourgeoisie class. On the other hand, the expectations from the impending revolution in Germany were far more reasonable. The working class and the soldiers in Germany were far more confident in organizing themselves as a part of their exercise in self-activity. The bourgeoisie in Germany, even while reeling under the deep economic crisis as a consequence of defeat in the war, was strong enough to prop up a smokescreen in the form of a "socialist" government that could effectively neutralize the revolution initiative of the workers.

In our view, the international nature and significance of the working class revolutions were inherent in the course of events explained above. We view the revolutions as inseparable *not* in their defeats, but *precisely* in their birth, in their happenings. The Bolsheviks and their chief protagonists Lenin and Trotsky were not unaware that the proletarian revolutions could survive only in an international battle for *socialism*. We have seen Lenin making the statement in the Third Congress of CI,

> We thought: either the international revolution comes to our assistance, and in that case our victory will be fully assured, or we shall do our modest revolutionary work in the conviction that even in the event of defeat we shall have served the cause of the revolution and that our experience will benefit other revolutions. It was clear to

> us that without the support of the international world revolution the victory of the proletarian revolution was impossible.

Their problem was retracing the path of capitalism that they were compelled to undertake in their attempt to hold on the newly acquired state-power under the sole authority of a *Party* when it was understood the revolutionary waves in Europe were receding. The Bolsheviks attempted to theorize and institutionalize the "Jacobin rule" with the anticipation that European proletarian revolutions would come forward soon to relieve them from retracing the path of capitalism. For that purpose, they led the one-eyed regimentation of CI in the light of the experience they had in Russia with the vain attempt to accelerate revolutions in Europe. On the other hand, they were looking for the avenues to stabilize Soviet Russia in the comity of nations after the WWI in the arena of world capitalism. For that purpose, CI was the platform for them to keep aloft the prestige of Soviet Russia among the workers of the industrialized nations of Europe and USA so as to maintain the pressure on their national governments for negotiation with Soviet Russia.

## II

The programs of CI, from their genesis, had a world view of "socialism" emanating from the practices in a country that was relatively underdeveloped compared to the contemporary industrialized countries such as Britain, France or Germany even after its humiliating defeat in the war. Lenin's interpretation of 'state capitalism' and the NEP under dictatorship of the proletariat was not only a bundle of contradiction of purposes, it was essentially a programme of *self-deception*. While exhorting for barter deal in the exchanges with the state as steps towards 'regular socialist exchange', Lenin wrote in the same breath during the NEP, 'Exchange is freedom of trade; it is capitalism.' Lenin's expectation from the NEP as the means to reach "socialism" via 'state capitalism' meant neither capitalism as production relation nor steps towards *socialism*, but were blatant coercion of the agricultural producers to hypothecate their produce to the state through barter deals.

The Bolsheviks and the working class in Russia, to their credit, faced for the first time the teething issues of transition of an underdeveloped capitalist society to *socialism*. To their credit, it was the first time in the sense that such issues of a *transitional society* were not present even in the conjectures of Marx and Engels. There are reasons (we argued elaborately on this topic in this essay) here to concur with Lenin when he wrote in 1922,

> Not a single book has been written about state capitalism under communism. It did not occur even to Marx to write a word on this subject; and he died without leaving a single precise statement or definite instruction on it. That is why we must overcome the difficulty entirely by ourselves.

The communists who took oath under the banner of the Third International were enmeshed with the firm belief that dictatorship of the proletariat was itself "socialism". Their belief was nurtured by Lenin prevarication in his celebrated work *The State and Revolution* where with a sleight of hand he justified "socialism" as the first stage of *communism* in Marx's conjecture. Thereby, unlike and much away from Marx and Engels, Lenin legitimized the institution of state to exist in the entire historical period of transition from "socialism" to a *communist* society. In our essay, we pointed out that this glaring and obvious prevarication could go on unchallenged even in the period of the 1970s debates among the "Marxists" as Marx and Engels (as noted in Lenin's above reference) were silent on the transitional nature of society from capitalism to *communism*. When Marx mentioned 'the *class dictatorship* of the proletariat as the necessary transit point' he had in mind a transitional *state* that was to wither away along with 'the class *dictatorship*' in a classless society. The dilemma and confusion in Lenin's explanation was this libertarian viewpoint about *state* being corroborated in his own work along with the prevarication, and in his thesis in the First Congress of CI. Not only Lenin, the first *Manifesto* of CI that was drafted by Trotsky echoed similar views, 'The dictatorship of the proletariat, which gives it the favoured position in the community, is only a provisional institution.' In a span of only one year, during the sessions of the Second Congress the prevarications took centre-stage of all deliberations, theorizations took about turn from the conjectures of Marx to the Bolshevik version of "socialism", to 'state capitalism', to the supremacy of the Central Committee of the *Party*, to the twenty-conditions for admission to CI, etc.

We have analysed in detail the reasons and the implications of such prevarications in the transformation of CI in the essay. Without repeating them again here we can say the "communist" movement under the leadership of CI lost the libertarian viewpoint of Marx right in its genesis as it was meant to pursue the Russian model in the international arena, 'state capitalism' under the hegemony of a *Party* in the name of "socialism". We have seen the celebrated "Marxist", Charles Bettelheim after spending three decades in Soviet Russia, was admitting the central theme of understanding of the European "Marxists" of his generation as,

> Hence the slogans of the period: "Technique decides everything" and "Catch up with and surpass the most advanced capitalist countries."....
>
> The fact is that this "understanding" dominated the ideological and political conceptions of the European sections of the Third International, and thereby helped to conceal the existence of classes and of class struggle in the Soviet Union, thus encouraging people to seek "elsewhere" than in class contradictions the causes of the grave difficulties being experienced by the Soviet Union.... [Bettleheim, 1977]

It was most unfortunate, that looking back after fifty years of the revolution, Bettelheim harped on the infallibility of leadership of the state in "socialism" as the panacea to the 'grave difficulties' faced by a *transitional society*, in the form of 'a Marxist-Leninist communist party'. To Bettelheim and to the "Marxists" of his genre who later stayed away from the cult of personalities in the name of "socialism", the institutions of revolutions like the *Soviets*, the *Workmen's Councils* were of secondary, or of least importance. Following the instances of the Paris Commune, these institutions were the spontaneous forms of organizations of political power evolving from the working class revolutions in Europe after the WWI. The significance of the institutions of revolution was lost simultaneously with the propaganda of infallibility of *Party* taking the centre-stage of CI. The very spirit of revolution, the sprouts of the *new* society that evolved in the "*mass*" initiative of the workers in their self-activity as direct producers to decide the modes of production and divisions of labour in the *new* order (for example, the *factory councils* in Soviet Russia, the *shop stewards committees* in

Germany and England, etc.) were simply missing in the suggestions offered by Bettelheim.

It was not Bettelheim alone, the contemporary critiques of Bolshevism from Europe were also at a loss to face the reality after Russian revolution; i.e. to confront the challenges of ushering *socialism* in a predominantly underdeveloped capitalist economy. In fact, except Luxemburg's brief article *The Socialization of Society* and the programme of the *Spartacus group* on the eve of the January Revolution in 1919, there was absolutely no material from the European "Marxists" those provided the contours of *socialist* organization of production in the society under dictatorship of the proletariat. However, even in this brief contour Luxemburg puts her exclusive focus on reorganization of industrial production. On the other hand, Lenin had these challenges of *transitional society* very much in mind and in action. He attempted to specifically answer the problems of "socialist" production relations, with strong recommendations for the financial institutions, the housing questions in his pamphlets [Lenin, 1972], [Lenin, 1974] before and after the October Revolution. In the detailed review of Lenin's programmes we have seen these recommendations were essentially meant to champion 'state capitalism'. At best, they were intended for deeper involvement of the workers in these state enterprises by labour conscription for speedier growth and accumulation of 'state capital' as observed earlier also by Bettelheim.

The stiff challenges that Russian revolution faced after stabilization of state-power in the hands of the Bolsheviks was from the petty-commodity producers whom Lenin identified as the 'rock bottom of capitalism'. This is where dictatorship of the proletariat faced the real challenge in overhauling existing production relations in society. We do not belittle in any way the challenges that came from *within* the working class in overhauling the divisions of labour in industrial production relations. However, post-Civil War, in the concrete reality of Russia, the challenges faced from the petty-commodity production and pre-capitalist production relations were of enormous proportion as the Bolshevik policy of 'grain monopoly of state' in the name of *War Communism* faced instinctive hostility from the agricultural producers.

Not only in Russia, the policy of "forced collectivization"

uniformly failed to motivate the peasants with small land-holdings and with limited ownership and access to the means of production towards "socialism" in all the colonies where "collectivization" was attempted in countrywide-scale following the Russian model, such as in the Chinese experiments of commune formation after revolution when the state-power was in the control of the "communists". It is noteworthy and ironical to find that both the critiques of Bolshevik land policy such as Luxemburg, Gorter or the "*Left* Communists" in Russia, and the supporters of Lenin like Bukharin, all of them banked heavily on the coercive instruments of the state for so-called "socialist" collectivization in the agrarian economy. The scale of human repression by these forced measures of "socialism" reached unparalleled proportion in Russia in later periods after the demise of Lenin. The narratives were similar also in the East European countries where the new state-powers claiming to be "socialist" came into existence after the Red Army marched through their lands at the terminal phase of the WWII.

It is very pertinent today to raise questions and introspect whether during the formative period of CI the leaders with revolutionary appeal to the international working class (not only in Russia alone!) were at all prepared to accept dictatorship of the proletariat as a *transitional society*. We have shown, the "*Left* Communists" were strongly advocating for *currency*-less economy. They were opposing Lenin for introducing state procurement and offering support prices for grains acquired by the state. Lenin found such policy of the "*Left* Communists" to be 'suicidal' for the existence of the Bolsheviks in Soviet Russia. On the other hand, when Lenin was advocating cooperative societies for the 'middle peasants' he had barter exchanges with the state in mind; that was compelling the cooperative societies to barter both the *tax* and *surplus* components *in kind* to the Soviet-state organization such as 'food supply organizations'. From the perspective of both the opponents and supporters of the NEP, capitalism in the form of market-based exchanges were intended to be restricted to bare minimum.

Contrary to these prevailing viewpoints, the agricultural economy of Russia was aspiring for more freedom of access to market. Russian agricultural society was definitely not aspiring for *socialism*, but for freedom of trading, for more avenues of circulation of money and growth of income. Among the Bolsheviks (we should say even within CI), Lenin was foremost in admitting this reality. Not only in Russia, while putting up the supplementary theses to Lenin's theses on the "Colonial Questions", M.N. Roy clearly advocated, 'Indeed, it would be extremely erroneous in many of the oriental countries to try to solve the agrarian problem according to pure communist principles.'

In this essay, we bring ourselves to the central question of *transitional society* while looking back at the human tragedy in the past century that was a direct result of determined pursuance of the so-called 'pure communist principles'. A substantial part of our effort is devoted to analysing particularly those societies including Soviet Russia where nation formation was the primary agenda of the society, and overhauling the feudal, pre-capitalist production relations were the main agenda of the agrarian revolutions.

In our view, the defeat of the working class revolutions in Europe to the reigning forces of capitalism was visibly an apparent phenomenon after the WWI. The more invisible, hidden defeat of the international proletariat happened in two accounts: first, the gross misunderstanding that prevailed was accumulation of capital in the hands of the state-power and stabilization of *currency* by artificial avenues to be synonymous with "socialism" and strengthening the coercive arms of the state was sacrosanct in such "socialism". Second, the vast "*masses*" of the peasantry engaged in petty-commodity production cannot be *forced* or *driven* to the realm of voluntary engagement in the society where all access to the means of production including *land* are subjected to the direct ownership of society; their private ownership cannot be usurped by the coercive instruments of the state. In fundamental terms, a society based on voluntary association of direct producers cannot be organized by alienating a large section of population to whom *land* is considered inalienable right of private property. By continuing the Bolshevik agricultural policies uniformly in all the colonies the "communist" movements under the leadership of CI essentially played the role of involuntary agents of recreating capitalism under the monopoly political rule of a hegemonistic association that was called *Party*. Even if we set aside the extreme social, political aberrations in the agrarian societies where democracy, both *before and after* the revolutions, was a rare phenomenon as oxygen is rare in the stratosphere, the political economy that was established uniformly in the course of the revolutions was the consolidation of primary accumulation of "state capital". In whichever way we name this "socialism" as " bureaucratic or state capitalism", these forms of capitalism co-existed and conformed to the rules and legacies of international capital, finances, monetary policies, etc. In this historical sense, the *transitional societies* offered capitalism as the lone, formidable choice for the socio-economic and political system after the revolutions. The tragic defeat of the working class happened in the process of their heroic efforts of nation building in these post-revolution societies where petty- commodity production dominated the agriculture scenario. All these efforts in the century-old legacy of CI only served the historical reality of abrogating the international *class identity* of the working class. They were destined to lose the revolutionary appeal of transformation to a society of *co-operative association of direct producers*. The avowed, holistic aim of the revolutions was to abandon the sole authority of *currency* in all societal exchanges that was destined to be dumped in the shadows of an unforeseeable future.

## III

All historical tragedies are poignant with bitter truth, whether it was the Paris Commune or the October Revolution. These modern revolutions were meant to be the anti-thesis, the positive rebuttal of the international working class to warmongering among the developed capitalist nations. The war hysteria among the nations was a direct fall out of the intense competition among the capitalist nation-states to occupy more and more territories in the colonies. Particularly the tragedy with the October Revolution was the egalitarian principles of the newly found state administration soon gave way to the totalitarian basis whose features and contradictions we discussed in this essay. However, when we look back from the advantage of hindsight we cannot rest only by realising the poignancy in the tragedy; in the stoic, resilient, heroic sacrifices of the million of marchers for the *new society*.

In the positive sense of response to the tragedy, we must realize and appreciate the dilemma the revolution posed before the new leaders of the society. We have seen during the Fourth Anniversary of the October Revolution Lenin only looked at a distant horizon for preparation of 'a small-peasant country' progressing over to "communist" society as,

> It appears that a number of transitional stages were necessary—state capitalism and socialism—in order to *prepare*—to prepare by many years of effort—for the transition to communism.

In a significant essay that remain unfinished but was thought-provoking in conceiving the nature of the *transitional society* Lenin initiated the discussion as,

> Theoretically, there can be no doubt that between capitalism and communism there lies a definite transition period which must combine the features and properties of both these forms of social economy. This transition period has to be a period of struggle between dying capitalism and nascent communism—or, in other words, between capitalism which has been defeated but not destroyed and communism which has been born but is still very feeble.

It must be brought to conclusion that although Lenin mentioned the 'transition period' all along in the passage, he definitely did not mean a time period of transition (going by the earlier reference 'to prepare by many years of effort') *alone*. He meant the character of 'social economy' under dictatorship of the proletariat where both the production relations 'dying capitalism and nascent communism' were in competition to survive. Such a scenario of society where hitherto non-existing *socialist* production relation faced bitter competition from existing capitalist nature of social exchanges for a number of stages of progression was definitely not present in the conjectures or vision of Marx, *or*, in later exposition by Engels on the subject. Engels, in fact, viewed the victory of dictatorship of the proletariat over the political – administrative institutions of the bourgeoisie state apparatus as the 'also its *last independent act* as a *state*.' To them, the last independent act, the coercive subjugation of the bourgeoisie under the political and administrative authority of dictatorship of the proletariat also would signal the death warrant for the institution of the state. In that sense, transition of an agricultural society where petty-commodity producers dominate the social exchanges to *socialist* production relations where circulation of *currency* becomes redundant as the medium of social exchanges was simply not in their vision.

Such an understanding of social development is not out of context in the current discussion going by the fact that the entire spectrum of the "Marxists" in Europe (including the Bolsheviks who vigorously pursued *War Communism* during the Civil War) considered "socialism" to be the immediate production relation that dictatorship of the proletariat could enforce in the society. We want to point out that there was no record of disagreement from the European "Marxists" when Lenin asserted confidently on the eve of October Revolution,

> because state-monopoly capitalism is a complete *material* preparation for socialism, the *threshold* of socialism, a rung on the ladder of history between which and the rung called socialism *there are no intermediate rungs.*

That the political economy of dictatorship of the proletariat was to be 'state capitalism' was repeatedly pronounced by Lenin at the various forums of the Bolsheviks and before the sessions of CI. Here, we want to point that there was no argument in the conjectures of Marx and Engels in favour of 'state-monopoly capitalism' as the political economy during dictatorship of the proletariat. Second, as Lenin stressed *'there are no intermediate rungs'* between 'socialism' and 'state-monopoly capitalism is a complete *material* preparation for socialism', the immediacy and seamless transformation of the two categories of production relations was apparent in the statement. Such directives by Lenin regarding the progress of "socialism" were not contested by his bitter critiques, starting from Kautsky to Luxemburg, or even Pannekoek or Gorter from the extreme end of the "*Left* Communists".

These historical facts lead us to the conclusion that the leading representatives of the Third International either did not have a clear idea of the political economy under dictatorship of the proletariat, *or*, had the wrong understanding of pursuing capitalist modes of exchanges under the state ownership of means of production. Such an understanding was an inheritance of the theory of "socialism" from the pedants of the Second International. The agenda of *transitional society* became apparent before Lenin *not* as a theoretical, conceptual phenomenon, but as a concrete reality when the Bolshevik rule in Russia faced the agrarian crisis and revolts of the peasantry against the Soviet administration. Lenin confessed before the delegates of CI,

> ...what we admitted soon after, a few weeks later, namely that the direct transition to purely socialist forms, to purely socialist distribution, was beyond our available strength, and that if we were unable to effect a retreat so as to confine ourselves to easier tasks, we would face disaster.

Therefore, in hindsight we want to appreciate and stand for Lenin's assertion, 'But theory and practice are two different things, and the practical solution of this problem is by no means the same as the theoretical solution'. This statement opens up the avenues for the huge, multifarious experiments that humankind can charter, and the challenges that remain open to the search for alternatives organization of society against the existing capitalist system so that exchanges *by currency* really turn out to be redundant and irrelevant in human society.

However, saying this, we also conclude the 'the practical solution' offered by the Bolshevik theory of "socialism" as 'state-monopoly capitalism is a complete *material* preparation for socialism' cannot be the character of the political economy under dictatorship of the proletariat. In fact, the *socialist* basis of production relations that were germinating in Soviet Russia in the midst of terrible anarchy and disorganization such as the *factory councils,* were nipped in the bud by the hegemony of the *Party*. As we have seen in the debates between the *Workers' Opposition group* and the *Party* central leadership, the significance of the Soviet institutions as the platform of debates and decision making was already lost in practice. The organization of the Soviets was transformed into the bureaucratic set up for administrative instructions and implementation just as the parliamentary institutions in the bourgeoisie state apparatus remain only show-pieces and caricature of democratic decision-making.

This brings us to the question of 'the material conditions

necessary' that Marx repeatedly harped in a number of places as the pre-condition for *socialism* to be victorious in Europe. It may not be out of place here to refer to the sharp and specific views of Marx in a polemic with Karl Heinzen on the conditions for withering away of the property relations in society.

> The property question, which is a world-historical question in "our time" therefore takes on meaning only in the *modern bourgeoisie society*. The more developed this society is, the more therefore the bourgeoisie has developed economically in a country, and the more the state power has assumed a bourgeoisie expression, then the more stridently does the *social* question come to the fore... [Marx, 1976]

While this polemical writing of Marx was in 1847, he was consistent even after a decade in laying out the conditions for resolution of antagonistic class relations. While introducing his work in 1859 on the productions relations in bourgeoisie society he wrote,

> The bourgeois mode of production is the last antagonistic form of the social process of production—antagonistic not in the sense of individual antagonism but of an antagonism that emanates from the individuals' social conditions of existence—but the productive forces developing within bourgeois society create also the material conditions for a solution of this antagonism. The prehistory of human society accordingly closes with this social formation. [Marx, 1859]

We have seen in the Introduction of our essay that in a eulogy to the Paris Commune in 1911, Lenin was certainly aware of this necessity of 'productive forces developing within bourgeois society' for *socialism* to be a material, living urge of the society. On the contrary, we have also seen how in 1923 an exasperated Lenin was invoking even Napoleon to justify the 'tenfold' intensity of labour conscription of the workers and peasants in Russia to increase the productive forces gigantically (e.g. the five year plan for electrification) in the name of "socialism". These heroic efforts later turned out to be the national slogans, as Bettelheim observed, 'Technique decides everything" and "Catch up with and surpass the most advanced capitalist countries.'

In this essay, our endeavour is to focus on the pathetic distortion of the vision of *socialism* under the theoretical formulation of the Third International. Under such formulation, the revolutionary nature of the *socialist* productions relations was given completely amiss, that is to completely overhaul the hierarchical, exploitative and wage-labour based participation of the workers in the production process. We must be able to assert today the profound understanding of Marx that dictatorship of the proletariat is essentially the unfettered freedom the proletariat exercises *as a class* to resolve the class antagonisms that hitherto 'prehistory' of class-divided society has bestowed upon the human civilization. Dictatorship of the proletariat is not for recreating the class antagonisms in newer forms under the pretext of developing the productive forces. It must be stressed that overhauling the production relations is not synonymous with the unchecked growth of the 'productive forces'; rather the productive forces have to be under the collective ownership of the direct producers in the society. In that sense, it is important to highlight that dictatorship of the proletariat is the 'necessary transit point' where human society can abrogate, can banish the 'productive forces' those continue to nurture the class antagonisms in the capitalist society to survive. An immediate case in point is the huge military-industrial complexes that have been created by every aspiring nation-state in their battle for survival under capitalism. These military-industrial complexes are to be overhauled instantly under dictatorship of the proletariat as the production processes associated with them are never meant for the collective ownership of the *free*, direct producers.

The fundamental feature of dictatorship of the proletariat is not to establish a new form of the institution of state, a new structure of power for extending the longevity of political authority in society. Rather, from *day one* of the *new power* in the society, the idea is to see how the organs of political authority that only bring upfront the accentuated class antagonisms in the society are made irrelevant in the organization of the society. Only by articulating such programmes, *socialism* transcends the realm of theory, the realm of conjecture, to the 'the direct programme of practical politics' that Luxemburg fervently looked forward from the October Revolution.

The most illuminating character of the working class is being the *only* constituent in the society that has the ability to transcend its own *class identity*. Only the proletariat has the self-ability to organize the society as the cooperative association of the *free*, direct producers as the wage-labour character of engaging labour in the production process becomes irrelevant in the society. Such a vision of direct exercise of social authority presupposes a necessary maturity in the conscious effort among the proletariat that enables them to revolutionize the existing production relations. Marx visualized the development of this revolutionary *class identity*, that was in his vision the proletariat 'constitutes itself as a class for itself', as a direct outcome of the accentuation of *class struggle* within the bourgeoisie society that goes together with the development of productive forces. Thus, to Marx, conscious, political participation of the proletariat in the accentuated forms of *class struggle* against the bourgeoisie and 'the material conditions necessary' for such political struggle to be victorious in the society were simultaneous possibilities before the political economy of capitalist Europe.

However, visualization and reality are different entities. The complex reality of the bourgeoisie society, of the property relations is such an entangled phenomenon that it encompasses not only so many different streams of knowledge and varied experience, but also involve so many contradictory pulls of activity happening simultaneously. None among the forty-two delegates from the ten countries of Europe who assembled in September 1915 in the First Anti-War Conference in Zimmerwald could contemplate that their call for non-participation of the working class in the ongoing WWI would become reality in March 1919 when the First Congress of CI was convened in revolutionary Moscow. In 1915, it was beyond their figment of imagination that four years later in the Sessions of CI the delegates will be charting the course of "socialism" not only in industrialized Europe, but also in the hinterlands of the colonies where the vast majority of the agrarian "*masses*" were striving for attaining nationhood. In their dream of hastening the impending revolutions and in their conviction to hold on to the fortress of "socialism" in an underdeveloped capitalist economy the laws of historical materialism, the history of development of capitalism and constitution of the antagonistic class interests in society, were all thrown out of the window. During the formative period of CI the rallying point that drew supreme attention was volunteerism; that sheer dedication of the revolutionaries would be able to surpass the laws of development of commodity production even when the working class failed in its endeavour to earn supremacy against the capitalist economy in Europe.

## IV

Finally, in drawing the curtains over this long essay we want to say none among the historical icons of international working class movement is unblemished, not even Marx. The fallacy that was maintained under the leadership of CI within the international working class movement was the imposition of preordained infallibility for the writings of Marx, Engels and Lenin. By that way the leadership of CI absolved themselves of the painstaking work in understanding the political economy of capitalism beyond the WWI. The only social law enunciated by Marx that withstood the acid test of human civilization beyond the time of Marx are his assertions on the fundamental exploitative nature of society based on commodity production, and accumulation of private property based on the exchanges of *value*. The very inner cycle of the political economy of capitalism represents *barbarism* outsmarting the prehistory of medieval times. Capitalism draws itself into crises in the frenzy of pursuit for "profit" that is of private interest to a minority class of people, and to safeguard the monopoly interests of the accumulation of wealth. One tested way for the bourgeoisie to mitigate the crisis between the two World Wars was to organize wars and war efforts by investing heavily in armament manufacturing, and whipping up chauvinism among the people by foisting any national issue. That strategy itself did not bring end to the crises of the "profit" cycle. At the same time, such crises of capitalism did not bring the downfall of *barbarism* by its own weight of doom.

In this essay, we have not charted the task of deeper analysis of the crises of modern capitalism except dwelling on the features of the crises as enunciated by Keynes at the end of WWI. After the WWII, capitalism in spite of its inherent crises could represent as the sole system of the political economy of the world, either under the monopoly control of private ownership, or under the state ownership of the privileged bureaucracy. Such complexities of modern capitalism were beyond the reach of Marx as was evident in the near absence of his views regarding the nature of the complexities of *transitional societies* aspiring to reach *socialism* from various stages of development of capitalism. History of the last century has proved beyond doubt that dictatorship of the proletariat is *not* the infallible instrument of political power in the hands of the proletariat from where society is destined to leap forward to *socialism;* a society beyond the realm of commodity production and wage-labour. In fact, the history of dictatorship of the proletariat so far has invariably proved that this is the realm where capitalism puts up its bitter, tortuous struggle in the form of the petty-commodity producers so that the last bastion of private property in the form of ownership of *land* can put up a fight back for survival. We are yet to see any worthwhile, meaningful programme to win over the resistance of these last vestiges of capitalism in the society towards collective ownership of the social wealth by the direct producers.

Similar was the limitation of the conjecture of Marx about political struggle in the *society* as can be found in his understanding of the phenomenon only through the prism of *class struggle*. The treaty of Brest-Litovsk by which the Soviet government in Russia was compelled to sign off vast areas of land to Kaiser Germany in March 1918 was the most ignominious surrender for a nation engaged in war. Soviet government signed the treaty in spite of bitter opposition within the Bolsheviks so as to stand by its promise of peace to the soldiers in the war front who were unwilling to continue the war. This was directly not a *class issue* of ownership of the means of production. Yet, the Bolsheviks in Russia moved beyond the national sense of dignity in signing off the treaty with the Kaiser administration with the hope that such a treaty will actually force the German reaction to stop its participation in war, and would invigorate the German working class towards revolution. Their hope was not just an imagination as the history of German workers' and soldiers' revolution from November 1918–March 1919 remained till today the horror for the international bourgeoisie.

Therefore, this review is to critically assimilate the lessons of defeat of the international working class in the light of the formulations and theories put forward during the formative period of CI. While reviewing such programmes one has to step back to understand Marx in the context of the factual account of the period of history, when possibly the last time, the international working class gloriously and defiantly presented before society its revolutionary *class identity*. Starting from the pundits of "socialism" to the worker on the street it was crystal clear during the revolutionary upheaval, what the workers were looking for was a *new* society where they are the leading architects. It took substantial passage of time to understand the limitations and defeat of their effort; this fact itself proves the historical significance of the effort to enact the revolution.

We just put two clarifications before we sign off. In our analysis, we consciously tried to remain balanced as the subject is highly polemical among the activist for *socialism*; one reason behind the extremely feeble voice of the workers in society. Still, by being balanced one cannot overlook nor can justify the defeat by the excuse of the adversity of situation. After all, the struggle for *socialism*, in itself, is a genuine adversity for the proletariat in the bourgeois society. Second, at the end of day, one can sill ask what was then wrong with Plekhanov and Kautsky when our own analysis proves that the heroic attempts of the workers in Russia was bound to be a failure in their isolation, and by the socio-economic programmes that were implemented in Soviet Russia in the post-Civil War period?

The direct answer is the defeat of the Paris Commune was also within the expectation of Marx and Engels as the insurrection of the communards were brought to a bloody end. That did not deter them or the generations of revolutionaries after them to wholeheartedly support the initiative of the Paris workers to bring for the first time before human society what was meant by *dictatorship of the proletariat*.

## REFERENCES

Sukumar Ghose, Editor. *Contemporary Bengali Literature: Poetry*. Academic Publishers, Calcutta, 1972.

Frederick Engels. Postscript: On the 20th Anniversary of the Paris Commune. In *The Civil War in France* by Karl Marx. Verso, New York, 2012.

Charles Bettelheim. *Class Struggle in the USSR, First Period: 1917-1923*. Part I. Monthly Review Press, New York, 1977.

V.I. Lenin. Can the Bolsheviks Retain State Power? *Collected Works*, Vol. 26, 2nd Ed. Progress Publishers, Moscow, 1972.

V.I. Lenin. The Impending Catastrophe and How to Combat It. *Collected Works*, Vol. 25, 4th Ed. Progress Publishers, Moscow, 1974.

Karl Marx. Moralizing Criticism and Critical Morality. *MECW* Vol. 6, 1976. URL: *http://marxists.anu.edu.au/archive/marx/works/1847/10/31.htm.*

Karl Marx. *Preface to A Contribution to the Critique of Political Economy*, 1859. URL: *https://www.marxists.org/archive/marx/works/1859/critique-pol-economy/preface.htm.*

# Index